Strategic Management

Dr. P. SUBBA RAO
Professor and Convener, Executive MBA Program
School of Business Administration
University of Papua New Guinea
Papua New Guinea (Australia).
Formerly: Professor and Dean
Faculty of Commerce and Management
Sri Krishnadevaraya University
Anantapur-515 003 (AP), India.

Assisted by,
Dr. K. ANIL KUMAR

Himalaya Publishing House
ISO 9001:2015 CERTIFIED

First Edition	:	**2009**
Second Revised Edition	:	**2010**
Third Revised Edition	:	**2011**
Edition	:	**2012, 2015, 2017, 2015**
Edition	:	**2024**

Published by : Mrs. Meena Pandey
for **HIMALAYA PUBLISHING HOUSE PVT. LTD.,**
Ramdoot, Dr. Bhalerao Marg, Girgaon, Mumbai - 400 004
Phone: 022-23860170/23863863; **Fax:** 022-23877178
E-mail: himpub@bharatmail.co.in; **Website:** www.himpub.com

Branch Offices :

New Delhi : "Pooja Apartments", 4-B, Murari Lal Street, Ansari Road, Darya Ganj, New Delhi - 110 002. Phone: 011-23270392, 23278631; Fax: 011-23256286

Nagpur : Kundanlal Chandak Industrial Estate, Ghat Road, Nagpur - 440 018. Phone: 0712-2721215, 2721216

Bengaluru : Plot No. 91-33, 2nd Main Road, Seshadripuram, Behind Nataraja Theatre, Bengaluru - 560 020. Phone: 080-41138821; Mobile: 09379847017, 09379847005

Hyderabad : No. 3-4-184, Lingampally, Besides Raghavendra Swamy Matham, Kachiguda, Hyderabad - 500 027. Phone: 040-27560041, 27550139

Chennai : No. 34/44, Motilal Street, T. Nagar, Chennai - 600 017. Mobile: 09380460419

Pune : "Laksha" Apartment, First Floor, No. 527, Mehunpura, Shaniwarpeth (Near Prabhat Theatre), Pune - 411 030. Phone: 020-24496323, 24496333; Mobile: 09370579333

Cuttack : Plot No. 5F-755/4, Sector-9, CDA Markat Nagar, Cuttack - 753 014, Odisha. Mobile: 09338746007

Kolkata : 3, S.M. Bose Road, Near Gate No. 5, Agarpara Railway Station, North 24 Parganas, West Bengal - 700 109. Mobile: 09674536325

DTP by : Sudhakar Shetty

Printed at : Geetanjali Press Pvt. Ltd., Nagpur. On behalf of HPH (P).

Preface

Intensified competition among domestic private and public sector companies and multinational companies consequent upon globalisation along with strides in information technology brough tparadigm shifts in the concepts of Strategic Management. In fact, principles of strategic management took a completely a new direction.

The overwhelming response from the students, Lecturers, Professors and heads of various Business Schools of various universities in India, Papua New Guinea and other countries to my various books, viz., Management and Organisational Behaviour, Business Policy and Strategic Management, Strategic Management (JNTU), International Business, Essentials of Human Resource Management and Personnel and Human Resource Management prompted me to write a separate book on 'Strategic Management'. In fact, we brought a customised book for Jawaharlal Nehru Technological University, based on its syllabus.

Mr. Niraj Pandey, Mrs. Ujjwala Pandey, Mr. Anuj Pandey, Mr. Vijay Pandey, Mrs. Poopathi and Mrs. Nimisha of Himalaya Publishing House have provided immense support in bringing out this revised edition. I thank all of them immensely.

My wife Mrs. Pulapa Rama Devi and my little friends Master Nitin Sai and Rohan Sai were put in inconvenience during the period of revising this book. I express my gratitude to them.

I request the students, teachers and other readers to write to me with their comments and suggestions via e-mail.

Port Moresby, Papua New Guinea

June, 2011

Pulapa Subba Rao

pulapas@rediffmail.com

Contents

Brief Contents

UNIT 1

UNIT 2

UNIT 3

UNIT 4

UNIT 5

Unit-1

Chapter - 1

The Strategic Management Process

Chapter Outline

(A) Why Strategy?

(B) What is Strategy?

(C) Why is Strategy More Complex?

(D) Strategic Management

(E) Strategic Management Process: Strategic Fit vs. Strategic Intent

— Points to be Remembered

— Keywords

— Questions for Discussion

— References

Learning Objectives

After studying this chapter, you should be able to:

- Understand the concepts of strategy and strategic management
- Describe the process of strategic management
- Explain the nature of business policy and strategic management
- Study the key areas in developing a strategy
- Explain why crafting a strategy is complex?
- Describe the need for strategic management
- Explain the benefits and challenges of strategic management
- Describe the strategic management process

(A) WHY STRATEGY?

Different organisations having similar opportunities and resources perform differently. Consequently, some organisations succeed while others fail though both are in the same business. Similarly, organisations dealing with the same product and catering to the same group of customers perform quite differently. For example, Singapore Airlines has been growing at a faster rate than that of US Air. Dell computers has been doing well in highly competitive personal computers market, while Compaq and Apple have been struggling behind. Mittal Steel company has been growing by leaps and bounds and could bag 9 per cent of global steel market whereas the giants like Arcelor SA in the steel industry have been lagging behind. Why does Toyota dominate the automobile market?

Why do Coca Cola and Pepsi Cola attract the taste of all ages of soft drink customers worldwide?, though their products may adversely contribute to the obesity of some of their customers. (See Box 1.1). Why has Southwest Airlines been progressing dramatically while United Airlines filed for bankruptcy in 2002, US Airways filed bankruptcy in late 2005? How did Maruti Automobiles over take the former market leaders like Ambasador and Padmini? How did Virgin Blue overtake the traditional giants like Qantas and British Airways? How did most of the mobile phone companies like Airtel, Hutch and Vodafone overtake the leader Reliance? The answer for all these questions is the strategic management of the organisations. Thus, the strategies formulated and implemented by the managers of a company make or mar the growth rate, efficiency and the long run survival and development of the company.

The immediate questions that arise are: what is a strategy? What is strategic management process? How do managers craft strategies? In fact, managers of different organisations craft different strategies though they are endowed with similar opportunities and resources and challenged by more or less similar threats and weaknesses. Some strategies result in high efficiency, while some others lead to disaster. Why and how these drastic variations take place? An analysis management process would assist us to understand the abnormalities in the ultimate outcome.

Now, we shall study the meaning of a strategy.

Box 1.1: Obese People Have 'Severe Brain Degeneration'

Obesity takes big toll on the brain

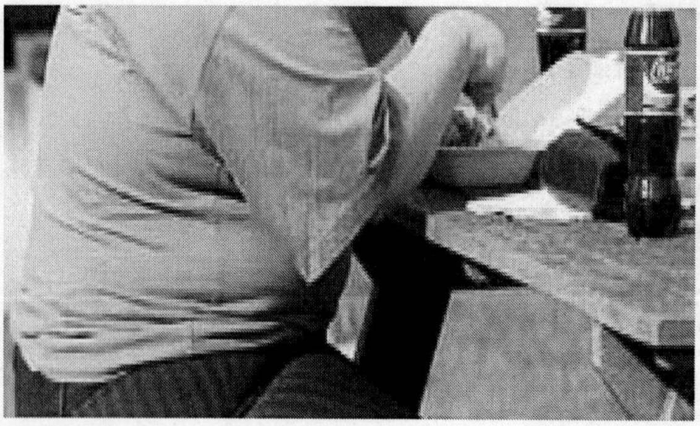

A new study finds obese people have 8 percent less brain tissue than normal-weight individuals. Their brains look 16 years older than the brains of lean individuals, researchers said today. Those classified as overweight have 4 percent less brain tissue and their brains appear to have aged prematurely by 8 years. The results, based on brain scans of 94 people in their 70s, represent "severe brain degeneration," said Paul Thompson, senior author of the study and a UCLA professor of neurology. "That's a big loss of tissue and it depletes your cognitive reserves, putting you at much greater risk of Alzheimer's and other diseases that attack the brain," said Thompson. "But you can greatly reduce your risk for Alzheimers, if you can eat healthily and keep your weight under control." The findings are detailed in the online edition of the journal, Human Brain Mapping. Obesity packs many negative health effects, including increased risk of heart disease, Type 2 diabetes, hypertension and some cancers. It has also been shown to reduce sexual activity. More than 300 million worldwide are now classified as obese, according to the World Health Organization. Another billion are overweight. The main cause, experts say: bad diet, including an increased reliance on highly processed foods. Obese people had lost brain tissue in the frontal and temporal lobes, areas of the brain critical for planning and memory, and in the anterior cingulate gyrus (attention and executive functions), hippocampus (long-term memory) and basal ganglia (movement), the researchers said in a statement today. Overweight people showed brain loss in the basal ganglia, the corona radiata, white matter comprised of axons, and the parietal lobe (sensory lobe). "The brains of obese people looked 16 years older than the brains of those who were lean, and in overweight people looked 8 years older," Thompson said. Obesity is measured by body mass index (BMI), defined as the weight in kilograms divided by the square of the height in metres. A BMI over 25 is defined as overweight, and a BMI of over 30 as obese.

Source:http://news.yahoo.com/s/livescience/20090825/sc_livescienceobesepeoplehaveseverebrain degeneration (Accessed on 26/08/09).

(B) WHAT IS STRATEGY?

In simple terms, strategy is a planned or emergent course of action that is expected to contribute to the achievement of organisational goals. Strategy can also be an idea or a thought that is viewed to be productive to complete a course of action. A strategy is defined as, "a unified, comprehensive, and integrated plan that relates to the strategic advantages of the firm and to the challenges of the environment. It is designed to ensure that the basic objectives of the enterprise are achieved through proper execution by the organisation." Alfred D. Chandler defines strategy as, "the determination of the basic long-term goals and objectives of an enterprise and the adoption of the courses of action and the allocation of resources necessary for carrying out these goals." Strategy by Arthur Sharplin as,"a plan or course of action which is of vital pervasive, or continuing importance to the organisation as a whole." James Brain Quinn defines the term strategy as, "the pattern of plan that integrates an organisation's major goals, policies and action sequences into a cohesive whole."

Should Strategy be a Plan?

Strategy is a long-run plan. Some authors view it as an integrated plan. Of late, it is viewed that strategy need not be a plan. Strategy sometimes emerges as a result of a situation or an incident as evident from some incidents that happened in various companies. One such incident happened in a biscuit manufacturing company.

One night at around 10 p.m., the production manager of a biscuit company received a telephone call from his neighbours informing him that his wife was sick and they admitted her in a hospital in the town and asked him to rush to the hospital. The production manager narrated the problem to his deputy production manager and explained the conflicting situation of wife's health versus production responsibility and irresponsibility of the deputy production manager of drinking habit even while on duty. The deputy production manager volunteered to take charge of the production department and requested the production manager to go to the hospital and take care of his wife. Further he informed that he would not consume liquor and take care of production unit with full commitment on that night. The production manager was convinced of the commitment of the deputy production manager and left for the hospital.

The deputy production manager out of his joy of becoming the Acting Production Manager on that night consumed liquor twice the quantity that he normally consumes and went around the factory. He informed most of the employees that he was the Acting Manager of the Production Unit and asked every one to work seriously and efficiently and returned to his chambers. He was drowsy and slipped while coming back to his chambers. One of his hands fell on a part of a machine. He told to himself that people complicate the machine designs and removed that part and threw it on the floor. Later, he went to his chambers and slept.

One of the employees, next morning while going home after his night duty observed the part on the floor and placed it in its right position without complaining with a view to avoid any possible risk of being identified as the initial culprit.

The marketing manager after two weeks of time received a surprising feedback from the salespeople who visited the retailers that the company produced a new and delicious product and discontinued the same. The retailers requested the company to restore the production of that new product. The marketing manager was irritated for not being informed of the introduction of the new product and hence picked-up an argument with the production manager. But the production manager countered the argument and categorically informed that the company did not introduce any new product in recent times. However, after prolonged arguments, the marketing manager informed his counterpart that he would produce batch number and date of manufacturing of the new product and provided the same to the production manager after a few days by obtaining the same from one of the retailers.

Production manager after analyzing the information provided by the marketing manger found that the new product was produced on the night when he left the production unit for hospital. Then he called the Deputy Production Manager and asked him about the incident. After detailed discussions and analysis of his minute-to-minute activities, deputy production manager recollected the incident that he removed the divider which divides the wheat floor mix into two parts – where one side sugar is added and the another side salt is added. The supply chain where the sugar is added is connected to sweet biscuit production line and the supply chain where the salt is added is connected to salt biscuit production line. The removal of the divider by the deputy production manager led to the addition of both sugar and salt at the same place and resulted in the production of sweet-cum-salt biscuits. Thus, the company by an accident could produce a new product, i.e., 'sweet-cum-salt biscuits'. And thereafter the company started commercial production of this new product that resulted in achieving the company's objectives and goals of enhancing market share and profit.

Therefore, it is felt that strategies need not be planned and they can be emerged. As such, strategy is viewed as a planned or emergent course of action that is expected to contribute to the achievement of organisational goals.

Analysis of Definitions of Strategy

The analysis of various definitions of strategy presents the following points:

- Strategy is a central understanding of the strategic management process.
- Strategy is the determination of basic long-term goals and objectives of an organisation.
- It helps in determining the courses of action to attain the predetermined goals and objectives.
- It points to allocation of necessary resources for implementing the course of action.
- It develops the company from its present position to the desired future position.
- It is a set of decision-making rules having a common thread.
- It sets a clear direction.
- It is a course of unified actions either planned and/or emerged.
- Enterprise knows its strengths and weaknesses compared with those of its competitors.
- Enterprise devotes its hard-won resources to projects that employ its set of core competencies, the primary skills within the organisation.
- Identifies factors in the political and social environment that requires careful monitoring.
- Recognises which competitor's actions need critical attention.
- The competitive firm should have a rational, clear-headed notion, purged of wishful thinking of *(i)* its mission *(ii)* its external competitive environment (for analysing opportunities and threats) and *(iii)* its internal capabilities (including strengths and weaknesses). Now, we turn our discussion to the dimensions of the strategy, criteria for effective strategy, forms and kinds of strategies.

Criteria for Effective Strategy

Although each strategic situation is unique, there are some common criteria that tend to explain an effective strategy. Criteria for effective strategy include:

(i) *Clear, decisive objectives:* All efforts should be directed towards clearly understood, decisive and attainable overall goals. All goals need not be written down or be chronologically precise but they must be understood and be decisive.

(ii) *Maintaining the initiative:* The strategy preserves freedom of action and enhances commitment. It sets the pace and determines the course of events rather than reacting to them.

(iii) *Concentration:* The strategy concentrates superior power at the place and time likely to be decisive. The strategy must define precisely what will make the enterprise

superior in power, best in critical dimensions in relation to its competitors. A distinctive competency yields greater success with fewer resources.

(iv) *Flexibility:* The strategy must purposely have built in resources, buffers and dimensions for flexibility and maneuvers. Reserved capabilities, planned maneuverability and repositioning allows one to use minimum resource while keeping competitors at a relative disadvantage.

(v) *Coordinated and committed leadership:* The strategy should provide responsible, committed leadership for each of its major goals. Care should be taken in selecting the leaders in such a way that their own interests and values match with the requirements of their roles. Commitment and not mere acceptance is the basic requirement.

(vi) *Surprise:* The strategy should make use of speed, secrecy and intelligence to attack exposed or unprepared competitors at an unexpected time. Thus, surprise and correct time are very important.

(vii) *Security:* The organisation should secure or develop resources required, securely maintain all vital operating points for the enterprise, an effective intelligence system to prevent the effects of surprises by the competitors.

Forms and Kinds of Strategies

Strategy is a plan — a consciously intended course of action. Some of them may be unrealised or some other actions may emerge meanwhile. These two form a realised strategy as shown in Figure 1.1. Kinds of strategies are presented in Exhibit 1.

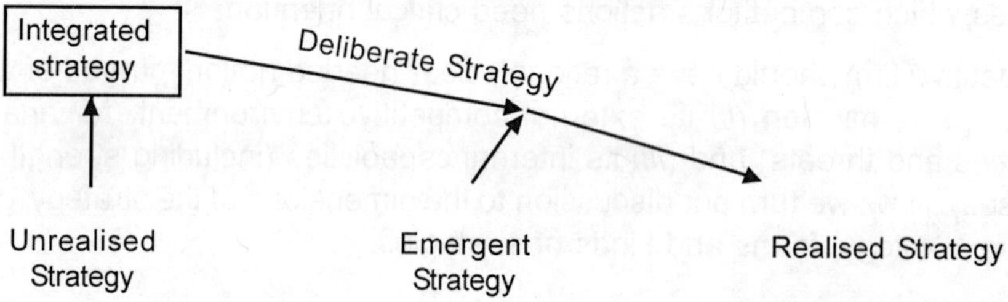

Fig. 1.1: Forms of Strategy

Exhibit 1.1: Various Kinds of Strategies, From Deliberate to Mostly Emergent

Planned Strategy: Precise intentions are formulated and articulated by a central leadership, and backed up by formal controls to ensure their surprise-free implementation in an environment that is benign, controllable, or predictable (to ensure no distortion of intentions); these strategies are highly deliberate.

Entrepreneurial Strategy: Intentions exist as the personal, unarticulated visions of a single leader, and so are adaptable to new opportunities; the organisation is under the personal control of the leader and located in a protected niche in its environment; these strategies are relatively deliberate but can emerge too.

Ideological Strategy: Intentions exist as the collective vision of all the members of the organisation, controlled through strong, shared norms; the organisation is often pro-active *vis-a-vis* its environment; these strategies are rather deliberate.

Umbrella Strategy: A leadership in partial control of organisational action defines strategic targets or boundaries within which others must act (for example, that all new products be high priced and at the technological cutting edge, although what these actual products are to be is left to emerge); as a result, strategies are partly deliberate (the boundaries) and partly emergent (the patterns within them); this strategy can also be called deliberately emergent, in that the leadership purposefully allows others the flexibility to maneuver and form patterns within the boundaries.

Process Strategy: The leadership controls the process aspects of strategy (who gets hired and so gets a chance to influence strategy, what structures they work within, etc.), leaving the actual content of strategy to others; strategies are again partly deliberate (concerning process) and partly emergent (concerning content), and deliberately emergent.

Disconnected Strategy: Members or subunits loosely coupled with the rest of the organisation produce patterns in the streams of their own actions in the absence of, or in direct contradiction to the central or common intentions of the organisation at large; the strategies can be deliberate for those who make them.

Consensus Strategy: Through mutual adjustment, various members converge on patterns that pervade the organisation in the absence of central or common intentions; these strategies are rather emergent in nature.

Imposed Strategy: The external environment dictates pattern in actions, either through direct imposition (say by an outside owner or by a strong customer) or through implicitly pre-empting or bounding organisational choice (as in a large airline that must fly jumbo jets to remain viable); these strategies are organisationally emergent, although they may be internalised and made deliberate.

Source: James Brain Quinn, Henry Mintzberg and Robert M. James (Eds.): *"The Strategy Process"*, Prentice-Hall, Englewood Cliffs, p. 16.

Need for Strategy

It is beyond doubt to state that every organisation necessarily formulate strategies. To state specifically, strategy is necessary in view of the following reasons:

(i) To have rules to guide the search for new opportunities both inside and outside the firm.

(ii) To take high quality project decisions.

(iii) To develop measures to judge whether a particular opportunity is a rare one or whether much better ones are likely to develop in the future.

(iv) To have an assurance that the firm's overall resource allocation pattern is efficient.

(v) To have and develop internal ability to anticipate change.

(vi) To save time, money and executive talent.

(vii) To identify, develop and exploit potential opportunities.

(viii) To utilise the delay principle, that is, delay the commitment until an opportunity is on hand.

Key Areas in Developing a Strategy

Managers have to consider the following key areas in developing a strategy:

(i) The type of goods and/or services that the firm will produce and will sell.

(ii) The mode of producing goods and rendering services.

(iii) Who are and will be the firm's customers.

(iv) The methods of financing the various operations of the firm.

(v) The amount of risk that the firm will take.

(vi) Methods of implementing the strategy.

(C) WHY IS STRATEGY MORE COMPLEX?

Globalisation along with strides in information technology brought paradigm shifts in the operations and modes of doing business in general and strategic management in particular.

The recent phase of globalisation after 1990 erased national political boundaries for the purpose of business. In addition, it set the phase for the emergence of global culture, global systems and practices, global products and services, standardisation of financial accounting principles and practices, logistics management systems like containerisation in case of sea transportation, establishment of manufacturing facilities throughout the world, preference for diversified human resources and sourcing the finance across the globe.

Significant shifts in globalisation have been due to the establishment of World Trade Organisation, (WTO), creation of regional integrations like European Union and ASEAN, declining trade and investment barriers, growth in foreign direct investment, growth in multinational companies (MNCs), transformations of MNCs into transnational companies that consider the entire world as a single country for doing business and changes in mindset and attitude of customers.

Global Economic Trends

Globalisation along with its drivers like World Trade Organisation, declining trade and investment barriers, enlarging regional integrations brought unprecedented shifts in the growth rates of various economies. The significant trends include:

1. USA is no more the world's single largest market with the enlargement of European Union.

2. The enlarged European Union has emerged as a single largest world market with its more than 700 million potential customers.

3. European Union along with Western European countries have per capita income higher than that of USA.

4. China's economy is larger than that of Canada.

5. India has also been growing rapidly and now has emerged as the fourth largest economy in the world.

6. World's largest economies by 2050 would be USA, China, India, Japan UK, France, Germany and South Korea.

7. Russia and Italy are expected to decline by 2050.

8. Most of the MNCs headquarters in USA, and Europe are expected to earn more than 60% of their revenue from China and India by 2020. Therefore, MNCs have been crafting strategies to invest in the emerging markets like China and India, where the growth would be fast and sustainable in the future years. General Electric is now investing in China and India while FedEx is investing in India and Brazil.

Paradigm Shifts that Affect Strategic Management

Change in Industry Boundaries: The shifts in globalisation and technology brought fundamental change in competition among the firms across the boundaries of industries and nations. In fact, the boundaries of industries have been changing due to the spectacular shifts in the nature of business strategies. For example, interactive computer networks and telecommunications have blurred the boundaries of the entertainment industry. Consequently, networks like ABC, NBC and Fox compete among themselves and also with AT&T, Sony and Microsoft. Similarly Coca Cola and Pepsi Cola fight not only between themselves but also compete with Bisleri and a number of national/local mineral water producers. ICICI competes with commercial banks, development banks and also insurance companies.

Shifts in Mindset: The shift in mindset of the customer from the traditional low cost product to flexibility, speed, innovation, integration of a wide range of functions and/or services and information revolution brought a change in the mindset of the strategist. The change in the mindset of the strategist led to the shift in strategy crafting from the conventional competitive advantage based on low cost, large scale economics and huge advertising budget to the innovation, differentiation and enlarging the product functions and conveniences.

Change in National Boundaries: Globalisation wiped out the national political boundaries for the purpose of business. As such most of the businesses have been spreading their operations to various foreign countries. Consequently national companies started competing with MNCs not only at home but even in various other countries in addition to competing with other national companies. For example, Tata Steel competes with Mittal Steel at home and in foreign countries in addition to competing with Visakha Steels, and other companies in India. Crafting and implementing appropriate strategy that fits the turbulent environment is paramount. In addition, the corporate strategy needs to be coordinated and aligned with business unit's strategies in decentralised corporate structures in various countries and/or regions.

Hypercompetition: The period post-1990s is marked by turbulent environment uncontrolled by any group of forces. "Assumptions of market stability are replaced by motions of inherent instability and change." Dynamics of strategic–maneuvering among the global and innovative combatants is caused by ever growing customer preferences, and partly due to the innovations of the competing firms. Hypercompetition is a condition of rapidly growing competition based on *(i)* price-quality positioning. *(ii)* innovative know-how *(iii)* establishing first-mover advantage and *(iv)* competition to protect their own brand and market and invade competitors' brands and markets. Thus, firms aggressively challenge the competitors' products and markets by enhancing their performance in order to improve their competitive position. As indicated earlier, the hypercompetition has been caused due to a number of interactive factors and the significant among them are globalisation and technology.

Box 1.2: Art of Hyper-competition

Is the idea of sustained competitive advantage dead? Richard D'Aveni, professor of business strategy at the Amos Tuck School at Dartmouth College, believes it is. According to Mr. D'Aveni, business has entered a new era of hypercompetition, shifting dramatically from slow-moving stable oligopolies to an environment characterized by a quick-strike mentality on the part of companies aimed specifically at disrupting the competitive advantage of market leaders. Mr. D'Aveni says, he discovered in his consulting work that traditional strategic concepts were making companies weaker, not stronger. "The old structure was: define an industry, reduce the level of competition and then avoid competition where possible," he says. "But I found that successful companies were not doing any of these things. The best performers were disrupting markets, acting as if there were no boundaries to entry." In his book, "Hypercompetition: Managing the Dynamics of Strategic Maneuvering" (Free Press), Mr. D'Aveni argues, that competitive advantage is no longer sustainable over the long haul. Advantage, instead, is continually created, eroded, destroyed and recreated through strategic maneuvering. The old goal, Mr. D'Aveni says, was to increase profitability by legally restraining the level of competition in an industry. Companies avoided price wars, segmented the market to avoid head-to-head competition and tried to keep the number of competitors low by putting up entry barriers around their industries. Today, he points out, this strategy is "literally impossible." He says, four driving forces are contributing to the new era of hypercompetition: customer changes, including fragmenting tastes; rapid technological change; falling geographic and industry boundaries as markets globalize; and deep pockets among competitors due to the rise of giant global alliances in a raft of industries. "The way to go about winning today is to obsolete the current advantages of the leader," Mr. D'Aveni says. The Microsoft Corporation, for example, has long been considered invincible because it controls the operating system market for most of the world's personal computers. But suddenly, Mr. D'Aveni says, three efforts are under way simultaneously to make Microsoft's hegemony obsolete. For one, chip manufacturers are imbedding software directly into semiconductor chips, doing away with the need for separate operating software. For another, there is the move toward a low-priced, dumb terminal-like device that hooks directly into the Internet and takes advantage of software such as Sun Microsystems' Java. And last, there are the voice recognition systems, offered by the likes of the telecommunications companies, that will circumvent the need for current operating systems. "Everyone thought I.B.M. was invincible at one time, as well," Mr. D'Aveni notes. The Dartmouth professor foresees the untapped distribution capabilities of the Internet and the World Wide Web as the perfect vehicle for "disrupting the apple cart" of a variety of industries. "What will happen to publishing, for example," he asks, "when reporters or authors can transmit their work directly to the reader over the Internet? Why does Michael Crichton need a publisher when he can eliminate the middle man? No doubt the C.E.O.'s of the publishing houses are worried." Most difficult for market leaders is that tomorrow's competitors are not even on the radar screens of most companies, Mr. D'Aveni says. With weak entry barriers to most markets, he adds, the "unconventional player attacks suddenly from outside the industry with unexpected methods, often with devastating effect." Despite these new parameters, Mr. D'Aveni suggests that long-term dominance of an industry is still possible even though sustainable advantage has gone by the boards. It is possible to win in hypercompetition by mastering the art of dynamically repositioning oneself in four key arenas: price/quality, know-how/timing, stronghold creation/invasion and deep pockets.

http://www.strategy-business.com/press/16635507/14886 (Accessed on 31/08/09).

Enlarged Opportunities: Globalisation enables the companies to source various inputs like material, finance, human resources, machinery and technology from different countries wherever the qualitative inputs at less cost and convenient terms and condition are available. For example, Dr. Reddy's Lab procure material from USA, human resources from India, machinery from Europe, produces in India and markets in Russia and African countries in addition to other developing countries. Wal-Mart has been contemplating procurement and production from many countries in the world to market in their 3,600 retail units. In fact, it treats operations in each country like a domestic company with local strategies with a global vision and mission.

Product Design, Quality and Service: Companies that go global design the products as per the preferences and conveniences of customers of foreign countries. In addition, they improve the quality of the product as well as the services due to the severe competition from the companies operating in the markets. For example, Toyota's product design, product quality and Jet Airlines – Boeing 777 has 132,500 major components and these components are produced in 545 different locations. A small optical company in the USA, *i.e.,* Swan Optical manufactures its eye wear in low cost factories in Hong Kong and China. Quality of service forced many automobile companies across the countries to improve their product and service including the Indian automobile companies.

Globalisation resulted in increase in, the efficiency of both MNCs as well as domestic companies producing quality product at less cost, supply of the product at the right time to the customer and provide better service as the customer buys the product from anyone who sells high quality product at less price with better service. In fact, customers today are secular and as such they are not loyal to any brand permanently.

Heavy Risks of Globalisation: Globalisation led to the closure of some of the domestic companies, particularly small companies in developing countries. In fact, thousands of small-scale companies were closed after globalisation due to their inability to compete with the MNCs. Further, even large-scale companies that had only a few products were forced to either expand or close down. Thus, globalisation complicates the process of strategic management due to the complex opportunities and threats created by the open of markets and severe competition.

Impact of Electronic Business (e-Business)

There have been dramatic developments in information technology during the last two decades. These developments enriches business communication, innovations in computer hardware and software, network of computers and network of production technology, machinery, product design, marketing systems, finance administration and human resource systems with computers. The next information technology breakthrough is the neural networks which will change the way the managers do their jobs. Neural networks combine computer software and chips that are capable of mimicking brain functions. For example, when a purchase order is issued to a vendor, he/she simultaneously enters the order in the online datebase. The entire activities in the operation result in receiving goods, a person at the receiving end checks a computer terminal to ensure that the shipment received is proper condition the employee clicks the mouse to issue a cheque, otherwise, the employee is empowered to refuse the shipment. Further, information technology brought significant and dramatic changes through various techniques like:

- Business Process Re-engineering
- Enterprise Resource Planning and
- Supply Chain Management

Electronic business (e-business) consists of three areas, *viz.*, *(a)* intranet within the organisation, *(b)* business-to-business (B2B) dealings and *(c)* business-to-customer (B2C) transactions.

Business-to-customer transactions include selling the goods and services through the internet to innumerable customers spread all over the world. Business houses establish virtual shops and offer goods and services to whoever visits their web sites. E-commerce is another aspect of e-business. Some other important aspects of e-business, which are successfully carried on through the internet are e-auctioning, e-banking, e-directories, e-engineering, e-travel services, e-operational resource management, e-supply and e-trading.

The emergence and growth of e-business has its impact on the way of doing business and thereby on the strategic management also as:

- **E-business provides with easy shopping:** Shopping on the internet provides with fascinating experience. A potential customer can turn to the web, browse different shops and place orders for a variety of goods and/or services without spending time and energy as it happens in traditional shopping.

- **E-business saves operating costs:** It saves operating cost by eliminating human intervention in order processing. (See Box 1.3).

- **E-business profoundly influencing the structure of business supply chains:** It changes the supply chains and their structure. For example, Chrysler Corporation by linking its supplies though a web-based network, reported savings of more than $3 billion in cost of materials in 2007.

- **Higher degree of personalisation:** E-business allows higher degree of personalisation and customisation of products, services and relationships.

- **Round the clock facility:** E-business is around-the-clock advantage to the customer. E-business allows a fast and flexible execution and response to the market opportunities. The web enables a company to introduce a new product, get immediate customer reaction, refine and perfect the product without investment with greater assurance of success.

Box 1.3: E-Business Strategies
E-Business Strategies explores the use of advanced technologies that change the business dynamics of the physical aspect of real estate: the design, construction, and delivery of buildings.The global real estate, design, and construction industries are highly fragmented and notoriously inefficient. This course explores the ways in which firms can gain economies of scale, coordinate design and construction on a multi-firm basis, capture the benefit of new technologies, and change the competitive landscape. A similar metamorphosis has happened in adjacent service industries which use real estate, including finance, insurance, retail, investing, food services, and consulting; this course explores they how these disruptive business models will also change the cost and differentiation dynamics in this sector. **E-Business Strategies** is an interdisciplinary research course which highlights the application of leading edge technologies being developed at MIT, Harvard, and elsewhere. These include visualization, remote sensing, 3D solid modeling, knowledge management, and sophisticated supply chain and logistics optimization.

Source: http://web.mit.edu/1.464/www/ (Accessed on 31/08/09).

Organisational Adaptation and Learning Organisation

Significant environmental dynamism dominated by globalisation and information technology led to the organisational adaptation and further creation and/or emergence of learning organisations. Institution theory of organisations propose that organisations can and do adapt to changing environment factors by restructuring their activities and by imitating the successful organisations. In fact, strategic choice perspective proposes that organisations not only adapt to the changing environment, but have opportunity and power even to reshape their environments. Organisational learning theory proposes that organisation reactively adapt to the environmental changes and proactively improve organisational structure to fit the same to the possible future environmental shifts either caused or created by using the knowledge they learned from the environment. Thus, the organisations have become learning organisations.

Synergetic Outcome: Organisations are congregations of individual human resources. Organisations learn and acquire knowledge through individual employees. Organisational learning output is the synergetic outcome of individual learning of all employees. Organisations learn by creating conducive environment for knowledge creation and development through discussion, research, brain storming, etc. Organisations create conducive environment for their employees to analyse and foresee the environment and its influence on product design, demand, price and market share of the organisation.

Employees and Learning Organisations: Employees develop the knowledge for the organisation to prepare for the future by developing systems, structure and products. Flexibility allows the organisation to develop short-term thrusts within the long-term or a fixed period strategy, resulting in strategic flexibility. Strategic flexibility demands short-term flexibility due to environmental shifts in order to achieve the long-term strategic goal more efficiently and not be distracted by environmental turbulences.

Employees and Learning Organisations: Employees develop the knowledge for the organisation to prepare for the future by developing systems, structure and products. Flexibility allows the organisation to develop short-term thrusts within the long-term or a fixed period strategy, resulting in strategic flexibility. Strategic flexibility demands short-term flexibility due to environmental shifts in order to achieve the long-term strategic goal more efficiently and not be distracted by environmental turbulences.

Strategic Flexibility: Strategic flexibility takes place in learning organisation, where the knowledge is created, shared, acquired, transferred and used for understanding and foreseeing the future environment. Learning organisations, thus, prepare themselves for the future by changing the structure adequately before the environmental changes take place.

Knowledge is Competitive Advantage: Organisational learning has become imperative as organisational activities like product design, new product development, manufacturing, and supply chain have become competitive and intellectual. In addition, knowledge is accepted as competitive advantage. Procter and Gamble, Microsoft, and Reliance Industries encourage the employees to create and share information and knowledge and utilise the same for developing organisational competencies.

Learning Organisations and Competencies: Learning organisations develop competencies in problem solving logically, experimenting with new approaches, learning from past experiences, experiences of themselves and others and transferring the knowledge quickly and utilisation of such knowledge for their own and others experiences for efficient strategic implementation by arresting or mitigating the possible deviations.

Learning Organisations and Action Learning: Learning organisation adopt action-learning and action research techniques for knowledge creation. For example, Motorola through its action-learning tool allows the marketing, manufacturing, finance and human resource personnel to meet and argue through brainstorming sessions and agree on the new products, new markets, customer groups, customer needs and pricing before taking up commercial production. These sessions force the future possible issues and problems and provides for a successful strategy implementation.

(D) STRATEGIC MANAGEMENT

Introduction

One can generalise and say that the strategic management is the process of management of strategic decision-making, implementation and control. It is not a complete meaning of strategic management though as it fails to cover many important aspects of strategic management. One should know that the nature of strategic management is different from that of management. Managers in most cases deal with day-to-day issues and problems of operational control. These issues and problems include procuring raw materials, scheduling production process, inventory control, producing goods, procuring finances, investing, capital budgeting, working capital management, procuring human resources, settling their problems, selling the products, creating demand, advertising, sales promotion, marketing research and the like. All these tasks are important, but the managers perform these tasks based on general guidelines provided to them. Therefore, these tasks are vital for efficient implementation of strategy but it is not the entire scope of strategic management. Then, what is strategic management?

Definitions of Strategic Management

"Strategic management is concerned with deciding on strategy and planning how that strategy is to be put into effect." It can be thought of as having these elements within it, *viz.*, strategic analysis, strategic choice and strategic implementation as shown in Fig. 1.2 Strategic analysis seeks to understand the strategic position of the firm. Strategic choice is to do with the formulation of possible course of action. Strategic implementation is concerned with planning how the choice of strategy can be implemented. According to Samuel C. Certo and J. Paul Peter, "Strategic management is a continuous, interative, cross-functional process aimed at keeping an organisation as a whole appropriately matched to its environment." A series of steps that a manager must take are identified by this definition. These steps include performing an environmental analysis, establishing organisational direction, formulating organisational strategy, implementing organisational strategy and exercising strategic control.

Schellenberger and Bosenan define the term strategic management as, "the continuous process of effectively relating the organisation's objectives and resources to the opportunities in the environment." or, "strategic management is primarily concerned with relating the organisation to its environment, formulating strategies to adapt to the environment and assuring that implementation of strategies taken place."

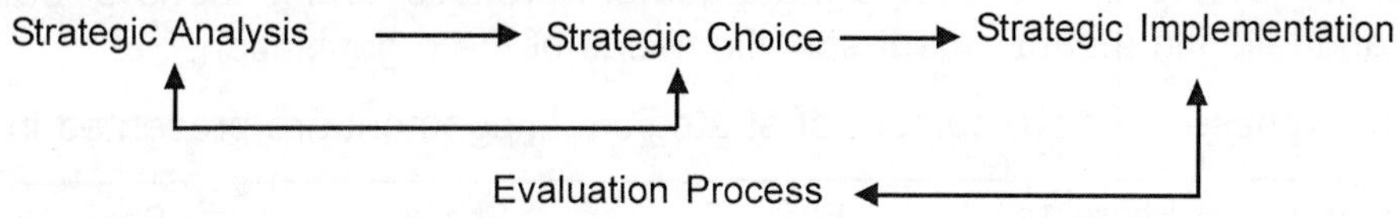

Fig. 1.2: Simple Model of Strategic Management Process

Analysis of the Definitions of Strategic Management

The study of the above mentioned definitions of strategic management presents the following analysis:

(i) Strategic management is a continuous process but that does not mean that the organisation never finishes its strategic work. Managers will always be focusing or reflecting on some aspect of strategic management, though different aspects of strategic management require different emphasis and effort of varying intensity at different times.

(ii) Though the process of strategic management starts with the step of performing an environmental analysis, and moves on to strategic control, it comes back as environmental analysis. Thus, strategic management consists of a series of steps repeated cyclically.

(iii) Various activities of strategic management draw the inputs from various functional areas of management. Thus, strategic management process integrates human resources with marketing, production/operations and finance. All these functional areas of management, in a comprehensive effort, contribute simultaneously to create an effective plan or output. Thus, the cross-functional team members work together and the organisation will enjoy the benefits of synergy. The members can visualise the overall position of where the firm is and what it needs to do in the future in order to achieve a sustainable competitive advantage. This process will encourage commitment of key executives to strategic plan.

(iv) Strategic management identifies its purpose as ensuring that an organisation as a whole appropriately matches its ever changing environment. Organisations must modify their strategies in accordance with the changes in its environment. For example, announcement of new economic policy by the Government of India in 1991 shook the environment and consequently most of the business firms modified their strategies. Similarly, the recent recession after 2008 also influenced business organizations to modify their strategies in the direction of reducing operations resulting in job cuts.

Historical Development of Strategic Management

Almost all the disciplines passed through different stages in their evolutionary process and reached their present stage. Strategic management is not an exception to this. Though the formulation of a strategy seems to be simple, it is very difficult to accomplish it. Many organisations develop their strategic management process over periods of several years, adjusting and tailoring them to meet specific needs of the organisation.

Different phases of development of strategic management are presented in Figure 1.3.

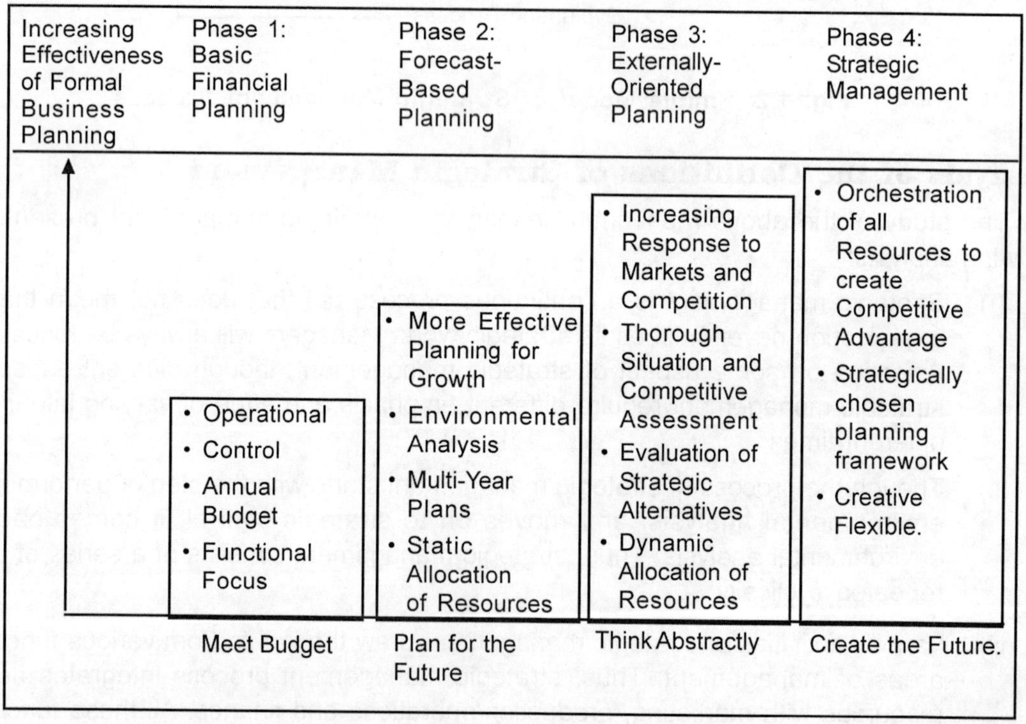

Source: Samuel C. Certo and J. Paul Peter, *op. cit.*, p. 14.

Fig. 1.3: Phases in the Development of a Strategic Management System

***Phase 1:* Basic Financial Planning:** The first phase of the strategic development is fairly a simple routine of basic financial planning. The main concern during this phase is simply meeting annual budget requirement, operational functions like production, marketing, finance and human resources and emphasising on the operational control.

***Phase 2:* Forecast-based Planning:** During this phase, the primary concern is mainly on effective plans, environmental scanning, plan for the future and allocation of resources.

***Phase 3:* Externally-oriented Planning:** There is a remarkable shift during this phase. The notable developments include: increasing response to markets and competition, complete situational analysis and assessment of competitive strength, evaluation of strategic alternatives and allocation of resources based on changing needs from time to time.

***Phase 4:* Strategic Management:** The focus shifts over time from meeting the budget to planning for the future, to thinking abstractly, to working to create desired future. To create future decision-makers, orchestrate and integrate all their organisation's resources to gain a competitive advantage. They build flexibility into the organisational planning process, and foster a supportive, participative climate within the organisation.

Thus, developing an effective and efficient strategic management process can be a long and difficult task. It requires sustained effort, enormous patience and sharp political skills. Strategic management requires efficient leadership.

Now, we shall discuss the need for strategic management.

Need for Strategic Management

Some managers argue that why should firms engage themselves in strategic management? They argue that firms can exist, develop and continue in business without strategic management. Some other managers argue that strategic management is essential in this competitive era. Exhibit 1.2 presents the reasons for and reactions to the value of strategic management. The following factors help us to know the need for strategic management.

Exhibit 1.2: Reasons for and Reactions to the Value of Strategic Management

Pros	Cons
1. Strategic management allows firms to anticipate changing conditions.	• Conditions change so fast, managers can't do any planning, especially long-term planning.
2. Strategic management provides clear objectives and direction for employees.	• Objectives must often be vague and general.
3. Research in strategic management is advancing so that the process can help managers.	• Managers pay little attention to research, and studies are not well done.
4. Business which perform strategic management are more effective.	• There are many reasons for success, and many firms are effective without formal planning.
5. Environment is not static. It is more dynamic and global environment also affects most of the firms. Strategic management helps in understanding environment and formulate strategy to suit to the environmental dynamism.	• Environmental dynamism can't be assessed.

Source: Adapted from Lawrence R. Jauch and William F. Glueck, "*Business Policy and Strategic Management*," McGraw-Hill Book Company, New York, p. 18.

1. Due to Change: Everything, except change is not permanent. It does mean that only change is permanent. Change makes planning difficult. But, firms may pro-act to the change rather than just react to it. Strategic management encourages the top executives to forecast change and provides direction and control. It will also allow the firm to take advantage of the opportunities provided by the changes in the environment and avoid the threats or reduce the risk as the future is anticipated. Thus, strategic management allows an enterprise to base its decisions on long-range forecasts.

2. To Provide Guidelines: Strategic management provides guidelines to the employer about the organisation's expectations from them. This would minimise conflict between job performance and job demands. Thus, it provides incentive for employer and helps the organisation in achieving its objectives.

3. Developed Field of Study by Research: Strategic management was just based on case studies or anecdotal evidence 30 years ago. But recently, there are methodological problem researches in this field of study. More systematic knowledge in this area is available at present. Therefore, today it is worthwhile to study strategic management.

4. Probability for Better Performance: There is no clear research evidence that strategic management leads to higher performance. But the majority of studies suggest that there is a relationship between better performance and formal planning. It is also stated that businesses which plan strategically have a higher probability of success than those which do not have.

5. Systematise Business Decisions: Strategic management provides data and information about different business transactions to managers and helps them to make decisions systematically.

6. Improves Communication: Strategic management provides effective communication of information from lower level managers to middle level managers and to top level managers.

7. Improves Coordination: Strategic management improves coordination not only among the functional areas of management, but also among individual projects.

8. Improves Allocation of Resources: Strategic planning helps in deciding upon most feasible and viable projects and thereby improves the allocation of resources to the viable projects.

9. Helps the Managers to have a Holistic Approach: Strategic management helps the managers to have complete understanding of the company and to have a holistic approach towards business problems and proportions.

Benefits of Strategic Management

Several corporations and institutions have been using strategic management. Organisations reap several benefits from effective strategic management. The benefits of strategic management include:

(i) Strategic management helps an organisation to be proactive rather than reactive in shaping its future.

(ii) It helps organisations not only to respond to its relevant environment, but also to initiate and influence its environment and thereby exert control over its destiny.

(iii) It helps organisations to make effective strategies through the use of a more systematic, logical and rational approach to strategic choice.

(iv) It helps the organisations to achieve understanding and commitment from all managers and employers. Managers and employers become creative and innovative when they understand and commit to the company's strategic management. This process results in employee empowerment. Empowerment is the act of strengthening an individual's sense of effectiveness.

(v) It encourages the organisations to decentralise the management process involving lower level managers and employees.

(vi) A significant number of research studies have suggested that a well-designed strategic management can boost profits.

(vii) A number of research studies have also indicated that systematic long-run planning resulted in high performance of the businesses.

(viii) It strengthens the employee commitment to and participation in formulating long-term goals.

(ix) Organisations foresee the environmental changes. Therefore, they reduce the chance of being affected by the changes in the environment, marketplace and actions of competitors.

(x) It helps for increased employee productivity, reduced resistance to change, clear understanding of performance-reward relationship.

(xi) It enhances problem-prevention capabilities of organisations as it promotes interaction among managers at all levels.

(xii) It often brings order and discipline to a firm.

(xiii) It allows for identification, prioritisation and exploitation of opportunities.

(xiv) It provides an objective view of management problems.

(xv) It represents a framework for improved control of activities.

(xvi) It minimises the effects of adverse conditions and changes.

(xvii) It allows major decisions and supports established objectives.

(xviii) It allows fewer resources and less time to be devoted for correcting erroneous or *adhoc* decisions.

(xix) It helps to integrate the behaviour of individuals into a total effort.

(xx) It provides a basis for the clarification of individual responsibilities.

(xxi) It gives encouragement to forward thinking.

(xxii) It provides cooperative, integrated and enthusiastic approach to tackling problems and opportunities.

(xxiii) It encourages favourable attitude towards change.

(xxiv) It gives a degree of discipline and formality to the management of business.

(E) STRATEGIC MANAGEMENT PROCESS: STRATEGIC FIT VS. STRATEGIC INTENT

As we have discussed earlier, strategic management is a process of series of steps. The basic steps in strategic management process are:

- Identify corporate vision, mission, objectives and goals.
- Analyse the corporate external environment to identify opportunities and threats.
- Scan the corporate internal environment to identify strengths and weaknesses of the company.
- Revise the corporate mission, if there is any drastic deviation in the external environment.
- Craft the strategic alternatives based mostly on the corporate opportunities and strengths. Also consider strategies for correcting company's weaknesses, when the opportunities are significant and distinct. Similarly consider crafting strategies by correcting the threats, as and when possible, and when the company has distinctive strengths or competencies.
- Select the best corporate strategy. Craft business unit level and functional level strategies based on corporate strategy.
- Implement the strategy.
- Evaluate and control the strategic implementation process in order to achieve the best performance. Fig. 1.4 presents the strategic management process.

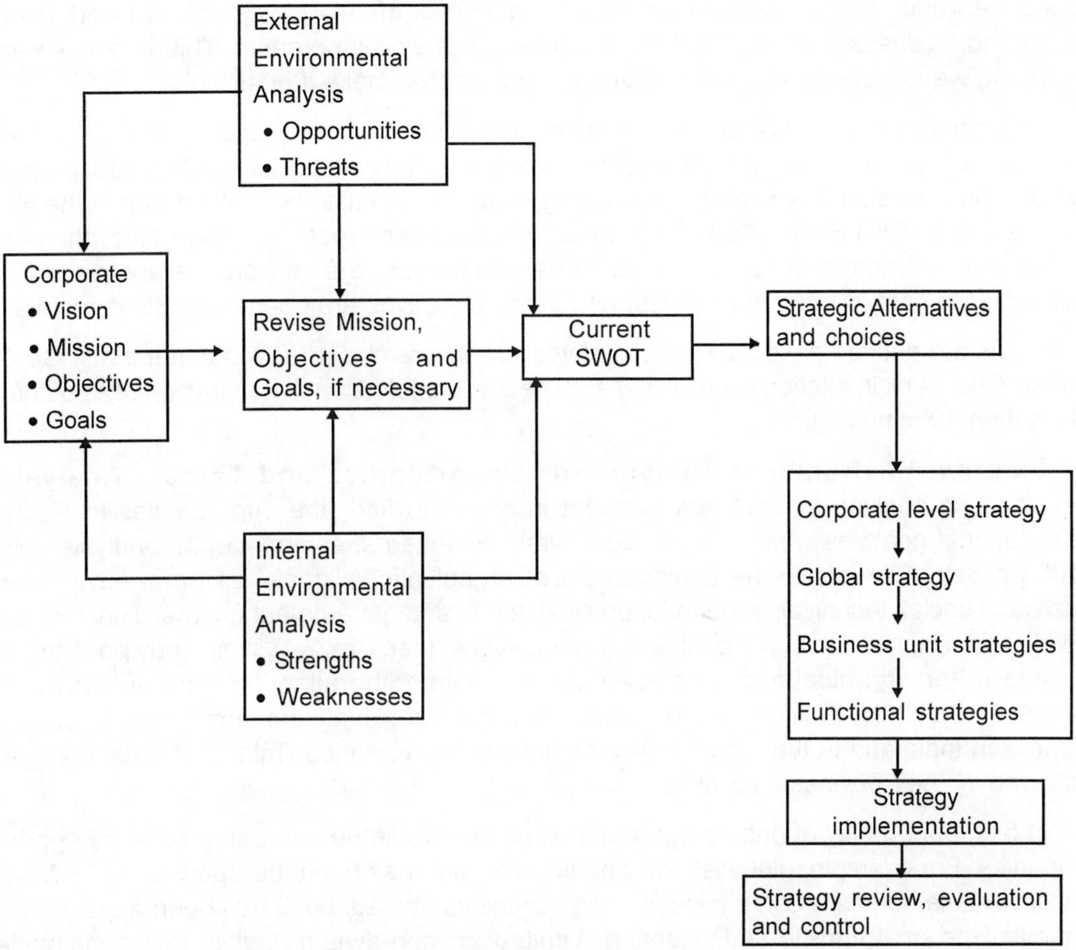

Fig. 1.4: The Strategic Management Process

Vision and Mission Statements

There is a confusion in the usage of the terminology of vision and mission as some companies use them distinctively, while others use them interchangeably. Thus, some companies define vision and mission statements separately, while others define only mission statement. These two terms are used separately in this book.

Vision statements visualise the future of the company. An organisation's vision statement answers the question: "What do we want to become?" or "What can we become?" Normally, mission statements are defined based on vision statements. Vision statement of a life insurance company is "To take care, your life's primary goal".

Mission statement defines the scope of business operations of a firm that distinguishes it from similar firms. The mission statement of **Ford Motor Company is:** "We are a global family with a proud heritage passionately committed to providing personal mobility for people around the world." While the mission statement of **Microsoft** is: At Microsoft, we work to help people and businesses throughout the world realize their full potential. This is our mission. Everything we do reflects this mission and the values that make it possible".

Organisation defines objectives based on its mission. Objectives specify the end towards which an activity is aimed at, long-range objectives specify the results that are desired in pursuing organisation's mission. For example, achieving high level of customer satisfaction is the long-run objective of ICICI Bank. The short-term objectives prefer targets normally of less than one-year's duration. Short-term objective of ICICI Bank is to make the transactions and procedures flexible for the convenience of the customer. Thus, objectives are open-ended statements.

Goals are defined based on the objectives. Goals are closed-ended statements. Goal in 2008 of ICICI Bank in relation to customer service is to complete each transaction of a customer in less than 10 minutes time.

External Environment Analysis (or Opportunities and Threats Analysis): Organisations analyse external environment in order to find the opportunities to achieve organisational goals as well as objectives. Similarly, external environmental analysis points out the possible threats to the achievement of organisational goals. External environment consists of social, technical, economic, political, legal, and government factors. These factors provide opportunities to certain business organisations, (see Box 2.4), while they pose threats to some other organisations. For example, economic liberalisation announced by the Government of India provided opportunities to various multinational companies to conduct business in India and to the Indian business houses like Reliance, Tata and Birla to expand and diversify their business activities.

In fact, opportunity of one category of companies would be a threat to other category of companies. For example, globalisation and liberalisation has been the opportunity for MNCs and large scale domestic companies in India as well as abroad, but it had been a great threat for most of the small firms like A.P. Lightings Limited and non-dynamic public sector companies like Hindustan Machine Tools in India and Banking Corporation of PNG in Papua New Guinea.

Box 1.4: Diplomats Provide Opportunity for World's Most Expensive Hotels

Starwood Hotels

The Royal Penthouse Suite at the President Wilson Hotel in Geneva commands $65,000 a night for its four-bedroom penthouse.

Amid the recession, rock stars, diplomats and other celebrities find solace from the doom and gloom by spending their time in sanctuary provided by the world's most luxurious and expensive hotels. While many of us are tightening our belts, shortening our summer holidays or even abandoning them, hoteliers to the rich and famous claim to have no trouble filling their most exclusive accommodations, and in the case of the most expensive suite in the world, managing to double its rate to $65,000 (€45,642) a night. In an annual survey by Financial News' sister publication Wealth Bulletin, the Royal Penthouse Suite at the President Wilson Hotel in Geneva, Switzerland, tops the list as the most expensive hotel room in 2009, commanding $65,000 for its four-bedroom penthouse — twice as much as patrons paid a year ago for its luxurious settings and views of Lake Geneva and Mont Blanc. The hotel's management puts the rise down to "buoyant demand" from government officials and U.N. diplomats. Last year's winner, the iconic Ty Warner Penthouse at the Four Seasons Hotel in New York, came second this time, at $35,000, $1,000 up from last year. New entries this year were the third-placed Presidential Suite at the Hotel Cala di Volpe in Sardinia, the Villa La Cupola Suite at the Westin Excelsior in Rome and the Presidential Suite at the Ritz-Carlton in Tokyo. Despite the past year's financial and economic turmoil, prices at the best hotel suites have risen by an average of 10% this year. Herbert Ypma, founder of the Hip Hotels brand, said: "The very high end hasn't suffered all that much. A lot of hotels used to having upmarket clientele are getting the benefit of them taking far more time off than usual — so they have more time to stay in hotels. Money was never the issue, time was."Hoteliers said that although the number of business travellers has fallen in the past year, government officials have taken their place in the best rooms and suites.President Barack Obama and his entourage took over the entire Ritz-Carlton Hotel in Moscow for three nights in June. The President Wilson Hotel said heads of state and other high-level government officials are fuelling demand for its hugely expensive Royal Penthouse Suite. Vivian Deuschl, spokeswoman for Ritz-Carlton Hotels, said demand is also coming from wealthy leisure travellers: "Last year they might have taken three or four cheaper holidays. This year they are taking one big vacation, but pulling out all the stops." The 10 most expensive hotel suites according to Wealth Bulletin's survey for 2009 are:

1. The Royal Penthouse Suite, President Wilson Hotel, Geneva — $65,000 per night: Complete with a cocktail lounge, the Royal Penthouse Suite at the President Wilson is so exclusive that bookings reportedly have to be made through the hotel's chairman. The suite occupies the entire top floor of the hotel. It is reached by a private elevator, has four bedrooms overlooking Lake Geneva and Mont Blanc and comes with six bathrooms. Equipped with bulletproof windows and doors, it is almost exclusively reserved for celebrities or state heads, ideal with the United Nations headquarters a five-minute drive away.

2. Ty Warner Penthouse, Four Seasons Hotel, New York — $35,000 per night: Business at the Ty Warner Penthouse at the Four Seasons Hotel in New York has remained as buoyant as when the suite opened in 2007, according to a spokeswoman. The nine-room suite has walls inlaid with thousands of pieces of mother-of-pearl. There is an indoor-outdoor Zen garden, a private spa room with a screen of living bamboo and a book-lined library, which has a grand piano at its centre.

3. The Presidential Suite, Hotel Cala di Volpe, Costa Smeralda, Sardinia — $34,000 per night: The Presidential Suite at Hotel Cala di Volpe near Porto Cervo, averages around $34,000 a night, although during the peak summer season will cost as much as $45,000. Located in the hotel tower, the multi-level Presidential Suite sprawls across 2,500 sq ft and has three bedrooms, three bathrooms, a private gym, a steam room and a wine cellar. It is crowned by a rooftop terrace with an outdoor saltwater swimming pool.

4. Villa La Cupola Suite, Westin Excelsior, Rome — $31,000 per night: Villa La Cupola Suite in Rome's Westin Excelsior embodies all things Roman and excessive: a cupola, a Pompeii-style Jacuzzi, frescoes and stained glass windows detailing allegories of a mythological figure paired with a modern one, such as Atlas and Television, Hypnosis and Neurosis, Hermes and Marketing and Hermaphrodite and Fashion. Located on the fifth and sixth floors, the suite covers 6,099 sq ft and has an additional 1,808 sq ft of balconies and terraces overlooking Via Veneto.

Ritz-Carlton

The Presidential Suite at Tokyo's Ritz-Carlton.

5. The Presidential Suite, Ritz-Carlton Tokyo — $25,000 per night: The Presidential Suite, on the top floor of the city's tallest building, has spectacular views of Mount Fuji and Roppongi Hills, as well as an expansive vista of Tokyo's impressive cityscape. It occupies 2,368 sq. ft., For refreshments, guests may enjoy the $18,000 Diamonds-Are-Forever Martini, which comes with a one-Karat Bulgari diamond at the bottom.

6. The Bridge Suite, The Atlantis, Bahamas — $22,000 per night: The 10-room Bridge Suite is actually a bridge spanning the two towers of the Atlantis Hotel. The 23rd-floor suite is decked with marble floors, a grand piano and a 22-carat gold chandelier. It was known in former times as "the Michael Jackson Suite" because of his regular stays. Prices have come down from $25,000 last year and fees are negotiable. Nevertheless, the suite is so exclusive the hotel does not even advertise it.

7. The Imperial Suite, Park Hyatt Vendôme, Paris — $20,000 per night: The Imperial Suite at the Park Hyatt in Paris provides guests with an "in-suite-spa" concept — with the bathroom/spa comprising a whirlpool bath, a steam shower room and a massage table. The 2,500 sq ft penthouse suite has a huge living room, a dining room, a kitchen and a work area.

Burj Al Arab

The Royal Suite at the Burj Al Arab in Dubai.

8. Royal Suite, Burj Al Arab, Dubai — $19,600 per night: Since it was built in the mid-1990s, the Burj Al Arab has become one of the world's most instantly recognizable hotels with its billowing sail-like structure stretching out on an artificial island into the Gulf of Arabia. The Royal Suite on the 25th floor has a marble-and-gold staircase, leopard print carpets, its own private lift and a rotating four-poster canopy bed.

9. Royal Armleder Suite, Le Richemond, Geneva — $18,900 per night: The Royal Armleder Suite at the Le Richemond Hotel is named after the wealthy family who used to own the famous hotel before Rocco Forte bought it in August 2004. The three-bedroom suite, which stretches over 2,500 sq ft on the seventh floor, has a 1,000 sq ft terrace with panoramic views of Lake Geneva, a real log fire and floor-to-ceiling bulletproof windows. Olga Polizzi, Rocco Forte's sister and well-known hotel interior designer, designed the suite.

10. The Ritz-Carlton Suite, The Ritz-Carlton, Moscow — $16,500 per night: To stay at the best suite in Moscow's Ritz-Carlton would cost around $16,000 a night — $500 less than last year. Furnished in Russian imperial style, the 2,370 sq. ft. suite has views of famous Moscow sites including the Kremlin and Red Square. The suite comes with the necessity for the security — conscious Russian billionaire — a panic room with its own energy and telecommunications facilities.

Source: http://finance.yahoo.com/real-estate/article/107608/diplomats-help-boost-rates-at-worlds-most-expensive-hotels.html(Accessed on 31/09/09).

Opportunities or threats depend upon perceptions as the same factor may be viewed as opportunity by one company while it may appear as threat to another. For example, more than one third of the low income group population in India was viewed as an opportunity by Coca Cola to introduce Coca Cola in a small bottle naming it "*Chota Cola*," *(Chota in Hindi language means small)* while its rival viewed the low income group as a loss of market. Environmental factors that may appear as threat at one point of time would turn out to be opportunities appearing at another point of time, once the company changes its strategy. For example the consumer goods giant Whirlpool introduced its washing machines in India in 1994. But it failed miserably because of the difference in women's clothing, *viz.*, the *saree* which was much thinner in material than those dress material used in US was not suitable for its machines. However, instead of accepting defeat, Whirlpool adopted to this cultural difference by coming up with a suitable model.

The model not only succeeded but also became a market leader. A cultural threat turned into a huge opportunity once Whirlpool changed its strategy.

On-time sales of most of the products including grocery would be a threat to most of the traditional sellers. Similarly, information technology creates opportunities for the fast moving and changing firms and but poses threats to the firms doing business with out dated technology.

Organisations analyse the external environmental factors and identify the opportunities and threats based on the company's current products, services systems and practices.

Internal Environment Analysis (or Strengths and Weaknesses): Internal environment consists of structures, resources, values, competencies, cultures, and systems of a company. Internal environmental analysis helps to identify company's strengths and weaknesses in relation to the market, customer needs and all other external environmental factors.

Internal environmental factors include organisation structure, finance, marketing, production/operations, human resources, information management and research and development capabilities of a company in terms of markets.

In fact, the same internal environmental factors seem to be strength in one kind of market and a weakness in other kind of markets. For example, the technology of Digicel, a mobile company is a strength of the company in smaller and relatively less developed and competitive markets like Papua New Guinea, Fiji and West Indies and is a weakness in highly competitive markets like USA, Europe and India. Therefore, companies have to assess their strengths based on the external environment under which they operate or propose to operate.

Companies identify their strengths and weaknesses in each of the functional area as well as overall organisational structure like producing high quality products, customised products and convenient products for the customers, efficient delivery of the products, efficient customer service, low cost and high productivity.

In addition, companies evaluate strengths and weakness against those of the competitors in order to find superiority or deficiency in each of the strengths and weaknesses. In addition, strengths and weaknesses are also identified against company's objectives and goals, in order to assess whether the company has capabilities to achieve its goals or not. For example, one of the objectives of Deccan Airlines is to provide passenger air travel at the lowest price compared to other domestic airlines in India. So Deccan Airlines evaluated its strengths in terms of low cost flights organisation structure that contribute to the low cost of operation per unit.

Thus, companies evaluate their strengths and weaknesses relative to the:

- external environmental factors
- markets in which currently operating and propose to operate
- objectives and goals of the companies and
- competitor's strengths and weaknesses.

Exhibit 1.3: presents some environmental factors to monitor strategic management process.

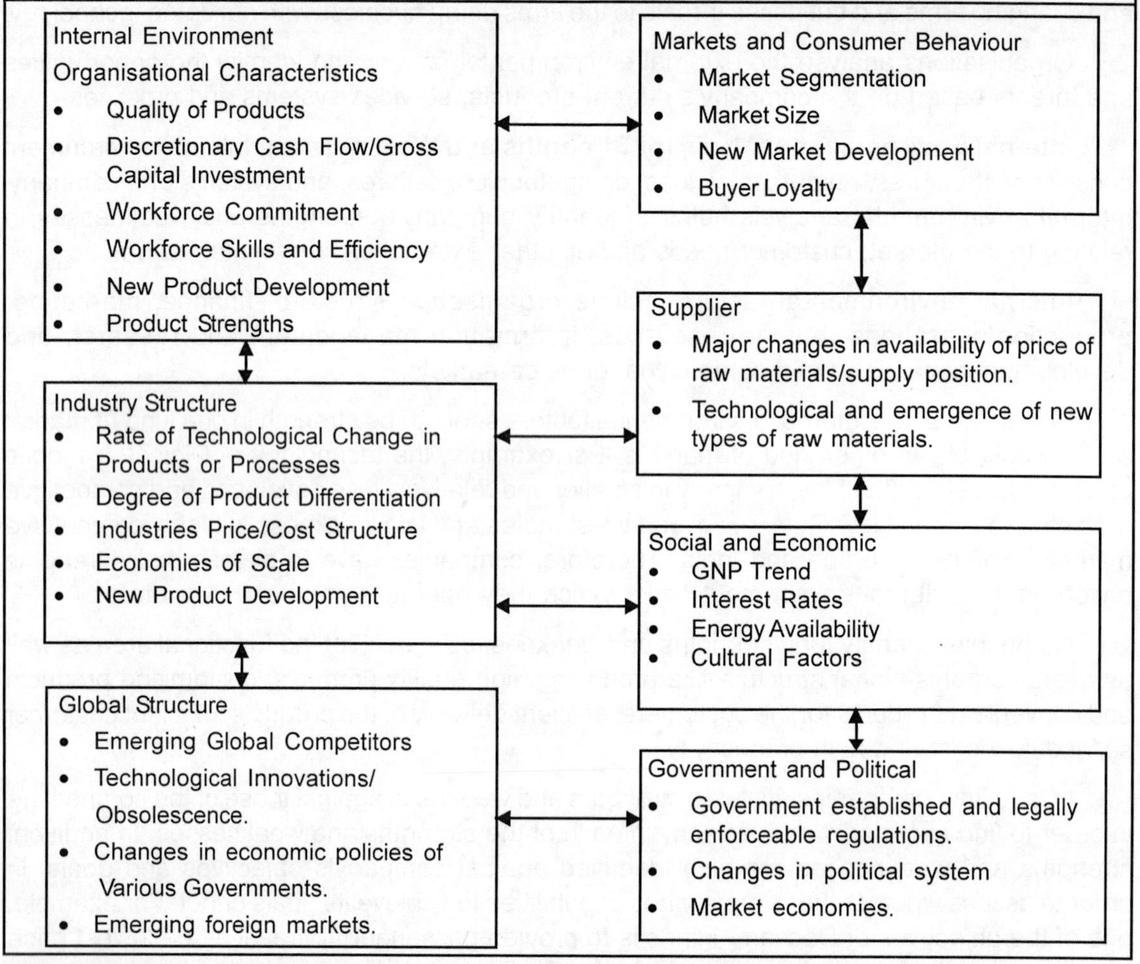

Source: Modified version from Samuel C. Certo and J. Paul Peter, *op.cit.*, p. 16.

SWOT Analysis and Strategy Formulation

The next logical step is to bring the alliance between opportunities and appropriate strengths, taking stock of weaknesses in relation to opportunities, study the possibility of correcting the weaknesses and study the threats, altering the strengths to convert the threats into opportunities. This process helps the organisation to make use of the opportunities to the full extent by aligning its strengths to the opportunities. This alignment further enables the company to formulate appropriate corporate strategies. The companies also strive to modify its products and/or correct their weaknesses in order to fit them with the opportunities and then formulate strategies. The example of Coca Cola's alternation in the bottle size and introduction of "Chota Cola" holds good in clarifying this concept. Thus, companies strive to bring the match among S-W-O-T in order.

Strategic Fit vs. Strategic Intent

Traditionally companies used to bring the fit between their current strengths and opportunities and formulate strategies in those areas where there is a fit between strengths and opportunities. C.K. Prahlad and Gary Hamel criticise the strategic fit model as it fixes the mindsets of the companies based on their current strengths and current environments and therefore fails to deals with the future environment and acquiring additional companies and resources.

Prahlad and Hamel argue that global leading companies like Toyota, Canon and Komastu acquired resources and capabilities necessary for the future environmental opportunities ahead of the change in the environment. These companies with their global leadership objective acquired the capabilities necessary to achieve such an objective. They prefer this situation of acquiring necessary resources and capabilities to achieve the objectives or goals under the circumstances of future environmental challenges and/or opportunities. According to them, strategic intent is more than unfettered ambition.

Companies under strategic intent process formulate challenging/ambitious goals, focus all organisational resources on winning, acquiring additional competencies, motivate and inspire employees towards the targets, sustain enthusiasm by providing new operational definitions based on perceived circumstances and towards the organisational transformation.

Beyond Strategic Fit and Strategic Intent

Certain organisations think beyond strategic fit and strategic intent by changing the current environment and/or creating new environments to their favour. This is by influencing the change process of the culture, altering the political factors by influencing the political parties, by introducing technological changes, by initiating different economic initiatives like granting loans, deferring payments and advance/delayed payments.

Normally companies initially craft corporate level strategies, which further become the basis for formulating global level strategies.

Corporate-level Strategies: Corporate level strategies link the opportunities, strengths/ competencies to the company's overall objective and goal. These strategies include expansion, diversification, mergers, joint ventures, takeovers, vertical and horizontal integration, entering into a new market and/or foreign country. Corporate level strategies affect the strategies and operations of all business units and functional level units.

Global Strategies: Global strategies include a decision to enter foreign markets. This strategy includes which countries to enter and the mode of entry. Global strategy is based on the corporate strategy.

Business level strategies: Business level strategies encompasses two or more functional units in crafting and implementing a strategy, for example, cost leadership strategy encompasses the integrated contribution of all functional areas. Other business level strategies include differentiation, niche market, total quality and fast delivery.

Fig. 1.5 presents strategic management process at different levels

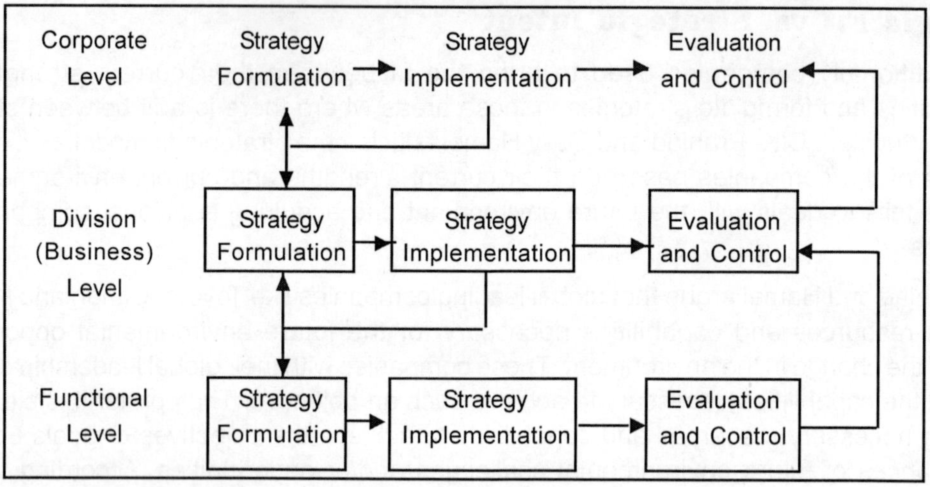

Fig. 1.5: Strategic Management Process at Different Levels

Functional Level Strategies: These strategies are more or less related to each function like production/operations, marketing, finance, human resource, information management and research and development. These are the ultimate strategies which are linked to corporate and business level Strategies. For example, managing cultural diversity is the human resource management strategy, while the merger is the corporate strategy.

Exhibit 1.4: Characteristics of Strategies at Different Levels

	Organisational Level	**Strategic Business Unit Level**	**Functional Level**
Purpose	Implement Mission	Achieve organisation strategies	Support business unit and organisational strategies
Internal Activities	Control contribution of divisions, business units to mission	Coordinate with other units developing distinctive competence	Manage daily operating problems
Key Questions	What business are we in? What business should we be in?	Are changes threatening or creating opportunities for our products or markets?	Are we on schedule?
External Activities	Monitor general and specific environment.	Focus on an industry, product, market.	Anticipate changes required from new business units and organisational strategies
Time Frame	Long-term (3 years plus)	Intermediate (1-3 years)	Daily (below one year)
Performance Measures	Vague, flexible	Measurable, moderately flexible	Detailed and specific

Source: Joe G. Thomas, "Strategic Management," Harper & Row, Publishers, New York, 1988, p. 46.

Strategic Evaluation and Control: The final step of strategic management process is strategic evaluation and control. It focuses on monitoring and evaluating the strategic management process in order to improve it and ensure that it functions properly. The managers must understand the process of strategic control and the role of strategic audit to perform the task of control successfully.

Challenges for Strategic Management

Strategic management faces different kinds of challenges, *viz.*, technological advancement and obsolescence, product or service innovations and development, etc. The recent additions to the challenges are: global issues consequent upon economic liberalisation, quality issues consequent upon the total quality management concept of the Japanese firms and social issues. We shall discuss these challenges for strategic management.

***(i)* Technological Advancements and Strategic Management:** As necessity is the mother of invention, competition and a host of other reasons are responsible for the rapid technological advancements and innovations. These advancements and innovations of one firm poses challenges for the strategic decision-making of the competing firms. Further, the continuous technological advancements led to the obsolescence of the existing technologies. It creates a challenge for the strategic management of those firms using obsolete technologies. The strategic managers should be fully aware of technological advances and innovations while formulating strategies.

Box 1.5: Technology and IBM

- IT strategy: establishing the overall IT strategy for an enterprise – including the SOA Strategy, Application Support Strategies, Governance models and innovative technology strategies.
- Enterprise and Service Oriented Architecture: helping to establish/evaluate an overall enterprise architecture and/or SOA for the business.
- IT performance management: helping to improve IT processes to deliver higher quality at reduced costs.

Why IBM

Technology strategy consultants provide the intersection of business and technology, supporting our clients in enhancing competitiveness and creating new sources of economic value from technology. Our consultants work with CIOs and their peers in the boardroom, seeking to close the gap between business and information technology. The Global Business Services technology strategy practice is a recognized market leader in innovative technologies, service-oriented architecture (SOA), and IT strategy. Our consultants have demonstrated experience creating value for clients and serving as trusted business advisors. And we can bring value to your organization through the unmatched worldwide capabilities, relationships and research of IBM. With nearly 3,500 strategy professionals worldwide, the IBM strategy and change practice is part of IBM Global Business Services, one of the worlds leading management consulting practices. Working across all major sectors, IBM has inherent business expertise across more than a dozen industries. This includes communications, distribution, financial services, and the industrial and public sectors. Our consultants have demonstrated experience creating value for clients and serving as trusted business advisors to our clients worldwide.

Source: http://www-935.ibm.com/services/us/index.wss/offerfamily/gbs/a1029389 (Accessed on 31/08/09)

***(ii)* Product/Service Innovation and Development and Strategic Management:** Technological advancements and innovations together with changes in consumer tastes and preferences, needs and conveniences led to the continuous product/service development and innovation of new products.

The firms with new products/services widely accepted by the customers enjoy distinctive strategic advantage whereas other firms in the same industry suffer from strategic disadvantage. This leads to further competition and creates new challenges for strategic management. Strategic managers are expected to be aware of these developments and innovations in the industry while formulating their strategies.

***(iii)* Global Issues and Strategic Management:** With the announcement of economic liberalisation in India and consequently opening up of the economy to the rest of the world in 1991, business activities have tended to cross national boundaries more intensely and frequently. Due to the increase in scale and variety of operations of multinational and transnational corporations in the country, even firms with no international operations are experiencing the impact of globalisation on their markets and operations. Since this trend is and markets will have to consider global issues in their strategic management process.

The strategic managers must be fully aware of critical international variables that might considerably affect their strategic operations, before they determine how their strategic management process can most effectively accommodate global environmental factors.

***(iv)* Quality Issues and Strategic Management:** The quality movement, spearheaded by W. Edwards Dening has had a significant impact on the method of strategic management process of organisations in the 1990s. Sea changes took place in the concept of quality. The concept of post-production quality control changed into Total Quality Management (TQM). It further changed to feed forward and zero-defect of the product. Further, quality today does mean an organisation — wide commitment to enhance the value of goods or services to the customer at each and every stage — from the stage of product design, raw material, every stage of production process, to the place of marketing (or selling) to post sale service. Japanese firms once produced cheap products, presently they are producing not only low cost but most qualitative products. In fact, today's customers feel happy to buy a Japanese-made product in view of its quality. Hence, Japanese firms enjoy strategic advantage position in this regard.

Box 1.6: Quality Strategy, Strategic Control Systems and Organizational Performance

Despite calls for the development of systems to control the implementation and monitoring of strategic plans, prior studies suggest that few American or European firms employ formal strategic control systems. Using survey data from the automotive and computer industries in Canada, Germany, Japan, and the

United States, we examine whether organizations following a quality-oriented strategy have adopted the strategic control practices discussed in the quality management literature. Our results indicate that organizations placing greater emphasis on quality in their strategic plan do tend to make greater use of quality-related strategic control practices. However, we find no evidence to support the claim that Japanese organizations link their control systems more closely to their competitive strategies than organizations in the other countries. Instead, Japanese manufacturers appear to make greater use of many of the strategic control practices regardless of their organization's strategic emphasis. The performance consequences of the strategic control practices vary somewhat by industry, suggesting that strategic control systems should be adapted to the organization's competitive environment. Finally, several strategic control practices are negatively associated with performance, consistent with claims that formal strategic control systems can actually hinder performance in some circumstances by focusing attention on formal and rigid action plans, targets, and information gathering when flexible and creative strategic responses may be more appropriate.

Source: http://knowledge.wharton.upenn.edu/paper.cfm?paperID=512(Accessed on 31/08/09)

Managers involved in the strategic management process at all levels are expected to understand the history of this movement and its day-to-day developments in order to appreciate the crucial role it plays in modern organisational strategy.

***(v)* Economic Boom and Recession:** Both economic booms as well as economic recession affect the strategic management process. Economic boom provides the opportunities for the increase in demand as well as business operations and economic recession in general create threats. Companies should foresee the trends that result in recession and formulate strategies accordingly. In fact, most of the companies failed to foresee the economic recession of 2008 and beyond.

***(vi)* Social Issues and Strategic Management:** Since the organisation is part and parcel of the society, most of the organisations are of the view that, social responsibility is the managerial obligation to act, protect and promote both organisational interests and welfare of the society. Strategic management process of an organisation will be affected by recognising this obligation.

The strategic managers should have a clear idea about *(i)* the societal constituencies that the organisation will serve us the obligation, *(ii)* the areas of the business to be affected by this obligation, *(iii)* method of conducting social audit to facilitate the strategic management process, and *(iv)* the areas of strategic advantages that the organisation will be enjoying.

Points to be Remembered

- Different organisations having similar opportunities and resources perform differently.
- Strategy is a unified, comprehensive and integrated plan/course of action that relates to the strategic advantages of the firm and the challenges of the environment.
- Strategy is necessary to have and develop internal ability.
- Globalisation and strides in information technology makes strategic management complex.
- Strategic management is concerned with deciding on strategy and planning how that strategy is to be put into effect.
- Strategic management passes through the stages of financial planning, external oriented planning and to strategic management.
- Strategic management is essential due to change and for better performance.

Keywords

- Strategy
- Strategic Management
- Forecasting
- Electronic Business
- Challenges
- Opportunities
- Change
- Financial Planning
- External Planning
- Business Decisions
- Environment
- Advantages

Questions for Discussion

(1) What is strategy? State a few definition of strategy.
(2) Should a strategy be a plan?
(3) What are the dimensions of strategy? Discuss different forms of strategy.
(4) Why do organisations need strategies?
(5) What are the key areas in developing strategies?
(6) State the historical developments of strategic management.
(7) Define the term strategic management.
(8) Discuss the need for and benefits of strategic management.
(9) What are the challenges to strategic management?

References

1. James Brain Quinn, "Strategies for Change" in James Brain Quinn, Henry Mintzberg and Robert M. James (Ed). *"The Strategy Process,"* Prentice-Hall, Englewood Cliffs, New Jersey, 1988, pp. 8-9.
2. Alfred D. Chandler, "Strategy and Structure," in the "History of American Enterprise,"M.I.T. Press, Cambridge, 1962, p. 13.
3. Thomas L. Wheelen, J. David Hunger and Krish Rangarajan, *"Strategic Management and Business Policy"*, Pearson, 2007, p.7.
4. James Brain Quinn, *"Strategies for Change,"* Richard D. Irwin Inc., Homewood Ill, 1980, p. 7.
5. Delivering the Goods at FedEx, *Business Week*, June 2005, pp.60-62
6. Michael A Hitt, Robert E. Hoskisson and R. Duane Ireland, *"Management of Strategy"*, Thomson, 2007, p.7.
7. R.M. Grant, "Strategic Planning in a Turbulent Environment: Evidence from the oil majors", *Strategic Management Journal*, 24: 491-517.
8. Thomas L. Wheeler, J. David Hunger and Krish Ramgarajan, '*Strategic Management and Business Policy*', Pearson, 2004, pp. 63-64.
9. R.A.D. Aveni, "Coping with Hypercompetition: Utilising the New 7's Framework", *Academy of Management Executive*, 9(3) 1995, p. 4b.
10. *R.A.D. Aveni*, "Corporate Spheres of Influence", *MIT Sloan Management Review, 2004, 45(4), pp. 38- 46.*

11. Wal-Mart at a Glance, 2005, www.walmart.com
12. Thomas L. Wheelen, J. David Hunger and Krish Rangarajan, "*Strategic Management and Business Policy*", Pearson, 2007, p.7.
13. *A.Y. Lewin and H. W. Voloberda*, "Prolegomena on Coevolution: A Framework for Research on Strategyand New Organisational forms", *Organisational Science, October 1999, pp. 519-534.*
14. D.A. Garvin, "Building a learning or mitigating the possible deviations", July-August 1993, p.80.
15. T.T. Bedwin, et.al., "The Evolution of Learning Strategies in Organisation", *Academy of Management Executive, November 1997, p. 47-58.*
16. James A.F. Stoner, "*Management*," Prentice-Hall of India (P) Ltd., New Delhi, 1984, p. 87.
17. Quoted in Chandan J.S., "*Fundamentals of Modern Management*," Vikas Publishing House (P) Ltd., New Delhi, 1986, p. 1.
18. Harold Koontz and Cyril O'Donnel, "*Essentials of Management*," McGraw-Hill Book Company, New York, 1978, p. 4.
19. Robert T. Justis, Richard J. Judd and David B. Stephens, "*Strategic Management and Policy*," Prentice-Hall Inc. New Jersey, 1985, p. 3.
20. Azhar Kazmi, "*Business Policy*," Tata McGraw-Hill Publishing Company Ltd., New Delhi, 1992, p. 4.
21. R.A. Gordon and J.E. Howell, "*Higher Education for Business*," Columbia University Press, New York, 1959.
22. Samuel C. Certo and J. Paul Peter, "*The Strategic Management Process*," Richard D. Irwin Inc., Chicago, 1993, p. 5.
23. R.A. Gordon and J.E. Howell, *op.cit.*
24. Gerry Johnson and Keven Scholes, *op. cit.*, p. 10.
25. Mathew J. Kiernam, "*The New Strategic Architecture*," The Executive, February 1993, pp.7-21.
26. H. Igor Ansoff, "*Implementing Strategic Management*," Prentice-Hall, New Jersey, 1984.
27. Lawrence R. Jauch and William F. Glueck, "*Business Policy and Strategic Management*," McGraw-Hill Book Company, New York, 1988, p. 4.
28. Ibid., p. 11.
29. Alfred D. Chandler, "*Strategy and Structure*," in the "*History of American Enterprise*," M.I.T. Press, Cambridge, 1962, p. 13.
30. Arthur Sharplin, "*Strategic Management*," McGraw-Hill Book Company, New York, 1985, p. 6.
31. James Brain Quinn, "*Strategies for Change*," Richard D. Irwin Inc., Homewood III, 1980, p. 7.
32. Samuel C. Certo and J. Paul Peter, *op.cit.*, p.6.
33. James Brain Quinn, "Strategies for Change" in James Brain Quinn, Henry Mintzberg and Robert M. James (Ed). "*The Strategy Process*," Prentice-Hall, Englewood Cliffs, New Jersey, 1988, pp. 8-9.
34. H. Igor Ansoff, "*Concept of Strategy*," in Ibid., pp. 12-13.
35. R.N. Anthony and J. Dearden, "*Management Control Systems*," Irwin, 1976 Quoted in Ibid, p. 10.
36. C.K. Prahalad and G. Hamel, "*The Core Competence of The Corporation*," Harvard Business Review, May- June 1990, pp 79-91.
37. *Ibid.*
38. Samuel C. Certo and J. Paul Peter, *op.cit.*, p. 8.

***

Chapter - 2

External Environment Scanning and Industry Analysis

Chapter Outline

(A) Introduction
(B) International Environment
(C) Social and Cultural Environment
(D) Technological Environment
(E) Economic Environment
(F) Political Environment
(G) Natural Environment
(H) Industry Analysis
— Keywords
— Questions for Discussion
— References

Learning Objectives

After studying this chapter, you should be able to:

- Analyse the need for environment scanning for formulation of strategies;
- Study the social and cultural environment in order to find out the business appropriateness;
- Analyse the economic environment in order to find out the influence of income and expenditure pattern;
- Discuss the technological environment to find out the appropriateness of the technology;
- Explain the influence of the political environment on the business;
- Discuss the industry analysis in order to find out the growth of the industry.

(A) INTRODUCTION

William F. Glueck defined the term environmental analysis as, "the process by which strategists monitor the economic, governmental/legal, market/competitive, supplier/ technological, geographic and social setting to determine opportunities and threats to their firms." "Environmental diagnosis consists of managerial decisions made by analysing the significance of data (opportunities and threats) of the environmental analysis."

Business Environmental Factors

Business environmental factors are broadly divided into external environmental factors and internal environmental factors. External environmental factors that affect the business include Social and Cultural factors (S), Technological factors (T), Economic factors (E), Political/ Governmental factors (P), International factors (I) and Natural factors (N) (STEPIN). Internal environmental factors influence/affect the business from within. They include: human resource management, trade unions, organisation structure, financial management, marketing management, production management, management/leadership styles, etc.

External environmental factors are further divided into micro external factors and macro external environmental factors. Micro external environmental factors include: competitors, customers, market intermediaries, suppliers of raw materials, bankers and other suppliers of finance, shareholders, and other stakeholders of the business firm.

External macro environmental factors include: social and cultural factors, technological factors, economic factors, political and governmental factors, international factors and natural factors. In recent times environmental protection has received greater attention in order to protect people, animals, plants and to maintain ecological balance. The analysis of internal environmental factors indicates the strengths and weaknesses of the business firm while the analysis of micro external and macro external environmental factors indicate the opportunities provided by the environment to the business. The strengths, weaknesses, opportunities and threats (SWOT) analysis helps to formulate strategies for the business firm. (See fig. 2.1).

Strategic Management and Environmental Analysis

Strategic management involves three levels of analysis, *viz.,* the organisation's macro environment/general environment, the industry in which the organisation operates, and the organisation itself. We will discuss the first two levels in this chapter and the third level in the next chapter. Every company operates within a complex network of external environmental forces both international and national.

Need for Environmental Analysis and Diagnosis

Environmental analysis is the process by which strategists monitor the environmental factors to determine opportunities for and threats to their firms. Analysis also involves studying each factor minutely to find its nature, function and relationship. Strategic manager essentially searches for opportunities and threats, their sources and their impact on the business. Environmental diagnosis consists of managerial decisions made by assessing the significance of the data (opportunities and threats) of the environmental analysis. A strategist examines the relationship between the company's strategy and the environment. Then, he/she forecasts

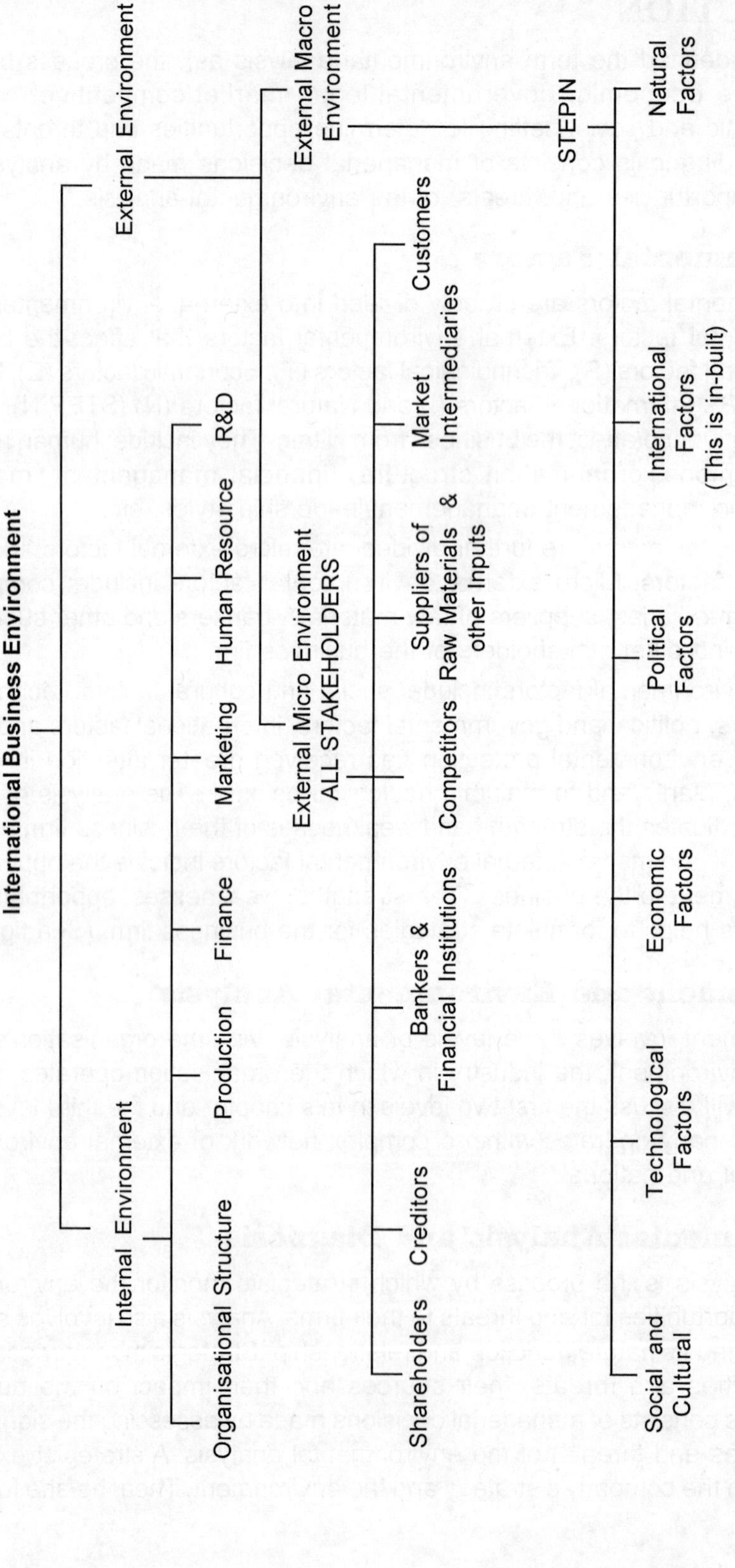

Fig. 2.1: Business Environment

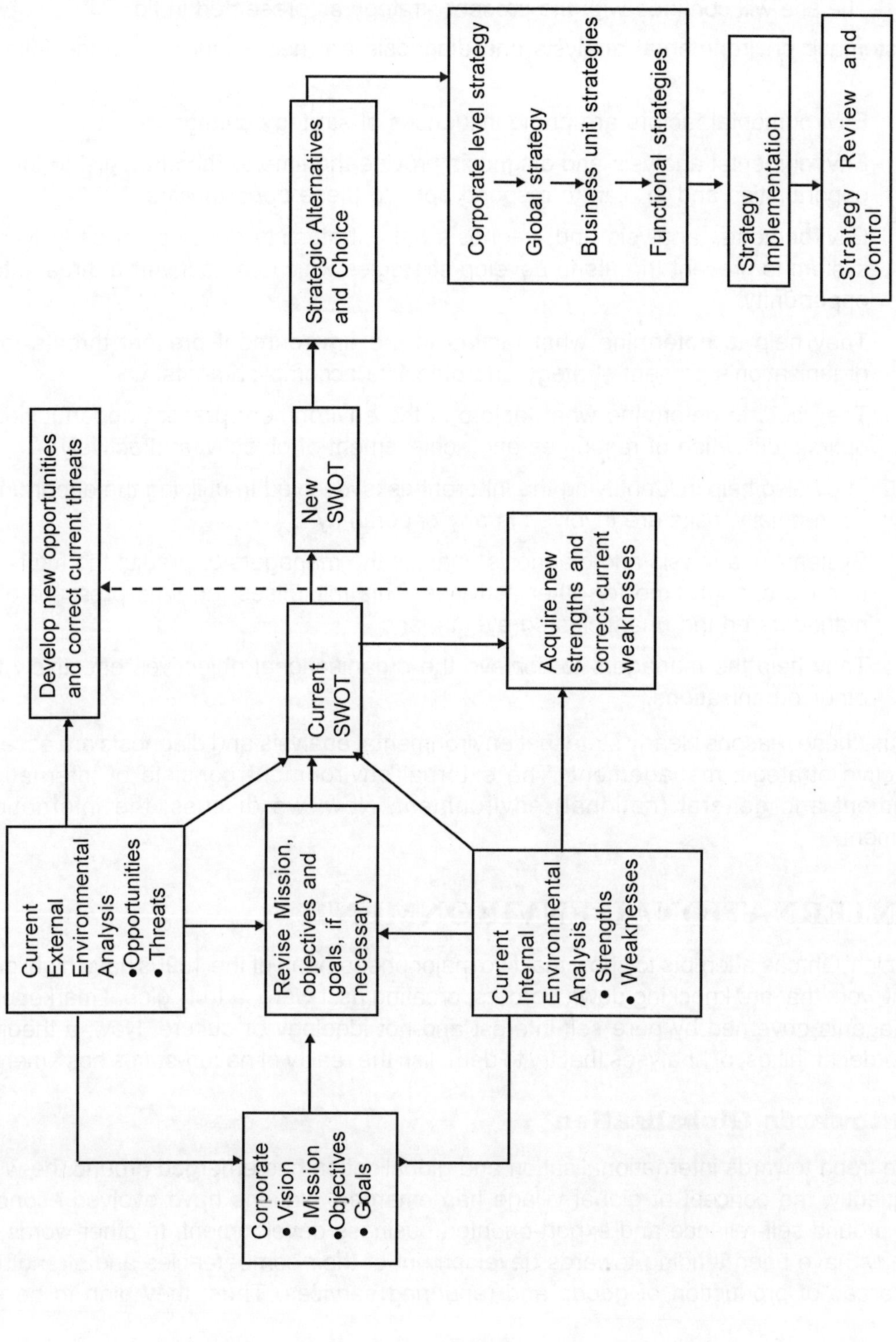

Fig. 2.2: Strategic Management Process

the future environment and compares the strategy with the future environment. If there are gaps, he/she reformulates the strategy after revising the business mission and objectives. Otherwise, he/she will continue with the present strategy as presented in fig. 2.2.

Systematic environmental analysis and diagnosis are necessary due to the following reasons:

(i) Environmental factors are prime influences of strategy change.

(ii) Environmental analysis and diagnosis provide the time to the strategist to forecast opportunities and to plan to respond aptly to these opportunities.

(iii) Environmental analysis and diagnosis help strategists develop an early warning system to prevent threats to develop strategies which can convert a threat into an opportunity.

(iv) They help to determine what factors in the environment present threats to the organisation's present strategy and objective accomplishments.

(v) They help to determine what factors in the environment present opportunities for optimal utilisation of resources and achievement of objectives effectively.

(vi) They also help in identifying the inherent risks involved in utilising the opportunities as, normally, risks are involved in any opportunity.

(vii) Systematic analysis and diagnosis enables the managers to predict the future and to have enough time for other activities. This minimises the time pressure of the managers on the unanticipated events, and

(viii) They help the managers to achieve the organisational objectives effectively than other organisations.

Thus, these reasons clearly state that environmental analysis and diagnosis are essential for effective strategic management. The external environment consists of international environment and general (national) environment. Now, we discuss, the international environment.

(B) INTERNATIONAL ENVIRONMENT

Kenichi Ohmae attempts to show that two major phenomena of the 1990s have highlighted forces at work that are knocking down borders, creating as it were, a truly global market place with its agents governed by pure self-interest and not ideology or culture. Now, a theory of cross-border affinities, of analyses that try to demolish the reality of nation-states has emerged.

Trend towards Globalisation

The trend towards internationalisation and globalisation has emerged around the world. Consequently, the concept of global village has emerged. Nations have evolved economic policies around self-reliance and export-oriented business development. In other words, the economies have been tending towards development of their competencies and strengths in certain areas of production of goods and rendering services. Thus, they plan to be self-reliant. Then, the economies find the opportunities to develop export-oriented business. Further, the economies opened their business to the rest of the globe. These changes have also been taking places in the erstwhile Socialistic/Communist countries. Thus, the business in different countries has become business in a global village. These factors resulted in the close and direct impact of international environment on the national business firms.

Nature of Globalisation: Globalisation refers to the process of integration of the world into one huge market. This type of unification calls for removal of all trade barriers among economies. At the organisational level, globalisation means: *(i)* the organisation commits itself heavily with several manufacturing locations around the world and offers products and/or services in several countries and *(ii)* ability to compete in domestic markets with foreign competitors.

A multinational company (MNC) or a transnational company (TNC) operates in more than one country, gains production, technology, marketing, financial, human resources and R&D advantages — in its costs and reputation over the domestic competitors.

Why do Companies go Global?

Companies go global due to the following reasons:

(i) Rapid shrinking of time and distance across the globe owing to the significant development of transportation and telecommunication facilities.

(ii) Inadequacy of and low purchasing ability in the domestic markets.

(iii) The short span of product life cycle in the domestic market.

(iv) To have diversified portfolio of markets.

(v) To secure reliable and cheap inputs like raw material, finance and human resources.

(vi) Due to political stability in some countries and political disturbances in other countries.

(vii) To reduce high transportation costs.

(viii) To set up plants close to the raw material.

Stages of Globalisation: There are four stages of globalisation as depicted in Exhibit 2.1. Companies at the first stage of globalisation have only passive dealings with foreign individuals and organisations. In the second stage, companies deal directly with their overseas interests. In the third stage, a company's international interests shape its overall make-up in an important way. In the final stage, the company sees its activities as essentially multinational as opposed to domestic.

Impact of International Environment on Domestic Business

Global environment consists of international political environment, policies of various governments, level of technology, social and cultural factors, level of economic development of different countries, level of industrial development, etc., has its impact on the business organisations of the domestic country. The impact is discussed hereunder.

(i) ***Configuring Anywhere in the World:*** An MNC can choose the location of its plants or business units in different countries on the basis of availability of raw material, consumer markets, availability of cheap labour, etc. Thus, an MNC competes with the domestic company for inputs as well as selling the output.

(ii) ***Interlinked and Interdependent Economies:*** Economic policy of most of the nations is to develop the countries through interlinkage and interdependence. Therefore, domestic industries also develop interlinkage and interdependency with the foreign companies.

(iii) ***Minimisation of Trade and Tariff Barriers:*** The recent trend towards globalisation in most of the nations in the world resulted in minimisation of trade and tariff barriers. Consequently, the protection provided to the home industry has been withdrawn. Therefore, the domestic industry is affected by the quality, price and convenience of the foreign products and services.

(iv) ***Effect on Related Industries and Ancillary Units:*** Globalisation may render many companies sick and defunct. This effect is more in case of ancillary industrial units and small scale industrial units compared to large scale industrial units. Globalisation of Indian economy in 1991 affected badly many ancillary industrial units.

(iv) ***Infrastructural Resources and Inputs at International Prices:*** The prices of infrastructural resources like banking, transportation and telecommunications and inputs like raw materials and human resources adjust at international prices. In other words, prices of these factors, which were lower before globalisation would increase due to increase in demand for the same.

(vi) ***Increasing Trend Towards Privatisation:*** Governments in many countries recently started withdrawing their capital from public sector industrial units and/or privatising these units after globalisation.

(vii) ***Entrepreneur and His Unit have A Central Economic Role:*** The trend of shifting the business from the bureaucrat to the entrepreneur has started consequent upon globalisation of business.

(viii) ***Mobility of Skilled Resources:*** The traditional factors of production, *viz.*, land, labour, capital and organisation are no more immobile. Globalisation has resulted in the inflow of these factors into the potential developing countries.

(ix) ***Market Side Efficiency:*** Integration of global markets implies that costs, quality, processing time and terms of business become dominant competitive drivers.

(x) ***Formation of Regional Blocks:*** A final corollary to globalisation is the formation of trade blocks like North American Free Trade Area (USA, Canada and Mexico), European Economic Community and South Asian Preferential Trading Agreements. These regional blocks provide the opportunities to the business from within and creates threats to the business from other areas.

Now, we shall discuss the macro internal environmental factor. We start our discussion with social and cultural factors.

(C) SOCIAL AND CULTURAL FACTORS

Social and cultural factors in various countries of the globe affect business. These factors include attitude of the people to work, attitude to wealth, family, marriage, religion, education, ethics, human relations, social responsibilities, etc.

Cultural Attitude and Business

Dressing habits, living styles, eating habits and other consumption patterns, priority of needs are dictated/influenced by culture of the land. Some Chinese and most of the Indians do not consume beef. Thailand Chinese believe that consumption of beef is improper and Indian (particularly Hindus) believe that eating beef is a sin as they believe cow is sacred *(Kamadhenu)*. The eating habits vary widely. Chinese eat fish stomachs and bird's nest soup, Japanese eat uncooked sea food, Iraqis eat dried, salted locusts and snakes while drinking. The French eat snails, Americans and Europeans eat mostly non-vegetarian food. Indian eat mostly vegetarian food. It was surprising to the rest of the world to know that there were pure vegetarians in India. However, the foreign culture regarding food has been adapted very openly. *Indian food items like Chapati, Masala dosa and Hyderabadi biryani* have become popular in Europe and the USA whereas pizzas have become popular in India. In fact, the culture around the world has been evolving as global culture.

Box 2.1: In India, Pizzas are Now The Flavour of The Season

Chicken tikka masala may be ruling the roost in Britain, but in curry country – India – pizzas are the flavour of the month. Take, for example, Neelam Mehta. Whenever she hears the question "What's for dinner, mum?" after she comes home from her Delhi office, her answer is often the same: "Pizza". "It's the easiest thing to do. Just pick-up the phone and order. I don't have to sweat it out in the kitchen at the end of the day," said Mehta, an Indian exporter with two teenage sons. Ever since India threw open its economic doors in the early 1990, a host of global pizza chains including Pizza Hut, run by Yum! Brands Inc., and Domino's Pizza have been fighting for a slice of the country's growing pizza market.

Source: Deccan Chronicle, July 22, 2003,

Similarly, dressing habits also vary from country to country based on their culture. We observe different dressing styles of the West, Middle East, India, Pacific, etc. Wearing '*saree*' by Indian women is influenced by the culture which in turn is influenced by the climate. However the *saree* culture in India is slowly decreasing with increase in women becoming more career oriented. Similarly, wearing 'burka/parda' by the women of the Middle East is another example of the influence of culture on the dressing habit.

Guidelines for the businessmen when they launch business in foreign countries: *(a)* resist the tendency to conduct business immediately on landing, and at all times, *(b)* offer favours as a business tool to generate allies, *(c)* contact, cultivate and conduct field work among at least one sample clientele to serve as an initial testing centre for the firm's product, *(d)* introduce the product line into the sample group by local firms of cause-related marketing and *(e)* extend product acceptance beyond the sample clientele into related market segments. Businessmen should follow these guidelines in order to prevent possible failures.

Box 2.2: Disney in France: Cultural Issues

Disney with its success in park business and entertaining children in USA entered Japan in 1983 and became successful there too so they decided to enter the French market too in 1986 owing to location advantage of Paris and availability of subsidies and incentives by French Government. However, Disney had problems negotiating with the French Government and faced unwillingness of French people to accept Disney. Despite these problems, Disney opened the park in 1992 summer. Soon after the opening, French farmers drove their tractors and blocked the entrance. Later, there were a number of operational disasters like Disney's policy of serving no alcohol, serving less quantity of breakfast, lunch timings, lack of teamwork for the employees of Disney of Paris. These problems resulted in a cumulative loss of $2 billion by the end of 1994.

Source: Adapted from Charles W.L. Hill, "International Business",: Tata McGraw-Hill, New Delhi, 2003, pp. 119-12.

Behavioural Factors Affecting Business

Cultural factors influence human behaviour. Cultural difference in various countries result in variation in human behaviour, consumer behaviour and behaviour of other stakeholders. Variation in behaviour can be ascertained through the social stratification of a country. Business should consider the behavioural patterns of social groups in hiring, marketing and in selecting suppliers of inputs and market intermediaries. Behavioural patterns can be studied based on ascribed group membership and acquired group memberships. Ascribed group membership is based on genders, age, family, caste, community, ethnic, racial and nation of origin. Acquired group membership is based on religion, political affiliation, professional and social associations. These memberships influence human behaviour of a society.

Behaviour based on Group Membership

Certain societies like USA reward people based on performance while other societies like Malaysia reward people based on ethnic group in addition to performance. Attitude towards female employment vary from country to country. Egalitarian societies do not discriminate employment of people based on sex whereas Arabian countries discourage females from seeking employment. Family membership is paramount rather than individual's achievements or traits — in certain societies like India, China and Southern Italy.

Impact of Culture on Consumer Behaviour

Culture influences the behaviour of the consumer though valid generalisations have not yet been developed. Montrose, Sommers and Jerome Kernan have made a beginning in this direction. They identify the value orientations that underline market behaviour as falling in six categories: *(1)* Egalitarian or elitist; *(2)* prone to lay stress on accomplishment or on inherited attributes; *(3)* expected material or non-material rewards; *(4)* evaluating individuals or products in terms of objective norms or of subjective standards; *(5)* focused on the distinctiveness of the parts (intensiveness); and *(6)* oriented towards personal rather than toward group's gain. The U.S. consumer tends to have the attributes described by the first term in each pair. British attitudes tend to fall on the opposite side. A number of examples illustrate the significance of these differences.

"When performance orientation is coupled with a predisposition to be intensive — *i.e.*, to perceive many separate and distinct needs to be acted upon as well as a variety of ways in which these needs can be served — the probability of accepting new contingencies as real is greater than when an extensive value orientation prevails. Americans see more separate and distinct activities plus more separate and distinct products which can be used in their performance than do Canadians, Australians or Britons. Such a disposition supports their market for gadgets, the great array of household appliances accessories".

Box 2.3: Culture-based Market Segmentation

A medium-sized Swedish engineering company manufactured fire-fighting equipment, but was incurring losses. In 1983 a new marketing director was appointed. After four years of work, turnover rose from £3 million to £10 billion and profitability was restored, mainly on the basis of a complete reappraisal of markets and marketing policy.

The marketing director found that the company had been dealing with about 100 country markets, but many produced orders only in small quantities, and these too intermittently. In total, the orders were a surprisingly small proportion of the turnover, but were just as costly and time-consuming to service as orders from the larger, steadier markets.

A careful process of selection showed that if the company concentrated more extensively on 50 markets, its chances of progress would improve, and of these 50, some 10 which looked the most promising were selected for constant and increasing attention; for example, visits were planned with increasing frequency. The company found that this core of key markets provided an almost ideal ratio, because only five or six countries accounted for 75 per cent of trade. A contraction of business in those few countries could prove very harmful. Recognising important national differences among the 10 key markets, with local issues and customer contracts, by reducing the total number of markets, but retaining those with significant trade, the company improved its profit performance.

Source: Edgar P. Hibbert, International Business, p.80.

Ageing Populations

Population ageing is constituted by a shift in the distribution of a country's population towards greater ages. An increase in the population's mean or median age, means a decline in the fraction of the population composed of children, or a rise in the fraction of elderly people.

Ageing population has seen an increase in many advanced countries as well as in some developing countries where advanced medical and health facilities are available. In addition, the baby-boom generation (people born in the 20-year period after World War II) in some countries like USA, UK and Australia continues to age. Added to this, the reduced birth rates in advanced countries and some developing countries like India and China has contributed to the ageing population.

Population ageing is a highly generalised process; it is most advanced in the most highly developed countries. Among the countries currently classified by the United Nations as more developed (with a population of 1.2 billion in 2005), the median age of the population rose from 29.0 years in 1950 to 37.3 in 2000 and it is estimated to rise to 45.5 by 2050. The corresponding figures for the world as a whole were 23.9 years for 1950, 26.8 for 2000 and 37.8 for 2050. Japan is one of fastest ageing countries in the world. There will be 9.3 people under the age of 20 for every person older than 65 by 2025. The ageing population would result in increased demand for medical care, pharmaceutical products and social security and decline in the demand for existing products like motor cycles, luxury cars and luxurious white goods.

Career Orientation of Women

Increase in career orientation of women particularly after globalisation has provided wider opportunities for fast foods and ready-made food industry, white goods, luxurious housing, automobile and the like. This trend is significant in India, China, Malaysia and Middle-East countries.

In Summary The Following Factors are to be Scanned to Assess The Social and Cultural Environment:

Demographic factors such as:

- population size and distribution
- age distribution
- education levels
- income levels
- ethnic origins
- religious affiliations
- gender distribution

Attitudes towards:

- materialism, capitalism, free enterprise
- individualism, role of family, role of government, collectivism
- role of church and religion
- consumerism
- environmentalism
- importance of work, pride of accomplishment

Cultural structures including:

- diet and nutrition
- housing conditions
- dressing habits
- work habits and work-culture
- punctuality

Source: Modified Version from: http://en.wikipedia.org/wiki/Environmental_scanning

(D) TECHNOLOGICAL ENVIRONMENT

Technological changes enabled business to take up the shape of transnational business through the concept of global business. International business, in fact, gained significance due to the amazing advancements in technology.

Technological environment has significant and direct influence on business in general and international business in particular. Technology is application of knowledge. J.K. Galbraith defines technology as "a systematic application of scientific or other organised knowledge to particular tasks." Technology advanced phenomenally during the past 50 years.

Technology changes are taking place at a faster rate. In fact, it brings changes in the society, economy and politics. Technology affects all walks of life, all countries and the entire globe. As stated by Alvin Toffler, "Technology feeds on itself. Technology makes more technology possible." Thus, technology is self-reinforcing. Technology brings the globe closer. Technology flows from the advanced countries to the developing world through the multinational corporations (MNCs), joint ventures, technological alliances, licensing and franchising.

Influence of Technology

Technology influences the way we live, we cook (electric rice cooker), we drink water (filtered and mineral water), communicate (telephone, fax, e-mail, videoconferencing, e-mail chatting, etc.), prepare for a class or a case, design or read a newspaper through the Internet, get marriage alliances (through the Internet), (computer aided), produce, sells (e-commerce), satellite networks electronic fund transfers, lasers, fibre optics, unmanned factories, miracle drugs, new diagnostic methods, new studies in technology like eye scanning for the password and using the remote for car will be changing our lives.

Technology and International Competition

Nations develop economically when they translate science into useful technology and in turn create wealth from innovations. Innovation is the useful adaptation of science or knowledge including invention of new products or processes. Invention is creation of entirely new things. A few companies or people invent but many companies adapt scientific knowledge to generate wealth by application and commercialisation.

Major inventions or discoveries do not remain private property for longer period. The inventions or innovation process and global competitiveness are two determinants of a nation's wealth. Japan concentrates on process innovation in automobiles, steel, telecommunication and microelectronics. Germany concentrates on innovations in chemicals, pharmaceuticals, automotive engineering, medical instruments and machine tools. Italy concentrates on innovations in textiles and leathers.

Scanning of Technological Environment

The level of technology is not the same in all the countries. Advanced countries enjoy the fruits of the latest technology while the developing nations face the consequences of obsolete or outdated technology. Therefore, MNCs have to understand technology, analyse it before entering the foreign markets. MNCs have to procure technological environmental information regarding:

- The level of technology of the industry in the home country.
- The level of technology of the industry in the proposed host country.
- Compatibility of the home country's technology with the host country's technology.
- If technology is not compatible, then select the appropriate technology for the host country, if possible. If not, select the host country's technology that suits the home country's technology.
- Study the compatibility of the technology to the culture of the host country including tastes and preferences of the host country's customers.
- Study the host country's Government policies regarding technology transfer.
- Study the modes of technology transfer like joint ventures, technological alliances, etc.
- Study the impact of technology on the environment of the home country including the laws pertaining to environmental pollution.

Technology and Globalisation

The Industrial Revolution resulted in large-scale production. The recent technological revolution took it further to the production of high quality products at lower costs. This forced the domestic companies to enter foreign countries in order to find markets for their products. Thus, technology is one of the important causes for globalisation.

Information Technology and Globalisation

As indicated earlier, information technology redefined the global business through developments like Internet, websites, e-mail, cyberspace, information super highways, Computer Aided Design (CAD), Computer Aided Production (CAP) and online transactions brought significant development in the global business. These facilities, according to M.J. Xavier, help the global companies in:

- Reducing the size of inventories
- Reducing delivery time
- Reducing unproductive waiting time
- Reducing the incidents of stock-outs and lost sales
- Responding to market changes at a faster rate
- Reducing rush orders
- Cutting down over production
- Reducing unnecessary movements of forwarding and back-tracking
- Reducing paper work and wasteful processes

- Planning production levels accurately
- Reducing/avoiding physical movement of employees, suppliers and customers.

MNCs have to understand and analyse more of economic environment of the foreign countries for strategy formulation.

Hence, we now discuss the economic environmental factors of the global countries.

In Summary the Following Technological Factors Need to be Assessed:
• Efficiency of infrastructure, including: roads, ports, airports, rolling stock, hospitals, education, healthcare, communication, etc. • Industrial productivity • New manufacturing processes • New products and services of competitors • New products and services of supply chain partners • Any new technology that could impact the company • Cost and accessibility of electrical power

Source: Adapted from: http://en.wikipedia.org/wiki/Environmental_scanning

(E) ECONOMIC ENVIRONMENT

The economic environment of various countries directly influences international business. In fact, international economic environment and global business interact with each other. Global economy has undergone a sea change during the last 50 years. The change revolutionary has been after 1990. The results of these changes are emergence of global markets, establishment of World Trade Organisation, emergence of global business houses and global competitors rather than local competitors.

Economic Systems

Economic systems is an organisation of institutions established to satisfy human needs/ wants. There are three types of economic systems, *viz.*, Capitalism, Communism and mixed. Economic systems are based on resource allocation in the system. They are market allocation in case of capitalistic, command/central allocation in case of communist and mixed allocations in case of the (Key questions to scan technological environment are given in Exhibit 2.1).

Exhibit 2.1: Key Questions of Technological Environment
• What are the technologies within the corporation? • Which technologies are utilised in the firm's business? Products? Components and Parts? • How critical is each technology to each of these products and business?

- Which of these technologies are shared among different products and businesses?
- Which technologies are contained in purchased parts and materials?
- Which of these external technologies might become critical and why? Will they remain available outside the firm?
- What was the evolution of these technologies over time? In which companies were these technological changes initiated?
- What is the likely evolution of these technologies in the future?
- What have been the firm's investments in critical technologies over time?
- What were the investments and investment patterns of its leading technological competitors? Historical? Planned?
- What has been the investment in the product and in the process side of these technologies? For the firm and for its competitors? Design? Production? Implementation and service?
- What is the subjective ranking of different firms in each of these technologies?
- What are the firm's business and products?
- What is the cost and value-added structure of these parts, components, products, and businesses?
- What has been the historical, financial and strategic performance of the business, and what are the implications of these trends? In terms of cash generation and earnings characteristics? Investment requirements? Growth? Market position and market share?
- What are the applications of the firm's technologies?
- In which technologies applications does the firm currently participate and why? In which does the firm not participate and why?
- How attractive is each of these applications as an investment opportunity in terms of its market growth, its potential for profit improvement, and/or its potential for increasing technological leadership?
  - — Underlying growth characteristics?
  - — Evolution of customer needs and requirements?
  - — Current and emerging market segments; segment growth rates?
  - — Competitive positioning and likely strategies of key competitors?
- How critical are the firm's technologies to each of these applications?
- What other technologies are critical to the external applications?
- How do the technologies differ in each of these applications?
- What other technologies are critical to the external applications?
- What are the competing technologies in each application? What are the determinants of substitution dynamics?
- What is and will be the degree of technological change in each of these technologies?
- What are the applications that the firm should consider entering?
- What should be the priorities of technological resource investment?

- What technological resources are required for the firm to achieve its current business objectives?
- What should be the level and rate of corporate technology investments?
- Which technological investments should be curtailed or eliminated?
- What additional technologies will be required in order to achieve the current corporate business objectives?
- What are the implications of technologies and business portfolios for corporate strategy?

Source: Fred R. David, *op. cit.*, pp. 115-117.

mixed economic system. In fact, there are no example of pure Capitalistic or Communist economics. All actual systems are mixed economic systems of varied degrees of market allocations and command allocations.

Capitalistic Economic System: Under this system, customer allocates resources. Customers' choice for product/services decide what will be produced by whom. This economic system provides for economic democracy, thus giving the customer, his choice for products/ services.

Mixed Economic System: Under this economic system, major factors of production and distribution are owned, managed and controlled by the state. The purpose is to provide the benefits to the public sector, agrarian reforms, control over private wealth, regulation of private investment and national self-reliance.

The trend that is taking place in the globe today is the move towards privatisation, *i.e.,* move towards market allocation. U.K. France, Holland and India, *for example,* have reduced their command sector after 1990.

Communistic Economic System : In this economic system, private property and property rights to income are abolished. The State owns all the factors of production and distribution. It provides less scope for foreign investment and business.

Box 2.4: Communism and Mcdonald's

After a long negotiations between McDonald's and Soviet officials, the former entered Russian market in 1990. Moscow city council was a partner of McDonald's in the Russian Joint Venture. But McDonald's faced severe shortages in supply of building materials to build the restaurant as these requirements were not included in the central plan. The company was not provided with sufficient supply of wheat flour, sugar, mustard either due to non-inclusion in the central plan or due to inability of Soviet manufacturers to deviate from their standard output or due to the strict control that Soviet manufacturers should sell to the Soviet companies. Another problem was that certain products like iceberg lettuce, pickled cucumbers and the Russet Burbank potatoes used for McDonald's French fries were not produced or consumed in Russia. McDonald's educated Soviet farmers and cattle ranchers on how to grow and raise the products it needed. McDonald's did not face any problem in respect to employees and customers and advertising. Russian television covered the event; it became almost impossible to accommodate the customers for the first time in January 1990 even though the Moscow's restaurant was biggest in the world. Customers favoured it though it was five times costlier than the normal local meal. Despite the crisis in 1998, McDonald's grew in Russia and had 73 stores by the end of 2001. McDonald's success in Russia enabled it to enter China and also become successful there.

Source: Adapted from John. D. Daniels, *et.al.*, '*International Business*', Pearson, Singapore, 2004, pp. 103-104.

Communism collapsed in the former USSR. Similarly, Communism collapsed in most of the African countries. This was mostly due to the changes towards privatisation. The degree of command allocation has been declining even in China. Cuba is an example of the last remaining predominantly Communist country. However, foreign, business faces a variety of problems in China.

Box 2.5: Problems of Microsoft in China
Microsoft entered China and planned to increased its sales to $100 million in 2000 from nil in 1994. Then Microsoft faced the problem of rampant piracy in China. It was estimated that about 90% of the software used in China was pirated. Even Government used pirated software. More so, China is an exporter of counterfeit software. China's judiciary also uses pirated software. Microsoft officials pressed Chinese officials to conduct raids but resulted in only collecting negligible penalties from those using pirated version even. It over backfired in some cases.
Microsoft then used the strategy of cutting the prices by 200 per cent and priced the software between US$ 100 to 200. But the pirated versions were sold at only US$ 5 to 20. So, Microsoft tried lobbying the US government to impress upon the Government of China to prohibit the use of pirated versions. At this time, China was trying to become a member of World Trade Organisation. Therefore, China accepted to protect the intellectual property rights of many US firms including Microsoft. US government signed for China's membership in World Trade Organisation in September 2000. US, however, lost its control over China in protecting intellectual property rights after signing for the China's membership in WTO.
Further, Chinese government declared that US could access the Chinese information system and network through Microsoft software. Chinese government encouraged the development of Chinese language version of the Linux operating system as an alternative to Chinese language version of Windows 2000.

Source: Adapted from Charles W.L.Hill, International Business. Tata McGraw-Hill, 2003, pp.81-92

Countries Classified by Income

The World Bank categorised economics into one of the following groups according to the per capita gross national income in 1999.

Low Income countries	US$ 755 or less
Lower Middle Income countries	US$ 756 to US$ 2,995
Upper Middle Income countries	US$ 2996 to US$ 9,265
Higher Income countries	US$ 9,266 or more

Macroeconomic Issues Affecting Business Decisions

Various macroeconomic issues like economic growth, inflation, balance of payments and transition to market economics affect business decisions.

(1) Economic Growth: The high economic growth rate of the countries lift the quality of life of their citizens in addition to providing an opportunity of expanding market share to international business firms. The stagnation or decline in economic growth of countries result in intense competition among the companies to retain their market share and/or to increase their market shares. The stagnation in global economy in 2001 and 2002 led to aggressive competition among the international business firms.

Managers of the multinational companies are interested in knowing the future economic growth rates of various countries in order to select the markets either to enter or concentrate or to commit more resources to the market. According to the Organisation of Economic Cooperation and Development (OECD), global economic recession in 2001 was highest in the last 20 years and European Union started recovering after this recession at a faster rate than that of Japan. However, China and India recorded continuous growth rates of around 7 per cent and 6 per cent respectively. Manager of multinational companies should know the growth rates of different countries on a continuous basis in order to avert the possible failures and enhance their market shares.

(2) Inflation: Inflation is another important factor that affects the market share of international business firms. Inflation affects rates, as the demand for money is high due to higher prices. Banks increase interest rates in order to attract deposits and governments raise interest rates with a view to combat inflation. Inflation also affects exchange rate of the domestic currency in terms of various foreign currencies. Inflation weakens the domestic currency and thereby makes exports dear and imports cheap.

Inflation forces people to spend their incomes immediately as happened in Brazil in the early 1990s when the inflation was rising at the rate of 1 per cent per day. High inflation affects exporting firms adversely and importing firms favourably. The rate of inflation has been declining since 1990. It came down from 4 per cent in early 1990s to 2.5 per cent in 2000 in advanced countries. International business managers have to continuously monitor inflation rates in order to manage cash flows in such a way that the adverse affects of inflation are kept at a minimum as managed by Pizza Hut in Brazil during 1990s.

(3) Balance of Payments: Balance of payments position of a country is an outcome of international business and also affects the future of the international business. Export and import trade in goods and services affects current account position and flow of capital affects the capital account position. Excessive imports of goods, services and capital over exports result in negative balance of payments. Continuous negative balance of payments will lead to currency instability and control over imports and incentives to boost exports.

Excessive imports over exports also lead to external debt from foreign countries and international financial agencies. Heavily indebted countries in the world are Brazil ($238.0 billion), Mexico ($150.3 billion), China ($149.8 billion), Argentina ($146.2 billion) and Indonesia ($150.3 billion). Most of these countries have GDP higher than the external debt. Many African countries have external debt in excess of GDP. Many foreign investors pumped money into Argentina as the currency was pegged to U.S. dollar even when the economy was in recession in 1996. Argentina kept spending heavily and this resulted in Argentina's default to the tune of US $155 billion in external debt — the largest default by any country in history.

Managers of multinational companies should monitor the balance payments positions of the countries where they operate in order to take preventive measures rather than becoming a part of the debt trap or its adverse effects as happened in the Asian crisis.

(4) Economic Transition: Many former Communist/command economies and mixed economies are undergoing transition to market economies due to the failure of central planning and public sector to generate economic development. The collapse of the former USSR and the breaking of Berlin wall and foreign exchange crisis in India in 1991 and opening up of China towards extensive international trade paved the way for increased globalisation of business. This process enhanced the interest of the multinational companies in carrying out business in many parts of the world and conversion of many national companies in various countries into multinational companies.

Economic Transition Includes:

- Liberalising economic activities, prices and market operations along with reallocating resources to their most efficient use.
- Dispensing with licensing system and regulated markets.
- Developing indirect, market-oriented instruments for macro-economic stabilisation.
- Achieving effective enterprise management and economic efficiency usually through privatisation.
- Imposing hard budget constraints which provide incentive to improve efficiency.
- Creation and establishment of institutional legal framework to secure property rights, the rule of law and transparent market entry regulations.

As indicated earlier, many countries initiated transformation from different economic systems like Communism/Socialism and mixed economies to market economies and they are in different stages of the transformation process. Most of these countries came across with various disabling factors such as:

- Opposition to liberalisation, privatisation and globalisation due to the vested interests of various groups and political parties.
- Ineffective enforcement of laws, rules and regulations due to the underground and virtual economy.
- Prevalence of corruption and illegal activities.
- Freezing of market transformation resulted in financial instability, low growth or reverse growth of the economy.

Many countries that faced these problems during the initial stages of transformation eventually overcame these problems. And some of the countries are in the process of overcoming these problems. Countries those overcame these problems experience the following environment or situation factors in the transformation process.

- Spread of benefits of market economy.
- Strong fiscal position in terms of increase in government income.
- Increase in confidence in banks and other financial institutions.
- Growth in industrialisation, employment and output.

- Increase in credibility and financial position of the government.
- Improvement in government's financial ability to finance and administer social safety net.
- Early recovery and adjustment to the market economic situations.
- Steady progress towards open and liberal markets.
- Development of market-friendly environment.
- Growth in foreign and domestic investment, further industrialisation, increase in employment, output, living standards and quality of life of the people.

Opportunity to MNCs

The process of liberalisation and transition provided significant opportunities to the multinational corporations to enter most of the countries of the world either by locating their manufacturing facilities or extending their markets or both. Privatisation helps multinational companies to acquire the pubic sector companies in the liberalised economies. Thus, MNCs are the immediate and greatest beneficiaries of liberalisation, privatisation and globalisation of world economies.

Transition Process

Transition processes vary from country to country. Russia changed both economic and political systems simultaneously. As such, the country faced severe consequences during its early stage of the process. Now, the country is comparatively comfortable in the transition process as the administrative constraints disappeared. In contrast, China opted for only economic transformation by strongly holding its political system of totalitarianism. China's economic growth rate is higher than that of other countries. India is the largest democracy in the world and it opted for economic transformation from mixed economy to market economy. India's economic growth rate is also significant compared to that of many countries in the world, though; it is a little bit less than that of China.

Economic vs. Social Issues in Transition

Though the transition has set trends for economic growth of at least some countries and the economic future of other countries seems to be bright, the contribution of transition to the social issues, widening gap between rich and poor, poverty, child care, medical facilities and HIV/AIDS would be the future challenges to the world.

These problems would be paramount in lower-income countries in general and lower-income African countries in particular unless certain measures are taken immediately; it would affect the cause of humanity unable to reap the economic benefits of transition to market economy.

Economic vs. Social Issues in Transition

Though the transition has set trends for economic growth of at least some countries and the economic future of other countries seems to be bright, the contribution of transition to the social issues, widening gap between rich and poor, poverty, child care, medical facilities and HIV/AIDS would be the future challenges to the world.

These problems would be paramount in lower-income countries in general and lower-income African countries in particular unless certain measures are taken immediately; it would affect the cause of humanity unable to reap the economic benefits of transition to market economy.

(a) Growth strategy
(b) Economic system
(c) Economic planning
(d) Industry
(e) Agriculture
(f) Infrastructure
(g) Financial and fiscal sectors
(h) Removal of regional imbalances
(i) Price and distribution controls
(j) Economic reforms
(k) Population
(l) Per capita and national income.

India is one of the major economies in the world. India has developed her economy in different areas. The important facets of Indian economic environment (Fig. 2.3) are discussed hereunder:

***(a)* Industrial Policy:** Industrial policy is the most important document which indicates the relationship between the government and business. The Industrial Policy Resolution previously laid emphasis on industrial development through the development of public sector. Industrial policy, 1991 was a major departure from the earlier policies. The significant objectives of this policy were: Self reliance, to build on the many-sided gains already made, removing regulatory system and other weaknesses, link the Indian economy to the global markets so that we acquire the ability to pay for imports, and to make us less dependent on aid, increasing competitiveness of industries for the benefit of the common man and ensuring running of public sector undertakings on business lines and to reduce their losses.

FACETS OF INDIAN ECONOMIC ENVIRONMENT

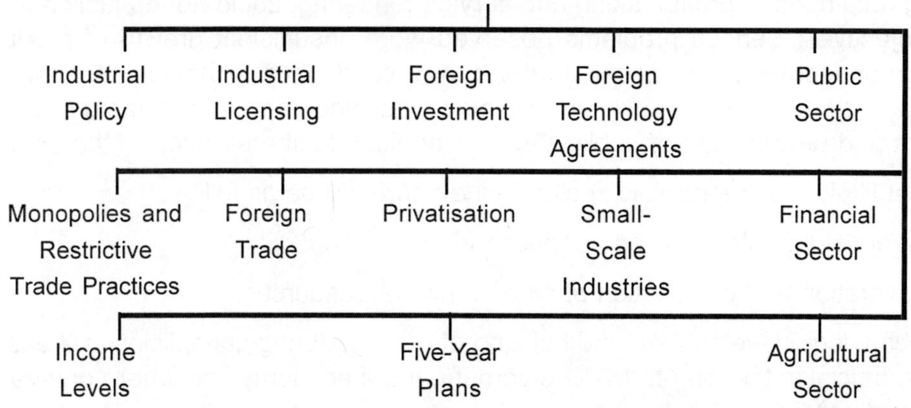

Fig. 2.3: Facets of Indian Economic Environment

***(b)* Industrial Licensing:** Abolition of industrial licensing for many projects except those specified (13 in number), irrespective of levels of investment is worthwhile. These specified industries will continue to be subject to compulsory licensing for reasons related to security, strategic concerns, social reasons, problems related to safety, overriding environmental issues, manufacturing of products of hazardous nature and articles of elitist consumption.

***(c)* Foreign Investment:** It has been decided to provide approval for direct foreign investment upto 51 per cent foreign equity in high priority industries requiring large investments and advanced technology. There shall be no hurdles in this process. This group of industries is generally known as the "Appendix-I Industries" and are areas in which FEMA companies have already been allowed to invest on a discretionary basis.

***(d)* Foreign Technology Agreements:** Government of India now, provides automatic approval for technology agreements related to high priority industries within specified parameters, in order to inject the desired level of technological dynamism in Indian industry. Other industries can also avail similar facilities, if the agreements do not require free foreign exchange. Indian entrepreneurs can negotiate the terms of technology transfer. The hiring of foreign technicians and foreign testing of indigenously developed technologies do not, now, require prior clearance.

***(e)* Public Sector:** The objective of the government before opening the Indian economy to the rest of the globe had been to establish socialistic pattern of society. This objective made the government to give top priority for public sector to develop industrial sector in the country. Public sector played a dominant role by establishing industries in the areas of public utilities, infrastructure, development banks, capital goods industries, core and key industries and industries requiring huge capital resources.

In fact, the government nationalised commercial banks, insurance industry and coal mines to achieve its objectives. Public sector was made responsible to achieve the objectives of the government like creation of employment opportunities, balanced regional development, providing infrastructural facilities and acting as a model employer. Public sector has played a crucial role in the country in the direction of these objectives. But, the public sector, in view of its conflicting dual roles of profit making and service rendering, could not do justice to any of these two objectives. Serious problems observed were: insufficient growth of productivity, poor project management, overmanning, absence of continuous technological upgradation, inadequate attention to R&D and human resource development. These factors led to the disinvestment and privatisation of public sector in addition to liberalisation of the economy.

The most likely areas for public sector, in the future will be as follows:

(a) Essential infrastructure and services.

(b) Exploration and exploitation of oil and mineral resources.

(c) Technology development and building of manufacturing capabilities in areas which are crucial in the long-term development of the economy and where private sector investment is inadequate.

(d) Manufacturing of products where strategic considerations predominate such as defence equipment.

***(f)* Monopolies and Restrictive Trade Practices:** The Monopolies and Restrictive Trade Practices Act, 1969 had two objectives before 1991. They were:

(i) Regulation of monopolies and prevention of concentration of economic power and

(ii) Prohibition of monopolistic, restrictive and unfair trade practices.

The economic liberalisation of 1991, aimed at achieving high productivity, competitive advantage to the domestic industry in the international market and economies of scale led to the amendment of the Act in 1991. The objectives of the amended Act are:

(i) Controlling monopolistic trade practices, and

(ii) Regulating restrictive and unfair trade practices.

***(g)* Foreign Trade:** It was widely recognised during the 1990s that the internationalisation of business, export-oriented industrial growth and self-reliance in the development of competencies were the highly essential factors for rapid economic development of the developing countries. Some countries believe in import substitution whilst majority of the countries believe in mutual dependence of the world nations for production and consumption. India recognised the significance of export and import trade for its development. This was quite evident in the new economic policy of 1991.

***(h)* Privatisation:** The word privatisation has been receiving much attention in business and government all over the world. Privatisation techniques have already been tried in countries like Great Britain, China, U.S.A., Turkey, Brazil, Eritrea, Mexico and Japan. The process of privatisation has already been started in India through disinvestment of government's shareholdings in public sector. The process of privatisation should be accelerated for effective functioning of public sector and rapid industrial growth. In fact, Government of India recognised the need for privatisation for rapid and efficient industrial growth.

***(i)* Small Scale Industries:** It was argued that 'small is beautiful.' It was further believed that small is efficient, innovative and productive. Further, government viewed that small scale sector solves the problems of the country like unemployment, and regional imbalance. Consequently, the government provided huge financial and non-financial facilities to this sector. But the government realised that this sector failed to a greater extent in playing its role and is a misfit in the market economies. Exhibit 2.2 shows the SWOT analysis of this sector. It is clear from this exhibit that the protection and assistance of the government to this sector is reduced at least in the magnitude, if not in direction.

***(j)* Financial Sector:** The financial sector consists of commercial banks, development banks, mutual funds, unorganised financial sector institutions, custodial service institutions, stock exchanges, underwriting and capital issue houses. The economic liberalisation brought significant changes in financial sector. The important ones among them are:

— Permission for Non-Resident Indians (NRIs) to enter the Indian stock market;

— Establishment of the Securities and Exchange Board of India;

— Setting up of the Investment Information and Credit Rating Agency of India (IICRA) and

— Establishment of Credit Rating Information Services of India Ltd. (CRISIL).

Exhibit 2.3: Small Sector: The SWOT Analysis

Strengths	• Flexibility in production volumes and design changes • Faster decision-making • Lower labour costs • Lower overheads
Weaknesses	• Often lack of management, marketing or financial skills • Technological obsolescence • Poor financing • Lack of marketing strength
Opportunities	• Large companies are outsourcing more to reduce their own costs • Promising export markets • Higher investment limits mean companies can expand and modernise • Big companies can take a larger equity stake in small ones
Threats	• With concessions disappearing, inefficient units will die • With de-reservation, competition will come from large companies • With import liberalisation, competition will come from MNCs and cheap inputs • Smaller, less aggressive companies will suffer.

Source: Business India, June 15, 1995, quoted in K. Aswathappa, *op. cit.*, p. 357.

***(k)* Infrastructure:** The infrastructural facilities improved significantly in India. But, India ranks very poorly in global competitiveness. This is a not welcome sign to invite foreign investment in a big way.

***(l)* Income Levels:** The high growth rate of income indicates the level of economic development of the country. National income in India increased from Rs. 1,10,685 crores in 1980-81 to Rs. 2,00,265 crores in 1993-94. The per capita income increased from Rs. 1,630 in 1980-81 to Rs. 2,255 in 1993-94. The slow growth of per capita income compared to that of national income is due to higher growth rate of population.

***(m)* Five-Year Plans:** Five-year plans were introduced from 1951-52 with a view to develop the economy on planned lines. The targets regarding national income were achieved during the First, Sixth and Seventh Five-Year Plans. Agricultural sector, industrial sector and service sectors were developed during the different five year plans.

***(n)* Agricultural Sector:** Agricultural sector is a major component of our economic environment. The agricultural sector has been developed by means of green revolution and white revolution. Agricultural productivity ranks second in rice and wheat in the world. India achieved self sufficiency in agricultural output. This development paved the way for the development of agro-based industries.

***(o)* Consumers:** Inflation and economic flux causes sweeping changes in consumer buying patterns. As consumers perceive that more money is buying them less, many people are adopting the much publicised "buy now, save later' motto at the expense of future security.

Economic factors have a direct impact on the potential attractiveness of various company strategies. The various important economic variables that often represent opportunities and threats for companies include: monetary policy of the Reserve Bank of India, share prices, interest rates, tax rates and policies, employment trends, price variations, etc. They are presented in Exhibit 2.2.

Exhibit 2.2: Key Economic Variables that often Represent Opportunities and Threats for Companies

- Shift to a service economy in India
- Level of development of commercial banks
- Level of growth of development banks
- Level of availability of credit
- Saving philosophy and trends
- Level of disposable income
- Propensity of people to spend
- Interest rates
- Inflation rates
- Economies of scale

- Money market rates
- Government budgets
- Gross National Product trends
- Consumption patterns
- Unemployment trends
- Worker Productivity Levels
- Value of Rupee in terms of other currencies
- Stock market trends
- Foreign countries' economic conditions
- Import/Export factors
- Demand shifts for different categories of goods and services
- Income differences by region and consumer groups
- Price fluctuations
- Monetary policies
- Fiscal policies and tax policies and rates
- Industrial and licensing policies
- Agricultural policies
- Labour policies
- Policies of various trading blocks like SAARC, EEC, NAFTA
- Policies towards joint ventures

Source: Modified Version Fred R. David, *op. cit.* p. 106.

(F) POLITICAL ENVIRONMENT

Political Ideologies

Political ideology is the body of complex ideas, theories and objectives that constitute a socio-political programme. Most of the countries at present are political by pluralistic as different people have various ideologies. Political ideologies of the people in the same country vary widely due to the variations in culture, ethnic groups, tribal groups, community groups, religious groups and the economic groups. These variations influence the people to form different political parties. Managers in multi-political party environment find it difficult to articulate the company's interest and formulae, its mission in order to balance them with the ideology of the political parties.

Democracy

The ideology of pure democracy aims that all citizens should be equal politically and legally, should enjoy freedom and participate in the political process. Pure democracy is not practically implemented and as such countries practice different forms of representative democracy, where citizens elect representatives to make decision on their behalf. Characteristics of contemporary and representative democracy include:

- Freedom of opinion, expression, press and freedom to organise.
- Freedom of electing the representative by voting.
- Limited terms for elected officials.
- An independent and fair judicial system with higher regard for individual rights and property.
- A non-political bureaucracy and defence infrastructure.
- An accessibility to the decision-making process.

Totalitarianism

Totalitarianism is extreme to democracy and is of two types, *viz.*, theocratic and secular. Religious leaders also assume the roles of political leaders and rule the country in theocratic totalitarianism, as is the case in Iran. One or a group of leaders or a single political party without aligning with any religion assume the power and rule the country with military force under secular totalitarianism as in case of Cambodia, Afghanistan before Taliban rule and Iraq under Saddam Hussein rule. Totalitarianism is also categorised as fascism, authoritarianism and communism. Fascism and authoritarianism are non-existent at present. Communism is also viewed as secular totalitarianism where political and economic systems virtually go together. Many former communist countries like Russia, Sweden and Estonia moved towards different degrees of capitalism and democracy. However, China, Vietnam and North Korea continue to be communist countries.

However, political and economic uncertainty prevails in those countries that shift from communism to capitalism and democracy due to their transition. These uncertainties cause problems to international business firms.

Political environmental factors also influence the operations of international business firms enormously. The influence of the political system of a country influences the business from multiple angles, *viz.*, deciding, promoting, fostering, encouraging, sheltering, directing and controlling the business activities. The success and growth of international business depend upon stable, dynamic, honest, people participative, secured political system in a country. (See Exhibit 2.3)

Countries with stable political system enjoyed the successful business operations. The USA is the best example for political stability and dynamism. Hence, business people prefer to locate their business operations in the USA. According to John Kenneth Galbraith, no country with a stable and honest Government has not had a reasonably satisfactory state of economic progress. The Government, in addition to being stable should also be efficient. Tanzania had a stable government during 1965 and 1985 with Nyerere as the head of the Government. He resigned in 1985 leaving a near-ruined country behind him. Zaire had similar experience with Mobutu and Zambia with Kenneth Kaunda.

John Kenneth Galbraith argues that, in all the advanced countries, "the early emphasis was not on capital investment but on political and then on cultural development. In USA, West Europe and more recently in Japan, a secure political context was stressed in both thought and action on economic development; it was considered the first requisite for economic progress."

In addition to the stable and dynamic governments, the political environment includes the policies and characteristics of political parties, the nature of the constitution and government system.

Some countries do not differ from other countries regarding the philosophies of the political parties, some other countries differ radically. Some countries are highly bureaucratic in decision-making regarding foreign investment, technology imports, etc., while some other countries have simple and quick decision-making mechanisms with their democratic approach.

The characteristics of bureaucratic and communistic countries include:

- Limitations, controls and curbs on private enterprises.
- Rule of the trade is state trading and counter trading.
- Many restrictions on imports and foreign capital both inflow and outflow.
- Restrictions on international/multinational corporations.

The trend has changed even in communistic countries. They have been progressively shifting towards liberalisation, privatisation and globalisation (LPG). As many as 8,500 public sector enterprises were brought under the umbrella of private sector in over 80 countries up to 1991. The erstwhile communist countries including the former USSR countries and the China are in the direction from Marx to the Market.

The political philosophy of the developing countries shifted from self-sufficient to self-reliant. As such they compete among themselves to woo foreign capital, technology and managerial expertise.

The political philosophy of most of the governments seem to be broadly one of convergence. However, they differ widely in imposing restrictions and regulations, scope, trade policies, procedures, taxes, custom duties, incentive systems, etc.

Political Relations and International Business

Political friendship/friendly diplomatic relations result in the growth of bilateral or multilateral trade. *For example,* the friendly diplomatic relations between India and the former USSR helped not only the Indian companies but also the MNCs operating in India to have close business linkages with the former USSR. Similarly, the friendly diplomatic relation between Pakistan and the USA helped Pakistan companies to have close business linkages with the USA.

Hostilities between countries also affect the international business among the companies of these countries. Arab countries did not prefer to carry on business with the business firms of Israel. These countries preferred business relations with those countries which boycott Israel. Hence, countervailing laws were adopted in USA to prevent the US companies from complying with this boycott.

In USA, the firms follow the policy of 'maintenance of arm's length' with the competing firms. But in other countries, particularly in Europe and India, they come to an agreement among themselves regarding price, product design, division of markets, etc. This difference is mostly due to the fact that, the US market is large enough to accommodate any number of firms to operate independent of competing firms. But the size of the European countries is very small and the firms cannot enjoy large scale economies. Therefore, European firms divide the market among themselves either in terms of products, geographical areas or customers in order to have large-scale economies.

Level of Economic Development and Political Stability: South Africa and Italy are economically developed countries. South Africa has been facing internal and external problems and Italy has been facing labour problems and internal dissension. Vietnam is politically stable but economically developing country. This is due to varied regional, ethnic, language, religious issues problems.

Political Risks: International business firms face political risks as and when there are changes in government policies and/or changes in political parties in power. Risks are based on the host government's actions like confiscation, expropriation, nationalisation, domestication and creeping expropriation.

- **Confiscation:** The process of nationalisation of a property without compensation is called confiscation. Chinese government's seizure of US property in 1949 when Chinese Communist party took power is an example of confiscation.
- **Expropriation:** Expropriation is the process of nationalisation of a property with compensation. Indian Government nationalised commercial banks with compensation in July 1969.
- **Nationalisation:** Nationalisation is the process of shifting the ownership of private property from private individuals or institution to the Government. Burma nationalised entire foreign trade. Poland and Czech Communists nationalised 100 per cent of their economy.
- **Domestication:** In domestication, foreign business firms relinquish control and ownership in favour of domestic investors either partly or fully. For example, Indian Leaf Tobacco Development Company Ltd., in India, Pepsi, General Motors and Barclays Bank in South Africa.
- **General Instability Risk:** These risks are due to social, political, religious unrest in the host country like the recent coup in Fiji and problems due to Muslim rebels in Philippines.

- **Operation Risk:** These risks are due to the imposition of controls on the foreign business operation (like production levels, marketing, finance and human resource) by the host government.

Indicators of Political Instability

Political instability can be viewed from the social unrest, attitudes of nationals and policies of host governments.

- **Corruption:** Corruption and bribery become acute and prevalent not only among bureaucrats but also among politicians during the early stages of political instability.
- **Social Unrest:** Social unrest is caused by clashes between or among community groups, religious groups and ethnic groups. For example, Christian-Muslim conflict in Lebanon, Hindu-Muslim conflict in India, White-Black conflict in the USA, the civil war between Serbs and Croats in 1991 in Yugoslavia, ethnic conflict between Christian in Armenia and Muslims in neighbouring Azerbaijan, etc.
- **Attitudes of Nationals:** The negative attitude of nationals towards foreign business and foreigners is a greater risk. These negative attitudes include exploitation, colonialism, repatriation, non-employment to foreigners, etc.
- **Policies of the Host Government:** Host Government's policies affect the operation of international business firms directly and internally or externally. For example, Janata Government in India asked Coca-Cola to leave the country in 1977 due to the policy of discouraging multinationals. The dispute between Chile and Argentina made Argentina to restrict exports (including the foreign companies operating in the country like General Motors, Peugeot and Renault) to Chile. The Enron Corporation's experience is another example.

Strategies to Minimise Political Risks

Political risks cannot be completely eliminated. However, they can be minimised by contributing to the change of the attitudes of the people and government of the host country like stimulation of the host country's economy, employment of nationals, sharing ownership, being civic minded, political neutrality, behind-the-scenes lobby, observation of political mood and reduction of exposure.

Stimulation of the Local Economy: The foreign company can stimulate the economic development of the host country by investing in their priority areas/portfolios. Further, the foreign company may encourage the local companies by purchasing the raw materials and other inputs from the latter, assist the local companies in technological aspects, using the local companies as ancillary units, etc. *For example,* IBM is the foreign company allowed to sell switchboards in France.

Similarly, the foreign company can stimulate the host economy by being export oriented. *For example,* AT&T entered France with an agreement with Generale de Electricity of France to produce digital switches and export to the USA.

Employment of Nationals: Most foreign companies feel that the people of developing countries are lazy, unintelligent, unmotivated, and less educated. As such foreign companies hire the people from advanced countries and do not employ the local people.

Multinational companies can minimise political risks by employing, developing and promoting the local people.

Sharing Ownership: If the multinational company owns the entire capital by itself, it magnifies political risks. Hence, it is suggested that the foreign companies should allow the domestic investors to invest and share the ownership by converting the company into a public limited company. In fact, some countries have imposed a condition that the foreign companies can enter the domestic country only with the participation of local investors. Eritrea is an example in this case. Ownership can be shared through joint ventures. Ford chose to merge its automobile operations in South Africa with Anglo American by reducing its share to a minority position of 40 per cent.

Being Civic Minded: US based MNCs sometimes encounter the 'Ugly American' label abroad. The MNCs in addition to doing business in foreign countries, should be good corporate citizens there. MNCs may help the foreign countries in different ways like constructing schools, hospitals, roads, water reservoirs, etc. Du Pont supplied 1.4 million water jug filters to eight African countries. H. J. Heinz spent US$ 94,000 to fund infant nutrition studies in China. IBM donated computer equipment and expertise worth $60,000 to Costa Rica.

Political Neutrality: It is criticised that the MNCs actively involve themselves in political affairs of developing countries. It is suggested that the MNCs should not involve in political affairs or disputes among the local groups of the host countries from the point of view of long-run interests. Brazilian companies, *for example,* do not get involved in the political activities of Central American countries.

Behind-the-Scene Lobby: Firms attempt to influence political decisions to help out the host countries. Mobil corporation issued newspaper advertisements urging US to sell missiles to Saudi Arabia. Pizza Hut came to China's rescue when the US mushroom industry asked for a quota against imports from China.

In summary the Following Political Factors Need to be Scanned:

- Political climate - amount of government activity
- Political stability and risk
- Government debt
- Budget deficit or surplus
- Corporate and personal tax rates
- Payroll taxes
- Import tariffs and quotas

- Export restrictions
- Restrictions on international financial flows

Source: Adapted from: http://en.wikipedia.org/wiki/Environmental_scanning

Legal Environment

Laws of the land directly affect the international business wherever they operate. Therefore, international business managers should be aware of the legal systems and laws that are in force in various foreign countries in addition to their home country as well as host country. Different forms of laws like common laws, civil laws, contract laws and theoretical laws and the degree of independence of the judiciary system vary from country to country. However, the countries in transition from Communism to market economy, mixed economic to market-economy and different types of totalitarianism to democracy and capitalism may not have perfect business laws. Therefore, international business managers should perform their activities cautiously.

Protection of Intellectual Property

The output of intellectual activity like an invention, a screenplay, computer software, chemical formula for a new drug and the like are intellectual properties of those involved. Patents, copyrights and trademarks establish ownership rights over intellectual property rights. Patent provides exclusive rights to the inventor of a new product or process for a particular period to produce and market the product/process. Copyrights provide exclusive rights to the authors, publishers, composers and the like to publish and market their works. Trademarks are designs, icons, names used by the producers and marketers to differentiate their products/ services from those of others. These trademarks are officially registered and become exclusive rights of the manufacture's who register them. Protecting intellectual property rights across the globe is a problem due to the volume of the task, cultural differences across the globe and limitations of various governments in enforcing the laws. World Trade Organisation is enforcing the intellectual property regulations. Governments in various member countries of the World Trade Organisation have been either formulating new laws or amending the existing laws in order to protect the intellectual property rights.

Product Safety and Product Liability

Products must adhere to certain safety standards as prescribed by product safety laws. Firms and its executives hold responsibility under product liability when injury, death or damage is caused by usage or consumption of product. These laws and standards are more comprehensive in USA compared to other countries. Differences in coverage of these laws among the countries result in variation in competitive advantage as well as non-uniformity of ethical standards to and among countries. Thus, the countries with less comprehensive product safety and product liability laws provide an opportunity to the business to reduce its cost and possess more competitive advantage than their counterparts in those countries, where the laws are more comprehensive.

Labour Laws: Labour legislations are enacted in various countries, mostly based on the resolutions of the International Labour Organisation. These legislations prescribe the minimum wages, trade union activities, employee-employer relations, collective negotiations, recruitment and employment practices, stipulations regarding working conditions, employee benefits, regulations and modalities of prevention and settlement of industrial disputes. However, MNCs force most of the governments to play an indifferent role with respect to implementation of labour laws. MNCs enter those countries where the cost of human resource is less in order to acquire competitive advantage through low labour costs. However, these practices sometimes result in exploitation of labour in developing countries.

Box 2.6: Nike in Vietnam: Failure of Implementation of Labour Laws

Nike subcontracted its manufacturing operations in Vietnam. The operation employed 25,000 employees and most of them were young women. Their wages were as low as $40 a month and the working conditions in the factories were quite inferior. Nike's practices were widely criticised by media. Consequently Nike hired Andrew Young – former US Ambassador to UN to enquire into the working conditions of employees and present a report. Mr. Young did not conduct detailed study but reported that Nike was doing a good job in treating the workers. Mr. Young was criticised widely for his improper reporting. Then Nike joined a taskforce including industry leaders, human rights groups and labour leaders that resulted in reaching an accord for payment of local minimum wages in foreign factories and establishment of Fair Labour Association – an independent association to monitor the wages and working conditions. Later, Nike announced a number of initiatives and incentives to employees working with its subcontractors. It was widely criticised that the Fair Labour Association was not an independent body and the labour practices in Nike were unfair even during 2001.

Source: Adapted "Right Group says Nike isn't fulfilling Promises". – Wall Street Journal, May 16, 2001 and Charles W.L. Hill, Tata McGraw, New Delhi, 2004, pp.131-134.

In Summary the Following Legal Factors Need to be Scanned:

- Minimum wage laws
- Environmental protection laws
- Worker safety laws
- Labour laws
- Copyright and patent laws
- Anti-monopoly laws
- Sunday closing laws
- Municipal licences
- Laws that favour business investment

Source: Adapted from http://en.wikipedia.org/wiki/Environmental_scanning

(G) NATURAL ENVIRONMENT

Natural environment consists of ecological factors and climatic conditions that affect business. Topography of the region, rivers, climatic conditions, humidity, weather conditions, etc., influence the business directly and indirectly. For example, the output and quality of products in cotton textile industry are affected by the humidity in the weather. Similarly ,availability of water influences the soft drinks industry as well as brewery and mineral water industry.

In addition to affecting location strategies, the natural factors affect cost strategies, investment strategies, green marketing strategies and quality strategies of different industries. Maintenance of pollution free environment, companies need to invest heavily on erecting additional machinery and equipment. Similarly, certain climatic conditions favour the maintenance of high quality of output while other climatic conditions disfavour the quality of the product. Further, the hilly geographical territories create problems for construction and maintenance of infrastructural facilities like roads, railway lines and telecommunication facilities. Therefore, companies have to scan natural environment to find out opportunities provided by and the threats posed by natural environment and to craft appropriate strategies.

Climate change is widely regarded as one of the most serious challenges the world faces with consequences that go far beyond its effects on the environment. Climate change has reached a tipping point in global awareness. Therefore, the companies need to maintain appropriate measures with regard to the challenges of climate change and its aftermath affects.

(H) THE INDUSTRY ENVIRONMENT

Industry is a group of firms producing (or rendering) the same or similar products (or services) which depend on others for inputs. The strategies of the firm will be affected by the attractiveness of the industry in which it chooses to do business and its relative competitive position within that industry. The important factors of this environment include:

Market, customer, demographic factors, geographic factors and competition.

The Market Environment

The market environment consists of all factors and groups having impact on the demand for the firm's products and/or services, competitors, etc. The factors influencing the firm's market environment include:

- Product design, configuration, demand, packing, uses, lifecycle, etc.
- Place of the market, special features of the market, etc.
- Place also includes customer related factors like customer taste, preference, needs, perceptions, values, bargaining abilities, satisfaction, dealers, distributors, wholesalers, retailers, etc.
- Price of the product, payment terms and conditions, special offers, discount, competitor's price, price of the substitute and complementary products etc.
- Promotional factors like expenditure and effectiveness of advertising, personal selling and sales promotion of the firm and competing firms.

Customer

The significant factor of the marketing environment is the customer. The strategists are mostly concerned with the customers of the firm and their needs and desires. In fact, the customer has become king to the strategists in the country with the liberalisation of the economy in 1991. The strategists are interested in not only the present customers but also the potential and future customers.

According to Lawrence R. Jauch and William F. Glueck, strategists include three factors as part of their industry analysis of customer sector, *viz.,* buyer identification, demographic factors and geographic locations of markets.

Buyer Identification: Markets normally indicate three distinct classes of customers. Different factors affect each class of customers in making their purchase decision as presented in Fig. 2.2. Strategists identify the nature of these customers and their utilities in order to avoid threats of loss of customers and to find or create opportunities for themselves to find new customers or to sell more to existing ones.

Demographic Factors

The demographic factors that influence the industry analysis include:

(i) Changes in population size and structure;

(ii) Age shifts in the population; and

(iii) income distribution and changes of the population.

FACTORS INFLUENCING DIFFERENT TYPES OF BUYERS

Consumers	Retailers and/or Wholesalers	Industrial and/or Institutional Buyers
• Availability	• Competitive product	• Cost vs Profitability
• Convenience	• Consumer recognition	• Financing
• Credit	• Product availability	• Legal conformity
• Price	• Product line breadth	• Price
• Quality	• Product turnover	• Product information
• Reputation	• Profit potential	• Product line
• Variety	• Promotional and merchandising support	• Product performance
• Warranty/Guarantee	• Supply dependability	• Source availability
		• Technical assistance

Source: Modified version from Lawrence R. Jauch and William F. Glueck, *op. cit.*, p. 117.

Fig. 2.2: Factors Influencing Different Types of Buyers

Geographic Factors

The strategists should also analyse the geographic environment to know the opportunities and threats as part of analysing customer sector. The strategist should think of extending the market to new locations.

Supplier: Suppliers provide material, capital and the likes to a firm. The strategist should analyse the supplier changes in the environment like price of the material, continuous supply of material, providing material on credit, etc. Michael Porter summarised this environment as follows:

(i) The power of the supplier to raise prices. The farther away the supplier is, the greater is his power.

(ii) The power of the supplier to raise the prices is less, if the buying firm is monopolist or oligopolist.

(iii) The power of the supplier to raise prices is greatest when the buyer is not an important customer or when the supplier can have forward linkage.

The power of the buyer can also affect the cost of suppliers. The power of the buyer can be maximum when *(i)* the buyer's firm is concentrated *(ii)* the buyer represents a significant portion of the supplier's business and *(iii)* if the buyer can virtually integrate backward.

Alternatively, the buyer's power would be minimum when *(i)* the buyer's firm is competitive *(ii)* the cost of switching to a substitute is high, *(iii)* the supplier's product is especially a vital part of the production process and *(iv)* the supplier can virtually integrate forward.

In addition to analysing the bargaining power of supplier and buyer, the strategist must analyse the environment to examine: *(i)* availability and cost of raw materials and sub-assemblies, *(ii)* availability and cost of energy, *(iii)* availability and cost of financial resources and *(iv)* availability and cost of labour.

Competitors

The strategist analyses the demand for and supply of the product that the firm produces. Further, he examines the level and nature of competition the firm faces and will face. Factors to be examined regarding competition are: *(i)* entry and exit of major competitors, *(ii)* substitutes and complements for current products and services and *(iii)* major strategic changes by current competitors (See Exhibit 2.2).

Barriers to entry or exit determine the entry or exit. Michael Porter contends that the following factors must be appraised with respect to their impact on barriers to entry in an industry.

(i) Product differentiation;

(ii) Economies of scale;

(iii) Absolute cost advantages;

(iv) Access to marketing channels; and

(v) Likely reaction of current firms.

According to Porter, the following are the barriers to exit from an industry:

(i) Managerial valves prevent it, *(ii)* Other products or services are related to exit candidates, *(iii)* Costs are sunk in assets *(iv)* direct exist costs are high and *(v)* Indirect costs may reduce exit behaviour. Exhibit 2.2 presents key questions about competitors.

Exhibit 2.2: Key Questions about Competitors

1. What are our major competitors' strengths?
2. What are our major competitors' weaknesses?
3. What are our major competitors' goals, objectives and strategies?
4. How are our major competitors most likely to respond to current economic, social, cultural, demographic, geographic, political, governmental, technological and competitive trends affecting the industry?
5. How vulnerable are our major competitors to our alternative company strategies?
6. How vulnerable are our alternative strategies to successful counter attack by our major competitors?
7. How are our products or services positioned relative to our major competitors?
8. To what extent are new firms entering and old firms leaving the industry?
9. What key factors have resulted in the present competitive position in the industry?
10. How have the sales and profit rankings of major competitors in the industry changed over recent years? Why have these rankings changed that way?
11. What is the nature of supplier and distributor relationship in this industry?
12. To what extent could substitute products or services be a threat to competitors in this industry?

Source: Fred R. David, p. 119.

The Concept of Driving Forces

Industry conditions change because important forces driving industry participants (competitors, customers, suppliers) alter their actions, the driving forces in an industry are the major underlying causes of changing industry and competitive conditions. Several different factors can affect an industry powerfully enough to act as driving forces. The important among them are:

- Changes in the long-term industry growth rate;
- Changes in who buys the product and how they use it;
- Product innovation;
- Technological change;
- Marketing innovation;
- Entry or exit of major firms;
- Diffusion of technical know-how;
- Increasing globalisation of the industry;
- Changes in cost and efficiency;
- Emerging buyer preferences for a differentiated instead of a commodity product;
- Regulatory influences and government policy changes;
- Changing societal concerns, attitudes, lifestyle; and
- Reduction in uncertainty and business risk.

Competitor Analysis

Studying the actions and behaviour of close competitors is essential. Unless a company knows what competitors are doing, it ends up "flying blind" into battle. Therefore, successful strategists take great pains in scouting competitors — understanding their strategies, watching their strategies, watching their actions, sizing up their strengths and weaknesses and trying to anticipate what moves they will make next. This activity includes the following actions:

1. Identifying competitor's strategies: Strategists can get a quick profile of key competitors by studying where they are in industry, their strategic objectives and their basic competitive approaches. (See Exhibit 2.2)
2. Evaluating who the industry's major players are going to be.
3. Predicting competitor's next moves.
4. Pinpointing the key factors for competitive success: Key success factors spell the difference between profit and loss and ultimately between competitive success and failure. A key success factor can be a skill or talent, a competitive capability or a condition a company must achieve, it can relate to technology, manufacturing, distribution, marketing or organisational resources. (See Exhibit 2.5).
5. Drawing conclusions about overall industry attractiveness. Whether an industry is relatively attractive or unattractive depends on several situational considerations.

Exhibit 2.5: Types of Key Success Factors

Technology-Related KSFs

- Scientific research expertise (important in such fields as pharmaceuticals, medicine, space exploration, other "high-tech" industries)
- Production process innovation capability
- Product innovation capability
- Expertise in a given technology

Manufacturing-Related KSFs

- Low-cost production efficiency (achieve scale economies, capture experience curve effects)
- Quality of manufacture (fewer defects, less need for repairs)
- High utilisation of fixed assets (important in capital intensive/high fixed-cost industries)
- Low-cost plant locations
- Access to adequate supplies of skilled labour
- High labour productivity (important for items with high labour content)
- Low-cost product design and engineering (reduces manufacturing costs)
- Flexibility to manufacture a range of models and sizes/take care of custom orders

Distribution-Related KSFs

- A strong network of wholesale distributors/dealers
- Gaining ample space on retailer shelves
- Having company-owned retail outlets
- Low distribution costs
- Fast delivery

Marketing-Related KSFs

- A well-trained, effective sales force
- Available, dependable service and technical assistance
- Accurate filling of buyer orders (few back orders or mistakes)
- Breadth of product line and product selection
- Merchandising skills
- Attractive styling/packing
- Customer guarantees and warranties (important in mail-order retailing, big ticket purchases, new product introductions)

Skills-Related KSFs

- Superior talent (important in professional services)
- Quality control know-how
- Design expertise (important in fashion and apparel industries)
- Expertise in a particular technology
- Ability to come up with clever, catchy ads
- Ability to get newly developed products out of the R&D phase and into the market very quickly

Organisational Capability

- Superior information systems (important in airline travel, car rental, credit card, and lodging industries)
- Ability to respond quickly to shifting market conditions (streamlined decision-making, short lead times to bring new products to market)
- More experience and managerial know-how

Other Types of KSFs

- Favourable image/reputation with buyers
- Overall low cost (not just in manufacturing)
- Convenient locations (important in many retailing businesses)
- Pleasant, courteous employees
- Access to financial capital (important in newly emerging industries with high degrees of business risk and in capital-intensive industries)
- Patent protection

Source: Arthur A. Thompson, Jr. and A.J. Strickland III, *op. cit.*, p. 82.

Michael Porter's Approach to Industry Analysis

According to Michael Porter, the business while analysing the environment should be concerned more with the intensity of competition is determined by various potential entrants, suppliers, industry competitors, rivalry among existing firms, buyers, substitutes, etc. (See Fig. 2.5).

The collective and interactive, "strength of these forces determine the ultimate profit potential in the industry, where profit potential is measured in terms of long run return on invested capital."

Strategists can identify opportunities and threats in each of these competitive forces and rate their strength as high or medium or low force. No force is regarded as an opportunity. However, the business firms in the long run can change the threats into either opportunities or neutral forces through their strategies. But they have to craft their strategies in the short run within the limitation of these forces.

For example, a soft drink company in India could currently rate as follows:

Force	*Rate*	*Comments*
Rivalry	High	Coca Cola and Pepsi cola.
Threat of potential entrants	Low	Industry reached maturity stage, sales growth is slow
Threat of substitutes	Low	Other soft drinks do not provide flavour close to Coca Cola or Pepsi Cola
Bargaining power of the buyers	Low	Large number of buyers with negligible share in the total sales
Bargaining power of the suppliers	Medium	Coca Cola and Pepsi Cola make large quantities of buying of sugar, water and carbon dioxide.
Development seconds market	Medium	Development of second market for books like www.amazon.com and cars
Threat of other stakeholders	Medium	Agitation against Coca Cola and Pepsi Cola environmental concern, ingredients of the products are on 'high.'

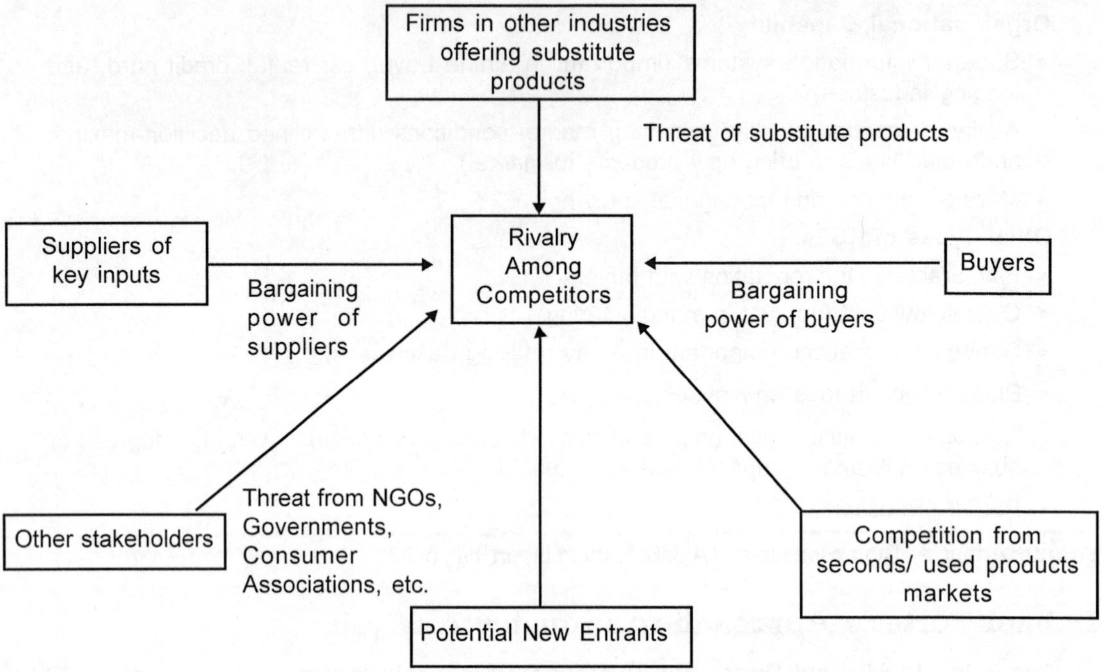

Fig. 2.5: Forces Driving Industry Competition

The soft drink industry is currently at high level of competitive intensity based on the above factors. In other words, the industry growth rate is low and the profit margins are narrowed down.

Now, we shall discuss each of these competitive focuses in detail:

Potential/threat of new entrants: Normally new entrants pose a threat to the existing firms as they enter the industry with new and creative management practices, new and improved product features, low price, latest technology, and write new promises to the customers. For example, Reliance mobiles entered mobile industry in India with latest technology, reduced price, wide area network and enhanced bandwidth. Similarly, Degicel entered mobile market in Papua New Guinea with wide area network, reduced price and latest technology.

However, the existing firms and/or the industry can create entry barriers: They include: Large scale operations sales and low prices provided, an advantage to Reliance mobile phones to prevent the entry of rivals in Indian mobile industry whereas the exorbitant tariff fixed by 'Be' mobile created an 'invitation to enter' the mobile market to Digicel mobiles in Papua New Guinea.

Product Differentiation: Product differentiation created by Coca-Cola like Sprite, Fanta, Diet coke, etc., created entry barriers to other companies and tough competition to Pepsi Cola.

Capital Requirement: The need for inventing large capital creates entry barrier for new entrants. For example, steel industry, airways and shipping companies need huge capital and therefore less number of new firms enter these industries.

Switching Costs: Entry barriers are created when the cost of switching to other businesses or systems is too high.

Accession to Distribution Channels: The existing firms can create a block to the access of the distribution channels by employing role distribution dealers.

Government Regulations: Government imposes entry barriers by imposing licensing and other regulations in certain industry like oil exploration, food processing, air travel, agro-based and chemical industry.

Rivalry Among Existing Firms

Actions of a firm affects the other firms of the same industry directly and the firms of some of the other industries indirectly. In fact, the moves of the French National Railways with regard to the enhanced speed affected the airlines industry in France. Thus, rivalry takes place even across the industries. The tariff reduction by domestic airlines in India affected the Indian Railways, which brought a variety of schedules to provide convenience to customers like *tatkal* tickets.

Thus, rivalry among firms are interdependent in their actions and counter actions. Intense rivalry, according to Michael Porter, is related to the presence of the following factors:

Number of Competitors: Presence of number of competitors depends upon the nature of industry and the size of the market. There are more than 10 competitors in mobile industry in India whereas there are only two competitors in mobile industry in Papua New Guinea owing to the small size of the market. In number of fast moving consumer goods industry, the firms watch the strategies and actions of the competitors very closely and craft their strategies when the number of competitors is less.

Industry Growth Rate: The war based on price, product improvement and differentiation is relatively more when the growth rate of the industry is slowed down. Indian mobile companies used to charge a tariff of more than Rs. 2 per one minute of the outgoing calls when the industry growth rate was high during late 1990s and early 2000. They reduced the same to around Rs. 0.50 when the growth rate slowed down by 2007. This is due to the fact that the firms compete for the same market whose growth is slowed down.

Product/Service Characteristics: The factors like availability and location proximity play vital role in the competition when the product/service characteristics are the same or do not matter much when compared to other factors like time and location proximity. For example, customers weigh the time and location proximity in buying food for immediate consumption and also when the product characteristics are the same.

Bargaining Power of Buyer

Current and potential bargaining power of the buyers determines the competitive strength of the firms for example, airlines, bargaining power in buying petrol is relatively high compared to that of a truck owner. Bargaining power of the buyer is relatively more in the following situations:

- **Purchases form A Larger Share of The Sales of Company:** For example, the quantity of books purchased by distance education department/centres of universities is larger, than publishing the total sales by a company. Similarly, the share of purloin of computers by colleges and universities is larger to the total purchases by a computer company.
- **Ability of The Buyer to Implement Backward Integration Strategy:** For example, the ability of Airlines Company or Indian Railways to have its own catering and the ability to start their own colleges and universities to educate the prospective employees like KIRLOSKER.
- **Availability of Alternative Suppliers:** Liberalisation of economies resulted in the alternative supply of products and services. For example, Air India was the major supplier of international air travel before 2000. Now, there are a wide range of alternatives.
- **High Share of The Value of Purchase:** The buyer prefers to reduce the cost of buying when the share of value of purchase is relatively high. This is true in case of purchase of barley by a brewery.

Low Margins of the Buyer in Sales

Market intermediaries when they are forced to maintain low margin bargain for low price. This is more applicable in case of fast moving consumer goods.

Bargaining Powers of Suppliers

Bargaining power of the supplier influences prices. Bargaining power of the suppliers of pharmaceuticals is more in Papua New Guinea and is one of the reasons for high cost of medical facilities in Papua New Guinea. Similarly, the bargaining power of OPEC is significant in supplying oil which resulted in increase in airfares in 2008.

The suppliers enjoy higher level of bargaining power under the following circumstances:

- When the suppliers in the industry is dominated by a few firms.
- When the supply of the product/service is less than the demand for it.
- When the product has distinctive attributes and difficult to switch over.
- When easy substitutes are not available like rail travel in India and air travel in Papua New Guinea.
- When suppliers can have forward linkage and direct dealing with customers like airline business.

Development of Second Market

Development of second/used products market poses a wide threat in some industries particularly in publishing and automobile industry. For example, www.amazon.com facilitates second market for a wide range of used books posing a threat to the publishing industry.

Similarly, a number of companies started the business in procuring such and supplying used cars to various foreign countries. Such trends pose competition to the firm in the publishing industry as well as automobile industry.

Relative Power of Other Stakeholders

Other stakeholders include political parties and non-government organisations. This is an additional factor for the Porter's model. For example; the products of Coca Cola and Pepsi Cola have been challenged by the Bhartiya Janata Party activists on the ground that natural fruits, tender coconut and juices are far better than the cola product, in terms of health issues and price. These activities posed challenges to Coca Cola and Pepsi Cola.

Some of the Papua New Guineans favour 'Be' mobile, a public sector unit, causing competition to Digicel mobile company in the country. Agitations by the consumer associations and voluntary organisations force governments to plan to enact special legislations and impose regulations to protect the consumer and the environment. These regulations enhance the cost of assets and production. The enhanced costs intensify the competition.

For example, water, air and sound pollution control measures imposed by the Government of India enhanced the cost of production of chemical industry.

Industry Boundaries

An industry is a group of firms that produce the same or similar products or render the same or similar services. Similar products indicate that they serve the same purpose for example, orange juice, grape juice, apple juice and mango juice serve the same purpose. So, firms producing different kinds of juices belong to the juices manufacturing industry. Different kinds of passenger cars like economy cars, luxury cars and cars-cum-truck serve similar purpose of conveyance. These firms belong to the automobile industry along with other automobile manufacturing firms. Sometimes, would be quite unclear to classify the industries for example, Coca Cola producers beverages as well as mineral water which can include mineral water under beverages. The answer is partly 'Yes' as both these products satisfy the need of thirsty and partly 'No' as the beverages satisfy the need for excitement, unlike water.

Similarly, some firms producing bicycles for riding also produce toy bicycles. How do we classify such companies? Such examples create a confusion over industry boundaries. These confusions complicate the task of crafting strategy as each operational area override other area of operations of the firm.

Industry definition is necessary:

(i) to determine the area in which the firm is competing.

(ii) to focus the attention of the strategies on the firm's competitors.

(iii) to identify the environment and common opportunities and threats.

(iv) to evaluate the strategies, goals and objectives of the firm.

Though industry definition is necessary, the following problems are involved in the process.

Growing competition forces companies to spread their operations to other industry. For example, universities spread their activities into publishing industry, hotel and transport industry.

Industry evolutions create industries within industries like telephone industry, mobile industry, e-mail and Internet within telecommunication industry.

Globalisation led to the creation of global industry.

Yet How to Draw Boundaries

Despite these problems, executives have to design boundaries in order to focus on strategic management. The executives, therefore, should examine the following issues:

- Identify the goals of each portfolio of the company.
- Focus on the critical success factors of each portfolio of the business.
- Scan the firm's strengths to compete in other areas of the industry and if not, acquire such strengths.
- Future opportunities and threats that force the firm to enter areas of other industries.
- Acquisition of new strengths and reduction of future threats of entering new industries.
- Reduction of conflict, overlap and gap areas of strategies that result owing the expanding industry boundaries.

Environmental Scanning

The process of environment scanning has been far from being systematic except with regard to information relating to current developments. Environmental scanning requires information inputs which can be devised from different strategies like:

- Verbal information from audio-visual media, suppliers, sales people, etc.,
- Written and documenting information from newspaper, journal and reports,
- Information from management information system
- Industrial spying
- Forecasting reports.

1. Key Sources of Information for Environmental Scanning

Once strategists have selected key environmental variables, the next step is to select key sources of environmental information for scanning. The sources of information include:

(i) The economic and business daily newspapers like The Economic Times, Business Standard, Business Line and Financial Express.

(ii) Journals and periodicals like Business India, Business World, Business Today, Update, Fortune India, Main Stream, Long Range Planning Journal, Economist, IMF

World Economic Outlook, Harvard Business Review, Foreign Trade, Finance and Development, Environmental Trends & Scenarios, etc.

(iii) Institutional publications like Mumbai Stock Exchange Directory, the Centre for Monitoring Indian Economy, Kothari Industrial Directory of India, Publications of Market Research, Agencies like Operations Research Group, the National Council for Applied Economic Research, etc., annual reports of various companies, publications of professional organisations like Federation of Indian Chamber of Commerce and Industry.

(iv) Government publications like Economic Survey, Guidelines to India Bulletins, ICICI Portfolio Studies, Business Intelligence and Data, The State of Nation Report, Quarterly Survey of Industries, Indian Trade Journal, Yojana, etc.

(iv) Other publications include: United Nations Publications, World Economic Survey, International Financial Statistics, Economic Survey of Asia and the Far East, Commodity Trade Statistics, Year Book of International Trade Statistics, etc.

2. Approaches to Environmental Scanning

The experiences of various pioneering companies reflect the emergence of four basic principles regarding effective implementation of environmental scanning function.

1. Environmental analysis must be linked, conceptually and practically to current planning and operations.
2. Environmental analysis serves a number of separate purposes, different analytic structures and systems may be required in order to achieve those different purposes.
3. Systems for environmental analysis must fit the culture and decision-making styles of the organisation and areas they serve.
4. Continuing support in spite of internal changes is required to sustain environmental analysis in an organisation over time.

3. Factors Affecting the Environmental Scanning

Several factors affect the environmental scanning. These factors are classified as *(i)* Strategist related factors, *(ii)* Organisation related factors and *(iii)* Environment related factors.

(i) Strategist related factors include: age, family background, educational background, experience, socio-cultural background, motivational level, perception and cognitive styles, ability to face challenges, ability to cope up with stress, ability to motivate and lead people, ability to adopt to different cultures and problem situations, ability to form and lead team work, ability to forecast, judgement, analytical and interpretation skills etc.

(ii) Organisation related factors include the nature of the business, product or services and markets, age, size and complexity of the organisation, organisation structure and its nature etc.

(iii) Environmental factors include: complexity, volatility or turbulence, hostility and diversity of the environment.

The strategist may face the problem of comprehending massive information and a number of environmental factors. Hence, the strategist should select priority based environmental factors to forecast the future or scanning the environment.

4. Scanning Systems

There are three types of scanning systems. They are:

(i) **Irregular Scanning Systems:** These consist of *ad hoc* studies in response to environmental crises.

(ii) **Regular Scanning Systems:** These consist of regular reviews of the environment or selected strategic environmental components. These reviews include annual planning exercises.

(iii) **Continuous Scanning Systems:** This is an ongoing activity. Established boundary, scanning offices often coordinate this activity. This is more future oriented system. Exhibit 2.6 compares these three scanning systems along several dimensions.

Techniques of Environmental Scanning

1. *Expert Opinion:* Knowledgeable people are selected and asked to assign importance and probability ratings to various possible future developments. The most refined version, the Delphi method, puts experts through several rounds of event assessment, where they keep refining their assumptions and judgements.

2. *Trend Extrapolation:* Researchers fit curves (linear, quadratic, or S-shaped growth curves) through past time series to serve as a basis for extrapolation. This method can be very unreliable if new developments alter the expected direction of movement.

3. *Trend Correlation:* Researchers correlate various time series in the hope of identifying leading and lagging relationships that can support forecasts.

4. *Dynamic Modelling:* Researchers build sets of equations to try to describe the underlying system. The coefficients in the equations are fitted through statistical means. Econometric models of more than 300 equations, for example, are used to forecast changes in the US economy.

Exhibit 2.6: Comparison of Scanning Models

Irregular Model	Regular Model	Continuous Model
Media for Scanning Activity		
Ad hoc studies	Periodically updated studies	Structured data collection and processing systems
Scope of Scanning		
Specific events	Selected events	Broad range of environmental systems
Motivation for Activity		
Crisis initiated	Decision and issue oriented	Planning process oriented
Temporal Nature of Activity		
Reactive	Pro-active	Pro-active
Time Frame for Data		
Retrospective	Primarily current and retrospective	Prospective
Time Frame for Decision Impact		
Current and near future	Near-term	Long-term
Organisational makeup		
Various staff agencies	Various staff agencies	Environmental scanning unit.

Source: Liam Fahey and William R. King, "Environmental Scanning for Corporate Planning," *Business Horizons*, August, 1977, p. 63.

5. *Cross-impact Analysis:* Researchers identify a set of key trends (those high in importance and/or probability) and ask, "If event A occurs, what will be the impact on all other trends?" The results are then used to build sets of "domino chains," with one event triggering others.
6. *Multiple Scenarios:* Researchers build pictures of alternative futures, each internally consistent and with a certain probability of happening. The major purpose of the scenarios is to stimulate contingency planning.
7. *Demand/hazard Forecasting:* Researchers identify major events that would greatly affect the firm. Each event is rated for its convergence with several major trends taking place in society and for its appeal to each major public group in the society. A higher convergence and appeal increases the probability that the event will occur. The highest-scoring events are then researched further.

5. Environmental Threat and Opportunity Profile: ETOP

Analysis of environmental information, data and factors, and determining opportunities and threats require a systematic technique. Lawrence R. Jauch and William F. Glueck suggest the technique of Environmental Threat and Opportunity Profile (ETOP). This technique conveniently summarises the diagnoses of all the various factors of the environment which is important to the strategic gaps facing the firm. The ETOP presents the impact of each environmental factor like economic, political and social on the organisation. Exhibit 2.7 presents an environmental threat and opportunity profile (ETOP) of a bank.

Exhibit 2.7: Environmental Threat and Opportunity Profile of a Bank

Environmental Factors	+	Continued emphasis on infrastructural facilities including telecommunications
	+	Increase in educational levels and income levels
	+	Increase in business activity.
	–	Establishment of financing companies
Technological	+	Increased computerisation
	–	Shortage of computer operators and engineers.
Government	–	Economic liberalisation allowed private banks to operate and compete with the existing banks
Customer	–	Shift from the present banks to the newly established banks with modern facilities.
Supplier	–	Source of technology will become scarce
Competitor	+	Less competition from the existing banks
	o+	No competition from cooperative banks.
	–	Strength of the foreign banks in terms of technology, people and funds.

Note: '+' Indicates opportunity '–' Indicates Threat, 'o' indicates neutral impact.

Points to be Remembered

- Strategic management involves three levels, *viz.*, the organisation's macro environment or general environment, the industry in which the organisation operates and the organization itself.
- Environmental factors are prime influences on strategy change.
- The trend towards globalisation has emerged around the world.
- Social and cultural factors influence business.
- Technological changes enabled business to take up the shape of transnational business through the concept of global business.
- Economic system is an organisation of institutions established to satisfy human needs/wants.
- Political ideology is the body of ideas. Theories and objectives constitute a socio-political programme.
- Industry is a group of firms producing the same or similar products vets.

Keywords

- Social Factors
- Cultural Factors
- Technological Factors
- Economic Factors
- Political Factors
- Global Factors
- Industry Analysis
- Competitor Analysis
- Multinational Companies
- Transnational Company
- Cultural Attitude
- Information Technology
- Economic Systems
- Balance of Payments
- Industrial Policy
- Small-scale Industry

Questions for Discussion

(1) Why do you scan the business environment?

(2) What is economic environment? How do you use economic factors in determining opportunities and threats?

(3) What are the global factors that affect the business?

(4) Why do companies go global?

(5) What are the social and cultural factors that affect the business?

(6) What are the technological factors? How do they influence business?

(7) What are the political ideologies? How do political factors influence business?

(8) What is industry analysis? Discuss the demographic factors that influence the business.

(9) What is competitor analysis?

(10) How do you identify opportunities and threats of a business?

References

1. William F. Glueck, *Business Policy and Strategic Management*, McGraw-Hill, 1980, p. 88.
2. *Ibid.*, p. 88.
3. Lawrence R. Jauch and William F. Glueck, *op. cit.*, p. 86.
4. *Ibid.*, pp.
5. Kenichi Ohmae, "*The End of the Nation State: The Rise of Regional Economies.*"
6. Arun Kumar Jain, "*Managing Global Competition*," Competence Publishing House, Dehradun, 1994, p. 30.
7. *Ibid.*, p. 31.
8. Philip Kotler, "*Principles of Marketing*", Prentice-Hall of India, p. 576.

9. K. Aswathappa, "*Essentials of Business Environment*", Himalaya Publishing House, Mumbai, 1996, pp. 34-35.

10. Arun Kumar Jain, *op. cit.*, pp. 33-37.

11. K. Aswathappa, *op. cit.*, p. 47.

12. Jeffrey A. Fadiman, "Should Smaller Firms Use Third World Methods to Enter Third World Markets": The Project Heads as Point Man Overseas, *Journal of Business and Industrial Marketing*, 4 (Winter/Spring 1989), pp. 17-28.

13. John D. Daniels, Lee H. Radebough and Daniel P. Sullivan, "*International Business*", Pearson Education, Singapore, 2004, p. 54.

14. Montose, Sommers and Jerson Kernan, "Why products flourish here": Fizzle There! *Columbia Journal of world business*, March-April 1967, p. 90.

15. Quoted in David H. Holt and Karen W. Wigginton, "*International Management*", Thomson, 2002, p. 51.

16. Warren J. Keegan, *op. cit.*, p. 80.

17. Quoted in John D. Daniels, *et. al.*, *op.cit.*, p.124.

18. Olech Havrylyshyn and Thomas Wolf, "Determinants of Growth in Transition Economies", *Finance and Development*, June 1999, p. 12.

19. Robert Wesson, "*Modern Government — Democracy and Authoritarianism*", Prentice-Hall, New Jersey, 1985, pp. 41-42.

20. John D. Daniels, *et.al.*, *op.cit.*, p. 88.

21. *Ibid.*, p. 11.

22. Sak Onkvisit and John J. Shaw, "*International Marketing*", Prentice-Hall, New Delhi, 1999, pp. 135-58.

23. Charles W.I. Hill, *op.cit.*, p. 11.

24. Lawrence R. Jauch and William F. Glueck, *op.cit.*, p. 117.

25. *Ibid.*, pp. 117-118.

26. *Ibid.*, p. 120.

27. Azhar Kazmi, *op. cit.*, p. 115.

28. Samuel C. Certo and J. Paul Peter, *op. cit.*, pp. 44-45.

29. James R. Bright and Milton E.F. Schoeman, "*A Guide to Practical Technological Forecasting*", Prentice-Hall, Englewood Cliffs, New Jersey, 1973. Quoted in Samuel C. Certo and J. Paul Peter, *op. cit.*, p. 11.

30. Lawrence R. Jauch and William F. Glueck, *op. cit.*, p. 138.

31. Michal E. Porter, "*Competitive Strategy*", Free Press, New York, 1980, p. 3.

32. John A. Pearce and Richard B. Robinson, "*Strategic Management*," Tata McGraw-Hill Publishing Co. Ltd., New Delhi, 2005, pp. 99-99.

***

Chapter - 3

Internal Environment: Capabilities and Competencies

Chapter Outline

(A) Resources and Capabilities
(B) Core Competencies
(C) Value Chain Analysis and Outsourcing
(D) Strengths and Weaknesses Analysis
(E) Competitive Strength Assessment
(F) Corporate Capability Factors
(G) Diagnosing Corporate Capabilities
— Points to be Remembered
— Keywords
— Questions for Discussion
— References

Learning Objectives

After studying this chapter, you should be able to:

- Analyse organisational analysis and capabilities;
- Discuss the core competencies of the company;
- Analyse organisational strengths and weaknesses;
- Study the organisational capabilities;
- Identify the opportunities and threats;
- Assess organisation's competitive strengths;
- Discuss various corporate capability factors in each of the functional areas;
- Diagnose the corporate capability factors.

(A) RESOURCES AND CAPABILITIES

Organisations formulate strategies based on corporate strengths and weaknesses. Corporate strengths and weaknesses are determined based on organisational resources, capabilities and competencies.

Resources

Resources are all kinds of inputs like material, components, parts, machinery, equipment, capital, human resources including talented employees, competent technical personnel and efficient managers. Though the resources are more essential to an organisation, they alone do not yield a competitive advantage. However, competitive advantage of a firm is created through unique blending, bundling and building of all kinds of resources. For example, Dell computers interlinked technology and human resources to build an efficient business model. This model helped Dell to sell computers directly to customers by eliminating market intermediaries like dealers and retailers, which in turn, created a distinctive competitive advantage for the Dell Computer Corporation.

Organisational resources are tangible and intangible resources. Tangible resources can be seen and quantified like buildings, machinery, equipment and vehicles. Intangible resources are those rooted deeply in the organisation's history and that have accumulated over time. Examples of intangible resources are employee's knowledge, trust, ideas, scientific capabilities, capacity to innovate and managerial competence, reputation with customers like brand name and perception of product quality, durability and reliability and reputation with suppliers for efficient, effective, supportive and mutually beneficial interactions and relationships.

Why Resources are Valuable?

Organisational resources determine strengths and weaknesses. Managers can structure the composition of resources in order to maximise strengths and minimise weaknesses. The following factors help to determine what constitutes a valuable asset, capacity or competence.

1. **Competitive Superiority:** Organisations with different resources have different degrees of competitive abilities. For example, the company with latest technology possesses competitive superiority over other companies. Similarly, companies with best talented and competent human resources enjoy the competitive superiority over other companies in terms of most efficient ideas, customer service, low cost and best quality. Similarly, patents determine the competitive advantage. For example, Coca Cola's cola formula brought competitive superiority to the company.
2. **Resource Scarcity:** When a particular resource contributing significantly to the value of the product/service is in short supply, such a resource determines the distinctive capability of a firm. Thus, the firms possessing such a scare resource possess distinctive capability over other firms.
3. **Inimitability:** If a particular resource possessed by a firm can't be imitated/copied easily by the competitors, such a resource provides distinctive capability to the firms in the long-run. In contrast the firms possess distinctive advantage only in the

short-run, when the resource can be copied/imitated easily. For example, Wendy's idea of providing 'drive through' facility in its hamburger business provided a distinctive capability to the firm in short-run as this idea was copied and practiced easily by other fast-food restaurants. Thus, competitors copy/imitate the distinctive competency of the firm at least in the short-run. Therefore, firms should develop unique resources based on the following characteristics in order to sustain the distinctive capability.

- **Physically Unique Resources:** Physically unique resources are virtually impossible to copy/imitate. Design of the Maruti cars, Cola formula of Coca Cola, beer ingredients, structure of ice beer of S.P. Brewery Limited, aroma of Bru Coffee are proved to be unique resources as their competitors could not copy them.

- **Path-dependent Resources:** Path-dependent resources are created by the firm over a period of time through their continuous effort. Therefore, it would be difficult for the competitors to acquire/imitate/copy of such resources. For example, Coca Cola developed the present coke formula over a period of time. Similarly, LG developed a distinctive variety of refrigerator that can store special Korean pickle for over a year. Farex baby foods, Dr. Reddy Lab's low cost pharmaceutical products and Toyota automobiles are examples of the distinctive resources developed by the companies that can't be copied by the competitors.

- **Casual Ambiguity:** Certain firms create and/or develop competitive advantage that can't be known exactly by others and therefore can't be understood and imitated by the competitors. Casual ambiguous resources arise from subtle combinations of tangible and intangible assets, social and cultural factors, processes and organisational attributes the company possesses. For example, employee freedom and risk-taking culture of a biscuit company enabled an employee to play with the production process and machinery and develop sweet-cum-salt biscuits. Similarly, South-West Airlines developed a number of new methods and approaches by casual ambiguity consequent upon the breaking culture adapted by the company.

- **Economic Deterrence:** Economic deterrence occurs when the requirement of capital for establishing manufacturing facilities is quite large and the size of the market is small only to accommodate a single player. Hence, competitors may not enter the market. For example, Air Niugini has no competitor due to the large size of capital requirement to establish an airline company and small size of airways market in Papua New Guinea. Similarly, Pepsi Cola Limited withdrew from the Papua New Guinea market due to the small size of the market and low rate of return on capital employed.

4. **Appropriate the Profits:** Different parties like owners/shareholders, human resources, input suppliers, output dealers contribute their resources to the success of the business and thereby to profits. Thus, the contributors of these resources are expected to share the profits created by the resource providers.

5. **Durability:** Durability deals with the extent of the time span that the value of resources remain. Value of some resources increase over time while the value of some other resources depreciates over the period. For example, the value of land appreciates

over the period due to scarcity of land while the value of technology depreciates over the period due to the invention of new technology and displacement of old technology by the latest technology. The value of brands of most of the varieties of wine appreciates while the value of computer technologies, mobile telephone technologies and technologies of electronic products depreciates.

6. **Substitutability:** Easy developmental of substitute products depreciates the value of the resource of the product and *vice versa*. For example, development of mobile phones depreciated the value of 'pagers' and 'land phones'. Similarly, development of computers depreciated the value of manual and electronic type writers. Development of photocopying machines depreciated to value of carbon paper technology. Limited scope for development of alternatives for land enhanced the value of land.

Resource-Based View and Organisational Analysis

Companies must evaluate their resources in order to estimate their future competitive advantage. Organisations should analyse various resources to gauge the value of each resource to the firm as well as to its competitive advantage. The following guidelines are helpful to analyse an organisation's resources.

- *Disaggregate Resources:* Organisations should disaggregate their resources into minute aspects and scan each aspect of resources in order to assess organisation's capabilities.
- *Utilise a Functional Perspective:* After breaking the resources into minute areas, attribute each minute area to a concerned functional perspective.
- *Look at Organisational Processes:* After minute resource analysis, combine the analysis in order to present an unified view of the total organisation.

Resources and Competitive Advantage

Competitive advantage of a firm as well as its sustainability depends upon the firm's resources. Grant proposes a five-step resource-based approach to internal analysis.

- Analyse the firm's resources in terms of strengths and weaknesses.
- Combine the firm's strengths into specific capabilities. Identify the capabilities that can help the firm significantly in achieving its mission. These corporate capabilities are viewed as distinctive capabilities, when the firm alone possesses these capabilities.
- Appraise the corporate capabilities in terms of their potential contribution to profit earning capacity of the firm as well as their sustainable contribution.
- Select the strategy that best exploits the firm's resources and capabilities relative to external environment.
- Identify resource gaps and bridge them for upgrading weaknesses.

Sustainability of Resource Advantage

As discussed earlier, resource advantage is not for ever. Some resource advantages sustain for a long period while some other resource advantages stay for a short period. Sustainability of resource advantage is determined by two characteristics, *viz.,* durability and inimitability.

Inimitability: Inimitability, as discussed earlier, is the rate at which a firm's resources are copied/duplicated by the competitors. Competitor's abilities to imitate include copying the product design by reverse engineering, copying the marketing strategies, scout the talent employees, suppliers of inputs and market intermediaries of the competitor and copying the production processes.

Imitation of a company's capabilities is dependent on three factors, *viz.,* transparency, transferability and replicability.

Transparency: Transparency is the degree of openness of a company's abilities, competencies and talent's that indicates the vulnerability for copying. For example, the formula of Coca Cola's cola is not at all transparent and as such the competitors could not copy.

Transferability: Transferability is the degree and speed at which the competitors can acquire the capabilities of a firm. Product design, technology as well as production process of biscuits can be easily imitated. As such, most of the biscuit companies are more vulnerable for copying.

Replicability: Replicability is the competitor's ability to use copied resources for the success of the firm. Many movie making companies copy the theme of already released movies of the competitors.

Now, we shall discuss another factor of resource, capabilities and core competencies, i.e., capabilities.

Capabilities: Capabilities are the firm's capacity to deploy resources that have been purposely integrated to achieve a desired state.

Capabilities

Capabilities are the organisation's capacity to deploy resources that have been purposely integrated to achieve desired end state. Capabilities are the outcomes of interactions among tangible and intangible resources. For example, IBM's capabilities are the interaction of its tangible resources like its employees, knowledge and ideas with regard to product development and the market strategies employed over the period.

Capabilities enable firms to create and exploit opportunities and develop sustained advantages. Dr. Reddy's Lab's capabilities enabled the company to create marketing opportunities in most of the developing countries particularly in Africa in addition to India. Capabilities are based on developing, carrying and exchanging information and knowledge through the firm's human capital. For example, Yahoo and Google's employees developed a number of products through exchange of information, knowledge, talent and expertise. Ranbaxy, Microsoft and Infosys believe in their intellectual capacity of their employees.

Intellectual Capabilities: In fact, it is felt that a company builds capabilities not based on technology, and other physical assets but from the knowledge, skills, talents, intellectual capital and commitment of its human resources. Therefore, companies should concentrate on providing congenial work environment, so that individual employee's intellectual capital would be synergised into organisation's knowledge, skill and commitment that forms the company's intellectual capability.

Organisations in order to enhance their intellectual capability have been shifting into learning organisations by enabling their existing employees to learn continuously, developing alliances with the people of consultant organisations, and employing more competent people. In addition, organisations employ 'Chief Learning Officers' and 'Chief Knowledge Officers', who in turn convert the individual knowledge and talents into organisation knowledge and skill.

Thus, a company's human capital — individual and synergised — in the form of knowledge, skills, talent and commitment form the capabilities and a key source of its competitive advantage during this current century. Human knowledge takes the shape of the innovations, creations, new ideas, effective strategies, new product/services and enhanced functions/uses of the existing product or service.

Organisations, in addition to human capabilities, build capabilities in other areas like manufacturing, marketing and research and development. Manufacturing capabilities include designing a new product, effective production process that reduces manufacturing cycle time and minimises cost of production. For example, Mazda developed an innovative production process that reduced the assembly time. Other manufacturing capabilities include sophistication of production technology, and designing quality. Marketing capabilities include effective use of logistics management techniques, building up of brands and developing customer relationships. For example, Reliance Fresh and More Super Markets build the capabilities around using effective logistics management techniques, whereas McDonald's and Singapore Airlines build capabilities around customer relationship management and Gillette builds effective brand images. Research and development capabilities include exceptional focus on innovation as developed by Sony, exceptional technological capability by Corning and development of deep knowledge in the development of alternative materials as is the case with Kodak.

The Body Shop developed the capabilities in motivating, empowering and retaining employees while Hewlett-Packard build the capabilities around effective execution of managerial tasks. Organisations strive to convert capabilities into core competencies.

(B) CORE COMPETENCIES

Core competencies are a company's resources and capabilities that enable the firm to build competitive advantage over the competitors. Companies build competitive advantage by procuring and multiplying resources, create abilities over them, and developing synergy of resources and capabilities. Core competencies enable the companies to formulate strategies and draw strategic actions by converting competencies into business activities. Thus, the companies achieve their goals of earning an expected profit, improve market share and satisfy their employees by using their core competencies.

For example, Vodafone India utilised its technical manpower and financial resources to build towers in Indian villages. This competency enabled the company to increase its share in the rural market and thereby its total market in India by 2% between 2005 and 2009. Similarly, Digicel (PNG) Ltd., also built towers in rural areas of Papua New Guinea in addition to urban centres by utilising its Financial, technical and resources. This capability enabled the company to acquire core competency over Be-Mobile Ltd., which was enjoying monopoly in mobile phone service in Papua New Guinea until 2007.

Thus, core competencies are those capabilities and resources that enable the company to perform and act to achieve its goals by adding or creating unique value to its goods and/or services better compared to its competitors in the long term. Therefore, all the resources and capabilities of a company need not result in competencies. It does mean that the resources and capabilities could be utilised in building a competitive advantage. These resources have competitive value and potential to serve as competitive advantage. Thus, some resources would represent a liability as the company may be weak over competitors in that resource area. Similarly, the firm may fail to utilise such resource during a particular time to build its competencies. For example, Deccan Airlines could not use its capabilities of seating capacity as its competitors like King Fisher due to its inabilities in maintaining punctuality during 2006.

When companies fail to convert certain resources into competencies, due to competition and external environmental threats, companies should find other markets or portfolios of business where such resources become capabilities. For example, Toyota introduced its outdated model and technology of home country in India and other developing countries.

How Many Core Competencies?

The mind boggling question at this juncture is how many core competencies are required for a company? It is obvious that a company can't have core competencies in all areas. McKinsey & Company identifies that their clients craft their strategies around them four core competencies. Core competencies of some selected companies are provided in the Exhibit 3.1.

Exhibit 3.1: Core Competencies of Some Selected Companies

Company	Core Competencies
McDonald	Real estate, restaurant operations, marketing and global infrastructure
Ford	Design, branding, sales, service operations
Honeywell	Technology, customer service
Brady Corporation	Safety, graphics, special products
Vodafone	Extensive coverage, technology, low cost
Dr. Reddy's Lab	Low cost, quality, wide range of product

Building Core Competencies

As indicated earlier, all capabilities need not be core competencies. Two tools help us to know whether a particular capability is a core competency or not. The first one consists of four specific criteria and the second one is value chain analysis.

Four criteria for determining core capabilities include:

- Valuable capabilities
- Rare capabilities
- Costly-to-imitate capabilities
- Non-substitutable capabilities

Valuable capabilities: Valuable capabilities create and add value by exploiting opportunities provided by external environment to the company. Digicel (PNG) Ltd.'s appropriate technical and financial capabilities enabled it to exploit the opportunities provided by the Papua New Guinea's environment like high cost of mobile services as well as instrument costs.

Similarly, non-availability of required quantity of petrol and other Petroleum products in Indian market were exploited by the technical, financial and skilled human resources of Reliance Petrochemicals Ltd. The vast experience of expertise of Wal-Mart in Retail Super-Market malls enabled it to exploit the retail market business in India.

The following exhibit presents the valuable capabilities of various companies and the opportunities that were exploited by them.

Exhibit 3.2: Value Capabilities and the Opportunities Exploited

Company	Value capabilities	Opportunities exploited
Sony Corporation	Expertise in designing, producing and selling	Portable disc players, easy to hold 8-mm video cameras market
Wal-Mart	Distribution capabilities	Market for low price for branded products. In fact, other retailers were charging high prices in USA.
J. Boag & Son Brewery	Brewing and marketing premium beer	Non-availability of premium beer
Vodafone (India)	Technical and financial capabilities	Entered rural mobile phone market in India by constructing towers in rural India.
Digicel (PNG) Ltd.	Technical and financial capabilities of medium level suitable for small markets.	High priced mobile services in a small market of Papua New Guinea.
Tata	Expertise in Automobiles	Small car market for low income group of India (Nano brand cars)
Dr. Reddy's Lab	Capabilities in bulk drugs, expertise in producing low cost pharmaceuticals	Exploited low-income customer markets in India and other Third World countries.

Rare: Rare capabilities are those that are possessed by the competitors rarely. In fact, many companies possess valuable capabilities, but not rare. Even having an innovative idea is also a rare capability. Companies with rare capabilities exploit external opportunities to a significant extent, compared to their competitors. The following capabilities possessed by the companies are viewed as rare capabilities.

Coca Cola	Idea of introduction of small size bottle of coke for low-income group	Successfully entered and exploited lower income group market
Coca Cola	Product formula	Market leader
L&G	Idea and development of special refrigerator for storing traditional Korean food	Turned around the sick company
Dell	Business model of selling the product directly to customers	Successfully exploited the market.
Computershare Ltd.	Idea of development of share registry software	Became global share registry.
Eureka Vacuum Cleaners	Special sales approach based on problems of Indian housewives product formula	Grabbed the household market for vaccum cleaners.

Costly to Imitate Capabilities: Costly to imitate capabilities are those capabilities that pose complexity and thereby heavy cost to competitors to imitate. These capabilities include unique organisational culture, brand name, interpersonal relations, trust, network with customers, suppliers, creditors, etc.

The following exhibit presents the capabilities that are costly to imitate of some selected companies.

Exhibit 3.4

Company/Product	Costly/Capabilities
McKinsey	Organisational culture
Tata Group	Historical reasons
Colgate Palmolive	Product brand
Airtel	Clarity of voice
McDonald	Taste of the food
Starbuck	Coffee flavour
3 Roses Tea	Aroma

Other reasons for the costly capabilities to imitate include:

- Casual ambiguity in linking a company's capabilities, competencies and competitive advantage.
- Social complexity: Social complexity involves complex social relations among managers, suppliers, creditors, market intermediaries and government officials.

Companies that developed social complexity as a competitive advantage include Tata group, Reliance Industries, Hewlett-Packard, Sony, Walt Disney Company, Merck, Harvey Norman, General Electric and Toyota.

Non-substitutable: Non-substitutable capabilities are those that do not have strategic equivalents. Non-substitutable capabilities include company's specific capacities like trust, relationships, product attributes, knowledge and expertise. Coca Cola's formula can be regarded as non-substitutable capability.

The following table presents the possible outcomes from combinations of criteria for sustainable competitive advantage.

Table 3.1: Possible Outcomes from the Combinations of Criteria for Sustainable Competitive Advantage

Value	*Rare*	*Costly*	*Non-substitutable*	*Competitive Consequences*	*Performance Implications*
No	No	No	No	Competitive Disadvantage	Below-average Returns
Yes	No	No	Yes/No	Competitive Parity	Average Returns
Yes	Yes	No	Yes/No Advantage	Temporary Competitive Average	About-average to Returns
Yes	Yes	Yes	Yes	Sustainable Competitive Advantage	Above-average Returns

Source: Adapted from Dallas Hanson, *et. al.*, p. 104.

(C) VALUE CHAIN ANALYSIS

Value is the amount buyers desire to pay for what a firm provides to them in the form of a product/service/product-cum-service. Creating value for buyers that exceeds the cost of manufacturing, marketing and other operations is one of the basic goals of any business unit's generic strategy. Business activities that transform inputs into desired output that customers value reflect the value chain. Value chain analysis examines and enhances the efforts of the business operations that contribute to the value to the customers. Value chain analysis views the business as a process of activities from the stage of raw material/inputs to the final stage of delivering the product including after sales service to the customer. Value chain analysis examines the areas of advantages of low cost and disadvantages of high costs. It further tries to further reduce the cost in the low cost areas and attempts to turn the high costs into low costs in order to reduce overall costs of all operations. Value Chain analysis, in addition to attempting to reduce the cost, also attempts to enhance the value to the customer. It enhances the value by contributing to the quality, convenience and comfort to the customer. Michael E. Porter contributed to identifying building blocks, assessing the value addition from each of the activities and linking their organisation's competitive advantage. The value chain display consists of total value of activities and margin. Value activities are of two types, *viz.*, primary activities and support activities (See Fig. 3.1)

Primary Activities: Primary activities are those business activities that relate and contribute directly to the manufacture, marketing of the product and creating and adding value in the chain of operations. Thus, primary activities form the sequence or chain through which raw materials/inputs are transformed into final product/service that the customers use including the post-sales service. Primary activities, thus, include:

- *Inbound Logistics:* These are the activities concerned with receiving, storing and issuing all kinds of raw materials and spare parts to the manufacturing/service centers. Materials handling, inventory management, stock control, storage, transportation are some of the functions involved in this activity.
- *Operations:* Production/operations activities aim at transforming inputs into products. These activities include machining, assembling, testing, packaging and delivering.
- *Outbound Logistics:* These activities include collection of finished goods, handling them, storing them, transporting them to marketing intermediaries and customers.
- *Marketing and Sales:* These activities include promotional programmes like advertising, personal selling and sales promotion, sales administration, product delivery and the like.
- *Service:* Service activities include pre-sales service to create demand and sales and post-sales service to enhance the value of product or service.

How do Primary Activities Add to The Value?

Primary activities add to the value of the product by reducing the cost as well as by improving the quality and convenience. Now, we shall discuss these aspects.

Inbound Logistics: Inbound logistics include quality verification of raw material at the source, transportation in good condition and efficiently, storage and warehousing economically and efficiently controlled. These activities ensure the quality of raw material that can contribute to the quality of the final product. In addition to performing these activities on time, ensure the timely distribution of the product to market intermediaries and the customer. Further efficient handling of these activities, better negotiations and maintenance of sound relationship with the supplier reduce the cost of inbound logistics. Inbound logistics contribute significantly to enhancement of value as raw materials account for more than 50% of product cost in majority of products.

Infrastructure and facilities for inbound logistics require heavy capital investment contributing significantly to the cost of final products. Therefore, firms employ modern techniques to reduce the investment requirement. For example, General Electric uses highly automated sorting and inventory systems that allow the material to move quickly from stores to the factory. This technique reduces the storage cost as well as inventory cost significantly. Some firms outsource these activities, and thus reduces the requirement of heavy investments.

Inbound activities play a vital role even in service industries like banking, insurance companies, hospitals, educational institutions, telecommunication services and transportation services. Procurement of medical equipment, pharmaceuticals and stationery influences the quality and cost of the services in hospitals. Similarly, efficient handling of inputs play vital role in determining quality, cost, convenience and customer satisfaction in hotel industry as well as in educational institutions.

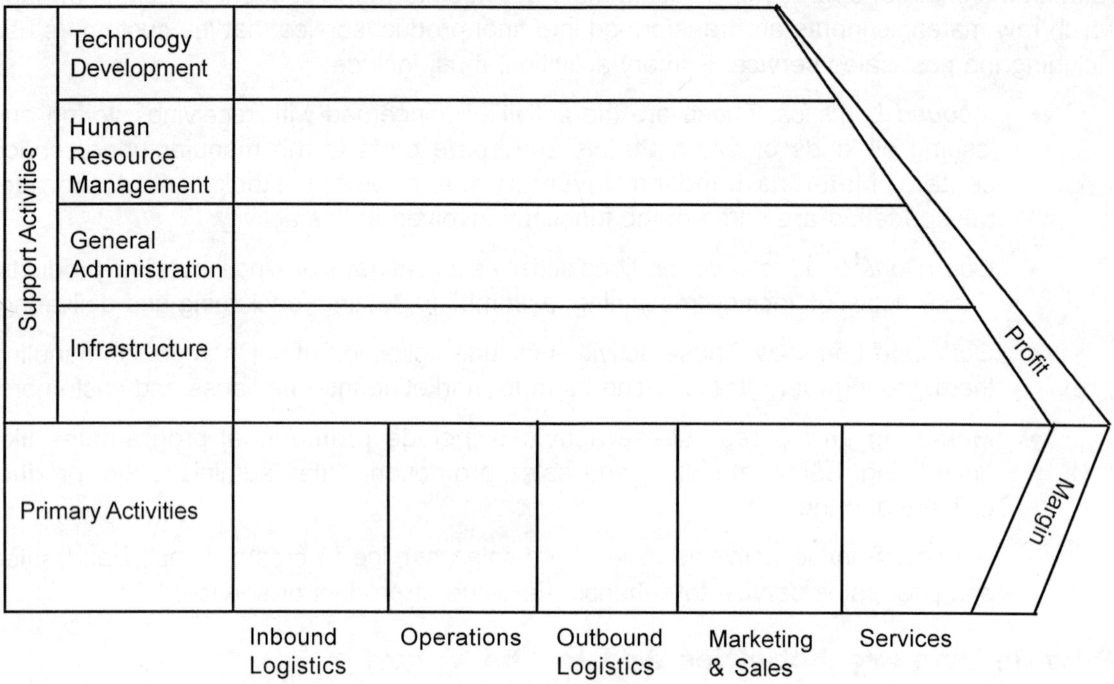

Source: Adapted from Michael E. Porter, "*Competitive Advantage*", Free Press, 1988.

Fig. 3.1: The Value Chain

Operations: Operations/production deal with the conversion process that transforms the inputs into output. Value is added or created when the input is converted into output. Operations aim at creation and innovation which in turn enhances the value of the product. Further the objectives of zero defect products ensure quality and dependability of the product.

Product design directly contributes to the value as customers that would pay higher price for the product designed in accordance with their unexhibited/unexpressed needs as well as conveniences. Appropriate type of process contributes to the cost reduction, speed of production and improved quality. Similarly, selection and practice of other production activities, appropriate technology, facilities like capacity, aggregate planning and scheduling of operations, efficient management of inventory and planning and control of quality contribute to the value.

Outbound Logistics: Outbound logistics begin after the completion of the production process and end with the distribution of the product either to the market intermediaries in case of indirect marketing and to the customer in case of direct marketing. Thus, the activities of outbound logistics include storage/warehousing, transportation, handling of products, negotiation with market intermediaries and inventory management. Efficient performance of these activities enables the firm to deliver on the products in taste to the customer, reduce delivery time and storage. Thereby, it reduces the cost of inventory.

Strides in information technology resulted in Internet-based marketing, helps the marketing intermediaries like wholesalers and retailers to maintain lowest level or close to zero level inventory. Some of the companies producing fast moving consumer goods track the inventory, orders, transportation, storage and the like. Dr. Reddy's Lab tracks the transportation, storage and inventory. P&G reduced the transportation time and the complexities in tracking the products by using Internet-based on-line inventory management. Efficient and fast outbound logistics of P&G enabled it to track the fast moving products, sharing the information with super markets about the customer tastes and demands and thereby develop new ideas for future product development. Thus, efficient and Internet-based online outbound logistic activities reduce cost, increases innovation and delivers the products intact.

Marketing and Sales: Marketing and sales activities include product development and mix, pricing, place of markets including channels of distribution like wholesalers, retailers, sales force and network marketing and promotional mix including advertising, personal selling and sales promotion. Companies select different marketing strategies like leader or follower strategies, total market or niche or focus strategies, single product line or multiple product line strategy, direct marketing or indirect marketing strategies and specified place marketing or online marketing. Companies select the strategies in order to reduce the marketing costs and enhance the convenience and comfort to the customers. Some of the hotels in India in order to enhance the convenience to the customer introduced phone ordering and home delivery. Even super markets follow this strategy. Most of the airlines including Singapore Airlines, Indian Airlines and Air Nuigini introduced online ticket booking in order to reduce the marketing cost and thereby ticket price and enhance customer convenience. Even Indian Railways and many road transport companies introduced online ticket booking. Firms also advertise online using Internet that reduces cost and reaches customers fast.

In fact, some companies design excellent marketing strategies that enable the customer to be willing to pay the price that is quite higher than the product cost, thus, enhancing the value. For example, Coca Cola, Pepsi Cola and other cola drinks as well as mineral water companies price their products significantly higher than the cost of the production of their respective products. They could do so mostly due to their marketing and sales efforts.

Service: Pre-sales and post-sales services are quite essential for consumer durable, convenience and luxury goods. Customers would be willing to pay more when the service and thereby the continuous and perfect functioning of the product is guaranteed and/or ensured. For example, automobiles, refrigerators, TVs, educational instruments like computers, overhead projectors/multimedia projectors and photocopying machines need after sales services. Excellent after sales service ensures continuous and perfect functioning of the product and thus, enhances customer's value.

In addition, the service reduces the replacement cost of the product as well as working cost. For example, the excellent service facilities provided by Maruti Udyog Limited throughout the country enhanced the running life and reduced running cost of its cars.

Support Activities: Other activities of the business are support activities which provide support to the primary activities of the business, and hence, they are referred to as support activities. Support activities help the company enhance the customer value and reduce the cost by bringing coordination among primary activities and providing necessary inputs for the primary activities. Support activities include:

- Technology development
- Human resource management
- General administration
- Infrastructure

Technology Development: Technology is improved continuously both in production and in other operations. It is developed through innovation and continuous upgradation. Technology revolution including the revolution in the information technology brought paradigm shifts in the production process, product functions and utilities, speed of manufacturing, quality of products in terms of zero-defect production, fast delivery of the products and information processing. Technology development enables the companies to add multiple functions to the product. For example, mobile phone today carries the functions of a clock, alarm, calculator, tape recorder, camera and video camera. Similarly, multiple functions are added to computers. Thus, technology development enhances the customer value by adding a variety of functions to the existing product. In addition, it reduces the cost of the product in terms of the utility of all functions put together. Technology development supports the primary activities. Inbound logistics are helped by transportation technology, materials handling technology, and storage technologies. For example, containerisation made the sea transportation become more convenient. Jet planes help fast movement and air conditioning of containers helps in the export of even perishable products to foreign countries.

Production and operations are directly helped by the technology development. Automation of production process, coding of stores activities and movement of the raw materials enable the production process to be economical, fast and of high quality. Designing and production of customised products, computer-aided design and computer-aided production became possible due to technology development. Technology enables outbound logistics for efficient and fast delivery in addition to intact delivery to the customer. As indicated in case of inbound logistics, containerisation, increase in speed of transport vehicles and other technologies relating to storage enhanced the efficiency of outbound logistics.

Product development, advertising, sales promotion and service activities are performed most efficiently due to technological development. Thus, developments in technology support the outbound logistics and service activities.

Human Resource Management: Human resource plays a dominant role in the successful and profitable performance of a firm. In fact, human resource makes or mars the performance of a company. The motivated, committed and efficient human resources significantly support primary activities. Skilled and trained human resources provide necessary support for all primary activities. In fact, all primary activities are performed by human resources.

Human resource is also referred to as human capital and asset. It determines the competitive advantage and distinctive competency of a firm. Efficient human resource management in terms of selection of right people, development, motivation, employee empowerment and the like provide required human effort for successful operation of all primary activities. Efficient human resource contributes towards increase in productivity which in turn reduces cost of production. In addition, efficient human resources contribute to the quality, customer convenience and comfort and thereby enhance value and profit margin of the company.

General Administration: General administration includes organisational structure, management style, leadership style, policies and procedures. General administrative policies and practice can be enabling or disabling. Enabling policies and practices include: flat and horizontal structure, employees empowerment, decentralisation, empowerment of employees in decision-making, strategy formulation and implementation, employee motivation, leading the employees progressively and development of commitment. These enabling policies of general administration support the primary activities, which in turn contribute to the reduction of cost and enhancement of value and profit margin.

Infrastructure: Infrastructural activities include accounting, finance, information system, pay roll, legal affairs, public relations and corporate governance. Expenditure on these activities is called overhead expenses as this expenditure can not be isolated. Infrastructure activities contribute to the value addition by supporting and enabling the primary activities. In addition, the efficient functioning of infrastructure activities contributes to the cost reduction, and thereby increase profit margin.

Outsourcing

Outsourcing is the long-term contracting out of mostly non-core business processes to an outside provider to help achieve increased value for the business. Availability of highly qualified skill pool and faster adaptation of well-defined business processes lead to higher productivity gains without compromising on quality. Outsourcing creates and adds value to the business by

- enabling the executives to concentrate on strategic areas,
- improving processes and saving money, and
- increasing business capabilities.

Outsourcing has been increasing in order to meet the growing international demand for lucrative and customer-interaction centres. Many organisations worldwide are outsourcing these services to locations like India, China, South Korea and Malaysia.

Many companies acquire the capabilities by outsourcing some of the business operations. Ford Motor Company could acquire the capabilities of reducing the cost of key parts by outsourcing. Nissan Motor Company outsourced the maintenance of its North American Computer Systems to IBM in order to reduce its costs. Dell Computers concentrates on creating value through its distribution channels by outsourcing most of its manufacturing and customer service activities. Nike and Reebok concentrates on their core competencies of designing and marketing by outsourcing production activities. In fact, small firms were developed in Vietnam and other countries due to the outsourcing of production activities by Nike and Reebok. These companies could further enhance their core capabilities and competencies by outsourcing the business processes in which they lack core competencies.

Organisational Analysis

Organisational appraisal is the process of monitoring an organisation's internal environment to identify strengths and weaknesses that may influence the firm's ability to achieve goals. The internal environment of an organisation includes forces that operate inside the organisation with specific implications for managing organisational performance. Internal environmental factors which come from within collectively define both trouble spots that need strengthening and the core competencies that the firm can build. An organisation can better analyse how much activity might add value or contribute significantly to shape an effective strategy by systematically examining its internal environment. Michael Porter has proposed a method for such an evaluation. This method is called value chain analysis. Value chain analysis can identify internal core competencies. Internal core competencies can be identified by analysing functional areas of business. The purpose of analysing an organisation's internal environment is to identify and evaluate organisational strengths and weaknesses.

(D) STRENGTHS AND WEAKNESSES ANALYSIS

Organisational analysis requires data and information about the internal environment. SWOT analysis refines this information by applying a general framework for understanding and managing the environment under which a company operates. (The acronym SWOT stands for strengths, weaknesses, opportunities and threats). A SWOT analysis consists of evaluating a company's internal strengths and weaknesses and its external opportunities and threats. SWOT analysis underscores the basic point that strategy must produce a good fit between a firm's internal capability (its strengths and weaknesses) and its external situation (its opportunities and threats).

1. Identifying Strengths and Weaknesses

A strength is a strong point for the company, *i.e.,* something a company is good at doing or a characteristic that gives it an important capability. A strength can be a skill, a competence, a valuable organisational resource or competitive capability or achievement that gives the company an advantage. A weakness is something the company does not have or does poorly (in comparison to competitors or standards) or a condition that puts it at a disadvantageous positions. A weakness may or may not make an organisation competitively vulnerable, depending on how much it matters in the competition battle.

SWOT analysis of a company is presented in Exhibit 3.5. The lists of strengths and weaknesses have to be evaluated after they have been identified. Important and crucial strengths are to be identified. These factors count more in determining performance, in competing efficiently and in formulating powerful strategy. Similarly some weaknesses can be fatal whereas others can be easily remedied. Such weaknesses should also be spotted out. Strengths are like strategic assets and weaknesses are like competitive liabilities. Unlike in financial balance sheet, the strengths/assets should be more than the weaknesses/liabilities in the strategic balance sheet.

A company's strengths are more significant. They can be used as cornerstones of the strategy. They are the basis for building competitive advantages. If a company does not have strengths to build competitive advantages, the management has to develop competencies quickly. These competencies can be the basis for building competitive advantages.

Successful strategists seek to exploit what a company does best — its expertise, strengths, core competencies and strongest competitive capabilities. At the same time, the successful strategists seek to correct the competitive weaknesses. Otherwise, these weaknesses hurt the company's performance, and disqualify it from pursuing an attractive opportunity. In essence, an organisation's strategy should be well-fitted to company's strengths, weaknesses and competitive capabilities. Thus, the company should build its strategy around the strengths and avoid the area of weaknesses.

2. Distinctive/Core Competencies

The company should consolidate its production, technological, marketing, finance and human resource know-how into competencies to enhance its competitiveness. A distinctive or core competence is something a company does especially well in comparison to its competitors. The distinctive competence is the unique capability it gives an organisation in capitalising upon a particular opportunity; the competitive edge it may give a firm in the market place and the potential for building a distinctive competence and making it the cornerstone of strategy. Thus, a distinctive competence is, "any advantage a company has over its competitors because it can do something which they cannot or it can do something better than they can."

Distinctive or core competencies empower a company to build competitive advantage. Core competencies include excellent quality maintenance, lowest production cost, latest technology utilisation, ability to provide required service, ability to develop new products, high creditworthiness, etc. The benefits of core competencies in formulating strategies include: (a) the company gets an added capability in going after a particular market opportunity, (b) the company gets the competitive edge it can yield in the market place, and (c) its potential for being cornerstone of strategy.

3. Identifying Opportunities and Threats

Opportunities and threats of a company can also be seen in Exhibit 3.5. There are differences between the industry's opportunities and a firm's opportunities except in one firm industry. Some firms are in better position than other firms in the same industry, in utilising the opportunities. This situation is based on the firm's strengths and weaknesses. The industry opportunities most relevant to a specific firm are those that offer significant avenues for growth and those where a firm has the most potential for competitive advantages. Certain external environmental factors pose threats to a firm. These threats include: adoption of latest technology by the competitors, inflow of high quality and improved products from foreign markets, entry of multinational and transnational corporations, change in the customer's preferences, change in governmental policies, failure of the markets, etc.

Strategy must be formulated to *(i)* pursue opportunities suited to the firm's strengths or competencies, and *(ii)* provide a defense against threats posed by the environment. The SWOT analysis should appraise a firm's strengths, weaknesses, opportunities and threats and draw conclusions about the firm's attractiveness. Exhibit 3.6 presents strategy-making questions.

Exhibit 3.5: SWOT Analysis — What to Look for in Sizing up a Company's Strengths, Weaknesses, Opportunities, and Threats

Potential Internal Strengths

- Core competencies in key areas
- Adequate financial resources
- Well thought of by buyers
- An acknowledged market leader
- Well-conceived functional area strategies
- Access to economies of scale
- Insulated (at least somewhat) from strong competitive pressures
- Proprietary technology
- Cost advantages
- Better advertising campaigns
- Product innovation skills
- Proven management
- Ahead on experience curve
- Better manufacturing capability
- Superior technological skills
- Others

Potential Internal Weaknesses

- No clear strategic direction
- Obsolete facilities
- Super profitability because?
- Lack of managerial depth and talent
- Missing some key skills or competencies
- Poor track record in implementing strategy
- Plagued with internal operating problems
- Falling behind in R&D
- Too narrow a product line
- Weak market image
- Weak distribution network
- Below-average marketing skills
- Unable to finance needed changes in strategy
- Higher overall unit costs relative to key competitors
- Others

Potential External Opportunities

- Serve additional customer groups
- Enter new markets or segments
- Expand product line to meet broader range of customer needs
- Diversify into related products
- Vertical integration (forward or backward)
- Falling trade barriers in attractive foreign markets
- Complacency among rival firms
- Faster market growth
- Others

Potential External Threats

- Entry of lower-cost foreign competitors
- Rising sales of substitute products
- Slower market growth
- Adverse shifts in foreign exchange rates and trade policies of foreign governments
- Costly regulatory requirements
- Vulnerability to recession and business cycle
- Growing bargaining power of customers or suppliers
- Changing buyer needs and tastes
- Adverse demographic changes
- Others

Exhibit 3.6: Strategy-Making Questions

1. Does the company have any internal strengths or core competencies on attractive strategy can be built around?
2. Do the company's weaknesses make it competitively vulnerable and/or do they disqualify the firm from pursuing certain opportunities? Which weaknesses does strategy need to correct?

3. Which opportunities does the company have the skills and resources to pursue with a real chance of success? (Remember: opportunity without the means to capture it is an illusion).
4. What threats should managers be worried about most, and what strategic moves should they consider in crafting a good defense?

Source: Adapted from Arthur A. Thompson Jr., and A.J. Strickland III, *op. cit.*, p. 90.

4. Strategic Cost Analysis

One of the critical strengths of a company is its cost position relative to competitors. Cost comparison is critical particularly for those companies producing consumer goods. Therefore, assessing whether a company's costs are competitive with those of its close rivals is a necessary and crucial part of a company's internal environmental analysis. Cost differences among rivals can stem from many factors like prices of raw materials, salary levels and cost of transportation. The lower a company's costs are below those of rivals, the company has an advantage over its competitors. Otherwise, it becomes competitively vulnerable to the company. Strategic cost analysis involves comparing a company's cost position relative to key competitors, activity by activity from raw materials purchase to the price paid by ultimate customers.

(E) COMPETITIVE STRENGTH ASSESSMENT

Systematic assessment of whether a company's competitive position is strong or weak relative to close rivals is an essential step in company's situational analysis. Particular elements to single out for evaluation are: (1) how strongly the firm holds its present competitive position, (2) whether the firm's position can be expected to improve or deteriorate if the present strategy is continued, (3) how the firm ranks relative to key rivals on each important measure of competitive strength and industry key success factor, (4) whether the firm has a net competitive advantage or disadvantage, and (5) the firm's ability to defend its position in light of industry's driving forces, competitive pressure, and the anticipated moves of rivals."

Exhibit 3.7 lists some indicators of strengths and weaknesses in a competitive position showing whether a firm's competitive position is improving or slipping. Competitive strengths and competitive advantages empower a company to improve its long-term market position.

Exhibit 3.7: The Signs of Strength and Weakness in a Company's Competitive Position

Signs of Competitive Strength	Signs of Competitive Weakness
• Important core competencies	• Confronted with competitive disadvantages
• Strong market share (or a leading market share)	• Losing ground to rival firms
• A pace-setting or distinctive strategy	• Below-average growth in revenues
• Growing customer base and customer loyalty	• Short on financial resources
• Above-average market visibility	• A slipping reputation with customers
• In a favourably situated strategic group	• Trailing in product development

• Concentrating on fastest-growing market segments	• In a strategic group destined to lose ground
• Strongly differentiated products	• Weak in areas where there is the most market potential
• Cost advantages	• A higher-cost producer
• Above-average profit margins	• Too small to be a major factor in the marketplace
• Above-average technological and innovational capability	• Not in good position to deal with emerging threats
	• Weak product quality
• A creative, entrepreneurially alert management	• Lacking skills and capabilities in key areas
• In position to capitalise on opportunities	

Source: Arthur A. Thompson Jr. and A.J. Strickland III, *op. cit.*, p. 96.

1. Scanning, Forecasting and Other Data Sources for SWOT:

Organisations require cross-functional cooperation to collect data about present and future environments. SWOT analysis becomes a team effort performed by functional specialists from finance, human resources, marketing, production etc. Information gathered from key employees can also help managers to better understand the internal environment of the organisation.

Scanning systems can take many different forms. They are:

(i) *Irregular Scanning Systems:* These consists largely of *ad hoc* studies, often in response to environmental crisis.

(ii) *Regular Scanning Systems:* These systems revolve around regular reviews of the environment or selected strategic environmental components.

(iii) *Continuous Scanning Systems:* These systems continuously monitor components of the organisational environment.

Internal environmental forecasting is a critical step in SWOT analysis. It is the process of identifying strategic issues that will affect an organisation's environment at some future time.

Strategic Issues Need To Be Addressed

Effective strategy-making requires a thorough understanding of the strategic issues a company faces. This step puts the company's overall situation into perspective and identifies the situation where management needs to focus its strategic attention.

Strategists should consider the following issues:

1. Whether the present strategy is adequate in light of driving forces at work in the industry.
2. How closely the present strategy matches the industry's future key success factors.
3. How good a defense the present strategy offers against the five competitive forces — future ones, not necessarily past or present ones.

4. In what ways the present strategy may not adequately protect the company against external threats and internal weaknesses.
5. Where and how the company may be vulnerable to competitive attack from one or more rivals.
6. Whether the company has competitive advantage or must work to offset competitive disadvantage.
7. Where the strong spots and weak spots are in the present strategy.
8. Whether additional actions are needed to improve the company's cost position, capitalise on emerging opportunities and strengthen the company's competitive position.

These considerations should indicate whether the company can continue the same basic strategy with minor adjustment or whether it should undertake a major overhaul.

(F) CORPORATE CAPABILITY FACTORS

Corporate capability is the inherent capacity or potential of a company to use its strengths and overcome its weaknesses with a view to avail the opportunities provided and face the threats posed by its external environment. Corporate capability factors are also called strategic factors, strategic advantage factors, corporate competence factors, etc. The areas of company capability factors include: general management, marketing, finance, human resource and research development.

Now, we discuss the corporate capability factors in general management and functional management areas, *viz.*, marketing management, financial management, production/operations management, human resource management and research and development.

1. Corporate Capability Factors in General Management

Management is the art of getting things done by the people. It is concerned with the accomplishment of organisational objectives by utilising physical, financial and human resources. Managers perform five basic functions, *viz.*, planning, organising, directing, staffing and controlling. (see Exhibit 3.8).

Planning: Planning is deciding in advance what do to, how to do it, when to do it and who is to do it. Planning bridges the gap from where we are, to where we want to go. Planning minimises the risk and maximises the advantages of opportunities. The purpose of every plan and all supporting plans is to facilitate accomplishment of organisational purpose and objectives. Planning is the cornerstone of effective strategy formulation. Planning is also essential for successful strategy implementation and strategy evaluation. In fact effective planning determines organising, staffing, motivation, leading and controlling. (See Fig. 3.2).

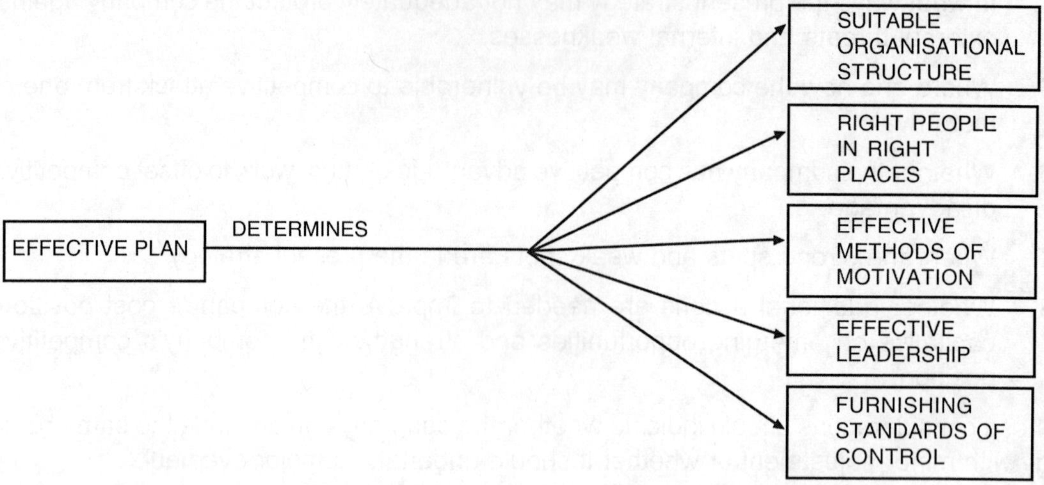

Fig. 3.2: Plans as Foundation for Strategy

Planning logically precedes the execution of all other managerial functions as managerial operations in organising, staffing, leading and controlling are designed to support the accomplishment of enterprise objectives. First, the top management must formulate an enterprise's mission, objectives, strategies before divisional and functional managers can effectively set goals. Therefore, planning to be effective, must begin at the top of an organisation and filter down. The three levels of planning analogous to the three levels of strategic management, are, corporate, strategic business unit and functional. Enterprises that use formal planning approaches are generally more profitable than those that do not.

The reasons for positive impact of planning on organisational and individual performances are:

(i) Planning allows an organisation to identify and take advantage of environmental opportunities, it permits an organisation to minimise the impact of environmental threats, as well. It also determines the likelihood that future trends and events could be harmful or beneficial to an enterprise.

(ii) An enterprise can develop synergy through planning. Synergy exists when members of a team pool together their knowledge and skills. In synergy, the sum of the efforts of all the members of a team is more than the total of all the individual efforts. It can be called the 1 + 1 = 3 effect. All members can work together towards the achievement of desired goals. Synergy can result in powerful competitive advantages.

(iii) Planning enables an enterprise to adapt to changing environments, and shape its own destiny. The strategy management is a formal planning process that allows an organisation to pursue proactive rather than reactive strategies. Thus, the efficient enterprises strive to control and mould their future, rather than merely reacting to external forces and events as they occur.

Exhibit 3.8: The Basic Functions of Management

Function	Description	Most Important at the Stage of Strategic Management Process
1. Planning:	Planning consists of all those managerial activities related to preparing for the future. It includes: forecasting, formulating objectives, policies and goals.	Strategy Formulation
2. Organising:	Organising includes all those managerial activities that result in a structure of task, authority and responsibility relationship. It includes: organisation, job design, span of control, unity of command, coordination, etc.	Strategy Implementation
3. Directing:	Directing involves efforts directed towards shaping human behaviour. It includes: leadership, communication, motivation, morale, organisational change, etc.	Strategy Implementation
4. Staffing:	Staffing activities are centred on human resource management. It includes: job design, job analysis, human resource planning, recruitment, selection., employee training and development, performance appraisal, salary, administration, employee safety, union-management relations, grievance procedure, disciplinary procedure, personnel research and records.	Strategy Implementation
5. Controlling:	Controlling refers to all those managerial activities directed towards assuring that actual results are consistent with planned targets. Key areas are: quality control, financial control, sales control, inventory control, expense control, etc.	Strategy Evaluation

Organising

An organisation is a means to an end. It is essential to carry out the pre-determined course of action. An organisation is a "structure and process by which cooperative group of human beings allocate its task among its members, identifies relationships and integrates its activities towards common objectives." Complex relationships exist between the specialised departments and the general departments as many top managers are seeking the advice from the specialist managers. Thus, organisation establishes relationships among the employees so that they can collectively contribute to the attainment of company goals.

An organisation structure facilitates the contribution of individuals to the attainment of company objectives. It does so by people with minimum unsought consequences or costs.

A well organised firm can formulate, implement and evaluate strategies effectively than a disorganised firm. The organisation function includes: combining the tasks into positions, positions into jobs, combining jobs to form departments, and bringing relationships among departments.

Jobs are analysed on the basis of tasks, positions, duties and responsibilities. Jobs are combined into departments based on enterprise function, territory, product, customers, process or equipment, etc. One of the increasingly used forms of organisation is referred to as matrix or project organisation. The essence of matrix organisation normally is the combination of functional and product forms of departmentation in the same organisation structure. As companies and customers have become increasingly interested in end results, there has been pressure to establish responsibility in someone to ensure results.

Organisations can also be structured on the basis of line and staff. Line and staff are viewed as relationships but not as departments. The relationship existing between two managers due to delegation of authority and responsibility and giving or receiving instructions or orders is called line relationship. The relationship between two managers is said to be a staff relation, when it is created due to giving and taking advice, guidance, information, help or assistance, counselling and the like, in the process of attaining organisational goals.

Staffing

The process of staffing is also called personnel management. Personnel management is planning, organising, directing and controlling and procurement, development, compensation, integration and maintenance of people for the purpose of contributing to the individual, organisational and social goals. It is also called human resource management. Human resource managers assist line managers in performing staffing activities like job analysis, human resource planning, recruitment, testing, interviewing, selecting, inducting, placing, appraising performance, training, developing, career planning and rewarding, disciplining, transferring, promoting, demoting, retrenching and dismissing employees.

The human resource management function is not only a significant task but also a complicated one. Hence, all organisations including the small organisations need to employ a special manager for this function. The increasing globalisation of business activity, expansion and diversification of the organisations both product/service-wise and geography-wise resulted in complexity of the task. These factors make the personnel manager to concentrate on managing cultural diversities, quality of work life and the like. The managers sometimes find it difficult to implement the strategies like joint ventures, mergers, etc., in view of the changing trends in human resource management. The strategists, particularly the chief executive officers are becoming increasingly aware of the vitality of human resources in strategic management.

Directing

The next logical function after completing planning, organising and staffing is the achievement of organisational objectives. The basic function of management is motivating, commanding, leading and activating people. The willing and effective cooperation of employees for the attainment of organisational objectives is possible under proper direction. Tapping the maximum potentialities of the people is possible through motivation and command. Coordination deals with the task of blending efforts in order to ensure successful attainment of an objective.

Controlling

The controlling function of management includes all those activities undertaken to ensure that actual performances confirm to planned performances. The controlling activities include:

(i) Establish performance standards,

(ii) Measure actual performance,

(ii) Compare actual performance to planned performance standards,

(iv) Take corrective actions.

The controlling function is particularly significant for efficient strategic evaluation. Exhibit 3.9 depicts check list of corporate capabilities in general management.

This list can be helpful in determining specific strengths and weaknesses in management. Positive answers to these questions indicate capabilities or strengths of the management in that area concerned. Negative answer to any of these questions indicates the weakness of the management in that area.

Exhibit 3.9: Corporate Capabilities in General Management: Checklist

Planning

1. Does the organisation have clearly stated goals and objectives?
2. Does the organisation have an overall strategy for competing in its basic industry?
3. Does the organisation monitor and anticipate competitor's actions and reactions in the marketplace?
4. Does the organisation monitor and anticipate the needs of key customers, suppliers, distributors, creditors, shareholders and employees?
5. Does the organisation have an effective budgeting process?
6. Does the organisation use a strategic management approach to corporate decision-making?
7. Does the organisation have a written mission statement?
8. Does the organisation have contingency plans?
9. Does the organisation have synergy?
10. Does the organisation allocate resources based on stated goals?
11. Does the organisation have objectives, strategies, goals, and policies that are mutually consistent, supportive, and clearly communicated?

Organising

1. Does the enterprise have a clear organisational structure as evidenced by a formal organisational chart?
2. Does the organisational chart reflect the most desirable structure for the firm?
3. Does the organisational chart exhibit acceptable spans of control?
4. Are similar activities appropriately grouped together in the organisational chart?
5. Are staff functions, such as personnel, shown appropriately in the organisational chart?
6. Is the unity of command principle adhered to in the organisational chart?
7. Do the organisation's managers delegate authority well?
8. Does the organisation have and use written job descriptions?
9. Does the organisation have and use written job specifications?
10. Are the organisation's jobs meaningful, rewarding and challenging?

Directing

1. Is employee morale high?
2. Is managerial morale high?
3. Is job satisfaction high?
4. Is a participative management style used?
5. Is creativity encouraged?
6. Are absenteeism rates in the organisation low?
7. Are turnover rates in the organisation low?
8. Have the managers identified the number and composition of informal groups in the organisation?
9. Are the norms of informal groups in the organisation favourable to management?
10. Does a good system for two-way communication exist in the organisation?
11. Are managers in the organisation good leaders?
12. Does the organisation have a good system of rewards and sanctions?
13. Does the organisation and its employees adapt well to changes?
14. Are employees able to satisfy individual needs through the organisation?
15. Are department policies reasonable and supportive of stated goals?

Staffing

1. Does the organisation have a personnel manager or human resource department?
2. Does the organisation hire employees only after careful recruiting, interviewing, testing and selecting?
3. Does the organisation provide employee training and management-development programmes?

4. Does the organisation provide reasonable employee benefits?
5. Does the organisation have an effective performance evaluation system?
6. Does the organisation have a good wage and salary administration system?
7. Does the organisation have stated grievance procedures?
8. Does the organisation have stated disciplinary policies?
9. Does the organisation have a career planning system for its employees?
10. Does mutual trust and respect exist between line managers and personnel managers in the organisation?
11. Are working conditions in the organisation clean and safe?
12. Does the organisation have equal employment opportunities?
13. Does the organisation have an affirmative action programme?
14. Does the organisation promote employees from within?
15. Does the organisation provide employee counseling?
16. Are union-management relations good in the organisation?
17. Does the organisation have a code of ethics?

Controlling

1. Does the organisation have an effective financial control system?
2. Does it have an effective sales control system?
3. Does it have an effective inventory control system?
4. Does it have an effective expense control system?
5. Does it have an effective production control system?
6. Does it have an effective management control system?
7. Does it have an effective quality control system?
8. Does it have computer-assisted control system?
9. Have the productivity standards been established in all departments of the organisation?
10. Does the organisation regularly monitor favourable and unfavourable variances in the control process?
11. Are corrective actions taken promptly to improve unfavourable variances?
12. Are rewards and sanctions in the organisation supportive of established control systems?
13. Is unethical behaviour effectively controlled in the organisation?
14. Are the organisation's control systems prompt, accurate and thorough?

Source: Adapted from Fred R. David, *op. cit.*, pp 157-159.

2. Corporate Capability Factors in Functional Areas of Management

Competitive advantage refers to all aspects of an organisation that allow it to compete more effectively than its rivals. Functional competence refers to the strengths of the organisation in the functional areas of management, *viz.*, marketing, finance, production/operations, human resources and research and development.

3. Marketing Management

Marketing has been defined as the human activity directed for satisfying needs and wants through exchange processes. Joel Evans and Barry Berman suggest that there are nine basic functions of marketing. They are: (1) Customer Analysis, (2) Buying, (3) Selling, (4) Product and Service Planning, (5) Price Planning, (6) Distribution, (7) Marketing Research, (8) Opportunity Analysis, and (9) Social Responsibility.

1. Customer Analysis: Examination and evaluation of customer needs, desires and wants is called customer analysis. Customer analysis involves administering customer surveys, analysing consumer information, evaluating market positioning strategies, developing customer profiles and determining optimal market segmentation strategies. Customer analysis information can be essential in developing an effective mission statement.

2. Buying: Buying means obtaining the goods and services needed to produce and sell a product. The function of buying includes evaluating alternative suppliers, selecting the best suppliers, arranging acceptable terms with suppliers and procurement.

3. Selling: Selling includes marketing activities like advertising, sales promotions, publicity, personal selling, sales forces management, customer relations and dealer relations.

4. Product and Service Planning: This function includes new product design and development, testing market, product and brand positioning, warranties, packaging, product options, product features, product style, product quality, scrapping old products and customer service.

5. Price Planning: Factors affecting pricing decisions include customers, government, channel members and competitors. Major pricing policies are penetration pricing and skim-the-cream pricing.

6. Distribution: This function includes warehousing, physical distribution channels, distribution coverage, retail site locations, sales territories, inventory levels and location, transportation carriers, wholesaling and retailing.

7. Marketing Research: Marketing research is systematic gathering, recording and analysing data about problems relating to the marketing of goods and services.

8. Opportunity Analysis: Opportunity analysis is an appraisal of the costs, benefits and risks associated with marketing related and/or strategic decisions.

9. Social Responsibility: Social responsibility includes organisation's obligation to offer products and services that are safe, ethical and reasonably priced.

Companies can identify marketing strengths and weaknesses by undertaking a comprehensive marketing audit. Exhibit 3.10 presents corporate capabilities checklist in marketing management.

Exhibit 3.10: Corporate Capabilities in Marketing — Checklist

A Marketing Systems Audit

1. Is the marketing intelligence system producing accurate, sufficient, and timely information about marketplace developments with respect to customers, prospects, distributors and dealers, competitors, suppliers, and various publics?
2. Are company decision-makers asking for enough marketing research, and are they using the results?
3. Is the company employing the best methods for market and sales forecasting?
4. Is the marketing planning system well conceived and effective?
5. Is sales forecasting and market potential measurement soundly carried out?
6. Are sales quotas set on a proper basis?
7. Are the control procedures adequate to ensure that the annual goals are being achieved?
8. Does management periodically analyse the profitability of products, markets, territories, and channels of distribution?
9. Are marketing costs periodically examined?
10. Is the company well organised to gather, generate, and screen new product ideas?
11. Does the company do adequate concept research and business analysis before investing in new ideas?
12. Does the company carry out adequate product and market testing before launching new products?

A Marketing Productivity Audit

1. What is the profitability of the company's different products, markets, territories, and channels of distribution?
2. Should the company enter, expand, contract, or withdraw from any business segments and what would be the short- and long-run profit consequences?
3. Do any marketing activities seem to have excessive costs? Can cost-reducing steps be taken?

Source: Philip Kotler, *Marketing Management: Analysis, Planning and Control*, Prentice-Hall Inc., Englewood Cliffs, New Jersey, 1984, pp. 767-70.

4. Financial Management

The best measure of a company's competitive position and overall attractiveness to investors is the company's financial position. Determining an organisation's financial strengths and weaknesses is essential in formulating strategies. Basic decision areas of finance are: the investment decision, the financing decision, and the dividend decision.

1. The Investment Decision: The investment decision (also called capital budgeting) is concerned with allocation and reallocation of capital to projects, products, assets and divisions of an organisation.

2. Financing Decision: The financing decision is concerned with determining the best financing mix or capital structure for the organisation.

3. Dividend Decision: Dividend decisions involve such issues as the percentage of earnings paid to the shareholders, the stability of dividend paid over the period to the shareholders, and the repurchase or issuance of stock.

Exhibit 3.11 shows useful financial checklist of corporate capabilities. The positive answers to the questions in the checklist are the financial strengths and the negative answers are the financial weaknesses of the company.

Exhibit 3.11: A Financial Checklist of Corporate Capabilities

Liquidity:

1. Have the firm's liquidity ratios been increasing over time?
2. Are the firm's liquidity ratios above industry averages?

Leverages:

1. Have the firm's leverage ratios been increasing over time?
2. Are the firm's leverage below industry averages?

Activity:

1. Have the firm's activity ratios been moving favourably over time?
2. Do the firm's activity ratios compare favourably with industry's average?

Profitability:

1. Have the firm's profitability ratios been increasing over time?
2. Are the firm's profitability ratios above industry's average?

Growth:

1. Have the firm's growth ratios been increasing over time?
2. Are the firm's growth ratios above industry's averages?

Source: Fred R. David, *op. cit.*, p. 177.

5. Production/Operations Management

The next element in evaluating the strategy of an organisation is its production or operations management. Operations management has been defined as managing the resources required to produce the products or render services provided by an organisation. One of the goals of a firm is to develop a distinctive competence which separates it from its competitors. Production decisions/strategies reflect decisions of quality, product design and configuration, cost, customer service, production efficiency, and response time. A firm, through operating strategies in these areas, may be able to develop its own reputation, differentiating it from its competitors.

Roger Schroeder suggests that production/operations management consists of five decision areas, *viz.*, process, capacity, inventory, human resource and quality. Corporate capabilities checklist in production or operations management is shown in Exhibit 3.12. The "yes" answer to some questions shows the strengths of an organisation in those areas and the "no" answer presents the weaknesses of an organisation in those areas concerned.

Exhibit 3.12: Corporate Capabilities in Production/Operations Management

Process

1. Are the facilities located effectively?
2. Are the facilities designed effectively?
3. Should the organisation be integrated backward or forward to a greater extent?
4. Are transportation costs for receiving and shipping excessive?
5. Is the process technology that is being used appropriate?
6. Is an effective and efficient flow or sequence of operations being used to convert inputs into outputs?
   - Line flow — characterised by a linear sequence of operations used to make the product or service; extremely efficient but also extremely inflexible. Examples are cafeterias and automobile assembly lines.
   - Intermittent flow — characterised by production in batches at intermittent intervals; equipment and labour are organised into work centres by similar types of skill or equipment. Examples are the flow operations used by fast-food restaurants and hospitals.
   - Project flow — characterised by a sequence of operations used to produce a unique product; no real product flow; used when there is a great need for creativity and uniqueness. Examples are developing a new product or building a ship.
7. Is the product or service being made to order, made to stock, or both? Is this activity most effective and efficient?
   - Made to order — processing activities are keyed to individual customer orders; process consists of customer placing an order, firm responding with a price and delivery date, and customer accepting or rejecting the offer. Delivery time and control of order flow are critical. Examples are a restaurant operation and painting a portrait.
   - Made to stock — process consists of producing a standardised product line; inventories are maintained to meet, say, a 95 per cent service level of orders. Forecasting, inventory management, and capacity planning are critical. Examples are a furniture plant and oil refinery.

Capacity

1. Is overall demand for the product or service regularly and effectively forecasted?
2. Are the appropriate economies of scale achieved?
3. Are the factories, warehouses, and stores located effectively?

4. Are there appropriate number of factories, warehouses, and stores?
5. Are the factories, warehouses, and stores of an appropriate size?
6. Have aggregate planning costs been determined and minimised?
   - Hiring and firing costs
   - Overtime and under-time costs
   - Inventory-carrying costs
   - Subcontracting costs
   - Part-time labour costs
   - Cost of stock-out or back order
7. Are loading, scheduling, and dispatching activities performed effectively?
8. Have strategies been developed for dealing with non-uniform demand?
9. Does the firm have an effective and efficient production control system?

Inventory

1. Have the costs of producing or buying needed inventories been examined?
2. Have inventory carrying costs been determined?
3. Have inventory ordering costs been determined?
4. Have purchasing, receiving and shipping costs been determined?
5. Have stock-out costs been determined?
6. Have service level versus inventory level considerations been examined?
7. Have appropriate production lot sizes been determined?
8. Does the firm have an effective inventory control system?
   - Single-bin system
   - Two-bin system
   - Card-file system
   - Computerised system
   - Economic Order Quantity (EOQ) system
   - Materials Requirements Planning (MRP) system
   - Order-point systems

Workforce

1. Have time and motion studies been completed on all operations-related jobs?
2. Have production jobs been designed effectively and efficiently?
3. Are production management employees competent, efficient, and motivated?
4. Are production standards clear, reasonable and effective?
5. Have the productivity rewards and sanctions been established?
6. Have reasonable and effective operations policies been established?
7. Are absenteeism and turnover rates low among production employees?
8. Is employee morale high among production employees?
9. Are the firm's operations managers effective leaders?

Quality

1. Does the organisation have an effective and efficient quality control system?
2. Have the following quality control costs been determined and evaluated?
   - Prevention costs, such as the cost of training and development programmes, and marketing studies to determine customers' quality needs and desires?
   - Appraisal costs, such as the cost of determining the quality of incoming raw materials, sampling procedures, finished goods inspections and tests, and operating laboratories?
   - Internal failure costs, such as the cost of scrap material, downtime, retesting, and inspections?
   - External failure costs, such as the cost of refunds, repairing products, replacing products and setting customer complaints?

Source: Fred R. David, *op. cit.*, pp. 182-184.

6. Human Resource Management

Human resource plays not only significant but a crucial role in building and developing an organisation. It is said that the difference between two organisations in terms of competencies is due to differences in the capabilities of their human resources. But management of human resources is more complicated than management of any other resources.

Human resource management consists of five important strategic decision areas, *viz.*, employment, human resource development, compensation, human relations and industrial relations.

A survey of CEOs spotlighted productivity improvement, employee communications and management succession planning as areas of strategies for human resource management. Exhibit 3.13 depicts corporate capabilities checklist in human resource management.

Exhibit 3.13: Corporate Capabilities in Human Resource Management

Human Resources Management (HRM)

(a) What are the corporation's current HRM objectives, strategies, policies, and programmes?

(i) Are they clearly stated or merely implied from performance and/or budgets?

(ii) Are they consistent with the corporation's mission, objectives, strategies, policies, and with internal and external environments?

(b) How well is the corporation's HRM performing in terms of improving the fit between the individual employee and the job? Consider turnover, grievances, strikes, layoffs, quality of worklife.

(i) What trends emerge from this analysis?

(ii) What impact have these trends had on past performance and how will they probably affect future performance?

(iii) Does this analysis support the corporation's past and pending strategic decisions?

(c) How does this corporation's HRM performance compare with that of similar corporations?

(d) Are HRM managers using appropriate concepts and techniques to evaluate and improve corporate performance? Consider job analysis programme, performance appraisal system, up-to-date job descriptions, training and development programmes, attitude surveys, job design programmes, quality of relationship with unions.

(e) What is the role of the HRM manager in the strategic management process?

Source: Thomas L. Wheeler and J. David Hunger, *op. cit.*, p. 43.

7. Research and Development

Research and development is concerned with the creation of knowledge, the design of goods and services and the operation of production process. Survival and development of most of the competitive firms depend upon the successful research and development activities. Research and development strategies should address: (1) the focus of R&D activities (pure or applied research), (2) the relationship of R&D activities to other functional areas (e.g., marketing, human resource, etc.), (3) the aggressiveness of the firm's R&D posture, (4) the time horizon for results expected from the R&D department, (5) new product development, and (6) pilot plans or prototype testing. Four approaches to determine R&D budget allocations have been used. They are: (1) financing as many project proposals as possible, (2) using a percentage-of-sales method, (3) budgeting for R&D about what competitors spend, and (4) deciding how many successful new products are needed and working backwards to estimate the required R&D investment. Exhibit 3.14 presents corporate capabilities in research and development. Like the previous checklists, "no" answers to the key questions indicate potential weaknesses and "yes" answers suggest areas of strengths.

Exhibit 3.14: Corporate Capabilities Checklist in Research and Development

1. Has the organisation examined the research and development practices in its basic industry?
2. Does the organisation have the personnel needed to conduct successful research and development?
3. Does the organisation have the facilities and equipment needed to conduct successful research and development?
4. Does the organisation have the information flows and resources needed to conduct successful research and development?
5. Has the organisation investigated the relative benefits of focusing R&D efforts on existing versus new products?
6. Has the organisation examined the trade-offs between developing new and improved products on the one hand, and developing new and improved production processes on the other?
7. Has the organisation established a research and development department?
8. Does the organisation allocate sufficient human capital resources to conduct successful research and development?

9. Does the organisation capitalise on available sources of new product ideas?
10. Is the organisation prepared to take the risk of instituting long periods of research without discovering ideas that have commercial value?
11. Is the organisation prepared to take the risk of financing long periods of product development and testing without eventual successful marketing of the product?
12. Does the organisation have, or can it obtain, needed capital to exploit discoveries if and when they are made?
13. Has the organisation examined the potential benefits of using outside agencies or individuals to conduct basic and applied research for the firm?
14. Has the organisation established clear research and development goals and policies?
15. Does the organisation understand the research and development strategies of is major competitors?
16. Has the organisation considered joint ventures in research and development?
17. Is the organisation knowledge about domestic and foreign licenses, royalty fees, patents, trademarks, and other regulatory concerns applicable to research and development activities in its basic industry?
18. Does the organisation have an overall research and development strategy?

Source: Fred R. David, *op. cit.*, p. 187-188.

(G) DIAGNOSING CORPORATE CAPABILITIES

There are two important methods of analysing and diagnosing corporate capabilities. They are: (1) Functional Area Profile and Resource Deployment Matrix and (2) Strategic Advantage Profile.

1. Functional Area Profile and Resources Deployment Matrix

This method requires the preparation of a matrix of functional areas with characteristics common to each other. This approach allows the firm to analyse the strategic deployment of funds and its strengths and weaknesses over time as compared with those of competitors. Each area must be considered with respect to what its policies and approaches were, are and will be. The analysis can be done on a piecemeal basis, with each area independently of others. However, the strengths and weaknesses must be compared in relation to one another. Weaknesses must be compared with strengths as weaknesses may prevent the company from taking advantage of an opportunity. Similarly, strengths and weaknesses may be compared to the external environmental factors. Most of the strategists are concerned with how their firms are placed strategically in relation to the competitors. It is also important to compare strengths and weaknesses relative to their overall significance to the strategy of the firm.

2. Strategic Advantage Profile

Once the corporate capability profile (CCP) is prepared and the key areas for diagnosis have been analysed, it is useful to prepare a strategic advantage profile (SAP). Strategic advantage profile provides, "a picture of the more critical areas which can have a relationship with the strategic posture of the firm in the future. Exhibit 3.15 presents an example of a SAP for a hypothetical firm. This exhibit indicates that, this firm has weaknesses in competition, mobilising finances by issuing equity capital, quality control, personnel managers and middle and junior managers with outdated management styles. These disadvantages preclude certain strategies such as competition based on quality, introduction of product changes, expansion of production and marketing. This company can go for the stability strategy. However, it requires the analysis of external environmental opportunities and threats to draw the conclusions on strategies.

Exhibit 3.15: Strategic Advantage Profile

Internal Area	Competitive Strength (+) or Weakness (–)
1. Marketing	+ Excellent pre-sales and post-sales service
	+ Complete understanding of consumer preference changes to sales representatives.
	– Close competition.
	+ Selling at consumer's door step.
2. Finance	+ High Rate of Profit
	+ Credit worthiness is favourable for raising loans
	– Low Rate of Dividend, Unfavourable Stock Market Conditions
3. Production/Operations:	+ Excellent Technology
	+ Excellent sources of raw materials
	– Poor Quality Control
4. Human Resources	+ Capable employees
	– Managers with personnel but not human resource management skills
	+ Favourable compensation package
5. Research and Development	0 Picking up now.
6. General Management	+ Top Management with Progressive Ideas
	– Middle and Junior Management with outdated management styles.

Note: + indicates Strength; 0 indicates neutral; – indicates weakness.

3. Company Situation Analysis

There are five steps to conduct company situation analysis. They are:

(1) Evaluating how well the current strategy is working.

(2) Doing a SWOT analysis.

(3) Identifying the corporate capability factors.

(4) Evaluating the company's cost position relative to competitors.

(5) Assessing the company's competitive position and competitive strength.

(6) Determining the strategic issues and problems the company needs to address.

Exhibit 3.16 provides a format for company situation analysis. The concepts and techniques discussed in this chapter are the basis for preparing the company situation analysis.

Exhibit 3.16: Company Situation Analysis

1. STRATEGIC PERFORMANCE INDICATORS

Performance Indicator	**20...**	**20...**	**20...**	**20...**	**20...**
Market share	....	....	....	....	....
Sales growth	....	....	....	....	....
Net profit margin	....	....	....	....	....
Return on equity investment	....	....	....	....	....
Others	....	....	....	....	....

2. INTERNAL STRENGTHS

INTERNAL WEAKNESSES

EXTERNAL OPPORTUNITIES

EXTERNAL THREATS

3. COMPETITIVE STRENGTH ASSESSMENT

Rating scale: 1 = Very weak; 10 = Very strong.

Key Success Factor/ Competitive Variable	**Weight**	**Firm A**	**Firm B**	**Firm C**	**Firm D**	**Firm E**
Quality/product performance	....	....	....	....	....	....
Reputation/image	....	....	....	....	....	....
Raw material access/cost	....	....	....	....	....	....
Technological skills	....	....	....	....	....	....
Manufacturing capability	....	....	....	....	....	....
Marketing/distribution	....	....	....	....	....	....
Financial strength	....	....	....	....	....	....
Relative cost position	....	....	....	....	....	....

Others	....	....	....	....	....	....
Overall strength rating	....	....	....	....	....	....

4. Conclusions Concerning Competitive Position
(Improving/slipping? Competitive advantages/disadvantages?)

5. Major Strategic Issues/Problems the Company must Address

Source: Arthur A. Thompson Jr. and A.J. Strickland III, *op. cit.*, p.100.

Points to be Remembered

- A strength is a strong point for the company.
- The distinctive competence is the unique capability it gives an organisation.
- Systematic assessment of whether a company's competitive position is strong or weak relative to close rivals is called competitive strength assessment.
- Corporate capability is the inherent capacity or potential of a company.
- Corporate capability in general management includes organisational structure, hierarchies and synergy.
- Resources are all kinds of inputs like material, components, parts, machinery, human resources, etc.
- Variable capabilities create and add value by exploiting opportunities provided by and threats posed by the external environment.
- Value is the amount buyers desire to pay for what a firm provides to them in the form of a products/service/product-cum-service.
- Core competencies are a company's resources and capabilities.

Keywords

- Strength
- Distinctive Competence
- Value Chain Analysis
- Opportunities
- Cost Analysis
- Replicability
- Intellectual Capabilities
- Outsourcing

Questions for Discussion

1. What are organisational resources and capabilities? Why are organisational resources valuable?
2. Discuss resource-based view of organisational analysis.
3. What are organisational capabilities? How do you identify then?
4. What are core competencies? How many core competencies are required for a company?

5. How do you build core competencies?
6. What is value chain analysis? How do primary activities add value?
7. How do you identify organisational strengths?
8. How do you identify organisational weaknesses?
9. How do you assess competitive strengths of an organisation?
10. How do you identify corporate capability factors of different functional areas?

References

1. Yeoh and Roth, "*An Empirical Analysis*", p. 638 in McGrath, Macmillan and Venkataraman, "*Defining and Developing Competencies*", pp. 652.
2. D. L. Deeds, D. Decarolis and J. Coombs, "Dynamic Capabilities and New Product Development in High Technology Ventures", *Journal of Business Venturing*, No. 15, 1994, pp. 211-29.
3. R. Hall, "The Strategic Analysis of Intangible Resources", *Strategic Management Journal*, No. 13, 1992, pp. 136-139.
4. John A. Pearce and Richard B. Robinson, "*Strategic Management*". Tata McGraw-Hill Publishing Company Limited, New Delhi, 2007, pp. 153.
5. R.M. Grant, "The Resource-Based Theory of Competitive Advantage: Implications for Strategy Formulation," *California Managers Review*, Spring 1991, pp. 114.
6. Thomas L. Wheelen, J. David Hunger and Krish Rangarajan, "*Strategic Management and Business Policy*", Pearson, 2006, pp. 77.
7. Dallas Hanson *et. al.*, "*Strategic Management*", Thomson Learning, Victoria, 2002, pp. 94.
8. Hilt, Nixon, Clifford and Coyne, "*The Development*", pp. 3.
9. B. Mc Evily and A. Zaheer, "Building Ties: A Source of Firm's Heterogeneity in Competitive Capabilities", *Strategic Management Journal*, 20, pp. 1133.
10. M.T. Hansen, N. Nhoria and T. Tierney, "What is Your Strategy for Managing Knowledge?", *Harvard Business Review*, 77(2), pp. 106-16.
11. Leonard Barton, Bower, Clark and Wheelwright, "How to Integrate Work and Deepen Expertise", *Harvard Business Review*, 72 (5), pp.123.
12. Brush and Artz, "Towards a Contingent Resource-Based Theory", *Strategic Management Journal*, 15, pp. 271-90.
13. C. Ames, "Sales Soft? Profits Flat? It's time to Rethink Your Business", *Fortune 25*, June, pp. 142-146.
14. Dallas Hanson *et. al.*, "*Strategic Management*", Thomson Learning, 2002, pp. 99.
15. *Ibid.*, pp. 100.
16. L.B.Ward "Dell Sales Overtake company", *Dalls Morning News*, 24 January 2000. pp.1-2.
17. Computershare 2001, Computershare Limited, Home Page, 19 February 2001, Quoted in Dalls Hanson, *op. cit.*, pp. 101.
18. Reed and De Fillippi, "*Casual Ambiguity*".
19. C. Eliezer, "Gudinski is back for a second Act", *Business Review Weekly*, 12 November 1999, pp. 161-165.
20. Robert A. Pitts and David Lei, "*Strategic Management*", Thomson, 2006, pp. 92.

21. Robert A. Pitts and David Lei, *op.cit.*, p. 95.
22. Burt, "*Ford expects to Farm Out*", p. 1.
23. P. Landers, "Nissan Retains IBM to Manage its Computers", *Wall Street Journal*, 29 October 1999, p. A15.
24. Samuel C. Certo and J. Paul Peter, *op. cit.,* pp. 36-37.
25. Michael Porter, "*Competitive Advantage*", Free Press, New York, 1985.
26. Samuel C. Certo and J. Paul Peter, *op. cit.*, p. 39.
27. Arthur A. Thompson Jr., and A.J. Strickland III, *op. cit.*, p. 87.
28. *Ibid.*, pp. 87-88.
29. C.K. Prahld and Gary Hamel, "The Core Competence of the Corporation", *Harvard Business Review,* 90:3, May-June 1990, pp. 79-93.
30. Arthur A. Thompson Jr., and A.J. Strickland III, (1984), p. 67.
31. Arthur Sharplin, "*Strategic Management*", McGraw-Hill, New York, 1985, pp. 93-94.
32. *Ibid.*, p. 90.
33. *Ibid.*, p. 95.
34. Samuel C. Certo and J. Paul Peter, *op. cit.*, p. 46.
35. *Ibid*.
36. Arthur A. Thompson Jr., and A.J. Strickland III, *op. cit.*, p. 98.
37. Fred R. David, "*Fundamentals of Strategic Management,*" Merrill Publishing Company, London, 1986, p. 151.
38. Z. Malik and Karger, "Does L.R. Planning Improve Company Performance", *Management Review,* September 1975, pp. 27-31.
39. Fred. R. David, *op. cit.*, pp. 151-152.
40. Philip Kotler, "*Marketing Management*", Prentice-Hall, Englewood Cliffs, New Jersey, 1984, p. 4.
41. J. Evans and B. Berman, "*Marketing*", Macmillan, New York, 1982, p. 17.
42. Fred R. David, *op. cit.*, pp. 160-167.
43. James Van Horne, "*Financial Management and Policy*", Prentice-Hall, Englewood Cliffs, New Jersey, 1974, p. 10.
44. R. Chase and N.J. Aquilano, "*Production and Operations Management*", Richard D. Irwin, Homewood, 1985, p. 5.
45. R.J. Schonberger, "*Operations Management*", Business Publications Inc., Plano, 1985, p. 34.
46. P. Subba Rao, "*Essentials of Human Resource Management and Industrial Relations*", Himalaya Publishing House, Mumbai, 1996.
47. Joe G. Thomas, *op. cit.*, p. 165.
48. Fred R. David, *op. cit.*, p. 185.
49. Lawrence R. Jauch and William F. Glueck, *op. cit.*, p. 170.

***

Unit-2

Chapter - 4

Strategic Analysis and Choice

Chapter Outline

Learning Objectives

After studying this chapter, you should be able to:

- Study the criteria for evaluating strategic alternatives;
- Analyse and match strengths and opportunities and weaknesses and threats;
- Discuss the criteria for analysing strategic alternatives by using various matrices like BCG, GE Nine-Cell matrix and the directional policy matrix;
- Study the selection of matrix in terms of industry attractiveness and business unit strength;
- Analyse the decision-making stage in terms of qualitative matrix.

(A) INTRODUCTION

The strategy formulation process involves environmental analysis, organisational analysis, development of strategic alternatives and analysis and selecting the most appropriate strategy from the alternatives developed. (Fig. 4.1) We have discussed, in Chapter 7, various strategy alternatives at corporate level. The corporate level strategies include:

(i) stability strategies,

(ii) growth strategies, viz., internal growth strategies, mergers, takeovers, horizontal integration, conglomerate diversification, vertical integration, joint ventures,

(iii) retrenchment strategies, viz., turn around strategy, captive company strategy, transformation strategy, divestment strategy and liquidation strategy, and

(iv) combination strategy or portfolio restructuring. We have also discussed, in Chapter 8, business unit strategies. These strategies include: (i) the Generic strategies, viz., a low-cost leadership strategy, differentiation strategies, focus and specialisation strategies, (ii) offensive strategies, (iii) defensive strategies, (iv) functional strategies, and (v) matching strategy to situation.

The logical next step is analysing these strategy alternatives both at corporate level and business unit and functional level and choosing/selecting an appropriate strategy. At this, situation, we should recall the business mission, objectives and goals. This is because, the strategy, we select should contribute for the achievement of organisation's mission and objectives. We also recall the objectives and goals of strategic business units and functional levels as the strategies we select also contribute to the achievement of objectives of these levels.

The process of analysis is concerned with understanding of what the future holds and how the company can sustain and grow. The process should analyse all types of strategies as in reality, low priority strategies, may be employed. The process should also identify the probable hurdles of strategy implementation, likely consequences or results of the plans. The firm's attitude towards risk plays an important role in the analysis and selection of a strategy.

(B) CRITERIA FOR EVALUATING STRATEGIC ALTERNATIVES

There are a number of different criteria for evaluating strategic alternatives. It would be very difficult to use all these criteria to get a satisfactory result simultaneously. However, to make the evaluation practically possible, all the criteria can be classified into three groups, *viz.*, criteria of suitability, criteria of feasibility and criteria of acceptability.

(i) Criteria of Suitability: These criteria attempt to measure the extent to which the proposed strategies fit the situation identified in the strategic analysis. The situation should indicate the list of the important opportunities and the threats that the firm faces and the particular strengths and weaknesses of the firm.

The evaluation should measure the suitability of the strategy to the situation. The evaluation of suitability is also called the criteria of consistency. The strategy to be selected should meet the following criteria:

- To what extent, the strategy can overcome the difficulties identified in the strategic analysis? For example, can the strategy increase the market share of the company?
- To what extent the strategy can exploit the environmental opportunities by using the company's strengths? For example, can the strategy provide the status of leader in introducing the new product, under the stable market conditions?
- Does the strategy fit in with the company's objectives and values? For example, would the strategy fit in the recently signed agreement with the members of the Chamber of Commerce and Industry in the country?

(ii) Criteria of Feasibility: These criteria, assess the practical implementation and working of the strategy. For example, will the strategy of price-cut result in hike in profits under the competitive environment? The following questions need to be assessed at the evaluation stage:

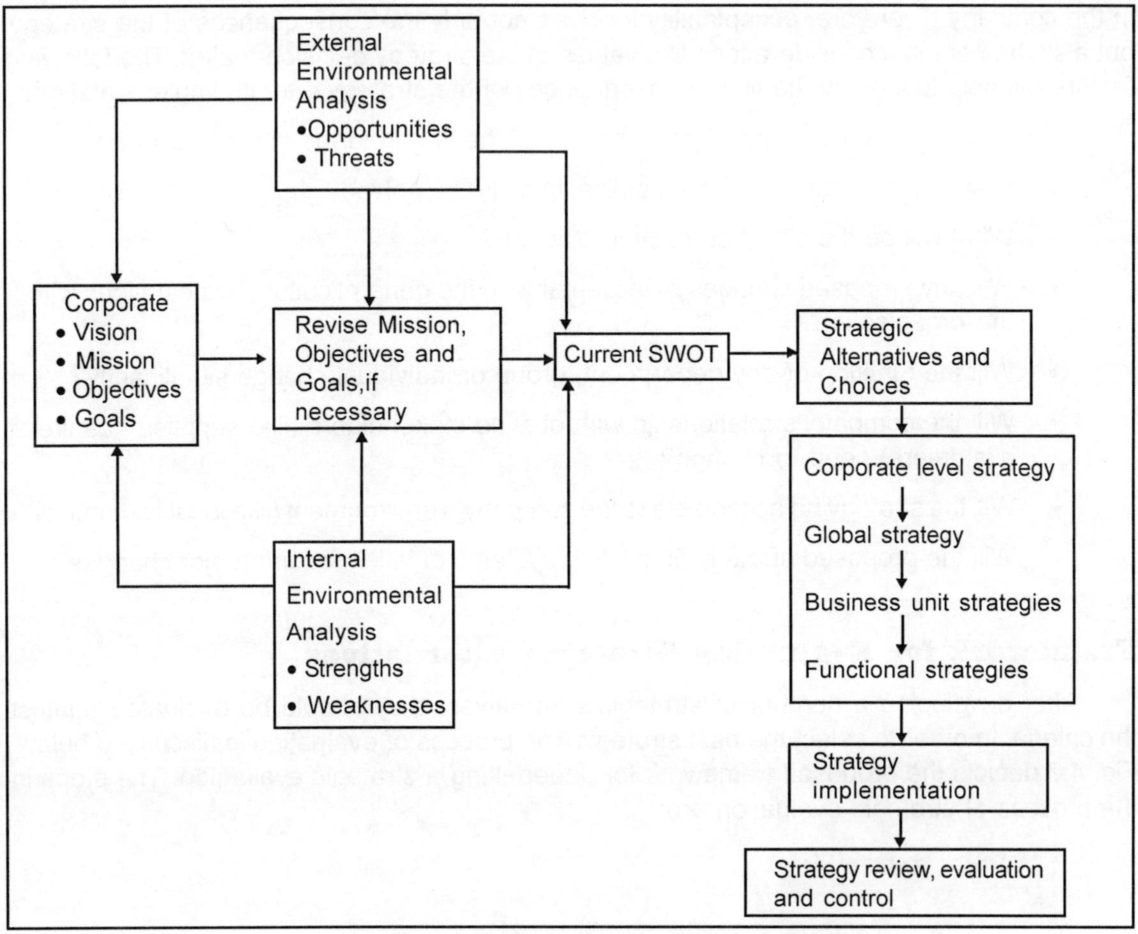

Fig. 4.1: Strategic Management Process

- Can the company provide enough financial resources to implement the strategy? This can be examined by analysing future cash flows, company's commitments, ability and willingness of the management to budget the funds.
- Is the company capable of performing to the required level?
- Can the necessary market position be achieved? Will the necessary marketing skills be available?
- Can competitive reactions be coped with?
- How will the company ensure that the required managerial and operative skills be available?
- Will the technology be available to compete effectively?
- Can the necessary materials and services be procured?

(iii) Criteria of Acceptability: The third measurement is acceptability of the strategy. The firm should assess the strategy to decide whether the consequences of proceeding with a strategy are acceptable. The strategy should be acceptable to the strategy decision-maker in the company. Therefore, acceptability involves not only the consequences of the strategy, but also the personal considerations like values of the strategy decision-maker. The following factors will help to identify the likely consequences of the strategy after its implementation:

- What will be the financial performance of the firm in terms of profitability?
- How will the financial problems (like liquidity) be solved?
- What will be the effect on capital structure?
- Will any proposed changes be acceptable to the general cultural expectations within the organisation?
- Will the function of any department, group or individual change significantly?
- Will the company's relationship with outside stakeholders (like suppliers, bankers, customers) need to change?
- Will the strategy be acceptable to the company's environment (like local community)?
- Will the proposed strategy fit existing systems or will it require major changes?

Framework for Evaluating Strategic Alternatives

After developing a number of strategic alternatives, they should be evaluated against the criteria, in order to select the best strategy. The process of evaluation is discussed below. Fig. 4.2 depicts the proposed framework for undertaking a strategic evaluation. The steps in the process of strategic evaluation are:

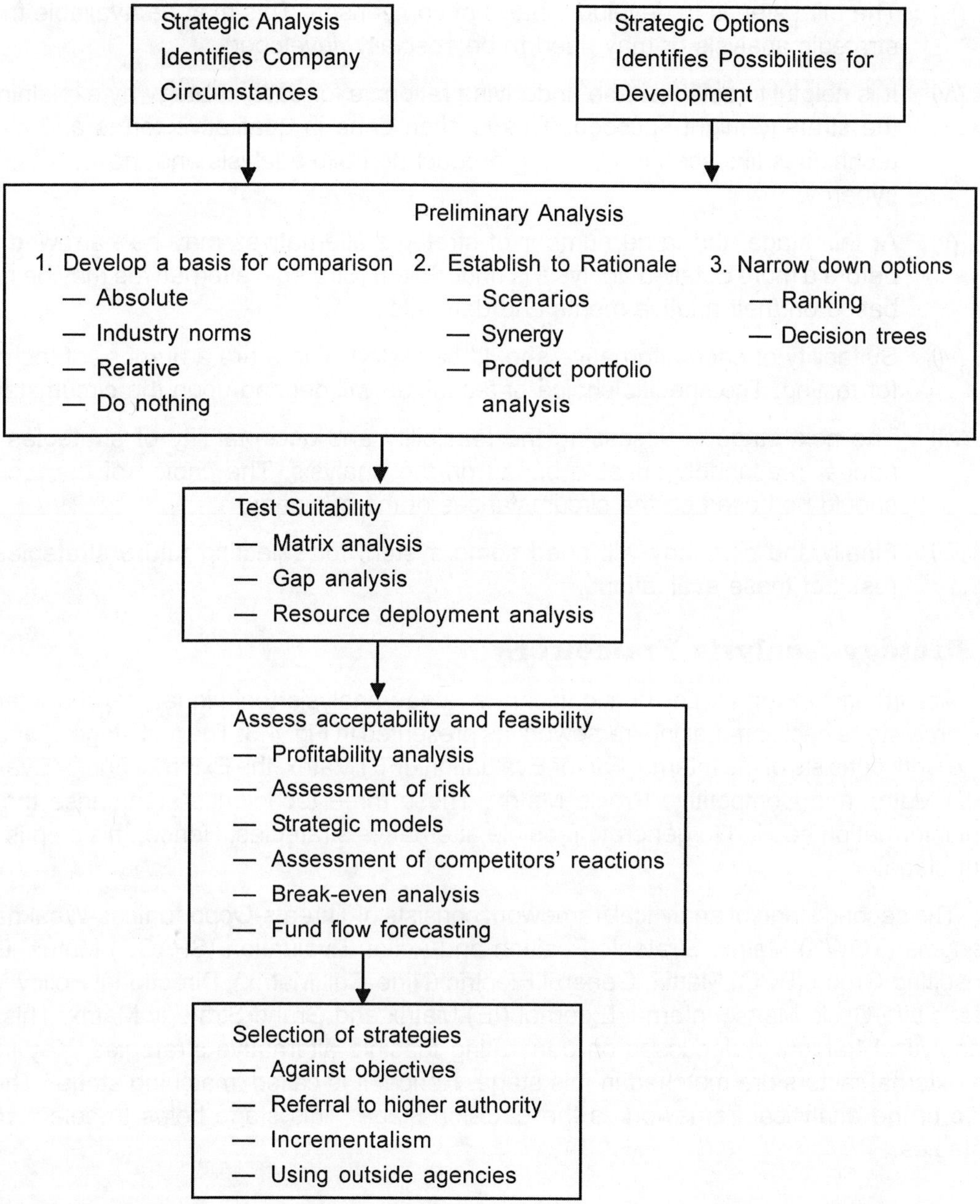

Source: Gerry Johnson and Kevan Scholes, *op. cit.*, p. 210.

Fig. 4.2: A Framework for Evaluating Strategic Options

(i) The first step is a strategic analysis in order to gain a clear understanding of the circumstances affecting the organisation's strategic situation.

(ii) The second step is to produce a range of strategic options.

(iii) The third step is to develop a basis of comparison. This may be available from the strategic analysis or may need to be specially developed.

(iv) It is helpful to establish the underlying rationale for each strategy by explaining why the strategy might succeed. This is often done in qualitative terms and by using techniques like scenario building product portfolio analysis and the assessment of synergy.

(v) At this stage, the large number of strategic alternatives may be narrowed down, before a more detailed analysis is undertaken. Strategic alternatives may be ranked, based on their relative merits and demerits.

(vi) Suitability of each alternative should be tested. There are a number of techniques for testing. The specific choice of technique will depend upon the circumstances.

(vii) The next stage is assessing the feasibility and acceptability of strategies which appear reasonably suitable based on the analysis. The choice of the technique should be based on the circumstances of the company.

(viii) Finally, the company will need some system for selecting future strategies as a result of these evaluations.

A Strategy Analysis Framework

According to Fred D. David, significant strategy analysis techniques can be integrated into three-stage decision-making framework as presented in Fig. 4.3. The first stage of analytical frame work consists of the Internal Factor Evaluation (IFE) Matrix, the External Factor Evaluation (EFE) Matrix and Competitive Profile Matrix. These three techniques summarise the basic input information needed to generate feasible alternative strategies. Hence, this step is called input stage.

The second stage of analytical framework consists of Threats-Opportunities-Weaknesses-Strengths (TOWS) Matrix, Strategic Position and Action Evaluation (SPACE) Matrix, Boston Consulting Group (BCG) Matrix, General Electric (Nine-Cell Matrix), Directional Policy Matrix, Hofer's Life Cycle Matrix, Internal-External (IE) Matrix and Grand Strategy Matrix. This stage of analytical framework focusses on generating feasible alternative strategies. Key internal and external factors are matched in this stage. Hence, it is called 'matching stage.' The third stage of the analytical framework is the decision stage. This stage helps to select specific strategies.

(C) THE INPUT STAGE

1. The Internal Factor Evaluation (IFE) Matrix

The Internal Factor Evaluation (IFE) Matrix summarises an organisation's key general management, marketing, finance, human resource, production/operations and research and development strengths and weaknesses. This technique is useful in answering four major questions about a firm's internal strategic position. They are:

(a) What are the company's key strengths and weaknesses?

(b) What is the relative significance of each strength and weakness to the company's overall performance?

(c) Does each factor represent a major weakness, a minor weakness, a minor strength and a major strength?

The weightages to the factors may be assigned as follows:

Factor	*Weightage*
A major weakness	–2
A minor weakness	–1
A minor strength	+1
A major strength	+2

(d) What is the company's total weighted score resulting from the internal factor evaluation matrix? Is the score above or below +0.10?

The internal factors should be stated in objective terms to the possible extent. The factors selected, would represent the internal bases from which an organisation's strategies will be formulated. The strategists should assign appropriate weights and ratings to each factor. An example of IFE Matrix is presented in Table 4.1.

Table 4.1: An Example of the Internal Factor Evaluation Matrix

	Key Internal Factor	*Weight*	*Rating*	*Weighted Score*
1.	The company's level of productivity has dropped to 65 percent	0.20	–2	–0.40
2.	The company's organisational structure is being totally revamped	0.05	–1	–0.05
3.	The company's earning per share (EPS) was lowest in the industry in 1992	0.10	–1	–0.10
4.	The company's return on investment (ROI) was only 2.2% in 1992, second lowest in the industry	0.10	–1	–0.10
5.	The company is boosting R&D expenditure to 20% of sales in 1993	0.15	+1	+0.15
6.	The company through 21 plant locations offers excellent customer service	0.15	+1	+0.15
7.	The company has established a reputation for technical excellence	0.25	+2	+0.50
	Total weighted score	1.0		+ 0.15

Sourcc: A modified version frorn: Relchhold's *Annual Report*, 1984. Quoted in Fred R. David, p. 201.

The company in example, has scored slightly more than the average in terms of overall internal strategic position.

2. The External Factor Evaluation (EFE) Matrix

The second technique of input stage of strategy formulation analytical framework is the External Factor Evaluation Matrix. This technique summarises an organisation's opportunities provided and threats posed by the external environmental factors, *viz.*, economic, political, technological, social, cultural, governmental, competitors and international. The External Factor Evaluation Matrix answers four questions. They are:

(a) What are the company's environmental opportunities and threats?

(b) What is the relative significance of each opportunity and threat to the company's overall performance?

(c) Does each factor represent a major threat, a minor threat, a minor opportunity or a major opportunity? The weightages to the factors may be assigned as follows:

Factor	*Weightage*
Major Threat	–2
Minor Threat	–1
Minor opportunity	+1
Major opportunity	+2

(d) What is the company's total weighted score resulting from the External Factor Evaluation Matrix? Is the score above or below the average of +0.10?

Table 4.2 presents an example of preparing the External Factor Evaluation Matrix. It is observed from the exhibit that the company has scored +0.25. Therefore, it can be viewed as the company has a strong external strategic position.

Stage 1: THE INPUT STAGE

1. Internal Factor Evaluation (IFE) Matrix
2. External Factor Evaluation (EFE) Matrix
3. Competitive Profile Matrix

Stage 2: THE MATCHING STAGE

1. Threats — Opportunities — Weaknesses — Strength (TOWS) Matrix
2. Strategic Position and Action Evaluation (SPACE) Matrix
3. Boston Consulting Group (BCG) Matrix
4. GE Nine Cell Matrix
5. Directional Policy Matrix
6. Hofer's Life Cycle Matrix
7. Internal-External (IE) Marix
8. Grand Strategy Matrix

Stage 3: THE DECISION STAGE

Quantitative Strategic Planning Matrix (QSPM)

Source: Modified version from: Fred R. David., *op. cit.*, p. 199.

Fig. 4.3: The Strategy Formulation Analytical Framework

The strategists should quantify subjectivity during the early stages of strategy formulation process. The strategists should have good judgement skills to determine appropriate weights and ratings. However, an absence of objective input information often results in biases, politics etc., in the strategy formulation process.[5]

Table 4.2: An Example of the External Factor Evaluation Matrix

	Key External Factor	Weightage	Rating	Weighted Score
1.	Due to heavy competition in the international markets, nearly 90% sales of the company were within India in 1996	0.25	–2	–0.50
2.	Due to the entry of many new firms into the industry, the company's market share has declined by 10%	0.15	–1	–0.15
3.	The Government, in its recent budget offered incentives to this industry	0.10	+1	+0.10
4.	The changing culture, will result in the increase in the total industry's sales	0.15	+1	+0.15
5.	The company's diversification into the new operations will increase the income by 30%	+0.25	+2	+0.50
6.	The decline in input prices will reduce the cost of production by 15%	+0.10	+1	+0.10
	Total Weighted Score	1.00		+0.25

3. The Competitive Profile Matrix

As analysed in the earlier chapter, identifying and analysing competitor's strengths, weaknesses and strategies are useful in the strategy formulation process. The Competitive Profile Matrix summarises significant information about competitors. Strategists should use only the factual information about competitors in strategy formulation. A Competitive Profile Matrix should answer the following questions:

(a) Who are our major competitors?

(b) What key factors are most important to being successful in the industry?

(c) What is the relative importance of each key factor to success in the industry?

(d) To what extent is each competitor strong or weak on each key success factor? (Where –2 = major weakness, –1 = minor weakness, +1 = minor strength and +2 = major strength)

(e) Overall, how strong or weak is each major competitor?

Table 4.3 presents an example of Competitive Profile Matrix.

Table 4.3: Competitive Profile Matrix: An Example

Key Success Factors		*Competitor 1*		*Competitor 2*	
	Weight	*Rating*	*Weighted Score*	*Rating*	*Weighted Score*
Customer service	0.22	+2	+0.44	+1	+0.22
Price	0.20	+1	+0.20	–1	–0.20
Product Quality	0.18	+1	+0.18	+1	+0.18
Technological Superiority	0.11	+1	+0.11	+2	+0.22
Dealer Relations	0.10	+2	+0.20	-1	–0.10
Financial Strength	0.10	+1	+0.10	+2	+0.20
Advertising Effectiveness	0.09	+2	+0.18	+1	+0.09
Total Weighted Scores	1.00	+1.41			+0.61

Source: Modified version from: Fred R. David, *op. cit.*, p. 204.

It is observed from the table 4.3 that both the competitors are strong and competitor 1 is more stronger than the competitor.

(D) THE MATCHING STAGE CORPORATE PORTFOLIO ANALYSIS

The matching stage of the analytical framework for strategy formulation is also called corporate portfolio analysis. Corporate portfolio analysis or the matching stage is a set of techniques useful in strategy formulation relating to individual products or business in a company's portfolio. The matching stage or the corporate portfolio analysis techniques include:

(a) The Threats-Opportunities-Weaknesses-Strengths (TOWS) Matrix,

(b) The Strategic Position and Action Evaluation (SPACE) Matrix,

(c) The Boston Consultancy Group (BCG) Matrix,

(d) The General Electric Nine-Cell Matrix,

(e) Hofer's Product Market Evolution Matrix,

(f) Directional Policy Matrix,

(g) The Internal-External (IE) Matrix, and

(h) The Grand Strategy Matrix.

Matching means aligning internal factors with external factors to generate alternative strategies.

1. The Threats-Opportunities-Weaknesses-Strengths (TOWS) Matrix

All firms must formulate appropriate strategies to win. A good offence strategy without a good defense strategy and *vice versa*, most often leads to defeat. Firms should use their strength to exploit the opportunities and/or to overcome the threats. Alternatively, companies may pursue defensive strategies to overcome weaknesses and avoid threats.

It is disastrous for the firm to face the threats posed by the environment, if it is already suffering from its weaknesses. However, a company can overcome its weaknesses, if the environment provides opportunities to it. It is rather difficult, but quite important to match key internal and external factors.

The TOWS Matrix helps to match the internal and external factors.

The TOWS Matrix tool results in the development of four types of strategies. They are:

(i) Strengths-Opportunities Strategies (SO),

(ii) Weaknesses-Opportunities Strategies (WO),

(iii) Strength-Threats Strategies (ST), and

(iv) Weaknesses-Threats Strategies (WT).

Companies would like to be in strengths-opportunity situation to exploit the opportunities provided by the external environment. Companies generally pursue WO, ST and WT strategies with a view to move to SO strategy. The TOWS Matrix is shown in Fig. 4.4.

Always leave blank	Strengths-S 1. 2. 3. 4. 5. 6. 7. 8. 9. 10. List strengths	Weaknesses-W 1. 2. 3. 4. 5. 6. 7. 8. 9. 10. List weaknesses
Opportunities-O 1. 2. 3. 4. 5. 6. 7. 8. 9. 10. List opportunities	SO Strategies 1. 2. 3. 4. 5. 6. 7. 8. 9. 10. Use strengths to take advantage of opportunities	WO Strategies 1. 2. 3. 4. 5. 6. 7. 8. 9. 10. Overcome weaknesses by taking advantage of opportunities
Threats - T 1. 2. 3. 4. 5. 6. 7. 8. 9. 10. List threats	ST Strategies 1. 2. 3. 4. 5. 6. 7. 8. 9. 10. Use strengths to avoid threats	WT Strategies 1. 2. 3. 4. 5. 6. 7. 8. 9. 10. Minimise weaknesses and avoid threats

Source: Fred R. David., *op. cit.*, p. 207.

Fig. 4.4: The TOWS Matrix

Steps Involved in Constructing a TOWS Matrix

1. List the company's key strengths.
2. List the company's key weaknesses.
3. List the company's key opportunities.
4. List the company's key threats.
5. Match the strengths with opportunities and record the resultant SO strategies in the appropriate cell.

6. Match weaknesses with opportunities and record the resultant WO strategies.
7. Match strengths with threats and record resultant ST strategies.
8. Match weaknesses with threats and record the resultant WT strategies.

2. The Strategic Position and Action Evaluation (SPACE) Matrix

The Strategic Position and Action Evaluation (SPACE) Matrix is an important matching tool. Fig. 4.5 presents SPACE Matrix. SPACE Matrix is a four quadrant framework and it suggests whether aggressive, conservative, defensive or competitive type strategies are more appropriate for a given company. The SPACE Matrix axes are: Financial Strength (FS), Competitive Advantage (CA), Environmental Stability (ES), and Industry Strengths (IS). The two internal dimensions, Financial Strength (FS) and Competitive Advantage (CA) and two external dimensions, Industry Strength (IS) and Environmental Stability (ES) can be considered the most important determinants of an organisation's overall strategic position.

There are a number of variables that could comprise each of the dimensions represented on the axes of the SPACE Matrix. Some example of variables, often included are presented in Exhibit 4.1. The recommended strategies for the four dimensions are presented in Fig. 4.6.

3. The Boston Consulting Group (BCG) Matrix

Autonomous divisions or profit centres of a company comprise what is called a business portfolio. The Boston Consulting Group — a leading management consulting firm devised a four-square grid. This grid was first portfolio matrix to be widely used. The BCG — type matrix is presented in Fig. 4.7. The matrix is formed using industry growth rate on the vertical axis and relative market share on the horizontal axis. Each business unit appears as a circle on the four cell matrix with the size of each circle scaled to the per cent of revenues it represents in the overall corporate portfolio.

Relative market share is the ratio of business's market share to the market share held by the largest rival company in the industry, with market share measured in terms of quantity of sales but not value of sales. In other words, relative market share is calculated by dividing a business's percentage share of total industry's sales volume by the percentage share held by its largest rival. For example, if business X has a 20 per cent share of the industry's total sales volume and its largest rival is business Y. Company Y's market share is 60 per cent. Then, the relative market share of business X is 20 ÷ 60 = 0.33. Alternatively, if X has a 40 per cent share of the industry's sales volume and Y has a 20 per cent share of the industry's sales volume, X's relative marketshare is 20 ÷ 40 = 2.00. It is clear from this definition that, only market-share leader businesses in their respective industries will have relative market share values greater than 1.0 and businesses with market share less than that of one or more rivals will have ratios below 1.0.

The border between high and low relative market shares is at 1.0, as shown in Fig. 4.7. Circles in the two left side cells (upper cell and lower cell), the matrix represent businesses that are market share leaders in their industry as the boundary is set at 1.0. Thus, the circles in the right side cells (upper cell and lower cell) of the matrix represent the portfolio members that are in runner-up positions in the industry. The size of the circle shows the degree to which the businesses trail is indicated by the size of the relative market share. A ratio of 0.20 indicates the business has a market share of 2/10 or 1/5 that of the largest business in the market and a ratio of 0.80 indicates a market share 4/5 of the largest business in the industry.

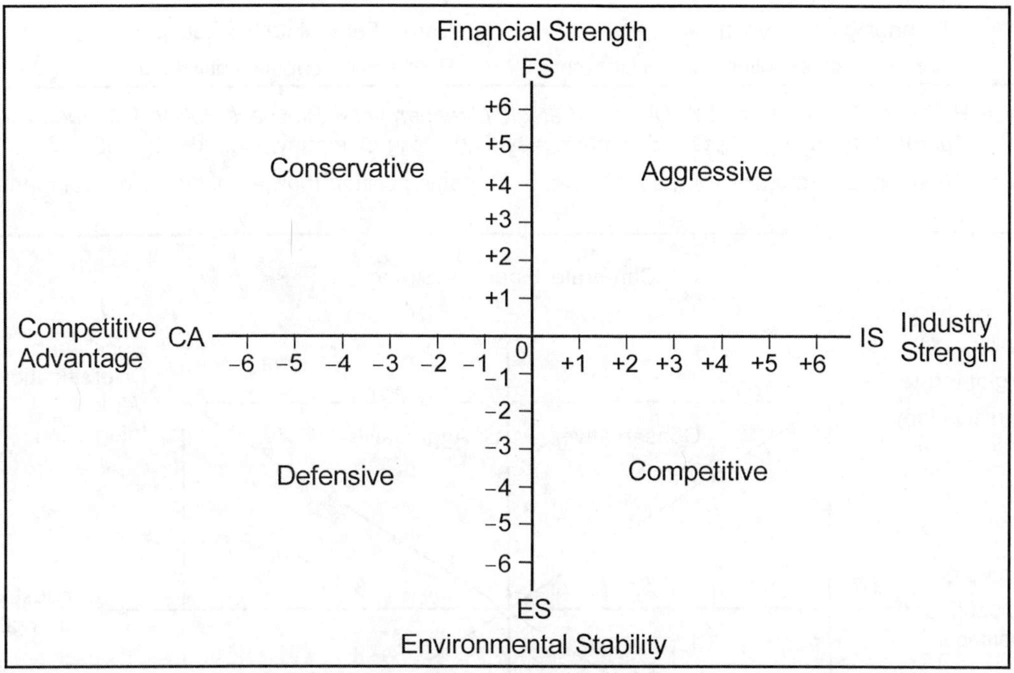

Fig. 4.5: The SPACE Matrix

Exhibit 4.1: Some example of factors that comprise the SPACE Matrix Axes

NTERNAL STRATEGIC POSITION	EXTERNAL STRATEGIC POSITION
Financial Strength (FS)	**Environment Stability (ES)***
Return on investment	Technological changes
Leverage	Rate of inflation
Liquidity	Demand variability
Working capital	Price range of competing products
Cash flow	Barriers to entry into market
Ease of exit from market	Competitive pressure
Risk involved in business	Price elasticity of demand
Competitive Advantage (CA)	**Industry Strength (IS)**
Market share	Growth potential

Product quality	Profit potential
Product life cycle	Financial stability
Customer loyalty	Technological know-how
Competition's capacity utilization	Resource utilization
Capital intensity	
Technological know-how	Ease of entry into market
Control over suppliers and distributors	Productivity, capacity utilization

Source: H. Rowe, R. Mason, and K. Dickel, *Strategic Management & Business Policy: A Methodological Approach* (Reading, Mass: Addison-Wesley Publishing Company, Inc., 1982), 155-156.

* A stable environment represents a better strategic position than an unstable environment.

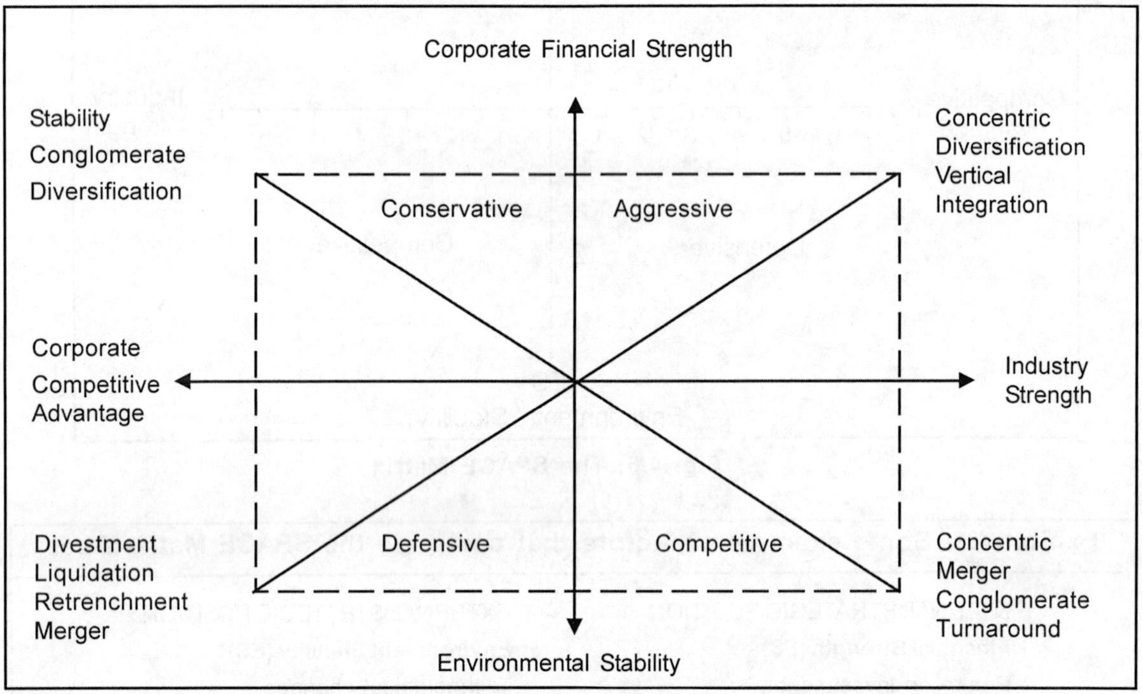

Source: A.J. Rowe, R.O. Mason and K. Dickel, "*Strategic Management and Business Policy — Methodological Approach*," Addison-Wesley, Reading, Mass, 1982, p. 164.

Fig. 4.6: SPACE Diagram: Recommended Strategies

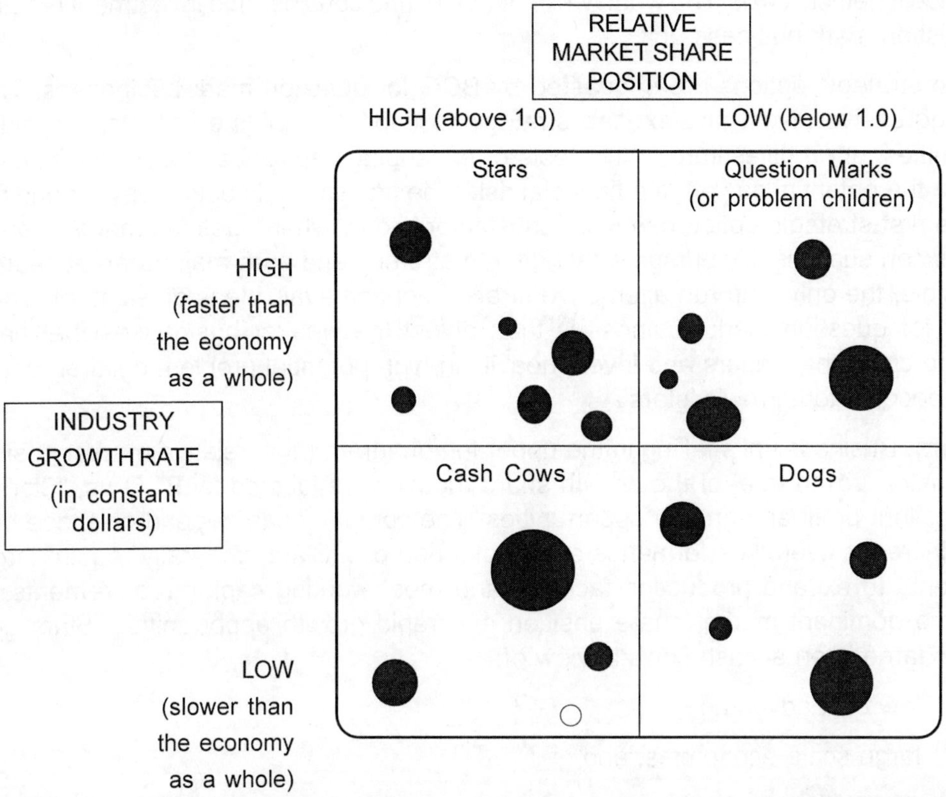

Note: Relative market share is defined by the ratio of one's own market share to the market share held by the largest rival firm. When the vertical dividing line is set at 1.0, the only way a firm can achieve a star or cash cow position in the growth-share matrix is to have the largest market share in the industry. Since this is a very stringent criterion, it may be "fairer" and more revealing to locate the vertical dividing line in the matrix at about 0.75 to 0.80.

Source: Arthur A. Thompson and A.J. Strickland, *op. cit.*, p. 194.

Fig. 4.7: The BCG Growth-Share Business Portfolio Matrix

Question Marks or Problem Children: BCG labeled the business units falling in the upper right quadrant of the growth-share matrix as "question marks" or "problem children." Rapid market growth makes such businesses attractive from an industry stand point. But their low relative market share raises a question about whether, they can compete successfully against larger and most cost-efficient rivals. Hence, the BCG designated such business units as question marks or problem children. Question mark businesses are also 'cash hogs' as the cash needs of such businesses are high. This is because of investment requirements of rapid growth and product development. Further, the internal cash generation of such businesses is low due to low market share, absence of large scale economies and low profit margins. Large inflow of cash is required for a question mark or cash hog businesses just to keep up with rapid market growth. If the question mark business wants to become an industry leader, it needs larger volume of cash infusions. The company of cash hog business has to analyse and decide whether, it would be worth while or not to fund considerable investment requirements of a question mark business unit.

Two strategic options are suggested by BCG for question mark businesses. They are: *(i)* an aggressive invest-and-expand strategy to capitalise on the industry's rapid-growth opportunities, or *(ii)* divestiture, if the costs of expanding capacity and building market share outweigh the potential pay off and financial risk. The first strategic option pay off and financial risk. The first strategic option can work satisfactorily only when question mark/problem child business can successfully pursue a fast growth strategy and earn major market share. If it is not feasible, the only long run alternative strategic option available is divestment. The viable strategy for question mark business is that: divest the weaker businesses that have less chance to catch the leaders and invest heavily in high potential problem children and groom them to become tomorrow's 'stars'.

Stars: Business units falling in the upper left quadrant (high relative market position and high industry growth rate) of the growth share matrix were labeled by BCG as, "Stars." They offer excellent profit and growth opportunities. The company can depend on these business units to increase overall performance of the total portfolio. Stars, generally require large cash investments to expand production facilities and meet working capital requirements. This is due to the dominant market share position and rapid growth opportunities. Stars generate their own large internal cash flows in view of:

(i) low cost advantage,

(ii) large scale economies, and

(iii) cumulative production experience.

Some stars can meet the investment requirements from their internal cash flows while others need cash from other businesses of the same company to stay ahead of rapid industry growth. Normally, old stars do not require cash flows from the company whereas, the young stars require substantial investment beyond what they can generate on their own like cash hogs.

Cash Cows: BCG designated the businesses with a high relative market share in a low growth market as "cash cows." Cash cow business units fall in the lower left quadrant of the Fig. 4.7.

Cash cow business units generate substantial cash surpluses than what it needs for reinvestment and expansion. This is due to the low industry growth rate and as much the fresh investment opportunities are less. The cash cow business unit generates more cash flows and profits due to high relative market share and industry leadership. But the reinvestment opportunities are less.

Due to the maturity of the industry demand, many of the yesterday's stars dropped into the lower cell of the left side area of the Fig. 4.7. Since the reinvestment opportunities are stagnated, the surpluses generated by the cash cows may be used to cover:

- Dividend payments
- Finance acquisitions
- Investing in emerging stars
- Investing in problem children that can be groomed as future stars.

The health and the efficiency to generate cash surplus of cash cows should be protected. However, weakening cash cows may be harvested and eventually disinvested.

Dogs: Business units falling under the lower right quadrant of the growth share matrix were labeled by BCG as "Dogs." Dogs are the businesses with a low relative market share in a slow growth industry. These business units are called dogs because of:

(i) their dim growth prospects,

(ii) their trailing market position,

(iii) squeeze that being behind the leaders.

These business units fail to generate cash flows on long-term basis. These units, sometimes fail even to generate cash flows that are necessary for working capital requirements. Therefore, BCG suggests that weak dog businesses be harvested, divested or liquidated depending upon the ability of the strategy to yield more cash.

BCG Matrix and Corporate Strategy: The important contributions of BCG Matrix are:

(i) It draws the attention to the cash flow and investment characteristics of various types of businesses.

(ii) It indicates how the company's financial resources can be shifted between/among businesses to optimise the returns/performance of the entire company portfolio.

According to BCG analysis, a sound long-term corporate strategy should utilise the surplus cash generated by cash cow businesses to:

(i) Finance market share increases for cash hog businesses.

(ii) Finance the young stars unable to generate cash to finance their own growth.

(iii) Finance the problem children having potentiality to grow into stars.

This strategy will help the cash hogs to become self-supporting stars. When the business of the stars reach the maturity stage, they become cash cows. The cash cows, when weaken will turn into dogs. Further the problem children without potentiality for growth will also turn into dogs. Dogs should be retained as long as they contribute duly to the overall performance of the company. The strong dogs which are close to '+1' may generate average cash flow and make average profits. BCG Matrix suggest harvest strategy for weakening or already weak dog businesses. A weak dog should be eliminated from the portfolio, if harvesting strategy is not attractive.

Disaster Sequences: There are two disaster sequences in BCG Matrix. They are: *(i)* when a star's relative market share is declined below +1 the star will be dragged to the position of a problem child. Further, if the situation of negative industry growth is added to the problem, the business will be dropped in the cell of dog. *(ii)* When the cash cow's relative market share declines below +1, the cash cow will turn into a dog.

The Possible Mistakes: Companies may commit the following mistakes in adopting strategies:

(i) Over-investing in a safe cash cow.

(ii) Under-investing in question marks.

(iii) Investing resources in all question marks rather than concentrating on the potential ones.

Strengths and Weaknesses of the BCG Matrix Approach

The BCG business portfolio matrix has the following strengths:

(i) It makes definite contribution to the strategist's tool kit.

(ii) It provides strategy-situation match by prescribing broad guidelines and providing direction to the companies.

(iii) It provides guidelines for maximising the financial performance of a diversified company.

(iv) It highlights the interaction within a corporate portfolio.

(v) It helps for fixing priorities for corporate resource allocation.

(vi) It provides rationalisation for both invest, expand and divest strategies.

However, the BCG Matrix has certain shortcomings.

Weaknesses of BCG Matrix

The legitimate shortcomings of the BCG Matrix are:

(i) This matrix based on high-low classifications ignores many businesses with an average growth rate.

(ii) The matrix has classified all businesses into four categories, *viz.*, stars, problem children, cash cow and dog. But, some market share leaders have never really been stars in terms of profitability. All businesses with low relative market shares are not dogs or question marks. In many cases runner-up firms have proven track records in terms of growth, profitability and competitive ability. Therefore, a key characteristic to assess a firm is the trend in a firm's relative market share. Is the firm gaining ground or losing ground and why? This shortcoming can be overcome by placing directional arrows on each of the circles in the matrix as shown in Fig. 4.8.

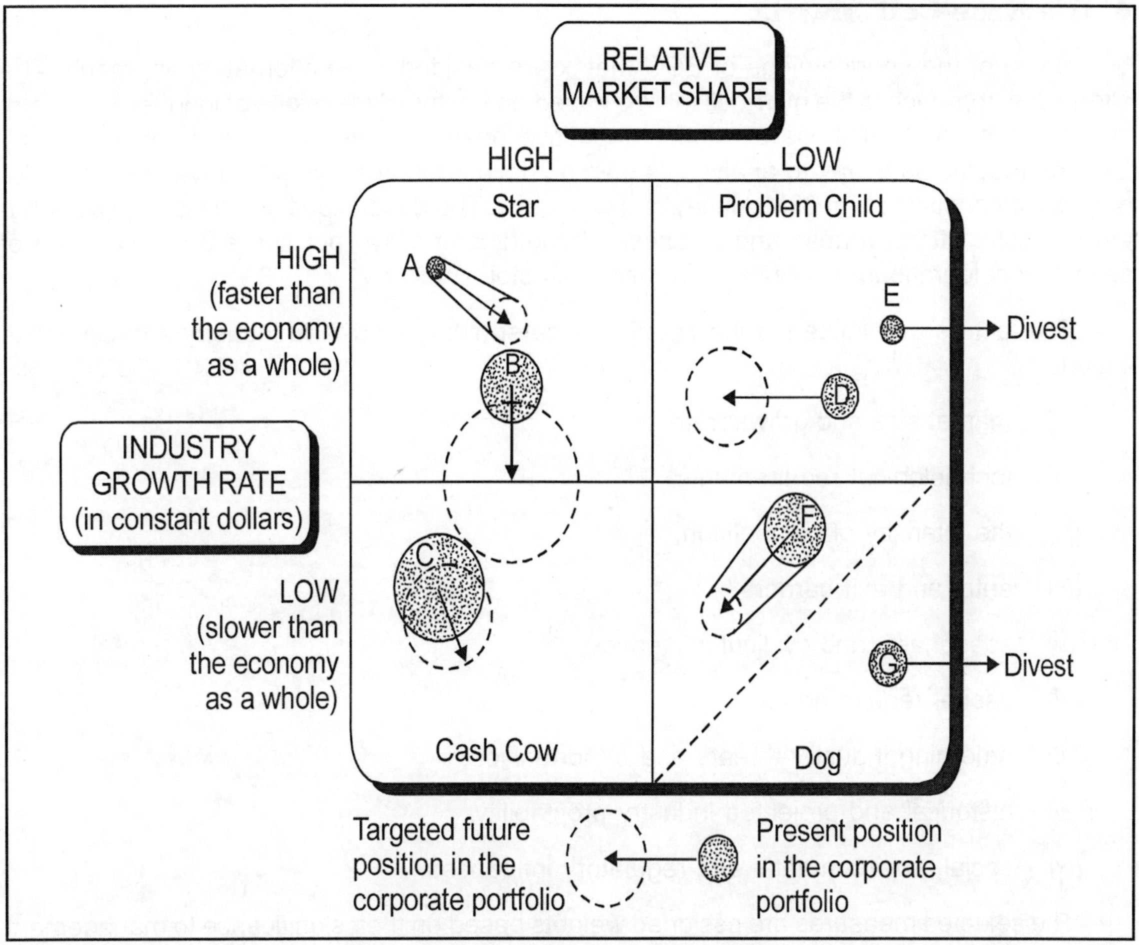

Source: Arthur A. Thompson and A.J. Strickland, *op. cit.*, p. 199.

Fig. 4.8: Present versus Future Positions in the Portfolio Matrix

(iii) The BCG Matrix is not a reliable indicator of relative investment opportunities across business units. For example, investing in a star is not necessarily more attractive than investing in a lucrative cash cow.

(iv) Being a market leader in a slow growth industry does not guarantee cash cow status.

(v) Strategists should examine more than just industry growth and relative market share variables to assess the long term attractiveness of the portfolio's business units.

(vi) The relationship between relative market share and profitability is not as tight as the experience curve effect implies. The significance of length production experience in lowering production cost per unit varies from industry to industry. Sometimes, the large market share is due to cost advantage and sometimes it is not.

4. GE Nine-Cell Matrix

Some of the shortcomings of BCG Matrix are avoided in an alternative approach. The alternative approach is the nine-cell matrix, based on the two dimensions of long-term industry attractiveness and business strength/competitive position. This approach is pioneered by General Electric as a way to analyse its own portfolio. This analysis was developed with the help of the consulting firm of Mckinsey and Company. The dimensions of the matrix, *viz.*, long-term industry attractiveness and business strength/competitive position are a composite of several considerations as opposed to a single factor.

The factors that influence the criteria for determining long-term industry attractiveness include:

(i) market size and growth rate,

(ii) technological requirements.

(iii) the intensity of competition,

(iv) entry and exit barriers,

(v) seasonality and cyclical influences,

(vi) capital requirements,

(vii) emerging industry threats and opportunities,

(viii) historical and projected industry profitability,

(ix) social, environmental and regulatory influences.

The selected measures are assigned weights based on their significance to management and their role in the diversification strategy. The sum of the weights must be 1.00. Use the 1-10 rating scale and assign appropriate weights to each factor. Then multiply the weights with the rating concerned. The product will be the weighted industry rating. Then add the weighted industry ratings of all the factors. The sum will be the industry attractive rating. Table 4.4 presents the procedure for calculation of industry attractiveness rating. Attractiveness ratings are calculated for each industry represented in the corporate portfolio. The position of each industry based on the industry's attractiveness score is placed on the vertical scale of Fig. 4.9.

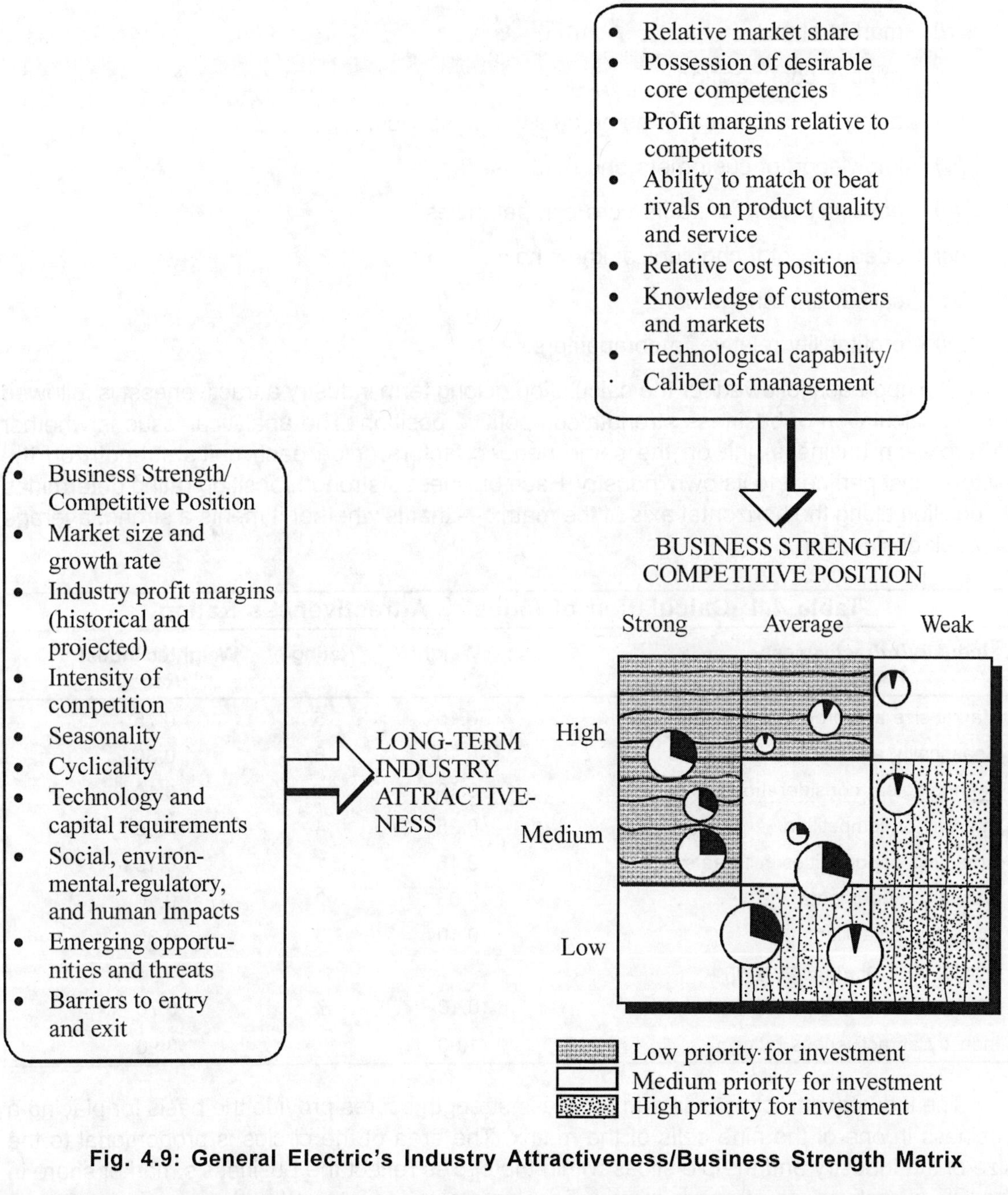

Fig. 4.9: General Electric's Industry Attractiveness/Business Strength Matrix

The factors that influence the business strength/competitive position include:

(i) market share,

(ii) relative cost position,

(iii) ability to match rival firms on quality and service,

(iv) knowledge of customers and markets,

(v) possession of desirable core competencies,

(vi) adequacy of technological know-how,

(vii) caliber of management,

(viii) profitability relative to competitors.

The approach followed for the calculation of long term industry attractiveness, is followed for the calculation of business strength/competitive position. The analytical issue is whether to rate each business unit on the same generic factors or on each unit's strength on the factors most pertinent to its own industry. Each business's strength/position rating determines its position along the horizontal axis of the matrix — that is whether it merits a strong, average or weak designation.

Table 4.4: Calculation of Industry Attractiveness Rating

Industry/Attractiveness Factor	Weight	Rating	Weighted Industry *Rating*
Market size and projected growth	0.15	5	0.75
Seasonality and cyclical influences	0.10	8	0.80
Technological considerations	0.10	1	0.10
Intensity of competition	0.25	4	1.00
Emerging opportunities & threats	0.15	1	0.15
Capital requirements	0.05	2	0.10
Industry profitability	0.10	3	0.30
Social, political, regulatory and environmental factors	0.10	7	0.70
Industry attractiveness rating	1.00		3.90

The industry attractiveness and business strength scores provide the basis for placing a business in one of the nine cells of the matrix. The area of the circles is proportional to the size of the industry and the pie slices within the circles reflect the business's market share in the GE attractiveness strength matrix. The long-term industry attractiveness is shown on vertical axis and from low to high. (*i.e.*, low, medium and high). Business strength/competitive position is shown on horizontal axis and presented from weak to strong (*i.e.*, weak, average and strong). Thus, three on horizontal and three on vertical lines make the total cells 3 × 3 =9.

Three cells are shown in vertical lines, three cells are shown in horizontal lines and the remaining three cells are shown in white colour in Fig. 4.9.

Corporate Strategy Implications: The attractive strength matrix helps in deciding investment priorities in different businesses of a company. The important strategic implications of the matrix are:

(i) Industry attractiveness and business strength/competitive positions are high in the upper left three cells. Top investment priority should be given to the businesses in these three cells. Therefore, the strategic prescription for the business in these three cells is "grow and build."

(ii) The second priority comes to the three diagonal cells stretching from the lower left to the upper right (*i.e.,* the lower-left cell, the middle cell and the upper right cell). Medium priority should be given to the businesses falling in these cells. Funds should be invested steadily in these businesses to protect and maintain their industry position. If any business in these three cells has high attractiveness, it should be given top priority in investment and be given go-ahead to employ a more aggressive strategic approach.

(iii) The business in the three cells in the lower-right corner do not receive any investment decisions. Rather, the strategies of harvest or divest may be employed for these businesses. However, if there are any exceptional cases for turnaround, the strategy of turnaround may be employed.

Strengths and Weaknesses of GE Matrix

Strengths: This matrix has three strengths:

(i) It allows for intermediate ranking between high and low and between strong and weak.

(ii) It incorporates a much wider variety of strategically relevant variables, whereas the BCG Matrix is based totally on two considerations — industry growth rate and relative market share.

(iii) It stresses the channeling of corporate resources to businesses with greatest probability of achieving competitive advantage and superior performance. That is top investment priority for the businesses in the three upper left cells, medium priority for the businesses in the three diagonal cells stretching from the lower left to the upper right and adopting turnaround, harvest and divest strategies for the businesses in the three lower right cells.

Weaknesses: Though the GE Matrix is better than the BCG Matrix, it also suffers from some weaknesses. They are:

(i) The nine-cell GE Matrix provides no real guidance on the specific business strategy. This matrix also suggests general strategy like — aggressive expansion, fortify-and-defend

or harvest divest. These strategies do not address the issue of strategic coordination between businesses, specific competitive approaches and strategies to be adopted at the business unit level.

(ii) The GE method tends to obscure business that are about to become winners because their industries are entering the take off stage.

5. Directional Policy Matrix

The directional policy matrix (DPM) was developed by Shell Chemicals, U.K. This matrix uses two parameters, *viz.*, business sector prospects and company's competitive abilities. Business sector prospects are rated on the basis of market growth, market supply and the like. Business sector prospects are judged as attractive, average and unattractive. Company's competitive abilities are judged as strong, average and weak. Business sector prospects represent vertical axis of the diagram of the directional policy matrix. Fig. 4.10 presents the directional policy matrix. There are 9 cells in the diagram. The business in the right lower cells deserve top priority for investment whereas, the business falling in the left upper cells deserve for divestment, withdrawal, etc. The businesses positioned in the three diagonal cells stretching from the lower left to the upper right are usually given medium priority. They merit steady reinvestment to maintain and protect their industry positions. However, the business with unusual attractiveness in these cells, should win higher investment priority.

Business Sector Prospects

Company's Competitive Abilities	*Unattractive*	*Average*	*Attractive*
Weak	Divestment	Imitation/Phased withdrawal	Phased Withdrawal/Cash generation
Average	Phased Withdrawal/ Merger	Maintenance of position/market penetration	Expansion/Product differentiation
Strong	Diversification/ Cash generation	Growth/market segmentation	Market leadership Innovation

Sources: Adopted from D.E. Hussey, "*Portfolio Analysis: Practical Experience with the Directional Policy Matrix," Long Range Planning*, August 1978, p. 3 and A.J. Rowe, R.O. Mason and K. Dickel, "*Strategic Management and Business Policy — A Methodological Approach*," Addison-Wesley, Reading, Mass, 1982, p. 154.

Fig. 4.10: The Directional Policy Matrix

6. Hofer's Life Cycle Matrix

Hofer developed a 15-cell matrix. In this matrix, businesses are plotted in terms of the industry's stage in the evolutionary life-cycle and the business unit's competitive position as shown in Fig. 4.11. The industry's stage in the evolutionary life cycle consists of the following stages: early development, industry takeoff, rapid growth, competitive shake-out, maturity, market saturation and stagnation, industry decline. The business unit's competitive position consists of strong, average and weak. The industry's stage in the evolutionary life cycle represents the vertical axis whereas the business unit's competitive position represents the horizontal axis. The circles in the matrix represent the sizes of the industries involved, and pie wedges denote the business's market share. The businesses shown in Fig. 4.11 could be labeled as follows:

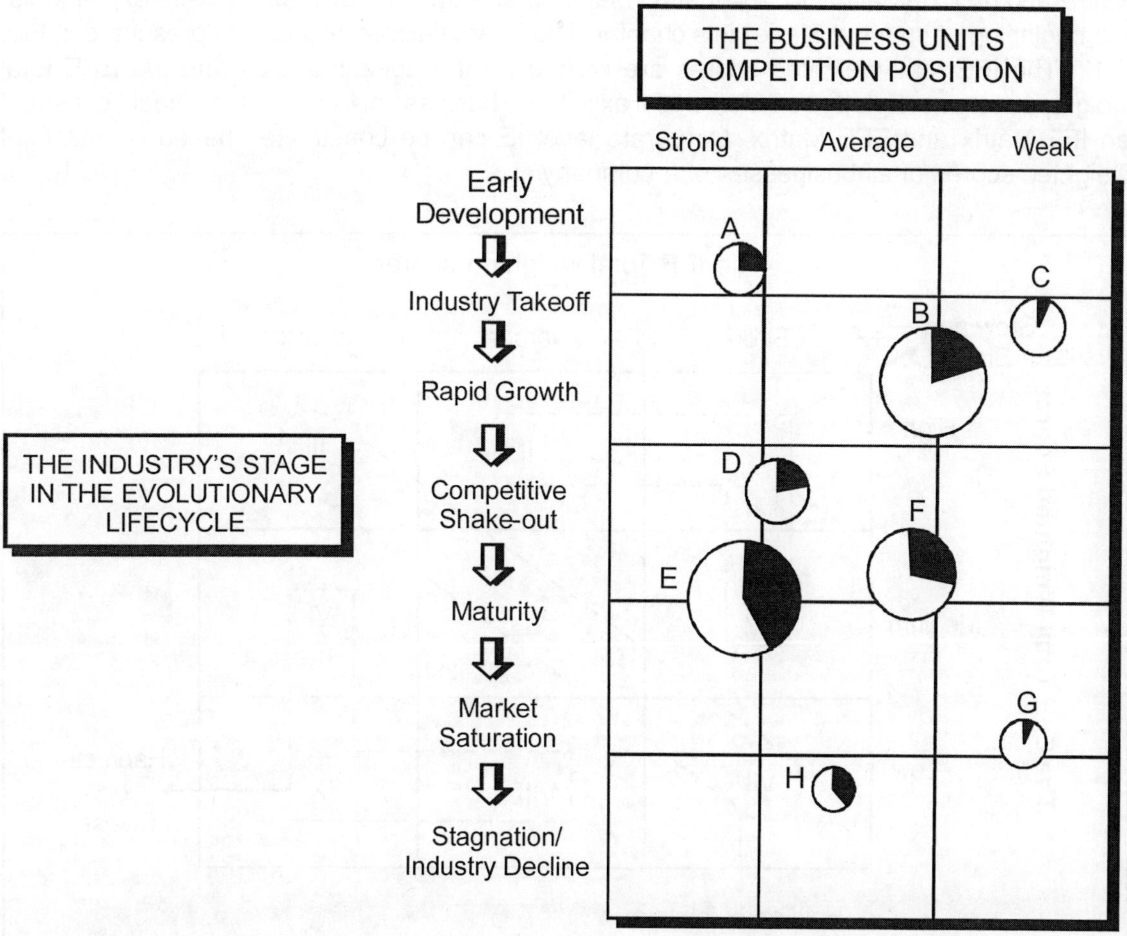

Fig. 4.11: The Lifecycle Portfolio Matrix

Business 'A' could be labeled as: developing winner

Business C " a potential loser

Business E " an established winner

Business F " a cash cow

Business G " a loser/dog.

The life cycle matrix has 15 cells and tells about the distribution of the company's business across the stages of industry evolution.

7. The Internal-External (IE) Matrix

The internal-external matrix is based on two dimensions *viz.*, *(i)* Internal Factor Evaluation Matrix and *(ii)* External Factor Evaluation Matrix. IFE matrix and EFE matrix were explained at the beginning of (in Input Stage) this chapter. The Internal-External Matrix is presented in Fig. 4.12. The IFE total weighted scores are plotted on the horizontal axis and the EFE total weighted scores are plotted on the vertical axis. Each business of the company should construct an IFE Matrix and EFE Matrix. Corporate level IE can be constructed based on the total weighted scores of all businesses of a company.

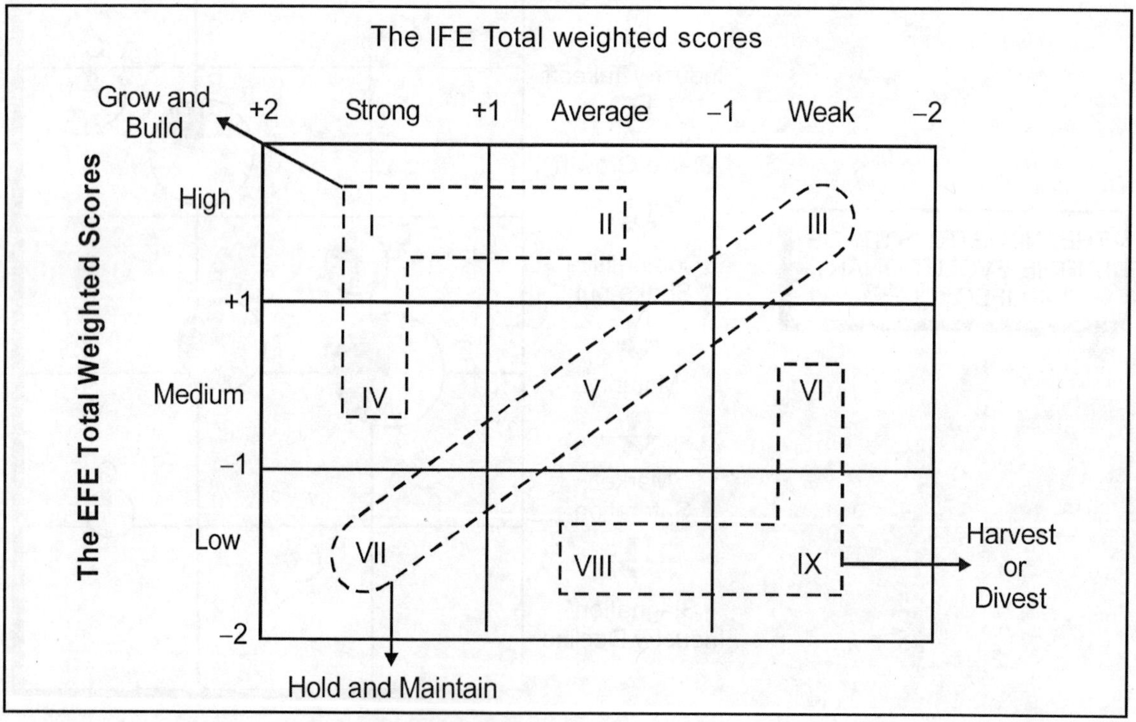

Source: Modified version from: Fred R. David, *op. cit.*, p. 219.

Fig. 4.12: The Internal-External (IE) Matrix

On the horizontal axis of the IE matrix, the IFE total weighted scores of –2 to –1 represent weak internal position, scores of –1 to +1 represent average position and scores of +1 to +2 represent strong position. Similarly, on the vertical axis an EFE total weighted scores of –2 to –1 represent low position, scores of –1 to +1 represent medium position and scores of +1 to +2 represent high position.

Strategy Implications: The IE matrix have nine-cell (3 × 3 = 9) display. The business falling in the left upper three cells (*i.e.,* cells I, II and IV) are accorded top investment priority. Therefore, the strategic prescriptions for these businesses can be 'Grow and Build'. Intensive (market penetration, market development and product development) or integrative (forward integration, backward integration and horizontal integration).

Next in priority come business positioned in the three diagonal cells stretching from the lower left to the upper right (businesses VII, V and III). These businesses are usually given medium priority. The strategic prescriptions for these businesses can be steady reinvestment to maintain and protect their industry positions. Market penetration and product development are two commonly adopted strategies for these types of businesses. However, if there is any business in these three cells, with an unusually attractive opportunity, it can be given higher investment opportunity and be allowed to go ahead to adopt a more aggressive strategic approach. The strategy prescription for businesses in the three cells (VIII, IX and VI) in the lower right corner is typically harvest or divest. In exceptional good business cases the strategy of turnaround can be employed.

The IE Matrix vs the BCG Matrix

The IE matrix seems to be similar with the BCG matrix.

(i) The tools involve in plotting businesses of a company in a schematic diagram,

(ii) The size of each circle represents the percentage sales contribution of each business, and

(iii) The pie slices reveal the percentage profit contribution of each business are similar.

There are some deviation between IE matrix and BCG matrix. The axes are different. The IE matrix is built with the help of more information about the businesses composed to that of BCG matrix. Further, the strategic implications of each matrix are different.

8. Porter's National Competitive Advantage

Competitive Advantages : A recent study concluded that competitive superiority is derived from four factors *viz.,* demand conditions, factor endowment, related and supporting industries and firm strategy, structure and rivalry. Fig. 4.13 presents the determinants of global competitive advantage. This figure is also known as the Porter Diamond.

We should understand the combined effect of these factors on the development and continued existence of competitive advantages. All the four factors need not always be favourable for a company to get global supremacy. But the interactive affect of these four factors need to be favourable if an industry/company in a country is to gain a global competitive advantage.

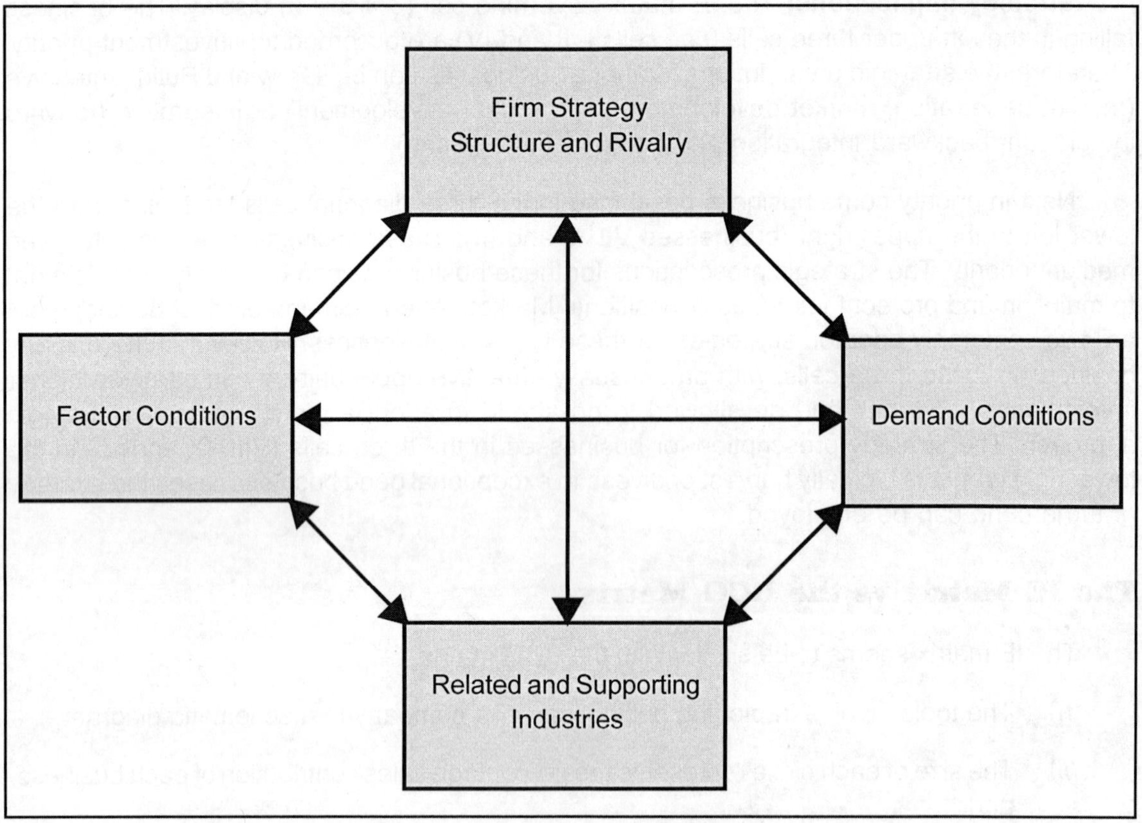

Source : Michael E. Porter, *"The Competitive Advantage of Nations, Free Press"* New York, 1990, p. 72.

Fig. 4.13: Porter Diamond

Now we shall discuss the four elements of the diamond.

- ***Factor Conditions:*** Factor conditions include factors of production. Hecksher-Ohlin theory deals with the classical factors *viz.*, land, labour, capital and organisation. Porter emphasises other factors like educational level of labour and quality of the country's infrastructure. Country's ability to compete globally depends upon the country's factor resources *viz.*, research, innovation and training. The USA has rich factor endowments and enjoys top position in world trade and world economy. *(See Box 4.4)*

Box 4.4 : Position of the USA in World Trade and World Economy

The USA has unique position in the world trade and world economy. Its unique positions include:

- Large size of the country
- Largest GDP with approximately $10 trillion
- Largest exporter and largest importer in the world
- Has world's largest financial market
- Large in having MNCs (16) out of top 500 MNCs in 2006
- Lost first positions of exports of merchandise in 2006.
- It started losing its position due to rapid development of some developing and recently emerging countries including South Korea, China, Malaysia and India.

- ***Demand Conditions:*** The existence of a large number of sophisticated domestic consumers who are economically able and willing to consume create and improve the demand for various products in the country. Companies improve the existing products and develop new products to meet the increasing demand. In addition, domestic companies compete with each other in developing existing and new products. As such some of the processing domestic companies would be ahead of the international companies and export to other countries. *For example,* Japanese companies developed camcorders, big screen TVs and VCRs better than the international companies and exported them to the European and North American countries after meeting the domestic demand.
- ***Related and Supported Industries:*** The emergence and growth of an industry provide the scope for the development of suppliers of raw material, market intermediaries, financial companies, consulting agencies, ancillary industries etc. These supporting service agencies compete among themselves leading to high input quality and lower prices. Availability of high quality inputs at lower prices in the domestic country enhances competitive advantage of the firm internationally.
- ***Firm Strategy, Structure and Rivalry:*** Firms continuously improve the quality, product design, invest in R and D in order to compete domestically. Firms also invest in human resource development, technology etc., in the domestic market. These developments result in high quality and lower prices in domestic country which are transferable to international markets. Intense competition for Japanese automobile manufacturers and electronics goods manufacturers led to their success in international markets. The same theory holds good in case of Indian garment manufacturers and US personal computer manufacturers.

9. The Grand Strategy Matrix

The Grand Strategy Matrix has become a popular tool for formulating corporate strategy. The Grand Strategy Matrix is shown in Fig. 4.13. There are four quadrants in the matrix. All companies can be positioned in one of four quadrants of the matrix. The businesses of the company can also be positioned on the similar ones. The matrix is based on two evaluative dimensions, *viz.,* competitive position and market growth. Appropriate strategies for a company to consider are presented in the quadrant concerned in the order of attractiveness.

Businesses/companies falling in the quadrant I are in the excellent strategic position. The firm in this quadrant may go for backward, forward or horizontal integration when they have excessive resources. These firms may also go for concentric diversification strategy in order to reduce the risks of narrow product line. These forms can also adopt aggressive strategies and exploit the opportunities provided by the external environment.

The businesses/firms falling in the quadrant II, *i.e.,* rapid market growth and weak competitive position, are unable to compete effectively at market place and exploit the opportunities offered by the external environment. These firms can employ the strategy of horizontal integration. As a last resort, the strategies of divestment and liquidation may also be considered. Alternative businesses may be developed from the funds generated by divesting the existing business.

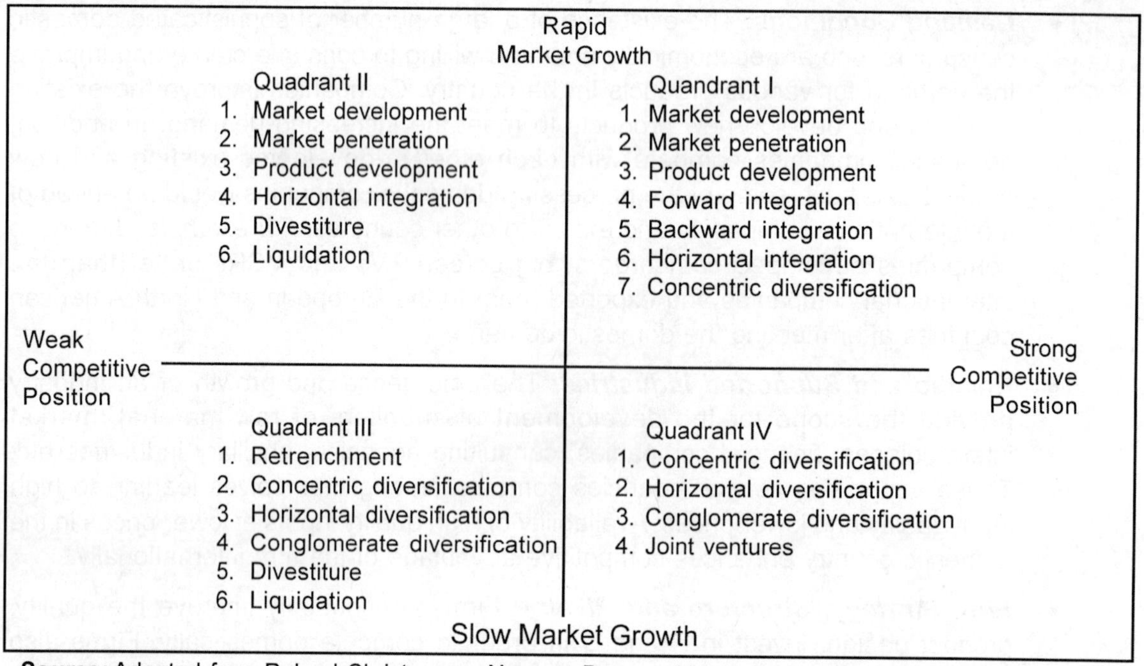

Source: Adapted from Roland Christensen, Norman Berg and Malcolm Sulter, "*Policy Formulation and Administration*," Richard D. Irwin, Homewood Ill., 1976, pp. 16-18.

Fig. 4.13: The Grand Strategy Matrix

The businesses/firms falling in quadrant III, *i.e.,* slow-market growth and weak competitive position, must make drastic and quick changes to avoid further loss and extinction. As a first step, these firms may reduce costs and assets. As a second step, the firms may shift resources away from the existing businesses to new businesses.

The business firms falling in quadrant IV, *i.e.,* slow market growth and strong competitive position — have strength to launch diversified programmes into more promising growth areas. These firms have more cash flows but less external opportunities to grow. These firms/ businesses can successfully pursue concentric, horizontal or conglomerate diversification. Another strategic option available for these firms is 'joint venture'.

(E) SELECTION OF THE MATRIX

Each matrix has its own strengths and weaknesses. It is not wise to restrict the analysis to one type of portfolio matrix. Therefore, it would be better to construct all the eight matrices, provided, adequate data is available. It will help to assess the company's portfolio from different perspectives. This process enables to achieve the analytical objective. The analytical objective is to understand:

(i) The portfolio's mix of industries.

(ii) The strategic position each business has in its industry.

(iii) The portfolio's performance potential.

(iv) The kind of financial and resource allocation considerations that have to be dealt with.

1. Comparing Industry Attractiveness

Judging the attractiveness of the industries in which the business is the central issue in evaluating a diversified company's strategy. Industry attractiveness can be judged from three perspectives:

(i) The attractiveness of each industry represented in the portfolio. The important consideration is that, "Is this a good industry for the company to have its business in?"

(ii) Each industry attractiveness is relative to the others. The company should find itself. "Which industries in the portfolio are the most attractive and which are the least attractive?" The allocation of resources will become easy by ranking the industries from the most attractive to the least attractive.

(iii) The attractiveness of all industries as a group. The company should find, "how appealing is the mix of industries?"

All the industries represented in the business portfolio should be judged on the following attractive factors:

(a) *Market size and projected growth rate:* Generally, faster growing industries are more attractive than slow growing industries.

(b) *The intensity of competition:* Industries with less competitive pressure are more attractive than industries with strong competitive pressure.

(c) *Technological and production skills required:* Industries where the skill requirements are closely matched to company capabilities are more attractive.

(d) *Capital requirements:* Industries with low or procurable capital requirements are more attractive.

(e) *Seasonal and cyclical factors:* Industries where demand is relatively stable, dependable and continuous are more attractive than that of industries whose demand is seasonal and/or cyclical.

Industry Profitability: Industries with high rates of return are more attractive than industries with low profit margins.

Social, political regulatory and environmental factors: Industries with fewer problems in these areas are normally more attractive.

Strategic fits with other industries with the firm has diversified into. The industries with valuable strategic fit relationship with other industries in the portfolio are more attractive.

Industries should be ranked from most to least attractive based on the calculation of industry attractiveness ratings for all industries in the corporate portfolio. A diversified company to be a strong performer, should get a substantial portion of its revenue and profits from businesses in attractive industries. The core businesses of the company should be attractive, good outlook for growth and above average profitability industries.

2. Comparing Business Unit Strength

Appraising each business unit's strengths and competitive position in its industry helps managers to judge a business unit's chance for success in its industry. Assessment of how a company's business compares in competitive strength should be based on the following factors:

(i) *Relative Market Share:* Business units with higher relative shares have greater competitive strengths.

(ii) *Ability to Compete on Price and/or Quality:* Business units that have cost advantage and have established brand names for quality will be more strongly positioned.

(iii) *Technology and Innovation Capabilities:* Business units with advanced technology and track record in innovations will be strong competitors.

(iv) *How well the business unit's skill and competences match industry key success factors:* The business units would be stronger, if their skills and competencies match with industry's key success factors, most exactly.

(v) *Profitability Relative to Competitors:* The business units that earn high rate of return consistently compared to the competitors will compete more strongly.

(vi) *Other factors include:* Knowledge about customers and markets, production capabilities, marketing skills, reputation and brand awareness and efficiency of management.

Shareholders' interests are normally served better, by concentrating company resources on business that can contend for market leadership in their industry.

3. Comparing Business-Unit Performance

After the businesses have been rated based on industry attractiveness and competitive strength, the business should be evaluated to know their performance prospects ranging from the best to the worst. The factors that should be considered in this respect are: sales growth, profit growth, contribution to corporate earnings, rate of return on the capital employed, cash flow generation, etc.

4. Strategic Fit Analysis

The strategic fit analysis studies, how well each business unit fits into the company's overall portfolio of business. This can be analysed from two angles:

(i) Whether a business unit has valuable strategic fit with other businesses the firm has diversified into.

(ii) Whether a business unit meshes well with corporate strategy or adds a beneficial dimension to the corporate portfolio.

The best strategic fit business in the overall corporate portfolio makes valuable financial contributions. It also contributes to the achievement of corporate objectives.

Ranking the Business Units on Investment Priority

Managers should rank the businesses in terms of priority for new capital investment based on the analysis given so far. First, the strategists should decide, whether the company will be investing additional funds or not? Once, it is decided that the business will invest additional funds, the strategist should rank the businesses based on their significance, competence, ability to generate cash flows, earn high rate of return, etc. They should rank the business from good to excellent prospects and investing minimally. Strategists should consider whether and how corporate resources and skills can be used to enhance the competitive standing of particular business units.

5. Formulating a Corporate Strategy

Strategist should, move to formulate a strategy to improve the performance of a diversified company. This is based on the overall mix of businesses in the portfolio. Key considerations in this regard include:

(i) Does the portfolio contain enough business in attractive industries?

(ii) How many businesses are question marks?

(iii) What is the proportion of mature businesses in the portfolio?

(iv) Does the portfolio contain enough cash cows to finance the stars and emerging winners?

(v) Does the core businesses of the company earn enough profits?

(vi) Seasonality and cyclical factors.

(vii) Are there too many weak portfolios?

(vii) Does the new corporate strategy improve the overall performance of the company?

The strategist should evaluate the company in terms of performance objectives with its current line of business in order to know the financial viability of the strategy. The strategist can pursue any five basic options to avoid a probable shortfall in financial performance:

(i) Alter the strategic plans for some or all of the businesses.

(ii) Add new business units. Strategists must decide about:

(a) Acquiring related/unrelated businesses. *(b)* Size of acquisitions. *(c)* Specific features of acquisition of business units. *(d)* Pattern of investing the new acquisitions.

(iii) Divest weak performing or money losing businesses.

(iv) Form alliances to try to alter conditions responsible for sub-par performance potentials.

(v) Lower corporate performance objectives.

Deploying Corporate Resources

Strategists must find the sources to finance the strategy. The funds from divestment, cash cows and harvest can be the sources of funds for the corporate treasury. Options for allocating these funds include:

(i) Invest in maintenance and expansion of existing businesses;

(ii) Invest in acquisitions;

(iii) Invest in long-range R&D;

(iv) Paying off existing long-term debt;

(v) Pay higher dividends; and

(vi) Repurchase of company's stock.

(F) THE DECISION STAGE

1. The Quantitative Strategic Planning Matrix (QSPM)

After the input stage and the matching stage, the decision stage follows. The QSPM is an important technique in the third stage strategy formulation analytical framework. This matrix suggests which alternative strategies are best. QSPM is the most current of the strategy formulation analytical techniques. QSPM utilises input information, matching results and analyses to evaluate alternative strategies quantitatively, based on specific organisational capabilities and limitations. It requires subjective decision in assigning weights and ratings. Table 4.5 presents the basic format of QSPM. The left column of the table consists of internal and external factors and the top row consists of feasible alternative strategies. The ratings of key factors are also recorded. Alternative strategies that are desired from TOWS Matrix, SPACE Matrix, BCG Matrix, GE Matrix, Directional Policy Matrix, IE Matrix and Grand Strategy Matrix are also considered. These matching tools, normally, generate feasible alternative strategies similar to each other.

Table 4.5: The Quantitative Strategic Planning Matrix — QSPM — Basic Format

Key Factors	Strategic Alternatives		
Ratings	Stage 1	Stage 2	Stage 3
Internal Factors:			
Management			
Marketing			
Finance			
Human Resource			
Production/operations			
Research & Development			
External Factors:			
Economy			
Political			
Social			
Technological			
Competitive			

Source: Fred R. David., *op. cit.*, p. 224.

The relative attractiveness of various strategies is determined by QSPM. It uses key internal and external factors in determining relative attractiveness. Though any number of sets of alternative strategies can be included in a QSPM and any number of strategies can comprise a given set, only strategies within a given set are evaluated relative to each other by QSPM. In other words, strategies in each set (like centric, horizontal and conglomerate diversification) are evaluated against each other. Therefore, strategies of the same set should be included in the table for the purpose of evaluation. Table 4.6 presents a sample and a more detailed example of QSPM.

Appendix 4.1 presents a direct application of QSPM.

Table 4.6: A Sample Quantitative Strategic Planning Matrix

Key Factors	*Rating*	*Strategic Alternatives* *Acquire Financial Services, Inc.* *AS**	*TAS**	*Acquire Food Services, Inc.* *AS**	*TAS**	*Rationale for Attractiveness Score*
Internal Factors						
Top management team has fifteen years' experience	3	4	12	2	6	Fifteen years' experience is in financial services
We have excess working capital of $2 million.	4	2	8	3	12	Food Services is valued at $2 million.

All of four twenty plants are located in the Northeast United States.	1	2	2	4	4	Food Services is located in the Sun-belt.
Our R&D department is outstanding.	3	—	—	—	—	This item does not affect the strategy choice.
Our Return on Investment (ROI) ratio of .12 is lowest in the industry.	1	2	2	3	3	ROI at Food Services is higher than at Financial Services.
External Factors						
Interest rates are expected to rise to 15 percent in 1987.	2	3	6	4	8	Rising rates will hurt the financial services business.
Population of the South is expected to grow by 15.3 million between 1980 and 2000.	3	4	12	2	6	Many new houses and apartments will be built and financed.
The financial services industry is expected to grow by 40 percent in 1986.	4	4	16	2	8	This 40 percent growth is in financial services.
Two major foreign competitors are entering the industry.	1	1	1	3	3	Food Services, Inc. is not affected by this entry.
President Reagan is expected to deregulate the industry.	2	—	—	—	—	This item does not affect the strategy choice.
SUM TOTAL ATTRACTIVENESS SCORE					59	50

*AS = Attractiveness Score; TAS = Total Attractiveness Score
Attractiveness Score: 1 = not acceptable; 2 = possibly accepted 3 = probably acceptable; 4 = most acceptable
Internal Ratings: 1 = major weakness; 2 = minor weakness; 3 = minor strength: 4 = major strength
External Ratings: 1 major threat; 2 = minor threat; 3 = minor opportunity; 4 = major opportunity

Note: Multiplying the rating times the attractiveness score is based upon the premise that to capitalize on strengths and take advantage of opportunities is more important for firms than improving weaknesses and avoiding threats. Some strategies do not agree with this premise and therefore, do not compute the total attractiveness score. They simply sum the attractiveness scores to determine the relative attractiveness of strategies using the QSPM.

Source: Fred R. David., *op. cit*., p. 225.

2. Guidelines for Strategy Formulation Process

Strategy formulation is not a simple process. Moreover, it is not purely a quantitative analysis. Quantitative analysis aid the process to some extent. Strategies in major diversified enterprises emerges incrementally over a period of time based on internal and external situations and experiences. This process is also the result of

(a) probing the future,

(b) experiments,

(c) gathering additional information from time to time,

(d) sensing problems,

(e) building awareness of various options,

(f) developing *ad hoc* responses to unexpected crisis,

(g) communicating partial consensus as it emerges and

(h) acquiring a "feel" for all the strategically relevant factors, their importance and their interrelationships.

Executives of major diversified companies do not formulate strategies all at once in comprehensive fashion. The strategic decisions in such organisations emerge gradually but not at one time in a full scale analysis. Top strategists make strategic decisions, "a step at a time, often starting from broad, intuitive conceptions and then embellishing, fine tuning and modify their original thinking as more information is gathered as formal analysis confirms or modifies emerging judgments and as confidence and consensus build for what strategic moves need to be made."

Politics and Strategy Formulation

Often, politics affect the strategy formulation. The following factors are responsible for politics:

(i) The organisational hierarchy, levels of authority and command.

(ii) Career goals of employees at different levels.

(iii) Problem of allocation of scarce resources.

(iv) Formation of coalitions and groups of individuals.

(v) Superiority of individual goals and group goals over organisational goals.

(vi) Ego clashes of top and middle level executives and line and staff executives.

Strategists have to spend most of their time and energy in nurturing the team concept and gain the support of key individuals and key groups. Internal support is crucial for strategists to manage the external forces. Sometimes, strategic decisions are based on the politics of the moment, when major groups of individuals do not support the best strategic alternative. Managing organisational politics is an integral part of building enthusiasm and team work. Strategists should ensure that all major power bases within an organisation have representation in or access to top management.

Board of Directors and Strategy Formulation

Often, the managing director of the company, in the capacity of chief executive officer and chief strategist, formulate the strategies without consulting the Board of Directors. The businesses to-day are more diversified, large in size and involve large amounts of financial resources. In view of these factors and also due to protecting the rights of shareholders, the board of directors should be informed and involved in the strategy formulation process. Exhibit 4.2 presents Board of Directors strategy audit framework.

Exhibit 4.2: A Board of Directors Strategy Audit Framework

- Is the company adequately informed about its markets? What further information would be worth the cost of getting? How should it be obtained?
- How well informed is the company about its competitors? How well is it able to forecast what competitors will do under various circumstances? Is there a sound basis for such competitive appraisals? Is the company underestimating or overestimating its competitors?
- Has management adequately explored various ways of segmenting its market? To what extent is it addressing market segments in which the company's strengths provide meaningful advantages?
- Are the products and services the company proposes to sell, ones that it can provide more effectively than competitors? What is the basis for such a belief?
- Do the various activities proposed in the strategy provide synergistic advantages? Are they compatible?
- Does the proposed strategy adequately address questions of corporate objectives, financial policy, scope of operations, organisation, and integration?
- What specific resources (personnel, skills, information, facilities, technology, finances, relationships) will be needed to execute the strategy? Does the company already possess these resources? Has management established programmes for building these resources and overall competence which will provide telling competitive advantages over the long run?
- To what extent does the strategy define a unique and appropriate economic rule for the company? How different is it from the competitor's strategy?
- Has the issue of growth rate been raised? Are there good reasons to believe that investment in growth will pay off? Does the company's track record support such a conclusion?
- Does the proposed dividend policy reflect the company's growth policy, based on a demonstrated ability or inability to reinvest cash flow advantageously? Or is it just a "safe" compromise, conforming to what others usually do?
- Is the management capable of implementing the strategy effectively? What leads to this conclusion?
- How and to what extent is the strategy to be communicated to the organisation? Is it to be distributed in written form? If competitors are aware of the company's strategy, will that help or hurt?

- What provision is to be made for employing the strategy as a guide to operating decisions? To what extent is it to be used by the board? How?
- How is it to be kept up-to-date? Are there to be regular reviews? How often and by whom?
- Has a set of long-range projections of operations following the strategy been prepared? Have the possible results of following alternative strategies been prepared?
- Does the strategy focus on the few really important key issues? Is it too detailed? Does it address genuine business questions (as opposed to "motherhood" statements)?
- In its strategic thinking, has management avoided the lure of simplistic approaches such as:

  Growth for growth's sake?

  Diversification for diversification's sake?

  Aping the industry leader?

  Broadening the scope in order to secure "incremental" earnings?

  Assuming it can execute better than the competitors without objective evidence that such is the case?
- Are there other issues, trends, or potential events that should have been taken into account?

Source: Milton Lauenstein, "Boards of Directors: The Strategy Audit," *Journal of Business Strategy* 4, No. 3 (Winter 1984): 90, 91.

Points to be Remembered

- Strategic alternatives at all levels, *viz*; corporate, strategic business unit level and functional level should be analysed and evaluated to rank them and to select the best strategy.
- The evaluation should measure the suitability of the strategy to the situation.
- The internal factor evaluation matrix summarises an organisation's key strengths and weaknesses.
- The matching stage of the analytical framework for strategy formulation attempts to match strengths with the opportunities and threats with the weaknesses
- Boston Consultancy Group's matrix evaluates based on industry growth rate and reactive market share position of the company.
- GE nine-cell matrix examines in terms of long-term industry alternativeness and business strength/competitive position.
- Selection of the matrix involves the portfolio mix of industries and portfolio performance potential

Keywords

- Internal Factors
- Competitive Profile
- GE Nine-Cell Matrix
- Hofer's Life Cycle Matrix
- Grand Strategy Matrix
- Strategic Fit Analysis
- External Factors
- Boston Consultancy Group
- Directional Policy Matrix
- Internal-External Matrix
- Industry Attractiveness
- Busines Unit Strength

Questions for Discussion

1. What type of criteria do you adopt to evaluate strategic alternatives?
2. Discuss the framework for evaluating strategic alternatives.
3. What is external factor evaluation matrix?
4. What is the matching stage corporate portfolio analysis?
5. How do you evaluate the strategic alternatives using the BCG criteria?
6. How do you evaluate the strategic alternatives using GE Nine-Cell matrix?
7. What is the internal-external matrix? Explain its strengths over other criteria.
8. What is selection of the matrix?
9. What is the decision stage? How do you use the quantitative strategic planning matrix to make a decision with regard to strategy selection?

References

1. Gerry Johnson and Kevan Scholes, "*Exploring Corporate Strategy*", Prentice-Hall, Englewood Cliffs, NJ, 1984, pp. 206-207.
2. S. Tilles, "How to Evaluate Corporate Strategy", *Harvard Business Review,* July-August 1963.
3. Gerry Johnson and Kevan Scholes, *op. cit.*, p. 211.
4. Fred R. David, *op. cit.*, pp. 198-200.
5. *Ibid.*, pp. 200-201.
6. *Ibid.*, pp. 202-203.
7. *Ibid.*, p. 203.
8. Heinz Weihrich, "The TOWS Matrix: A Tool for Situational Analysis", *Long Range Planning*, Vol. 15, No. 2, April 1982, p. 61.
9. Fred R. David, *op. cit.*, p. 208.
10. A Rowe, R. Mason and K. Dickel, "*Strategic Management and Business Policy, A Methodological Approach*", Addison-Wesley Publishing Co., Reading, Mass, 1982, pp. 155-164.

11. Arthur A. Thompson Jr., and A.J. Strickland III, *op. cit.* pp. 194-195.

12. *Ibid.*, p. 195.

13. *Ibid.*, p. 196.

14. *Ibid.*, p. 197.

15. *Ibid.*, p. 198.

16. Derek F. Abell and John S. Hammond, "*Strategic Market Planning*", Prentice-Hall, Englewood Cliffs, NJ, 1979, p. 212.

17. Michael G. Allen, "Diagramming G.E.'s Planning for What's WATT", in "*Corporate Planning: Techniques and Applications*", Robert J. Allio and Malcolm W. Pennington, AMACOM, New York, 1979.

18. Arthur A. Thompson and A.J. Strickland III, *op. cit.*, pp. 200-201.

19. Charles W. Hofer and Dan Schendel, "*Strategy Formulation: Analytical Concepts*", West Publishing, St. Paul Minn., 1978, p. 33.

20. *Ibid.*, p. 34.

21. Fred R. David, *op. cit.*, pp. 218-220.

22. Arthur A. Thompson and A.J. Strickland III, *op. cit.*, pp. 205-206.

23. *Ibid.*, pp. 206-207.

25. *Ibid.*, p. 209.

26. Hofer and Schendel, "*Strategy Formulating: Analytical Concepts*," p. 80, Quoted in *Ibid.*, p. 210.

27. Barry Hedley, "Strategy and the Business Portfolio," *Long Range Planning,* Vol. 10, No. 1, February 1977, p. 13.

28. Fred R. David, "Evaluating Alternatives Growth Strategies – An Analytical Approach," *Long Range Planning,* Spring 1986.

29. Fred R. David, *op. cit.*, pp. 223-224.

30. Michael E. Porter, "*Competitive Advantage,*" p. 58 and p. 196. Quoted in Thompson and Strickland, *op. cit.*, p. 213.

31. Arthur A. Thompson and A.J. Strickland, *op. cit.*, p. 213.

32. Fred R. David, *op. cit.*, pp. 230-231.

33. *Ibid.*, p. 232.

*****

Unit-3

Chapter - 5

Structural Implementation

Chapter Outline

(A) Analysing Strategic Change
(B) Managing Strategic Change
(C) Issues in Strategy Implementation
(D) Organisational Structure
(E) Approaches to Organisational Structure
(F) Matching Structure and Strategy
(G) Assessment of Organisational Structure
(H) Perspectives on the Methods of Organising
(I) Strategies for Competing in Global Markets
— Points to be Remembered
— Keywords
— Questions for Discussion
— References

Learning Objectives

After studying this chapter, you should be able to:

- Analyse the need for strategic change;
- Study various issues in strategy implementation like project, procedural implementation and organisation implementation;
- Discuss strategy and structure relationship and Structure-follow-strategy thesis;
- Analyse different approaches to organisational structure like product, geographic and strategic business unit structures;
- Explain various approaches match the structure to the strategy;
- Study the assessment of organisational structures.

(A) ANALYSING STRATEGIC CHANGE

The strategist should find out to what extent the organisation will have to change in order to succeed in the strategic implementation. Different kinds of strategies require different change in the business process, nature and size. For example, a stability strategy affects the present business and organisation to the least extent. Similarly, a new pricing strategy affects only the people in the marketing department and brings a few changes in the day-to-day business operations. In fact, the joint venture strategy brings radical changes in the organisation, *viz.*, replacing the existing organisational structure, introducing a more flexible, cross-functional organisational structure based on team building, new production process, technology, new markets and market practices, dropping existing products and adding new products and/or services.

Strategic change can be a continuum varying from no variation in strategy to a complete and radical change in the project procedure, organisational mission, objectives and organisational structure. Samuel C. Certo and Paul Peter divide strategic change into five discrete stages. They are stable strategy, routine strategy change, limited strategy change, radical strategy change and organisational redirection. Exhibit 5.1 presents levels of strategic change.

Exhibit 5.1: Levels of Strategic Change

Strategic Change	Industry	Organisation	Products	Market Appeal
Stable Strategy	same	same	same	same
Routine Strategy Change	same	same	same	new
Limited Strategy Change	same	same	new	new
Radical Strategy Change	same	new	new	new
Organisational Redirection	new	new	new	new

Source: Samuel C. Certo and J. Paul Peter, *op. cit.*, p. 113.

The implementation process of strategy involves many people, tasks, business units and products when it moves from stable strategy to organisational redirection. The implementation process becomes more complex when it moves towards organisational redirection.

Stable Strategy

Stable strategy is continuation of stability in all aspects of the business. Therefore, mostly, it requires continuation of strategy from the previous planning period. It requires running of the business and performing the same tasks with the same skills. Successful implementation of stability strategy requires monitoring the activities to ensure that the objectives are achieved. The learning from previous experiences (experiences curve effects) will help to achieve the objectives effectively.

Routine Strategy Change

In the routine strategy change, a firm seeks to attract customers, by making normal, predicted adjustments in the methods. The strategy changes include: Changing advertising appeals, update packaging, using different pricing tactics, change the distributors, distributing channels and methods, adding gifts, etc. Managers should integrate and coordinate the activities with various agencies and intermediaries in order to implement the strategies successfully. Similarly, the strategists should also co-ordinate the activities within the company. For example, the strategy of price reduction will enhance the demand for the product. Hence, the strategist should coordinate the activities of marketing department and production department to increase production, capacities of distribution channels and distributors. This strategy does not require major efforts and major changes for its successful implementation.

Limited Strategy Change: This strategy involves offering new products to new markets within the same general products class. Products are new, though, they belong to the same general class. Hence, the managers have to perform many new activities. These activities include: designing the new products, procurement of new kinds of inputs, new machinery, producing new products, arranging new market intermediaries (if necessary), new market channels and the like.

Radical Strategy Change: This strategy involves a major shift for the firm. The radical strategy change is necessary, when the firm adopts the strategies like mergers and acquisitions in the same basic industry. These strategies create complex problems in integrating the two firms into one firm. These complex problems include: restructuring the organisation, organisational change, change in the organisational culture, change in the positions of key personnel, change in the distributors and distributing channels, etc.

Organisational Redirection

This strategy involves mergers and acquisitions of firms in different industries. The magnitude of strategic change depends on the degree of variation of the nature of industries and the degree of centralisation of the new firm. Another form of organisational redirection involves when a firm leaves one industry and enters a new one. For example, a firm enters the hot drinks industry by leaving the soft drinks industry.

(B) MANAGING STRATEGIC CHANGE

The board of directors should actively involve like catalyst (See Exhibit 5.2) in the implementation process. The managing director can get a sense of the magnitude of a newly implemented change from the broad categories of change discussed above. However, these strategies will not provide the details of actually managing a strategic change effort. James Brian Quinn provides an outline of the steps that effective leaders often use to manage strategic change. Exhibit 5.3 presents three major sequential steps, along with the specific activities in each. Quinn's approach emphasises the essential analytical and political roles of the executives in managing strategic change. Effective leaders also need political and leadership skills to sell those interpretations to others.

Exhibit 5.2: Degree of Involvement of Board of Directors in Strategy Implementation

Low (Passive)					High *(Active)*
Phantom	**Rubber Stamp**	**Minimal Review**	**Nominal Participation**	**Active Participation**	**Catalyst**
Never knows what to do, if anything, no degree of involvement.	Permits officers to make all decisions. It votesas officers recommend on action issues.	Formally reviews selected issues that officers bring to itsattention.	Involved to a limited degree in the performance of review of selected key decisions, indicators, or programmers of management.	Approves, questions, and makes final decisions on mission, strategy, policies and objectives; Has active Board committees. Performs fiscal and management audits.	Takes the leading role in establishing and modifying the mission objectives, strategy and policies. It may have a very active strategy committee.

Source: Adapted from P.K. Ghosh, "*Business Policy*," Sultan Chand & Sons, New Delhi, 1994, p. 288.

Exhibit 5.3: Managing Strategic Change

INITIATING STRATEGIC CHANGE

- Build networks to sense needs
- Improve and lead the formal information system
- Amplify understanding
- Build awareness
- Change symbols
- Legitimise new viewpoints
- Develop partial solutions
- Broaden support

MOVE FROM CONCEPT TO STRATEGY

- Overcome opposition to change by finding zones of indifference and no loss situations
- Building comfort levels; change perceived risks
- Structure flexibility
- Test trial concepts

SOLIDIFY COMMITMENT

- Create key pockets of commitment
- Keep political exposure low
- Eliminate options

- Crystalise focus and consensus; management coalitions
- Formalise commitment, empower champions
- Design continuous strategic change process.

Source: Samuel C. Certo and J. Paul Peter, *op. cit.*, p. 116.

Formulation and Implementation of Strategy

The strategy formulation and the relationship between strategy formulation and strategic implementation should be studied. This is because, the formulation and implementation process are intertwined in real life. The two linkages exist between strategy formulation and strategy implementation are: *(i)* forward linkage, and *(ii)* backward linkage. The forward linkage deals with preparing the organisational activities including organisational structure, leadership, culture, etc., necessary for the strategic implementation.

The backward linkage deals with the influence of implementation on strategy formulation. In other words, once the strategy is selected and implemented, it is found in the reality that there are certain deviations due to the different ground realities. These deviations force the strategist to reformulate the strategy based on the ground realities. Therefore, the past strategic actions and experiences should be taken into consideration in formulating strategies.

(C) ISSUES IN STRATEGY IMPLEMENTATION

A number of issues are normally involved in strategy implementation. The important issues are: project, procedural, organisational structural, behavioural considerations, production/operations, human resources, financial and marketing.

1. Project Implementation

Project is defined by the Project Management Institute of the US as, "a one-shot, time limited, goal-oriented, major undertaking, requiring the commitment of varied skills and resources." Thus, a project is a highly specific programme for which the time schedule and specific costs are determined in advance. Projects create all necessary conditions and facilities for the strategy implementation.

2. Procedural Implementation

Strategy implementation also requires executing the strategy, based on the rules, regulations and procedures formulated by the government. Though, many procedures are simplified with the liberalisation, privatisation and globalisation of Indian economy, certain procedures are still applicable in the process of strategy implementation. Therefore, the strategists should study the following procedural aspects before implementing the strategy. They are: licensing procedures, foreign collaboration procedures, Foreign Exchange and Regulation Act requirements, environmental requirements, Monopolies and Restrictive Trade Practices requirements, import and export requirements, incentives and benefits, requirements of labour laws and other legislations.

Box 5.1: Shell offers business model on profit-sharing to ONGC

In order to overcome any bottlenecks on their joint co-operation in exploration and production (E&P) activities Royal Dutch Shell has offered ONGC a business model of profit sharing for any enhancement in productivity. Sources told *Business Line* that ONGC is considering Shell's proposal based on a framework outlined by the latter. The two companies have been holding high-level discussions on the issue. Indications are that ONGC was not open to going beyond Government prescribed norms on making joint investments and giving operatorship of the fields. However, ONGC has said that it was ready to share any enhancement made on planned profile of a field with Shell. Opportunities The steering committee set up by the two entities to manage co-operation between the two companies, following a memorandum of understanding inked between the oil sector behemoths, is looking into these aspects. Opening the doors for a possible participation in overseas projects as well as domestic ventures, earlier this year ONGC and Shell Exploration Company B.V. (subsidiary of the world's third largest petroleum group Royal Dutch Shell) had inked an understanding to examine significant opportunities for future co-operation both in India and other countries. The MoU covered wide areas of cooperation across the full range of upstream and downstream activities, including exploration and production, coal gasification, natural gas, oil products, refining and petrochemicals. The areas of cooperation in the upstream sector included investigation of increasing and enhancing production from existing producing fields in the country, joint bidding in exploration acreage rounds in India. The cooperation also includes farming into existing, but undeveloped Indian exploration blocks, investigation of opportunities for cooperation and joint participation in international upstream ventures from Shell and ONGC's portfolios, and evaluation of a joint project for coal gasification facilities in the country.

Source: http://www.blonnet.com/2006/09/29/stories/2006092904270200.htm

3. Organisational Growth

Organisational structure is a means to an end of achieving organisational mission and objectives. Thus, it is an important means for strategic implementation. Organisational structure refers to the methods of allocating duties and responsibilities to individuals, and the ways that individuals are grouped together into units, departments and divisions. The formal organisational structure represents the relationships between people and functions as designated by management and conveyed in the organisation chart. It also defines the number of levels in the organisational hierarchy. The informal organisational structure represents the web of social relationships among various members of a company.

4. Organisational Structures and Strategies

Companies build structures for their organisations based on their strategies. There are a number of methods/ways that the organisations can be structured. The simple strategies require simple structures whereas the growth strategies require flexible structure and complex strategies necessarily influence to build matrix structures. In fact, the stable strategies require a mechanistic organisation and a growth strategy require an organic structure.

5. Entrepreneurial Structure

Generally, the small businesses and businesses when they are started consist of an owner-manager and few employees. (Fig. 5.1) These types of organisations do not require an organisational chart and formal assignment of responsibilities. Organisation structure is fluid with each employee often knowing how to perform more than one task and with owner-manager involved in all aspects/areas of business.

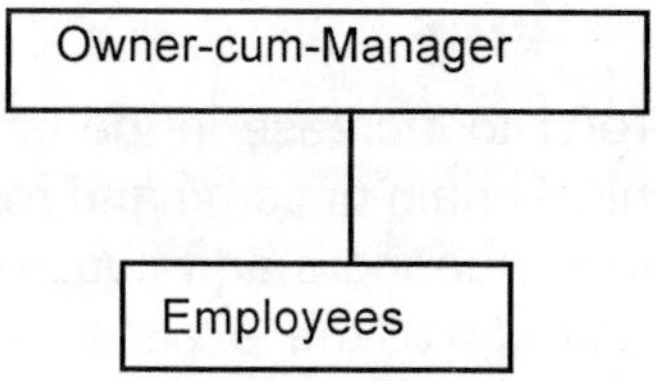

Fig. 5.1: Entrepreneurial Organisation Structure (Start-up)

The small firms, if, they are successful during the first years of crucial periods, it would be due to the increased demand for products or services. The entrepreneurs develop the business and increase the size of the firm to meet the increased demand. The business begins to evolve from fluidity to a status of more permanent division of labour due to the growth. The owner-manager, who was performing all functions in the initial stage now finds that he has to perform more managerial activities than operational activities. The growth demands the owner to employ new candidates and this results in assignment of specialised functions to these employees.

The business growth results in expansion of organisational structure both vertically and horizontally. The entrepreneurial organisational structure with growth is depicted in Fig. 5.2. As can be seen from this figure, the operative functions of manufacturing are assigned to manufacturing manager and the operative functions of marketing are assigned to the marketing manager. These two managers perform the activities with the help of employees. The owner-manager performs managerial and strategic functions.

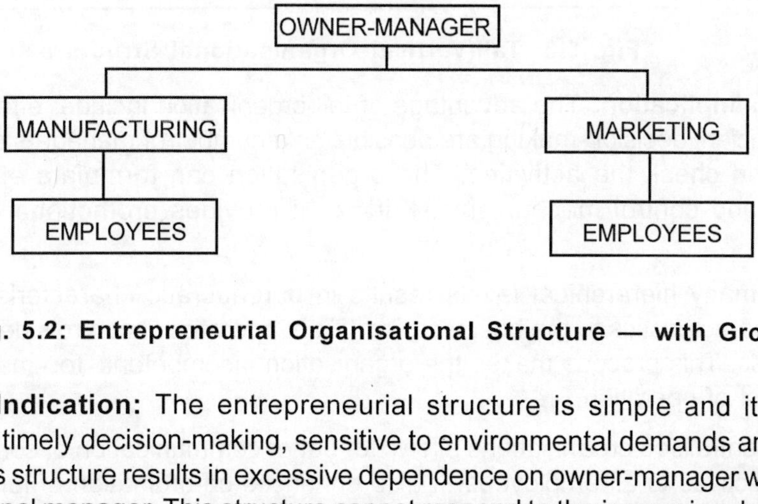

Fig. 5.2: Entrepreneurial Organisational Structure — with Growth

Strategic Indication: The entrepreneurial structure is simple and it offers some advantages like: timely decision-making, sensitive to environmental demands and operational flexibility. But, this structure results in excessive dependence on owner-manager who is normally is not a professional manager. This structure cannot respond to the increasing demand beyond a point. Thus, this structure is mostly suitable to the strategy catering to the needs of a local market by being small.

6. Vertical/Tall Organisations

Vertical/Tall organisations refer to increase in the length of the organisation's hierarchy chain of command. The hierarchical chain of command represents the company's authority – accountability relationship between superiors and subordinates. Authority and responsibility flows from the top to the bottom through all the levels of the hierarchy. Accountability flow from the lowest level to the highest level. Fig. 5.3 shows the vertical/tall organisation. Employees at each level should report to their superior, who in turn should report to boss. Thus, the activities are reported to the top. Authority is more centralised in tall organisation.

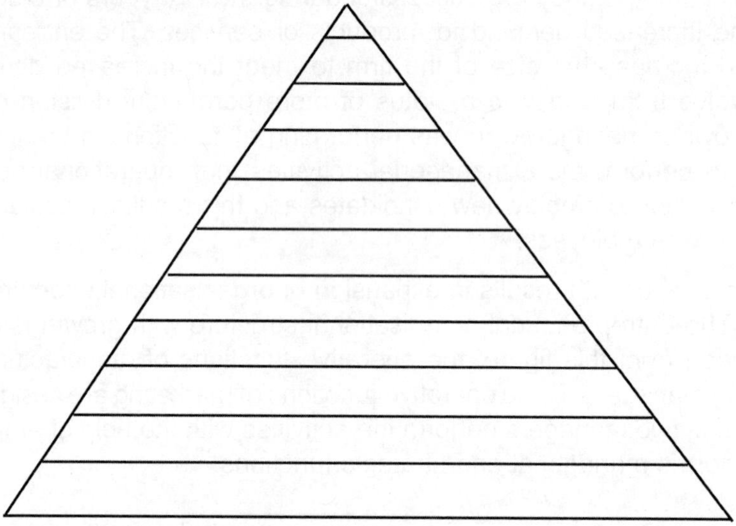

Fig. 5.3: Tall/Vertical Organisational Structure

Strategic Implication: The advantage of tall organisation include: effective analysis of factors and efficient decision-making are possible as a number of managers at different levels supervised and check the activities. The organisation can formulate effective policies, programmes and control mechanisms. Further, it provides promotional avenues to the employees.

But, too many hierarchical levels results in bureaucratic characteristics rather than commercial characteristics to the business firm. Tight operational controls delay the decision-making process. This process makes the organisation incompetent. Too many controls may reduce the cost of operation.

Tall and centralised organisations allows for better communication of company's mission, goals and objectives to all employees. It also enhances co-ordination of functional areas to ensure that each area will work closely with the other functions. Since, all employees are centrally directed, co-ordination becomes possible.

Tall organisational structure is appropriate for the firms having bleak growth opportunities, problem children and dogs. Further, firms with cost minimisation strategy and firms in maturity stage can adopt tall organisations. Thus, this type of structures are well suited for environments that are relatively stable and predictable.

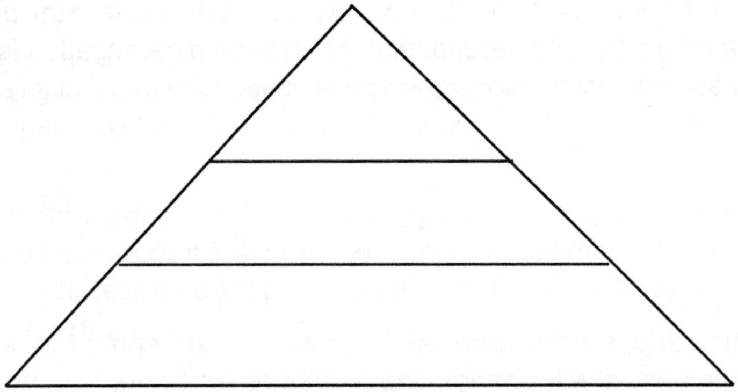

Fig. 5.4: Flat/Horizontal Organisational Structure

Horizontal/Flat Organisations: Horizontal/flat organisations refer to an increase in breadth of an organisation's structure. Fig. 5.4 presents the model of horizontal/flat organisation. The number of levels in the organisational hierarchy are a few. The span of control is relatively large.

The increasing bio-professionalisation and multi-professionalisation and wide acceptance for empowerment allowed even the large business firms to reduce the number of hierarchical levels of their organisations. Consequently, large sized firms also started adopting horizontal/flat organisation by delayering. In fact, this structure is well suited for the small size business firms.

Authority is more decentralised in relatively flat structures. Managers with broad span of control must grant more authority to his subordinates. Decisions are more likely to be made by the employees who are at the helm of affairs and more familiar with the situations and ground realities. Organisational activities are mostly performed informally. Professional managers are treated as real professionalists.

Strategy Implications: The major advantage of flat structure is quick decision-making. Thus, it enables the management to take decisions in right time. Other advantages of this structure include: low administrative costs, freedom and autonomy to the managers to operate, decision-making by the managers who are at helm of affairs and empowerment of managers. These benefits motivate the managers to accept responsibility and commit themselves towards organisational objectives. Further, these characteristics enable the organisation to be duly sensitive to the environmental demands. The employees also become innovative and creative.

The horizontal/flat organisational structure are appropriate for the organisations with horizontal and vertical growth strategies, stars and cash cows. Thus, these structures are useful for competitive and dynamic business firms.

(D) ORGANISATIONAL STRUCTURE

Organisational structure is an established pattern of relationships among the component parts of an organisation. Structure is made up of three component parts, *viz.*, complexity, formalisation and centralisation. Complexity refers to horizontal differentiation, vertical differentiation and locational differentiation. Horizontal differentiation is horizontal separation between units based on occupations and specialisations. Vertical differentiation is the potential for communication distortion. Locational differentiation refers to the degree to which the location of an organisation's offices, plants and personnel are geographically spread.

Formalisation refers to the degree to which the jobs within the organisation are standardised. High standardisation of jobs results in less freedom and discretion. Centralisation refers to the degree to which decision-making is concentrated at a single point in an organisation.

Initially, firms adopt a structure. As it grows, in size, spread into new businesses, new geographical regions, it will change the structure and adopt new type of organisational structures. Many companies change their structures as and when there is a change in their strategies and/or size.

Efficient strategy implementation largely depends on appropriate organisational structure. Structuring an appropriate organisation should be a top priority for the strategist.

Matching Organisation Structure to Strategy

Every strategy is grounded in its own set of key success factors and critical tasks. Therefore, the internal organisation structure should be designed around the key success factors and critical tasks. The following five-sequence procedure is a useful guide for fitting organisational structure to strategy.

1. Pinpoint the key functions and tasks necessary for successful strategy execution.
2. Reflection on how strategy-critical functions and organisational units relate to those that are routine and to those that provide staff support.
3. Make strategy-critical business units and functions of the main organisational building blocks.
4. Determine the degrees of authority needed to manage each organisational unit bearing in mind both the benefits and costs of decentralised decision-making.
5. Provide the co-ordination among the various organisational units.

1. Strategy-critical Activities

Some activities and skills are generally critical in the execution of a strategy. In fact, much of the activities are performed in a routine manner even in the process of strategy implementation. The critical tasks to be performed only for strategy implementation include: tight cost control when the firm adopts the strategy of low-cost producer, special promotional appeal, tight quantity control to produce zero defect products, critical skills to produce distinctly qualitative products, and special design of the produce, when the company adopts the strategy of market leader. The critical activities in high-tech industries include: research and development, product innovation, developing new products, developing new uses of existing products, taking the laboratory results into the market quickly, testing the new products in the market, etc. Thus, the strategy-critical activities vary according to the nature of the firm and competitive situation of the firm.

The firm in order to decide on the type of organisation structure should know the special tasks/functions to be performed and the right time for effective strategy execution. Further, the firm should also find out the vulnerable areas where malperformance of the tasks/functions seriously endanger strategic success. This effort will enable the management to concentrate on the crucial areas in organisation building efforts.

Understanding the Relationships among Activities

The strategic relationship among the critical, supportive and routine activity groups should be analysed and scrutinised. Activities or functions can be related by the flow of material, production process, types of customers served, distribution channels used, the intermediaries used, technical skills and know-how necessary to perform the activities, sequence or the order in which the activities must be performed, geographical location help in grouping and regrouping of activities in the organisation restructuring or redesigning process.

Grouping Activities into Organisation Units

The strategy critical activities should be used as the main building blocks in structuring the organisation. The strategy-critical activities must receive the attention and be the prominent parts in the organisation rebuilding scheme. The role and power of the key and critical groups should be duly recognised. Further, adequate resources should be allocated to these critical activities. All this would be possible by grouping the key and strategy-critical areas. Top management should be informed about the significance of the strategy-critical areas in the strategy execution. The managers in charge of these areas should be given influential position in the newly built organisational structure.

Determining the Degree of Authority and Independence to Each Unit

The tall organisations are normally centralised. The decision-making authority in these firms is highly centralised. The strategies are formulated by only top management. Even the policy decisions are made at top management level. The lower level managers are delegated with the limited authority to make operational decisions.

The flat organisations are highly decentralised. Enough authority to formulate strategies, modify strategies, make policy and operational decisions is delegated to the managers at all levels. In fact, some organisations empower their managers to function independently, with little direct authority exerted by corporate staff.

Guidelines for Delegating Authority: Strategies have to be implemented by the managers at different levels, but not only by the top management. In fact, the middle and lower level managers play a key role in strategy implementation. Hence, adequate authority should be delegated to the middle and lower level managers. The guidelines include:

(i) Activities and organisational units with a crucial role in strategy implementation process should not be subordinate to routine and non-key activities.

(ii) Revenue-producing and results producing activities should not be subordinate to internal support or staff functions.

(iii) Authority to make strategic and policy decisions should be delegated to the level of helm of affairs, particularly, when lower level managers can make better decisions, in right time than high level managers.

(iv) However, the final authority to make strategic decisions should rest with the top management for consistency and uniformity.

(v) Select the key jobs and competent managers and appoint the right and competent manager as head of each unit.

(vi) Delegate enough authority to these competent managers to formulate and implement strategies.

(vii) Do not delegate authority to incompetent managers, managers who consistently produce unsatisfactory results and managers who have a poor track record in strategy formulation and implementation.

(viii) Centralise the authority of strategy formulation, execution and decision-making in diversified companies with related businesses in their portfolio.

Co-ordination among Units

Co-ordination among key units and between key units and other units is important in the process of strategy execution. Generally, the managers with authority should perform this task. The chief executive, the chief operating manager, the strategic business unit level managers should perform the co-ordination tasks as their positions have enough authority over the entire unit. The strategy formulation procedure should take care of co-ordination among all the units and/or managers. The functions of co-ordination should be centralised even in case of diversification strategies into related and unrelated areas.

2. The Structure-Follows-Strategy Thesis

The practice of matching organisation structure to the particular needs of strategy is a fairly recent and research based management development. Alfred Chandler, in his research study found that changes in a company's strategy bring about new administrative problems, which in turn, require a new or refashioned structure for the new strategy to be successfully implemented. A company's internal organisation should be reassessed whenever strategy changes. Otherwise, internal problems would crop-up and result in failure in strategy implementation. Structure follows strategy as organisational structure is only a means to an end rather than end itself. Organisational structure is a managerial tool in the process of achievement of organisational objectives. It is easy to coordinate strategic moves across functional areas, if functions, activities and responsibilities are efficiently organised to link strategy and structure.

(E) APPROACHES TO ORGANISATIONAL STRUCTURE

There are six approaches to structure the organisation. They are: (1) Functional organisation structure, (2) Product organisation structure, (3) Geographical organisation structure, (4) Decentralised business divisions, (5) Strategic business units, (6) Matrix organisational structure, (7) Team Structure and (8) Virtual Structure.

1. Functional Organisation Structure

Functional organisation structure is most widely used structure. Each functional department consists of those jobs in which employees perform similar jobs at different levels. The commonly used functions are: marketing, finance and accounting, human resources, manufacturing, research and development and engineering. Fig. 5.5 illustrates a typical functional structure.

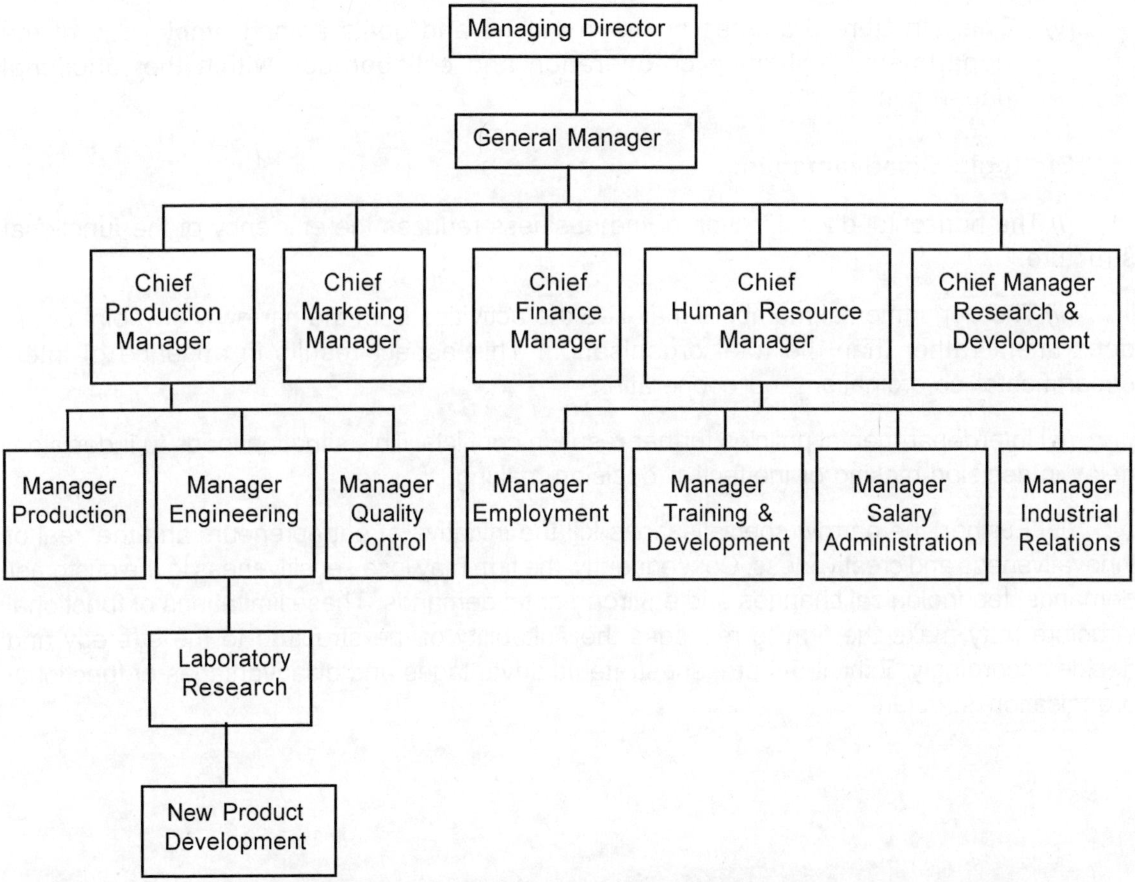

Fig. 5.5: A Functional Organisation Structure

Strategic Advantages:

(i) A functional structure would be effective in single business firms where key activities revolve around well defined skills and areas of specialisation.

(ii) Indepth specialisation and focussed concentration on performing functional tasks can enhance operating efficiency and the development of core competencies.

(iii) This type of structure promotes maximum utilisation of up-to-date technical skills and enables the firm to capitalise on specialisation and efficiency. These are strategically important considerations for single business companies, dominant product companies and vertically integrated companies.

(iv) The functional structure is most appropriate when firms compete on the basis of technical specialisation or efficiency in a relatively stable environment.

(v) This structure promotes common values and goals among employees of the department, facilitating co-operation and collaboration within the functional department.

Strategic Disadvantages:

(i) The horizontal diversification of the business reduces the efficiency of the functional structure.

(ii) The departmental members may see the activities from the narrow view point of the department rather than the total organisation. This aspect results in absence of inter-departmental co-ordination and cooperation.

(iii) Interdepartmental policies further result in conflicts. This situation leads to indecision, delay in decision-making or ineffective decision-making.

(iv) Further, the narrow specialisations kill the initiative of entrepreneurs and the zeal of innovativeness and creativeness. Consequently, the firm may lose sensitiveness to the customer demands, technological changes and environmental demands. These limitations of functional structure may make the firm to reassess the suitability of the structure to the strategy and decide accordingly. Exhibit 5.4 present strategic advantages and disadvantages of functional organisation structure.

Exhibit 5.4: Strategic Advantages and Disadvantages of Functional Organisational Structure

Strategic Advantages	Strategic Disadvantages
• Permits centralised control of strategic results. • Very well suited for structuring a single business. • Structure is linked tightly to strategy by designating key activities as functional departments. • Promotes in-depth functional expertise. • Well suited to developing a functional based distinctive competence. • Conducive to exploiting learning/experience curve effects associated with functional specialisation. • Enhances operating efficiency where tasks are routine and repetitive. • Encourages collaborative work. • Results in economies of scale. • Minimises duplication. • Permits congruence of goals.	• Poses problems of functional co-ordination. • Can lead to inter-functional rivalry and conflict, rather than co-operation. • May promote over-specialisation and narrow management view points. • Hinders development of managers with cross-functional experience because the ladder of advancement is up the ranks within the same functional area. • Forces profit responsibility to the top. • Functional specialists often attach more importance to what is best for the functional area than what is best for the total business — can lead to functional empire building. • Functional myopia often works against creative entrepreneurship, adapting to change and attempts to restructure the activity-cost chain. • Effective only in stable environment. • Results in slower response to change. • Results in poor co-ordination. • Results in absence of accountability.

Source: Modified version: Thompson and Strickland, *op. cit.*, p. 225.

2. Product Organisation Structure

Activities are divided on the basis of individual products, product line, services and are grouped into departments in product organisation structure. All important functions, *viz.*, marketing, production, finance and human resource are contained within each department. This type of organisation structure overcomes many of the major limitations of functional organisational structure. Fig. 5.6 presents the product organisation structure.

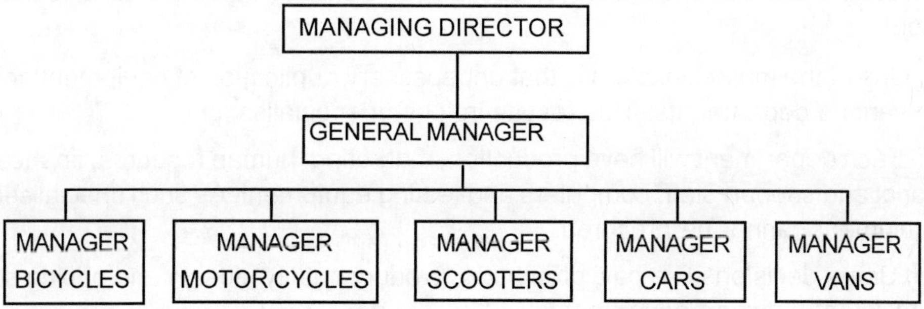

Fig. 5.6: Product Organisational Structure

Strategic Advantages:

(i) The product organisation structure is more appropriate than the functional form of organisation for firms producing multiple products.

(ii) Co-ordination among functional areas like product design, producing, distributing, marketing is effective as all functions are performed in each department.

(iii) Since, each department is independent, most of the decisions can be made at departmental level without involving the top management in this process. It will result in fast decisions, enhancement of organisational competency to compete in rapidly changing environment.

(iv) Responsibility and accountability for market share, sales, profit/loss is clearly fixed. Thus, either the credit for the success or blame for the failure of a product can be clearly attributed to a particular department. This advantage cannot present in case of functional organisation structure. Exhibit 5.5 present strategic advantages and disadvantages.

Exhibit 5.5: Strategic Advantages and Disadvantages of Product Organisation Structure

Strategic Advantages	Strategic Disadvantages
• Appropriate for organisations with multiple products. • Improves coordination across functions. • Suited to a more dynamic environment. • Moves decisions close to the problem. • Release Managing Director's time • Clarifies profit/loss accountability.	• Result in inconsistent decisions from one department to another. • Involves difficulty in allocating overheads. • Results in duplication of equipment and personnel. • Encourages dysfunctional competition for resources. • Results in loss of specialisation. • Emphasises departmental rather than organisational goals.

Source: Modified Version: Joe G. Thomas, op. cit., p. 266.

Strategic Disadvantages: Product organisational structure is also not free from limitations:

(i) One of the major limitation is that unnecessary duplication of equipment and personnel among various departments. This results in loss of specialisation.

(ii) Each department will have production, marketing, human resource, finance managers, secretarial and support staff, computers and testing equipment. As such specialised personnel and equipment cannot be procured.

(iii) Some decisions like pay, promotion, product quality, design and pricing strategy may be inconsistent between departments.

(iv) Interdepartmental conflicts arise regarding sharing of common resources, allocation of common and overhead expenses, etc.

3. Geographical Organisation Structure

The activities or functions are grouped into departments based on the activities performed in the geographical areas/regions. Each geographical unit includes all functions required to produce and market the products in a particular geographical area. Figure 5.7 presents a geographical organisation structure. Multinational organisations, enterprises operating in diverse geographic markets or serving an expansive geographic area are organised based on the geographic structure. This structure is also used by chain stores, power companies, restaurant chains, dairy products, banking companies, insurance companies, etc.

Strategic Advantages: The advantages of this type of organisational structure are:

(i) Products and services are better designed to the climatic and cultural needs of specific geographical regions.

(ii) A geographical structure allows a firm to respond to the technical needs of different international area.

(iii) Producing and distributing products in different national or global locations may give the organisation to serve better the consumer needs of various nations.

(iv) This organisation structure enables a company to adapt to varying legal systems.

(v) It also allow firms pinpoint the responsibility for profits or losses.

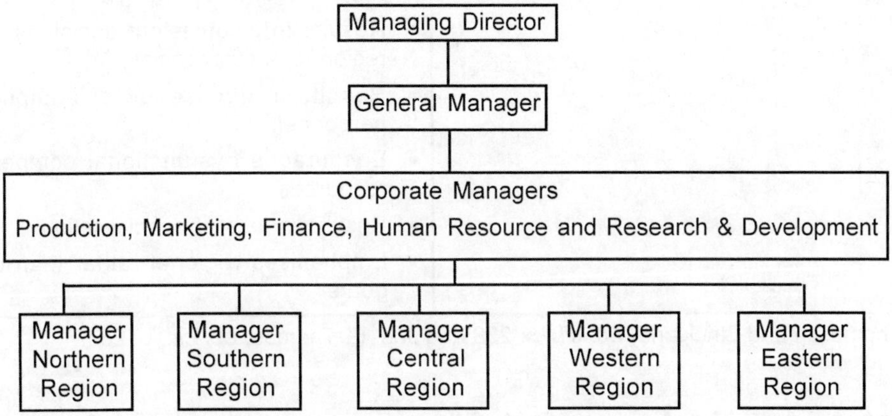

Fig. 5.7: Geographical Organisation Structure

Strategic Disadvantages: This organisational structure is also not free from limitations. The limitations of this structure are similar to those of product structure.

(i) Often more functional personnel are required. The firm cannot appoint specialists unlike in functional structure due to duplication of personnel.

(ii) There would be duplication of equipment and facilities.

(iii) Co-ordination of company-wide activities would be difficult.

(iv) There would be a problem of imposing a degree of uniformity and diversity.

(v) It is difficult to maintain consistent company image or reputation.

(vi) This structure adds another layer of management to run the geographic units. Strategic advantages and disadvantages are presented in Exhibit 5.6.

Exhibit 5.6: Strategic Advantages and Disadvantages of Geographical Organisation Structure	
Strategic Advantages	**Strategic Disadvantages**
• Allows tailoring of strategy to needs of each geographical market. • Delegates profit/loss responsibility to lowest strategic level. • Improves functional coordination within the target market. • Takes advantages of economies of local operations. • Area units make an excellent training ground for higher level general managers. • Clarifies profit/loss accountability. • Results in good functional co-ordination.	• Poses a problem of how much geographic uniformity headquarters should impose versus how much geographic diversity should be allowed. • Greater difficulty in maintaining consistent company image/reputation from area to area when area managers exercise much strategic freedom. • Adds another layer of management to run the geographic units. • Can result in duplication of staff services at headquarters and regional levels, creating a relative cost disadvantage. • Results in inconsistent decisions from one region to another region. • Results in duplication of equipment and personnel. • Encourages dysfunctional competition for resources. • Results in loss of specialisation. • Emphasises regional rather than company goals.

Source: Thompson and Strickland, *op. cit.*, p. 226 and Joe. G. Thomas, *op. cit.*, p. 267.

4. Decentralised Business Unit Structure

Grouping activities based on product lines has been a trend among diversified companies since 1920. In a diversified firm, the basic organisational building blocks are its business units, each business is operated as a stand-alone profit centre. Fig. 5.8 presents decentralised line of business type of organisational structure.

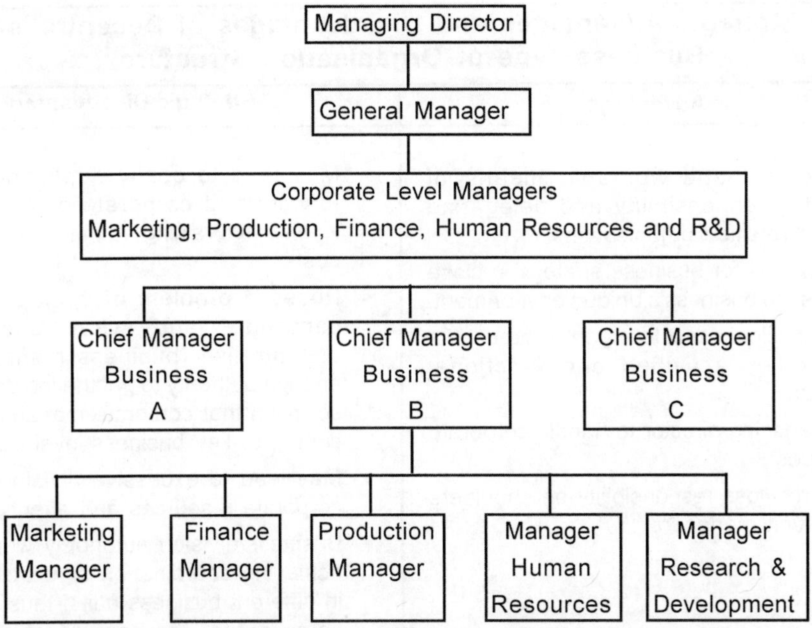

Fig. 5.8: Decentralised Line of Business Type of Organisation Structure

Strategic Advantages: Functional structure and geographic structure are standard organisational building blocks in a single business firm. But, in multi-business firms, the businesses are diversified.

(i) Diversification is generally managed by decentralised decision-making and delegating authority and responsibility to a manager at each business unit.

(ii) Each business unit should be managed by an entrepreneurially oriented general manager who is delegated with authority to formulate and execute business strategies.

(iii) Each business unit operates as a stand-alone profit centre. Each business unit is structured on the basis of either functional structure or geographic structure depending upon strategy, key activities and operating requirements.

Strategic Disadvantages: The strategic advantages and strategic disadvantages of a decentralised line-of-business type of organisation structure are presented in Exhibit 5.7. The disadvantages are:

(i) The major problem of this type of organisation structure is absence of mechanism for coordinating related activities across business units.

(ii) General manager in-charge of each business unit functions independently. It makes co-ordination a complicated task. Therefore, corporate headquarters must devise some internal mechanism for achieving strategic co-ordination and to capture strategic benefits. Co-ordination can be achieved by developing corporate R&D department, corporate sales force, sales force of closely related businesses, merging the order processing and shipping functions of businesses with common customers and consolidating the production of related parts.

Exhibit 5.7: Strategic Advantages and Disadvantages of Decentralised Line of Business Type of Organisation Structure

Strategic Advantages	Strategic Disadvantages
• Offers a logical and workable means of decentralising responsibility and delegating authority in diversified organisations. • Puts responsibility for business strategy in close proximity to each business's unique environment. • Allows each business unit to organise around its own set of key activities and functional requirements. • Frees the managing director to handle corporate strategy issues. • Puts clear profit/loss responsibility on shoulders of business-unit managers.	• May lead to costly duplication of staff functions at corporate or business unit levels, thus raising administrative overhead costs. • Poses a problem of what decisions to centralise and what decisions to decentralise (business managers need enough authority to get the job done, but not so much that corporate management loses control of key business-level decisions). • May lead to excessive division rivalry for corporate resources and attention. • Business/division autonomy works against achieving coordination of related activities in different business units, thus blocking to some extent the capture of strategic fit benefits. • Corporate management becomes heavily dependent on business-unit managers. • Corporate managers can lose touch with business unit situations, end-up surprised when problems arise, and not know much about how to fix such problems.

Source: Thompson and Strickland, *op. cit.*, p. 229.

The corporate managers can also build up strategic fit relationship involving skill transfer and technology transfer across business units. Corporate office can set up inter-business task forces, standing committees, or project teams for the purpose of skills transfer and technology transfer.

5. Strategic Business Unit Structure

A single chief executive cannot control a number of decentralised units of a broadly diversified company. The business can be effectively controlled, if the related businesses are grouped into strategic units and the efficient and senior executive is delegated with the authority and responsibility for its management. The senior executive will in turn report the matter to the chief executive. This arrangement will improve strategic planning and implementation, though, it adds one layer in the organisational hierarchy. Top management coordinates the interests of the diversified business units.

A strategic business unit is a grouping of business subsidiaries based on some important strategic elements common to each. The common or related elements could be an overlapping set of competitors, a closely related strategic mission, a common need to compete globally, an ability to accomplish integrated strategic planning, common key success factors and technologically related growth opportunities. Fig. 5.9 presents SBU type of organisation structure.

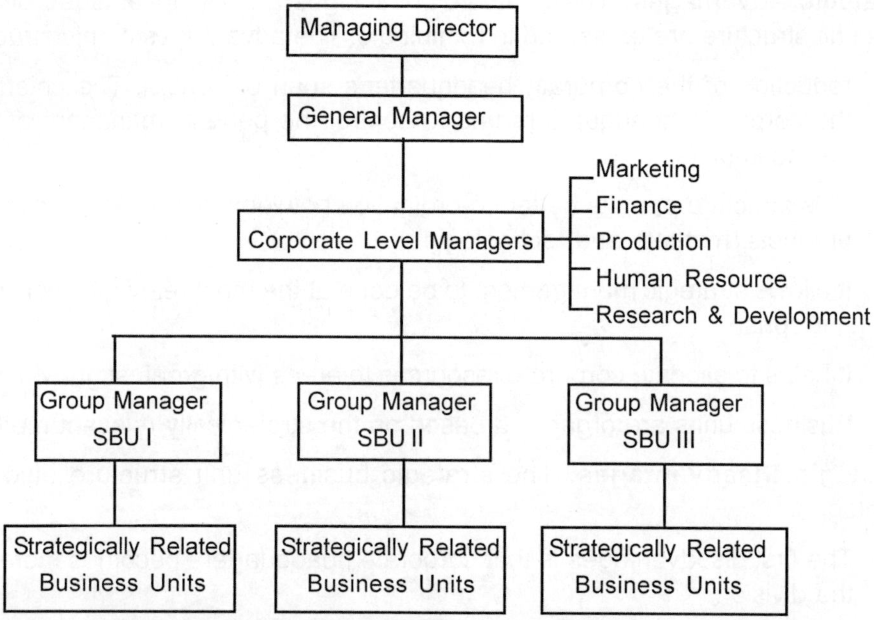

Fig. 5.9: Strategic Business Unit Type of Organisation Structure

Exhibit 5.8: Strategic Advantages and Disadvantages of Strategic Business Unit (SBU) Type of Organisation Structure

Strategic Advantages	Strategic Disadvantages
• Provides a strategically relevant way to organise the business unit portfolio of a broadly diversified company. • Facilitates the coordination of related activities within an SBU, thus helping to capture the benefits of strategic fit in the SBU. • Promotes more cohesiveness among the new initiatives of separate but related businesses. • Allows strategic planning to be done at the most relevant level within the total enterprise. • Makes the task of strategic review by top executives more objective and more effective. • Helps allocate corporate resources to areas with greatest growth opportunities. • Improves coordination among businesses facing similar strategic issues.	• It is easy for the definition and grouping of business into SBUs to be so arbitrary that the SBU serves no other purpose than administrative convenience. • If the criteria for defining SBUs are rationalisations and have little to do with the nitty-gritty of strategy coordination, then the groupings lose real strategic significance. • The SBUs can still be myopic in charting their future direction. • Adds another layer to top management. • The roles and authority of the managing director, general manager, SBU level managers have to be carefully worked out. • Unless the SBU head is strong willed, very little strategy coordination is likely to occur across business units in the SBU. • Performance recognition gets blurred; credit for successful business units tends to go to corporate managing director, then to business unit head, last to group manager. • Increases layers of management. • May result in SBU goals that differ from corporate goals.

Source: Thompson and Strickland, *op. cit.*, p. 231.

Strategic Advantages: The strategic advantages and disadvantages of the strategic business unit structure are presented in Exhibit 5.8. The advantages of this structure include:

(i) reduction of the corporate headquarter's span of control. The chief executive at the corporate headquarters has to control the general managers of the strategic business units.

(ii) This structure permits better co-ordination between divisions with similar missions, products, markets and technologies.

(iii) It allows strategic management to be done at the most relevant level within the total enterprise.

(iv) It helps to allocate corporate resources to areas with greatest growth opportunities.

(v) Business units are organised based on the strategically relevant method.

Strategic Disadvantages: The strategic business unit structure also has certain disadvantages.

(i) The first disadvantages is that corporate headquarters becomes more distant from the division.

(ii) conflicts between/among the strategic business unit managers for greater share of corporate resources can become dysfunctional.

(iii) Corporate portfolio analysis becomes complicated one in this structure.

6. Matrix Organisation Structure

Organisational structures discussed earlier have possessed a single chain of command. In other words, employees in those structures reports to only one manager. But, the organisation structure possesses a dual chain of command. Both functional and project managers exercise authority over organisational activities, in matrix structure. Thus personnel in this structure have two superiors, *viz.,* a project manager and the manager of the functional department. Fig. 5.10 presents the matrix organisational structure.

A matrix organisational structure is appropriate when:

(i) Management attention must be focussed on two or more key issues (technical issues, consumer needs, functional efficiency).

(ii) Large amounts of diverse information need to be processed.

(iii) Problem solving is complex (environmental uncertainty, interdependence among organisational units, complex products or technology).

(iv) Economies of scale require the sharing of human resource expertise to achieve high performance.

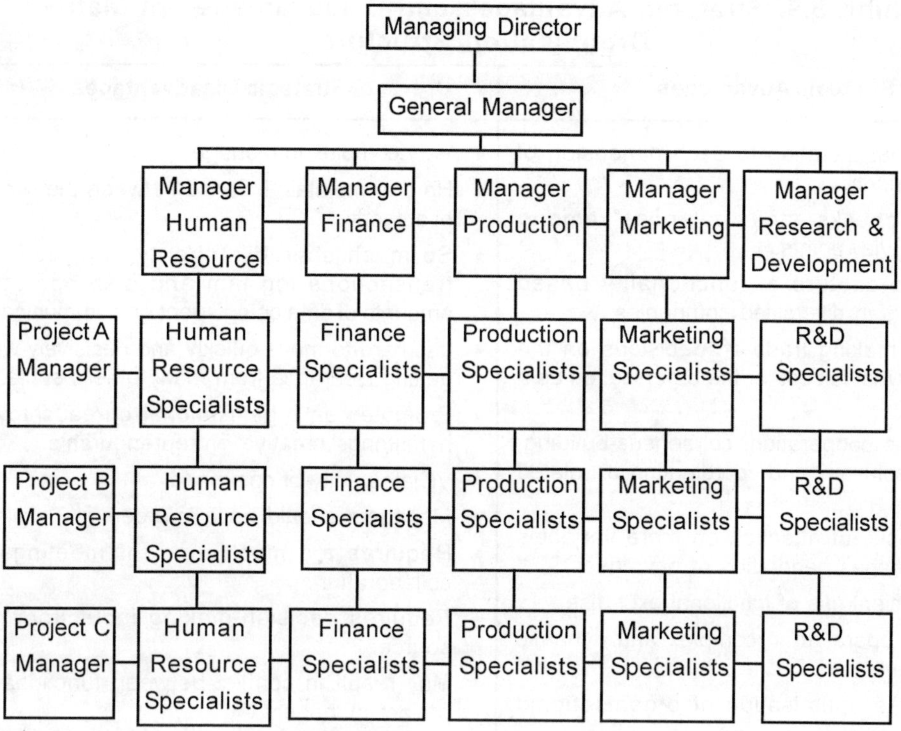

Fig. 5.10: Matrix Organisation Structure

Strategic Advantages: The matrix structure is commonly used in the firms whose technological change is rapid. The advantages of matrix structure include:

(i) the company can have the advantages of both project type of organisational structure and functional organisation structure.

(ii) Functional personnel are paid for their services whenever they are used by project managers. This practice enables the management to reduce the cost.

(iii) This structure has considerable flexibility. The personnel can be transferred from one project to the other depending upon the need of the project.

(iv) The lower level functional employees are highly motivated and satisfied with their job as they are involved in decision-making.

(vi) Each project manager is in-charge of a unit. Therefore, he can be developed as a general manager through performing general managerial functions. Exhibit 5.9 presents the strategic advantages and strategic disadvantages of matrix organisational structure.

Exhibit 5.9: Strategic Advantages and Disadvantages of Matrix Organisation Structure

Strategic Advantages	Strategic Disadvantages
• Gives formal attention to each dimension of strategic priority. • Creates checks and balances among competing viewpoints. • Facilitates capture of functionality based strategic fits in diversified companies. • Promotes making trade-off decisions on the basis of, "What is best for the organisation as a whole." • Encourages cooperation, consensus-building, conflict resolution and coordination of related activities. • Permits focus of attention on more variables and encourages generation of new ideas. • Makes efficient use of functional expertise. • Facilitates operation in complex and dynamic environment. • Encourages optimisation of organisational goals. • Managers are aware of strategic issues.	• Very complex to manage • Hard to maintain balance between the two lines of authority. • So much shared authority can result in a transactions log jam and disproportionate amounts of time being spent on communications. • It is hard to move quickly and decisively without getting clearance from many other people. • Promotes an organisational bureaucracy and hamstrings creative entrepreneurship. • Violates unity of command. • Managers should have interpersonal skills. • Requires too much time for meetings and collaboration. • Requires decision-making input from many sources. • May result in conflict between functional and project managers.

Source: Thompson and Strickland, *op. cit.*, p. 232 and Joe G. Thomas *op. cit.*, p. 269.

Strategic Disadvantages: The significant strategic disadvantages of matrix organisational structure include:

(i) greater administrative costs associated with its operation. Personnel spend much of their time in meetings and exchanging of information to coordinate functional areas with projects.

(ii) In view of the two forms associated in this structure, they are characterised by conflicts. The most critical conflict is between functional managers and project managers.

(iii) Functional employees experience stress by working in matrix structure. Reporting to two bosses, creates role ambiguity and role conflict. Some companies reverted their organisational structures back to traditional structures from matrix structures due to these problems.

7. Team Organisation Structure

Strategies of business are not always static. They go on changing depending upon internal and external environmental factors. Hence, a single type of organisational structure is not suitable for all situations. Blending the basic forms of organisation to match the structure to strategy in the units concerned in essential. Another option is to supplement special situation devices to the basic organisational structure. This option is Team structure.

Team structure takes three forms, *viz., (i)* Project Team, *(ii)* Task Force Team, and *(iii)* Venture Team.

(i) *Project Team:* Project teams are created to handle special kind of situations with a finite life expectancy. Project teams are self-sufficient work groups. These are created to supervise the completion of a special activity. The special activities include: setting up a new technological process, starting up a new venture, producing a new product, initiating and completion of a joint venture and the like.

(ii) *The Task Force Team:* Interdisciplinary assignments necessitate the formation of task force team. A task force team consists of top level executives and specialists in different areas from the organisation. The advantages of special task force team include: increased opportunity for creativity, open communication, cross-functional authority, effective integration of talents, quick conflict resolution, collaborative approach for problem solving.

(iii) *The Venture Team:* Venture team is a group of individuals. The purpose of forming this team is to bring a specific product or a new business into being. The problems of venture team are: *(i)* Difficulty of deciding the manager to whom the report should be made, *(ii)* Source of funding to the venture, *i.e.*, is the source from department or business or corporation *(iii)* problem of coordinating large number of different ventures.

8. Virtual Organisational Structure

There is a Footwear Company. But it does not produce footwear. Small industries in Kanpur, Kharagpur, Tamil Nadu, etc., produce shoes for this company. Shoe Design and Quality Company's executives prescribe the shoe designs, models, specifications, etc., and communicate the same to the small industries through internet. Shoe Design and Quality Company's quality control inspectors inspect the quality of the shoes produced by the small industries and certify them. This company does not sell the shoes to the customers. But the shoe retailing shops throughout the country sell this company's shoes. Transport Corporation of India transports the shoes for this company from the manufacturing points to the retailing outlets. Commuiq Ads advertises for this company. Thus several agencies perform various business functions relating to shoe company, i.e., design, production, logistics and marketing of sales which are connected through a social network which operate in physically dispersed locations by different electronic devices like phones, mobile phones, internet, etc. This company is called virtual organisation.

Virtual organisation, according to Biswajeet Pattanayak, is a "social network in which all the horizontal and vertical boundaries are removed. It consists of individuals working out of physically dispersed workspaces, or even individuals working from mobile devices and not tied to any particular workspace. It is the co-ordination intense structure, consisting primarily of patterns and relationships, and this form needs the communication and information technology to function."

Virtual organisation is an organisation that exists in the minds of stakeholders, as a network or alliances of independent companies that collaboratively pursue a particular business.

Business Week describes virtual organisation as follows:

Technology: Virtual partnerships are based on electronic network among independent companies, some times located in different places.

Excellence: Virtual partnerships draw on the core competencies of each member to create and deliver the best final product and/or service like medical services.

Opportunism: Virtual organisation is based on opportunities available. Once, the opportunities disappear some or all the partners may separate from the network/strategic alliance.

Trust: Partner companies of virtual organisation build and maintain network based on mutual trust and confidence.

No Borders: Partners of the virtual organisation, with their complex network of relationships, make it hard to identify the boundaries among themselves.

Virtual Workplace: People/employees of various partners of virtual organisation, some time may not have a common workplace. They can work from any place and coordinate their activities through internet. Telecommuting/tele-work is quite common in virtual organisations.

Characteristics of Virtual Organisations:

Characteristics of virtual organisations include:

- Flexi-work, Flexitime and Flexi-workplace
- Part-time work
- Job sharing
- Home-based working
- Dependency on information technology like e-mail integration, voice-mail, mobile phone network, computer-telephony integration, etc.
- Loose organisational boundaries
- De-jobbing
- Multi-skilling
- Flexibility in power, work, etc.
- Goal directed
- Customer centred.

Virtual Organisations and Behavioural Implications:

Behavioural implications trends in virtual organisations include:

- Organisation's human resources are the loose web of people;
- Knowledgeable people are hired for short term projects depending upon market demand;
- Employees have autonomy at work but are accountable to the targets, performance, etc.;
- Employees can work from their homes (home-cum-office) or from any other place as such social and work environment do not draw much attention of HR Manager;
- Career planning and development are based on projects;
- Employees are selected based on not only technical skills but their ability to work in teams; and
- Emotional and attitudinal quotient (EAQ) is the prime factor in employee selection rather than intelligence quotient (IQ).

Employees' features in virtual organisations include:

- Self-motivation, adaptability, self-commitment, effective communication, goal/result-orientation, technical competency, multi-skills, etc.;
- Employee performance is managed based on three dimensions *viz.*;
  - (i) Setting performance standards/requirements;
  - (ii) Facilitating performance by providing required facilities, resources, eliminating obstacles, etc.;
  - (iii) Encouraging the employees to perform successfully; and
- Create a network of employees and enable them to create and share information and knowledge.

Advantages:

(i) These structures enable for doing business with less capital, less human resources and other inputs

(ii) These structure provide for flexibility of operations

(iii) These structures react to the environment demands most efficiently

(iv) These structures develop the ancillary industries.

Disadvantages:

(i) Companies do not have strong foundations or strengths in their operations,

(ii) Organisations have to heavily depend on outsourcing,

(iii) Failure in the network results in the failure of the entire organisation.

(F) Matching Structure and Strategy

The suitability of structure to strategy is dependent on a number of situational factors. Absence of fit between strategy and structure leads to inefficient functioning of the company. The stages of organisation development is an important factor that influence the match between strategy and structure.

Stages of Organisation Development

Generally successful companies grow larger in size and diversify their activities. The growth of the company brings a number of changes. These changes include:

(i) Increase in financial resources (gross profits and investments)

(ii) Increase in resource needs (human resources, financial resources, material resources).

(iii) Increase in number of products and markets.

(iv) Increase in operating and managerial specialisation.

(v) Increase in size, complexity and risk of operating and managerial problems.

As organisations develop, the dominant strategic issues change with organisation's developmental changes. The three most frequently discussed stages of development models are those developed by Thain, Cannon and Greiner.

1. Cannon's Stages of Development Model

Cannon developed comprehensive stages of development model. His model consists of five stages of development. He argues that firms are found in one of these five stages of development. Though, Cannon does not contend that firms move through stages, strategic issues facing a firm move with each stage.

Stage I: The Entrepreneurial Stage: As discussed earlier, this stage represents the small business, generally operated by the owner-manager. The market of the firm in limited to a specific geographical area.

Stage II: When the company grows in size, the owner-manager cannot perform increased volume of managerial functions. Therefore, the owner-manager, hires an accountant, sales representatives and other agents. The other functional managers will also be hired with the further increase in the organisational size. A functional form of organisation structure will be adopted. But the problems of functional structure will come to the surface with the further increase in the company's operations. These problems include: delay in getting approval for new products and other innovations. These problems may push the company to the next stage.

Stage III: Organisation will be restructured either based on product or geographic or customers. Control may become difficult when each division develops its own view of product quality, pricing, etc.

Stage IV: To regain control of the organisation, management may employ additional human resources to assist top management.

Stage V: This stage involves increasing involvement of top management in strategic decision making. This move to recentralisation may be as part of a cutback and turnaround strategy.

Exhibit 5.10 depicts Cannon's stages of development model.

Exhibit 5.10: Summary of Cannon's Stages of Development

Characteristics	Entrepreneurial I	Functional Development II	Decentralisation III	Staff Profiteration IV	Recentralisation V
Strategic decisions	Made mostly by the top person	Made more and more by other managers	May have loss of control	Corporate staff assists in decisions	Corporate management makes decisions
Organisation structure	Informal operations	Specialisation based on functions	To cope with problems of functionalisation	Corporate staff assists chief executive	Similar to Stage 1
Communication and climate	From leader down. Informal communication	Internal communication is important, is difficult	By industry or product division	Conservatism may result in slower communications	
Control system	Minimal need for coordination and control	Concerned with everyday situations	Problems with control	May be problems between line and staff	Tightening of control

Source: Adapted from J. Thomas Cannon, *op.cit.*, pp. 525-528. Quoted in P.K. Ghosh, *op. cit.*, p. 302.

2. Thain's Stages of Corporate Development Model

Thain proposed a different conceptualisation of organisational stages of development. Exhibit 5.11 presents Thain's model. It identifies three stages of organisational development with different factors relevant to top management in each stage.

Stage I: Stage of Thain is similar to Cannon's entrepreneurial stage. The manager maintains absolute ownership and control. The company's strengths, weaknesses, and performance are shaped by the owner-manager's personality, ability and style. The increase in the size of the business forces the owner to appoint managers for different functions.

Exhibit 5.11: Thain's Key Management Factors by Stage of Development

Key Factors	Stage I	Stage II	Stage III
1. Size up major problems.	Survival and growth, dealing with short-term operating problems.	Growth, rationalization, and expansion of resources, providing for adequate attention to product problems.	Trusteeship in management and investment and control of large, increasing, and diversified resources. Also important to diagnose and act on problems at division level.
2. Objectives.	Personal and subjective.	Profits and meeting functionally oriented budgets and performance targets.	ROI, profits, earnings per share.
3. Strategy.	Implicit and personal; exploitation of immediate opportunities seen by owner-manager.	Functionally oriented moves restricted to "one-product" scope; exploitation of one basic product or service field.	Growth and product diversification; exploitation of general business opportunities.
4. Organization, major characteristic of structure.	One-unit "one-man show."	One-unit functionally specialized group.	Multi-unit general staff office and decentralized operating divisions.
5. *(a)* Measurement and control.	Personal, subjective, control based on simple accounting system and daily communication and observation.	Control grows beyond one man, assessment of functional operations necessary, structured control systems evolve.	Complex formal system geared to comparative assessment of performance measures, indicating problems and opportunities and assessing management ability of division managers.
(b) Key performance indicators.	Personal criteria, relationships with owner, operating efficiency, ability to solve operating problems.	Functional and internal criteria such as sales, performance compared to budget, size of empire, status in group, personal relationships, etc.	More impersonal application of comparisons such as profits, ROI, P/E ratio, sales, market share, productivity, product leadership, personnel development, employee attitudes, public responsibility.
6. Reward-punishment system.	Informal, personal, subjective; used to maintain control and divide small pool of resources to provide personal incentives for key performers	More structured, usually based to a greater extent on agreed policies as opposed to personal opinion and relationships.	Allotment by "due process" of a wide variety of different rewards and punishments on a formal and systematic basis. Company-wide policies usually apply to many different classes of managers and workers with few major exceptions for individual cases.

Source: D.H. Thain, "Stages of Corporate Development," *Business Quarterly*, Winter 1969.

Stage II: In this stage, there is the existence of a management team built around one business and selling primarily to one market. The company in this stage specialises in one product and concentrates in one area. These characteristics, may threaten the survival of the firm consequent upon changes in consumer preferences or ability to buy. Companies try to overcome this danger by diversifying the activities.

Stage III: The firms in this stage are conglomerate diversified with multiple operating units controlled by corporate office. Companies in this stage can often operate independently of outside resources. But the organisation adopts a bureaucratic structure to manage and control a large size and diversified business.

3. Greiner's Phases of Organisational Growth

Greiner explains how growth affects management style. There are two stages in each phase of Greiner's model. Those stages are: evolution-steady organisational growth period and revolution periods upheaval or turmoil. The accumulated problems in each phase will be solved only when a breaking point is reached. This breaking point causes revolutionary change in organisational structure. Managers should prepare revolutionary change by identifying the phase through which the organisation is passing. Exhibit 5.12 presents the five phases and organisational issues in each phase of Greiner's model.

Exhibit 5.12: Greiner's Five Phases of Growth

Category	Phase 1	Phase 2	Phase 3	Phase 4	Phase 5
Management focus	Make and sell	Efficiency of operations	Expansion of market	Consolidation of organisation	Problem solving and innovation
Organisation structure	Informal	Centralized and functional	Decentralised and geographical	Line-staff and product groups	Matrix of teams
Top management style	Individualistic entrepreneurial	Directive	Delegative	Watchdog	Participative
Control system	Market results	Standards and cost centres	Reports and profit centres	Plans and investment centres	Mutual goal setting
Management reward system	Ownership	Salary and merit increases	Individual bonus	Profit sharing and stock options	Team bonus

Source: Quoted in Joe G. Thomas, *op. cit.*, p. 277.

Phase 1: in this phase, creativity centres around the development of products and markets. Management spends most of the time in solving operating problems, rather than in managing the company. Organisational structure is mostly informal and authority for decision-making is centralised. The growth of the company in size makes the informal organisation ineffective and crisis in management and leadership. The revolution ends this phase by employing functional specialists.

Phase 2: Functional managers improve the organisational efficiency and performance. However, decision-making is centralised among the functional managers. The absence of strategic decision-making authority among the lower level managers results in revolution in autonomy.

Phase 3: This phase is concerned with delegation. Lower-level managers are delegated with strategic decision-making authority for particular products or markets. Top level management concentrates on business growth and diversification. Absence of co-ordination among business units relating to products or markets creates revolution. This revolution leads to Phase 4.

Phase 4: Improvement and maintenance of co-ordination is the main concern in this phase. Co-ordination systems are introduced. Decentralised units are combined into strategic business units. The co-ordination efforts will result in formalised communication system, centralised decision-making, formulation of rules, regulations and controls. These factors result in a bureaucratic organisation, which causes a crisis and brings Phase 5.

Phase 5: This phase strives to enhance collaboration. Behavioural orientation, group working, project teams and matrix structures are adopted to improve problem solving.

Greiner argues that only a limited number of firms have reached Phase 5. Phase 5 brings organisational changes due to the emphasis on behavioural skills and behavioural modification.

4. Leontiades Stages of Growth Model

Leontiade's growth model is one of the recent model. Leontiades states that growth is best understood by examining single business and multi-business firms. Two sub-categories of strategies exist within each classification as presented in Exhibit 5.13.

Exhibit 5.13: Leontiades' Stages of Growth

Single Business Firms

- Small Business
- Dominant Business.

Multi-Business Firms

- Concentric Diversification
- Conglomerate Diversification.

Organisational structure appears to vary between single-business and multi-business firms. Single business firms follow a functional design and multi-business firms use a divisional structure.

(G) ASSESSMENT OF ORGANISATIONAL STRUCTURE

The crucial question is: how a company can implement its strategy by designing appropriate organisational structure. There are no hard-and-fast rules for evaluating the appropriateness of a company's organisation structure. However, the following questions (as presented in Exhibit 5.14) will help in assessing the organisation structure.

Exhibit 5.14: Checklist for Determining Appropriateness of Organisational Structure

1. Is the structure compatible with the corporate profile and the corporate strategy?
2. At the corporate level, is the structure compatible with the firm's business units?
3. Are there too few or too many hierarchical levels at either the corporate or business unit level of analysis?
4. Does the structure promote co-ordination among its parts?
5. Does the structure allow for appropriate centralisation or decentralisation of authority?
6. Does the structure permit the appropriate grouping of activities?

Source: Peter Wright, Charles D. Pringle and Mar J. Kroll, *op. cit.*, p. 165.

1. *Is the structure compatible with the corporate profile and the corporate strategy?*

Companies may be in one business or several related businesses or several unrelated businesses. Functional structure may be viable for single business firms but not viable to the multi-business firms. For the multi-business firms, product or divisional and multi-divisional structure may be appropriate. Therefore, the company should adopt the suitable structure based on its corporate profile.

If the company wants to remain small, a functional structure may be suitable. Alternatively, the multi-divisional structure is appropriate for the continuously growing companies. Therefore, the company's structure should also be compatible with its corporate level strategy.

2. *At the corporate level, is the structure compatible with the firm's business units?*

The firms producing different technical products, should opt for the organisational structure based on product divisional structure. Each division produces the distinct products and markets them. However, the firm producing related products in terms of production and/or marketing, can go for geographic organisational structure. Thus, the structure should be compatible with the firm's business units.

3. *Are there too few or too many hierarchical levels at either the corporate or business unit level of analysis?*

Flat organisations with a few hierarchical levels and wider spans are suitable for dynamic and fast changing firms. Tall organisations with more hierarchical levels and narrow spans are suitable for the stable firms or stable and predictable environments. Different business units of the same company operate in different environments like dynamic and stable. Therefore, different business units of the same company can have different types of organisational structures.

4. *Does the structure promote co-ordination among its parts?*

Different divisions of the organisation need co-ordination at varying degrees. If the company has diversified and unrelated businesses, the minimum level co-ordination among these units is necessary. However, high degree of co-ordination is essential within each business unit. Similarly, high degree of co-ordination is necessary, if the company's has related diversified business units. The co-ordination may become difficult in the complex business organisations. Special permanent co-ordinating units may be established in such organisations.

5. *Does the structure allow for appropriate centralisation or decentralisation of authority?*

The delegation of authority of decision-making depends upon a number of factors. One among them is organisation size. Authority is delegated downward in large organisations compared to the small organisations. The second factor is the number and types of business units. If the company has a number of unrelated business units, the authority is delegated downward compared to that of the company with a number of related business units. The third factor is the type of environment. Companies in relatively changing environments decentralise the authority compared to the companies in relatively stable environment. Therefore, depending upon the environment, the strategy should allow the centralisation or decentralisation.

6. *Does the structure permit the appropriate grouping of activities?*

Structure may be appropriately designed to group the activities appropriately. It facilitates the implementation of the strategy successfully.

(H) PERSPECTIVES ON THE METHODS OF ORGANISING

The above analysis brings two aspects, *viz., (i)* there is no perfect or ideal organisational design, and *(ii)* there are no universally applicable rules for matching strategy and structure. Further, it can be concluded that, two or more organisational structures can be used for different business units of the same company at the same time like functional, geographic and product structures. "The best organisational structure is the one that fits the firm's situation at the moment."

Peter F. Drucker sums up the intricacies of organisation design as:

"The simplest organisation structure that will do the job is the best one. What makes an organisation structure "good" are that it does not create. The simpler the structure, the less that can go wrong.

Some design principles are more difficult and problematic than others. But none is without difficulties and problems. None is primarily people-focussed rather than task-focussed, none is more "creative", "free" or "more democratic". Design principles are tools and tools are neither good nor bad in themselves. They can be used properly or improperly, and that is all.

To obtain both the greatest possible simplicity and the greatest "fit", organisation design has to start out with a clear focus on key activities needed to produce key results. They have to be structured and positioned in the simplest possible design. Above all, the architect of organisation needs to keep in mind the purpose of the structure he is designing."

(I) STRATEGIES FOR COMPETING IN GLOBAL MARKETS

Strategies for competing in global markets include:

(i)	Indirect Exporting	*(ii)*	Direct Exporting	*(iii)*	Licensing
(iv)	Joint Ventures	*(v)*	Direct Investment	*(vi)*	Acquisitions
(vii)	Production Sharing	*(viii)*	Management Contracts	*(ix)*	Turnkey Operations

(i) ***Indirect Exporting:*** Indirect exporting means exporting through independent intermediaries to various countries. There are four types of intermediaries, *viz.,*

(a) *Domestic based exporter:* Domestic based exporter buys the products from the manufacturer and he in turn exports them to various countries.

(b) *Domestic based export agent:* Domestic based export agent negotiates with the domestic producers and foreign purchasers for exports. He co-ordinates the domestic producers and foreign purchasers. He collects commission for his services.

(c) *Co-operative organisation:* A number of producers producing the same or similar products form into a co-operative organisation. This cooperative organisation will carry on exporting activities on behalf of the member producers. This type of arrangement is used by the producers of agricultural products.

(d) *Export management company:* This company manages the exports by charging a fee.

Indirect exports cost less to the producers and the producers can concentrate on the manufacturing as the export arrangements are taken care by the intermediaries.

(ii) ***Direct Exports:*** Companies depend on indirect marketing during the early stage of their exports. Eventually, they may decide to export directly in order to get more benefits and economies of scale. The investment and risk will be greater compared to the indirect exports. Therefore, companies develop a relationship with all stockholders of the foreign market, even before they enter the foreign market.

The methods of direct exports are as follows:

(a) *Domestic Based Export Department or Division:* A separate export department or an export division within the marketing department may be created by the company to look after the exports. This department/division will perform all the functions and complete the procedures relating to exports.

(b) *Overseas Sales Branch or Subsidiary:* The company may establish overseas sales branch(es) in one or more foreign countries. These sales branches perform the functions of export marketing and also fulfil the procedural formalities. These branches also make the host countries to feel the presence of the company. These branches perform customer service in addition to performing other marketing functions in the host country.

(c) *Travelling Export Sales Representatives:* The company can send the sales representatives to various foreign countries to explore business and also to execute the business.

(d) *Foreign Based Distributors or Agents:* The company appoints foreign based distributors or agents to deal with the exports and sell the company's products. These distributors or agents may be given exclusive rights to represent the company and its products. Alternatively, they may be given limited rights as well as responsibilities.

Companies have to participate in international exhibitions and trade fairs and exhibit their products.

(e) *E-Business:* The domestic company can sell directly to the various foreign customers through electronic business by making portals or websites on the internet. Most of the companies have their own websites which are also linked to various search engines of other popular websites like *www.yahoo.com, www.rediff.com, etc.* The companies should make their websites worldwide and worldly-wise. *(See Box 5.5).*

(iii) **Licensing:** Under this approach, the licensor licenses a foreign company to use its production process, trade mark, patent, trade secret or other item value for a fee or royalty. The manufacturer enters a foreign market with a little risk. The foreign company gains the advantages of production expertise or technology or a well-known product without having to start from scratch. Coca-Cola enters different foreign markets by licensing bottlers around the globe. It supplies them syrup, trains the personnel of the foreign companies in producing and selling the product.

There are different forms of licensing arrangement. One form of licensing is management contract. Under this arrangement, a company sells a management contract to the owners of a foreign hotel, airport, hospital or other organisation to manage these businesses for a fee. The firm provides management expertise.

The second form of licensing is contract manufacturing. Under this method, the firm engages local manufacturers to produce the product. The third form of licensing is franchising. The franchiser offers a franchisee a complete brand concept and operating system. The franchisee pays certain fees to the franchiser.

(iv) ***Joint Ventures:*** The Foreign investors and the local manufacturer join together to form a joint venture. The joint venture involves technological transfer, market sharing and investment sharing. The foreign investor and local producer share ownership and control. Joint venture is an appropriate strategy for technological, economic and political reasons. Some governments need a domestic manufacturer's participation in ownership and control in allowing the foreign firm to enter the domestic market. The two firms substitute their resources, skills and expertise in forming a joint venture. Some joint ventures are successful and run for many years. But, some foreign investors after gaining the knowledge of marketing conditions, consumer behaviour and culture of the people may divorce the local investor and start its independent company. Similarly, the local investor after getting the technology transferred may divorce the foreign company and have his complete ownership and control. The other problems of joint ventures include: cultural variations of the two companies, variations in the policies of reinvestment of profits, competition between the two firms for critical managerial positions and the like. Further, joint ownership may hamper a multinational company from carrying out specific manufacturing and marketing policies on a worldwide basis. *(See Box.5.2).*

Box 5.2: Vodafone, Essar Sort Out Differences Over Indian Jv

Vodafone Group and India's Essar Group have reached an agreement on running Hutchison Essar, the Indian mobile phone operator in which Vodafone plans to acquire a controlling interest.

Under the agreement, Vodafone will have operational control of the joint venture, while Essar, which holds 33 per cent of the equity, will have rights consistent with its shareholding, including proportionate board representation, Vodafone said.

Hutchison Telecommunications International Ltd. (HTIL), announced in February that it had entered into an agreement to sell its 67 per cent direct and indirect equity and loan interests in Hutchison Essar to a subsidiary of Vodafone for a total cash consideration of $11.1 billion.

Under the agreement announced, Hutchison Essar will be renamed Vodafone Essar, and in due course the business will market its products and services under the Vodafone brand, Vodafone said. The services are currently being marketed under the Hutch brand.

Ravi Ruia, vice chairman of the Essar Group, will become chairman of Vodafone Essar, and Arun Sarin, CEO of Vodafone, will become the joint venture's vice chairman.

The appointment of Ruia as chairman appears to be a concession to the demand of the Essar Group that they run the Indian company jointly with Vodafone. Essar said it would cede operational control to Vodafone, but wanted to be consulted on strategic decisions relating to the joint venture.

Essar will also have certain liquidity rights. Between the third and fourth anniversaries of completion of the transaction, and subject to regulatory requirements, it will have an option to sell its 33 per cent shareholding in Vodafone Essar to Vodafone for $5 billion, or an option to sell between $1 billion and $5 billion worth of Vodafone Essar shares to Vodafone at an independently appraised fair market trading value, Vodafone said.

Vodafone needs Essar as a partner because of the Indian government restrictions limiting foreign equity holdings in Indian companies to 74 per cent.

Source: Adapted from http://www.infoworld.com

(v) ***Direct Investment:*** Direct investment is the ultimate way of going internationally. The direct investment includes involvement of a company in ownership and control of foreign based assembly or manufacturing or service facilities. The foreign company

(i) can buy part of the local manufacturing facilities, or *(ii)* can buy full interest in the local company, or *(iii)* can build its own facilities on its own. The company after producing in a foreign country can meet the customer needs in that country and export to other countries. This strategy helps the company to widen the market and get distinct advantages.

The Advantages of Direct Investment include:

(a) Getting raw material, labour and other inputs at cheaper prices.

(b) Getting foreign government incentives like cheap finance, tax concessions, subsidies and the like.

(c) Savings in cost of transportation of products to other countries.

(d) Creating jobs in the host country and build up a positive image in the host country.

(e) Building-up of closer relationships with host country's government, customers and market intermediaries makes its products more acceptable in the local market.

(f) Acquiring full control on its investment and market and develop manufacturing and marketing policies to serve the long-term needs and international objectives.

Disadvantages: In spite of these advantages, direct investment suffers from the risks and disadvantages. The disadvantages include:

(i) The company exposes its large investments to political risks, and commercial risks like blocked or devalued currencies, worsening markets or expropriation.

(ii) The laws of foreign government require the company to employ people without required skills, payment of higher salaries and payment of higher rates of taxes.

(iii) The host country may impose discriminative conditions on the foreign companies.

(iv) The political instability in host country also affect the foreign company's business.

(vi) ***Acquisitions:*** A foreign company rather than starting the business from scratch, acquires an already established company in the host country. The foreign company can buy the established company in its entirety rather than on piecemeal basis. Synergistic benefits can be enjoyed by the foreign company if it acquires a firm strong complementary product lines and efficient distribution network. If information about the potential companies in the host country is not available, it would be difficult for the foreign company to acquire. The government's restrictions on the ownership and control is a limiting factor for acquisition. *For example*, the Government of Eritrea imposes a restriction that foreigners cannot have 100 per cent ownership. Instead, they should have a joint ownership with Eritrean investors. *(See Box 5.3)*.

Box 5.3: Tata Buys Corus Group: Largest Acquisition by an Indian Company

The most dramatic change in the Indian business in the past decade has been the surge in ambition. Take Ratan Tata, the Mumbai based tycoon who won the race to buy Britain's Corus Group, beating his Brazilian rival Benjamin Steinbruch in a closely contested auction.

At £6.2 billion, or $12 billion, Tata Steel's offer may be a pygmy by U.S. standards of deal making.It is, however, the largest ever attempted by an Indian company and, when completed, may just make the league table of Top 30 all cash transactions globally. Ratan Tata calls it "a moment of great fulfilment."

Several analysts are suggesting that Tata has gone overboard in trying to best Steinbruch's Companhia Siderurgica Nacional, or CSN. Tata Steel raised its offer to 608 pence a share, from 455 pence initially. CSN bid 603 pence. The leveraged deal, they say, may have put the 100 years old Indian company's finances at risk. Tata Steel shares fell by almost 11 per cent in Mumbai after this.

If Tata Steel were to create, from scratch, 19 million tons of steelmaking capacity comparable in quality to what Corus possesses, it would end up investing 70 per cent to 85 per cent more than it is paying now. Or at least that's what Tata's own calculations show.

Besides, setting up a new factory, a three to five year project if everything goes well, has a great execution risk.

Even in a developing country such as India — which you would assume would welcome the jobs associated with a new steel plant — it isn't easy to make such investments. Invariably, the iron ore exists in places where the poorest of the poor live. And they are nervous about displacement.

Acquiring Corus will also give Tata access to the European customers of steel, especially in the automobile and aerospace industries.

Corus will benefit from access to Indian iron-ore reserves as well as a virgin market for steel. India's per capita steel consumption is still about 35 kilograms, or 77 pounds, a year, or about one-tenth of a developed country levels.

The Tata-Corus combination will be the world's fifth biggest steel producer.

(vii) ***Production Sharing:*** The term production sharing combines the higher labour skills and technology available in the developed countries with the lower cost labour available in the developing countries.

(viii) ***Management Contracts:*** Large MNCs may have a large amount of management talent at its disposal. Management contracts offer a means through which an MNC may use part profits and personnel to assist a firm in a host country for a specified fee and period of time. MNCs earn some income from their investment and continue the operations until the local management is trained and developed. These arrangements help the developing economies that have the capital but do not have skilled manpower, and managerial skills necessary.

(ix) ***Turnkey Operations:*** Turnkey operations are typically contracts for the construction of operating facilities in exchange for a fee. The facilities are transferred to the host country or the firm when they are complete. Normally, the customer is a government department or agency. The foreign company supplies some of its own equipment for the project.

These strategies are explained in detail in the chapter on *"Modes of Entering Global Markets"*.

The strategist of a global firm has to formulate business unit level strategies for the global firm.

5. Formulation of Alternative Business Unit Level Strategies

The global companies formulate business unit level strategies based on the corporate level strategies, organisational strengths and environmental opportunities. The important strategies at this level include:

(a) Low cost leadership strategy

(b) Focus or Niche strategy

(c) Differentiation strategies.

(a) **Low Cost Leadership Strategy:** The global companies plan to reduce the cost of production, cost of marketing, etc., by locating the firms close to the raw materials or close to the markets, adopting latest technology, etc. The strategy of low cost leadership provides the global company two options, viz., fix the price at a lower level compared to that of the competitors or to increase the profit margin or both.

(b) **Focus or Niche Strategy:** Transnational companies formulate specific strategies for specific markets whereas international and multinational corporations apply the same strategy in a number of countries. The transnational companies are expected to think globally and act locally. Thus, they become global companies. The niche strategy refers to focussing on a small market. Transnational companies adopt the focus strategy for each local market in order to compete with the domestic companies.

(c) **Differentiation Strategy:** Transnational companies mostly adopt the differentiation strategy. They differentiate the product policies, price policies, service policies from country to country and from one customer group to other customer group, etc. This strategy helps them to compete with the local companies and also create a positive impression among the customers of various countries.

In addition to these strategies, the business unit level strategies of global business include other strategies.

(d) **Offensive Strategies:**

- Attacking competitor's strengths
- Attacking competitor's weaknesses
- Simultaneous attacks on many fronts
- End-run offensives
- Guerrilla offensive strategies
- Pre-emptive strategies

(e) Defensive Strategies:

Defensive strategies include:

- Protecting company's competitive position, and
- First mover advantage.

The important business unit level strategy is international product portfolio.

Points to be Remembered

- Firms seek to attract customers by making normal predicted adjustment in the methods
- Organisational structure is to be adjusted or modified according to the strategy requirements.
- Structural systems include entrepreneurial, tall and horizontal structures.
- Structural approaches include: product, functional, geographic, matrix, team, virtual, etc.
- Organisational structure should be assessed in order to know its comparability with the strategy.

Keywords

- Routine Strategy Change
- Project Implementation
- Entrepreneurial Structure
- Horizontal Structure
- Geographic Structure
- Strategic Business Unit Structure
- Team Structure
- Radical Strategy Change
- Procedural Implementation
- Vertical Strategy
- Functional Structure
- Decentralised Structure
- Matrix Structure
- Virtual Structure

Questions for Discussion

1. What is strategy implementation?
2. What is strategic change? How do you manage it?
3. What is project? How do you implement it as a part of strategy implementation?
4. What are the systems of organisational structure?
5. What is procedural implementation?
6. What are the strategic advantages of:
   (a) Product structure
   (b) Strategic business unit structure
   (c) Matrix structure
   (d) Virtual structure

7. Discuss structure-follows-strategy theory.
8. How do you match structure to the strategy?
9. Discuss the assessment of organisation structure.

References

1. Samuel C. Certo and J. Paul Peter, "*The Strategic Management Process*", Richard D. Irwin Inc., Homewood, Illinois, 1995, p. 113.
2. *Ibid.*
3. *Ibid.*, p. 114.
4. James Brian Quinn, "*Strategies for Change*," Richard D. Irwin, Homewood Ill, 1980.
5. Michael Beer, Russel Eisenstat and Bert Spector, "*The Critical Path to Corporate Renewal*", Harvard Business School Press, Boston, 1991.
6. K. Andrews, "*The Concept of Corporate Strategy*," Taraporevala & Sons, Bombay, 1971, p. 179.
7. *Project Management Journal*, Project Management Institute, USA, August, 1984.
8. Azhar Kazmi, *op. cit.*, p. 213.
9. J. Child, "*Organisation: A Guide for Managers and Administrators*," Harper & Row, New York, 1977, p. 10.
10. Peter Wright, Charles D. Pringle and Mark J. Kroll, *op.cit.*, p. 149.
11. La Rue T. Hosmer, "*Strategic Management: Text and Cases on Business Policy*," Prentice Hall, Englewood Cliffs, NJ., 1982 and J. Thomas Cannon, "*Business Strategy and Policy*," HarCourt Brace Jovanovich, New York, 1968, p. 316. Quoted in Thompson and Strickland, p. 220.
12. Arthur A. Thompson and A.J. Strickland, *op. cit.*, p. 220.
13. Peter F. Drucker, "*Management: Tasks, Responsibilities, Practices*," Harper & Row, New York, 1974, pp. 530, 535.
14. Arthur A. Thompson and A.J. Strickland, *op. cit.*, pp.220-221.
15. *Ibid.*, p. 222.
16. Alfred Chandler, "*Strategy and Structure*," MIT Press, Cambridge, Mass, 1962. Quoted in Ibid.
17. Raymond Corey and Steven H. Star, "*Organisational Strategy: A Marketing Approach*," Harvard Business School, Boston, 1971.
18. Arthur A. Thompson and A.J. Strickland, op. cit., p. 223.
19. R. Duncan, "*What is the Right Organisation Structure*?" Organisational Dynamics, Winter 1979, pp. 59-80, J.W. Lorsch and A.H. Walker, "*Organisational Choice: Product Vs. Function*," Harvard Business Review, November/December 1968, pp. 129-138.
20. Joe G. Thomas, *op. cit.*, pp.265-266.
21. Arthur A. Thompson and A.J. Strickland, *op. cit.*, pp.227-228.
22. *Ibid.*, p. 228.
23. Peter Wright, Charles D. Pringle and Mark J. Kroll, *op.cit.*, p. 160.
24. S. Davis and P.R. Lawrence, "*Matrix*," Addison Wesley, Reading, Mass, 1977, pp. 11-24.
25. Arthur A. Thompson and A.J. Strickland, *op. cit.*, pp.233-235.
26. P.R. Lawrence and J.W. Lorsch, "*Organisation and Environment*," Richard D. Irwin, Homewood Ill, 1967, p.138.

27. D.H. Thain, "*Stages of Corporate Development*," Business Quarterly, Winter 1969, p. 34.

28. M. Leontiades, "*Strategies for Diversification and Change*," Little Brown, Boston, 1980, Chapter 2. Quoted in Joe G. Thomas, *op. cit.*, p. 271.

29. J.T. Cannon, "*Business Strategy and Policy*," HarCourt Brace Jovanovich, New York, 1968, pp. 525-528.

30. Joe G. Thomas, *op. cit.*, pp. 272-273.

31. D.H. Thain, "*Stages of Corporate Development*," Business Quarterly, Winter, 1969, pp. 33-45.

32. *Ibid.*, pp. 39-40.

33. Joe G. Thomas, *op. cit.*, p. 273.

34. L.E. Greiner, "*Evolutions and Revolutions as Organisations Grow*," Harvard Business Review, July-August 1972, pp. 37-46.

35. Joe G. Thomas, *op. cit.*, pp. 227-278.

36. Leontiades, "*Strategies for Diversification and Change*," pp. 36-46.

37. *Ibid.*, p. 39.

38. Peter Wright, Charles D. Pringle and Mark J. Kroll, *op. cit.*, pp. 164-166.

39. Arthur A. Thompson and A.J. Strickland, *op. cit.*, p. 236.

40. *Ibid.*

41. Peter F. Drucker, "*Management*," pp. 601-602.

***

Chapter - 6

Behavioural Implementation

Chapter Outline

(A) Positive Attitude and Mindset
(B) Leadership
(C) Corporate Culture
(D) Values
(E) Power
(F) Organisational Changes
(G) Organisational Development
— Points to be Remembered
— Keywords
— Questions for Discussion
— References

Learning Objectives

After studying this chapter, you should be able to:

- Analyse the positive attitude and discuss the approaches to enhance positive attitude among employees to smoothen the strategy implantation process;
- Study the leadership styles and to develop and use the appropriate leadership style based on the strategy;
- Discuss the corporate culture that is appropriate for the chosen strategy;
- Explain values in different countries and values appropriate for the strategy;
- Discuss power and methods of assessing power;
- Analyse the process of organisational change and development.

(A) POSITIVE ATTITUDE AND MINDSET

Attitude and mindset are evaluative statements — either favorable or unfavourable — concerning objects, people or events. They reflect how one feels about something. Belief is the cognitive component of an attitude. Emotional or feeling segment is affective component of an attitude. Behaviourial component of an attitude is an intention to behave in a certain way towards someone or something.

Positive attitude is viewing and thinking realistically or positively with regard to strategy implementation. Positive attitude helps to cope more easily with the daily affairs of strategy implementation. It brings optimism into strategy implementation process and makes it easy to overcome all kinds of obstacles in the strategy implementation process. Employees see the bright side of the strategic change, become optimistic and expect the best to happen. Positive attitude is a state of mind that is worth developing and strengthening for efficient strategy implementation.

Therefore, organisations before implementing strategies should develop and strengthen positive attitude and mindset. Organisations can manifest positive attitude in the following ways:

- Understanding the situations positively
- Creative thinking
- Thinking optimistically
- Try again and again until succeed
- Anticipating success
- Foreseeing the possible problems
- Develop all possible solutions to solve the possible anticipated obstacles
  - Thinking and acting proactively
  - Anticipate and chase opportunities
  - Create opportunities
  - Minimise/avoid threats
  - Inspire subordinates, customers and all other stakeholders
  - Energise the employees
  - Develop the attitude of 'I Can Do!
  - Communicate most effectively and frequently
  - Open communication
  - Enable the subordinates, customers and all other stakeholders

- Motivate employees towards their goals
- Eliminate all kinds of deviations of employees in the process of strategy implementation
- Inspire the existing abilities and skills of employees
- Empower employees toward strategy implantation.

Development of positive attitude and mindset of the employees enable companies to seek unsolicited cooperation and collaboration of employees. In addition, employees think and take care of strategy implementation. Further, all kinds of hurdles in the process of strategy implementation are removed. In addition, employees stop resisting the strategic changes.

(B) LEADERSHIP

Leadership is the relationship in which one person (the leader) influences others to work together willingly on a related task to attain goals devised by the leader and/or group. Leadership is the key factor in strategy implementation. Some people equate leadership with management. But these two concepts are not synonymous. In fact, leadership is a part of management, but not all.

Leaders require and use three different skills in influencing and interacting with people to attain goals, *viz.,* technical skills, human relations skills and conceptual skills. Manager exhibits leadership when he or she secures the cooperation of others in accomplishing objectives. Organisational leadership plays a significant role in the changing business environment.

The competitive environment and remaining competitive require an organisation to develop an appropriate leadership. The changing business and its consequences for the leadership factor are presented in Fig. 6.1. Leadership can be felt throughout an organisation. It provides pace and energy to the work and empowers the employees. Though efficient leadership is essential for organisational success, it is not just sufficient to achieve the organisational effectiveness. This is because of the fact that organisational effectiveness depends on several factors. However, the appropriate style of the leader helps for successful implementation of the strategy.

1. Leadership Styles

Leadership is practised by its styles which may be positive or negative. The way in which a leader uses power also establishes leadership styles. There are three popularly known styles, *viz.,* free-rein, autocratic, participative and democratic.

Free-rein or *Laissez-faire* Style: The leaders, in this style, avoid authority and responsibility. They mostly depend upon the group to establish objectives and goals, formulate policies and programmes. The group members train and motivate themselves. Contrary to autocratic style the leader plays minor or negligible roles and depends upon the group. It is, however, concluded that there is no direction and control by the leader.

Autocratic Style: Autocratic leader or leaders in the autocratic style centralise power of decision-making in themselves. The followers have no say either in decision-making or implementation. They have to completely obey and follow the instructions of the autocratic leaders. The leaders take full authority and responsibility. Autocratic leaders are classified into:

(i) Strict autocrat who follows autocratic style completely where the method of influencing subordinates is thoroughly negative.

(ii) Benevolent autocrat typically gives awards to subordinates and motivates them to achieve the goals.

(iii) Incompetent autocrat, who adopts autocratic style with a view to hide his/her incompetency.

Participative Style: Participative leaders decentralise authority and encourage subordinates to express their opinion in decision-making as well as in implementing decisions. Leaders solicit the opinions and idea of the subordinates and make the decisions by themselves. Thus, the authority to make decisions is reserved by the leaders. However, decisions are arrived at by consultation.

Democratic Style: Democratic leaders decentralise authority and encourage subordinates to participate and involve in decision-making and implementation process. Decisions are made jointly by the leader and subordinates as a group.

It is, however, concluded that there is no clear-cut and single leadership style which is applicable universally and in all circumstances. Leaders adopt different styles in different situations depending upon situational requirements.

Situational Approach: Hersey and Blanchard's approach identifies two major styles, *viz.*, tasks style and relationship style. Hersey and Blanchard incorporated the maturity of the followers into their model. The level of maturity is defined by the degree of achievement motivation, willingness to take responsibility and amount of education and/or experience. The key for leadership effectiveness in this model (Fig. 6.2) is to match up the situation with the appropriate style.

The four styles are:

(i) **Telling Style:** This is a high task, low relationship style, it is effective when followers are at low level of maturity.

(ii) **Selling Style:** This is a high task, high relationship style. It is effective when followers are on the low side of maturity.

(iii) **Participative Style:** This is a low task, high relationship style. It is effective when followers are on high side of maturity.

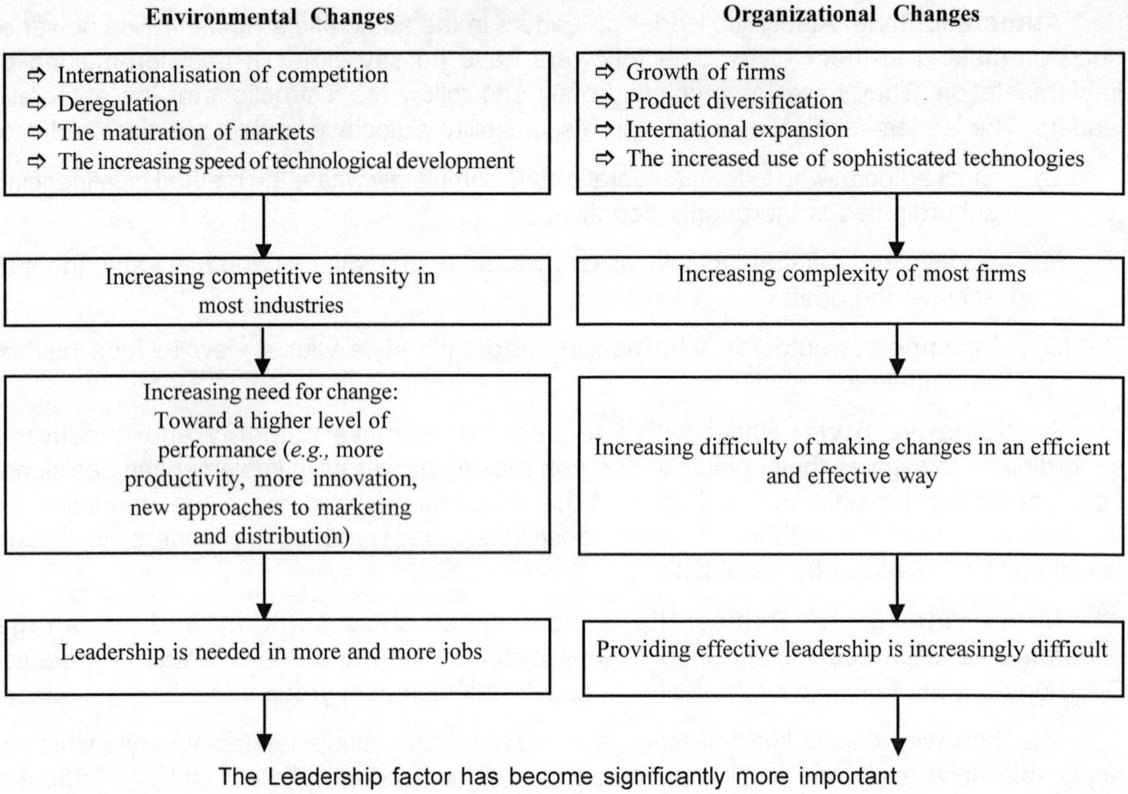

Fig. 6.1: The Changing Business Scene and Its Consequences for the Leadership Factor

Source: John P. Kotler, "The Leadership Factors," quoted in Wright, Pringle and Kroll, *op. cit.*, p. 175.

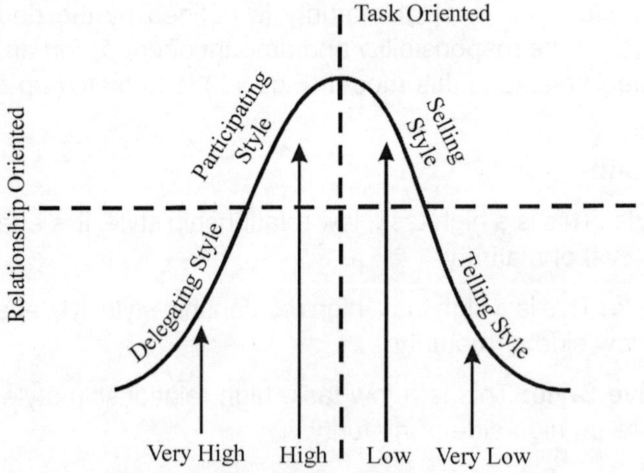

Maturity Level of followers (need for achievement, willingness to accept responsibility, and education/experience)

Fig. 6.2: Hersey and Blanchard's Situational Leadership Model

Source: Paul Hersey and Kenneth Blachard, *Management of Organisational Behaviour: Utilisation of Human Resources*, Prentice Hall, Englewood Cliffs N.J., 1977, p. 170.

(iv) **Delegating Style:** This is a low task, low relationship style. It is effective when followers are at a very high level of maturity.

The most appropriate leadership style is a matter of controversy. Current research indicates that contingency-based leadership or situational leadership is the most effective. In other words, leaders are advised to adopt a style that is best for the particular situation that they are facing. Upper level leadership is qualitatively different from leadership at lower levels. The most pertinent body of knowledge available is the recent work on transformational and transactional leadership styles.

Transformational and Transactional Leadership Styles

Transactional leaders use the authority to exchange rewards like pay, fringe benefits, status for employees' contribution to the job and organisation. By contrast, transformational leaders, inspire involvement in a mission, giving followers, a 'dream' or 'vision' of a higher order than the followers' present reality. In other words, the transformational leaders inspire followers to contribute more than they originally expected to do by stretching their abilities and increasing their self-confidence. Employees are 'transformed' by becoming more aware of the significance of their contribution and by being helped to transcend their own self-interest for the sake of organisational mission.

Bernard M. Bass proposes that most leaders exhibit both transactional and transformational styles. But they do so in different amounts. Transactional leaders improve their organisations step-by-step. Transformational leaders lead their organisations toward a future that may result in significantly different processes and levels of performance. (Fig. 6.3 and Fig. 6.4) Transactional leadership is tied to the past and is hypothesised to enhance organisation's performance steadily, but not dramatically. These two leaders exhibit the well-known leadership styles, *i.e.*, the task oriented leadership and the relationship oriented leaderships directing employees, encouraging employee participation in decision-making.

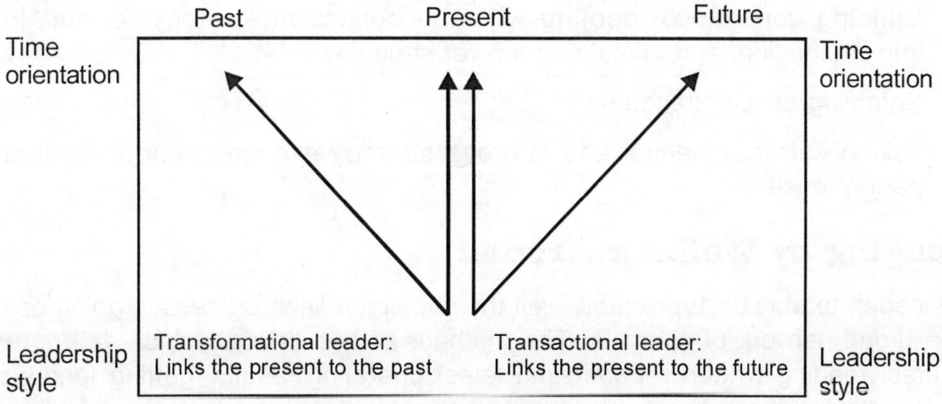

Fig. 6.3: The Perceptual Difference Between Transactional and Transformational Leadership

Source: Wright, Pringle and Kroll, *op.cit.*, p. 179

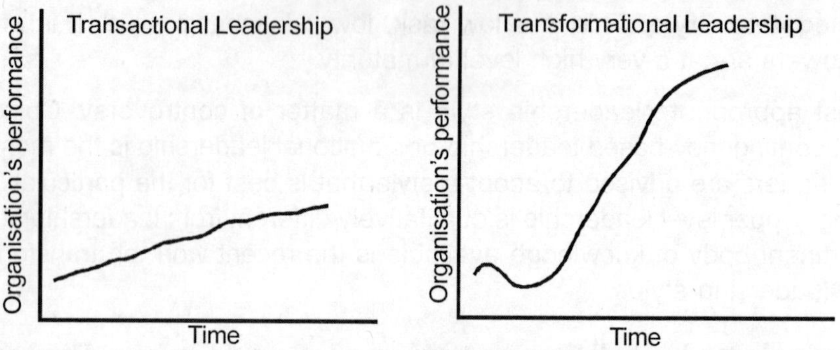

Fig. 6.4: Hypothesised Results of Transactional and Transformational Leadership Styles

Source: Weight, Pringle and Kroll, *op.cit.*, p. 179.

2. Exerting Strategic Leadership

Strong leadership is almost always essential for successful strategy implementation. The strategist has different leaderships roles to play. They include: chief entrepreneur, crisis solver, taskmaster, figurehead, spokesperson, resource allocator, negotiator, motivator, adviser, inspirationalist, consensus builder, policymaker, mentor, and head cheerleader.

The strategic leader has to diagnose the situation and select the best way to handle it. There are six important roles for strategic leader. They are:

(a) Staying on top of what is happening and how well things are going.

(b) Promoting a culture in which the organisation is "energised" to accomplish strategy and perform at a high level.

(c) Keeping the organisation responsive to changing conditions, alert for new opportunities, and bubbling with innovative ideas.

(d) Building consensus, dealing with the politics of strategy formulation, and implementation, and containing "power struggles".

(e) Enforcing ethical standards.

(f) Taking corrective actions to improve strategy execution and overall strategic performance.

3. Managing by Walking Around

The leader, to stay on top of how well the implementation process is going on, should develop a broad network of contacts. The methods of networking include: talking with key subordinates, reading written reports, and latest operating results, getting feedback from customers, watching the competitive reactions of rivals, tapping into grapevine, listening to rank-and-file employees, etc. These methods have their own limitations. The leader, in order to overcome the limitations may visit the field regularly and talk with many different people at different levels. The leaders normally attach great importance to informal communication to gain quick and easy access to information. The leaders tend to become isolated if they stay in their offices.

Fostering a Strategy-Supportive Climate and Culture

The leader should spend much of his time in personally leading the major strategic changes. The leaders should play a leading role in pushing ahead and prodding for continuous improvements in values and culture into in tune with strategy. Leaders should convince people that the selected strategy is right and it should be implemented to the best of the company's ability. Words inspire people, infuse spirit and drive, define strategy. Supportive cultural norms and values. Deeds add credibility to the words, create strategy-supportive symbols and set example. The leader's role depends on the degree of strategic shift in cultural norms. Walking around gives the leader a feel for how things are progressing, opportunity to encourage employees, lift spirits, shift attention from the old to new priorities, etc.

Keeping the Internal Organisation Responsive and Innovative

Though, the strategy implementation is the responsibility of the leader, it is difficult to one person to generate fresh ideas, identify new ideas, identify new opportunities and respond to changing conditions etc. Therefore, the leader should develop dependable supply of fresh ideas from rank-and-file, managers at different levels, entrepreneurs, etc. A flexible, responsive, innovative internal environment is essential as is fast moving high technology industries. The leader should take special pains to develop, nourish and support employees who come forward with new ideas, better services, new product ideas and product applications, ideas of new divisions, new industries, etc.

Empowering Champions

The leaders need to do the following things where champions can blossom and thrive, in order to promote organisational climate. They are:

(i) encouraging the individuals and groups to bring their ideas forward, be creative and exercise initiative.

(ii) the champion's maverick style has to be tolerated. Do not look at people with creative ideas, as disruptive or troublesome.

(iii) leaders should induce and promote attempts and be willing to tolerate mistakes and failures.

(iv) leaders should use different kinds of *ad hoc* organisational forms like venture teams, task forces, groups, etc., to support ideas and experimentation, and

(v) leaders should ensure the champions should be rewarded adequately.

Dealing with Company Politics

A leader cannot formulate and implement strategy successfully in view of organisational politics. The leader should be perceptive about company politics and adopt to political manoeuvring. Organisational politics play a dominant role in strategy formulation and implementation. Groups and their coalitions press for modification of strategic plan. Internal politics influence in selecting a strategy against the other. Organisational politics also affect organisational structure, staffing decisions and budget allocations. The politics affect primarily the strategy in stimulating options, nurturing support for strong proposals and killing weak proposals, guiding the formulation of coalitions on particular issues and achieving consensus and commitment.

According to a research study, successful executives used the following political tactics:

(i) Letting weakly supported ideas and proposals die through inaction.

(ii) Establishing additional hurdles or tests for strongly supported ideas that the manager views as unacceptable but that are best not opposed openly.

(iii) Keeping a low political profile on unacceptable proposals by getting subordinate managers to say no.

(iv) Letting most negative decisions come from a group consensus that the manager merely confirms, thereby, reserving personal veto for big issues and crucial moments.

(v) Leading the strategy but not dictating it — giving few orders, announcing few decisions, depending heavily on informal questioning and seeking to probe and clarify until a consensus emerges.

(vi) Staying alert to the symbolic impact of one's actions and statements best a false signal stimulate proposals and movements in unwanted directions.

(vii) Ensuring that all major power bases within the organisation have representation in or access to top management.

(viii) Minimising political exposure on issues that are highly controversial.

4. Enforcing Ethical Behaviour

Strategic manager must exercise ethical leadership in different aspects. They are:

(i) He/she must set an excellent ethical example in his/her own behaviour and establish a tradition of integrity.

(ii) He/she must educate the managers and employees about what is ethical and what is not,

(iii) top management should clearly refer to the company's ethical code and take a strong stand on ethical issues.

Leading the Process of Making Corrective Adjustments

Making adjustments or "mid-course" corrections is a normal and necessary part of strategic management. Corrective adjustments in the company's approach to strategy implementation should be made on an "as-needed" basis strategy. Leaders should be proactive as well as reactive in reshaping strategy and how it is implemented.

5. Leadership Implementation

According to Lawrence R. Jauch and William F. Glueck, organisations accomplish leadership implementation in several ways:

(i) Through changes in current leadership at appropriate levels;

(ii) By developing appropriate leadership style and climate;

(iii) By getting involved in career development of future strategists; and

(iv) By adopting organisation development techniques to effect changes.

Leader Choice and Assignment

After selecting the strategies at different levels, the top management should place the right strategists at right places including at SBU levels. The questions relating to leadership are:

(i) Who holds the current leadership positions?

(ii) Do they have the right characteristics to assure that the strategy will work well?

(iii) Who should be assigned what and which type of tasks?

The company must examine the strategist's education, abilities, experience, and personality to implement the selected strategy. The firm must examine the match between the new strategy and the chief executive officer.

Style and Climate

Leadership style is one of the important aspects of leadership implementation. The questions relating to leadership style include:

(i) Can the strategist lead the SBU efficiently with his or her present style?

(ii) Can the strategist change the leadership style if that is necessary to make the new strategy work?

(iii) Can the strategist develop the right climate and culture for the strategy?

There should be the match between the strategy and the climate of managerial values and leadership style. Fig. 6.5 suggests that different managerial skills appear to be relevant depending on the job requirements for a given strategy and SBU. A SBU in the cash cow stage require leadership styles and characteristics different from that of another SBU in the significant expansion stage. Leader is responsible for developing a climate conducive for the

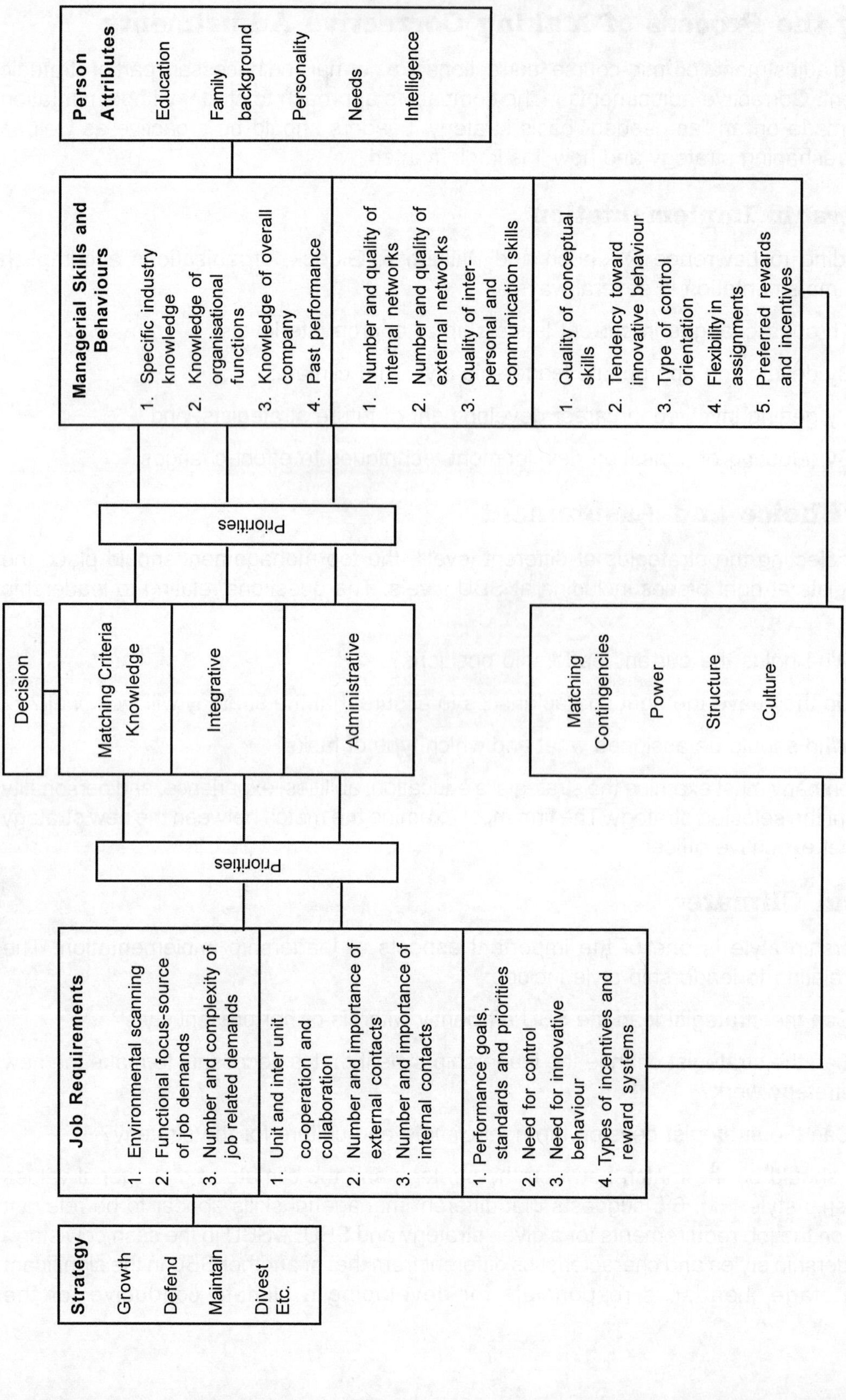

Fig. 6.5: A Suggested Framework for Strategy-Manager Matching

Source: Lawrence R. Jauch and William F. Glueck, *op. cit.*, p. 356.

implementation of the strategy. Climate can be viewed from the point of the nature of leadership, motivation, decision, communication and control process. Review of these aspects is presented in Exhibit 6.1. The aspect of corporate culture is a dimension of climate that leaders help to develop. These aspects of leadership implementation are essential components of the administrative system which can make or break a strategy. They can be used to engender commitment and loyalty to the organisation and its strategies.

Exhibit 6.1: Development of Conducive Climate for Strategy Implementation by the Leader — Ways of Viewing it

Leadership processes as a component of climate refer to the following types of questions:

1. To what extent do superiors have confidence in and trust subordinates? (No confidence to complete trust.)
2. To what extent do superiors behave in a manner that encourages subordinates to feel free to discuss important matters their jobs? (No discussion to full discussion.)
3. To what extent do superiors try to get ideas and opinions from subordinates and use them constructively? (Never or seldom to always.)

Motivational processes as a component of climate can be represented by the following:

1. What types of motives are used? (Fear, threats, punishment, economic rewards, noneconomic rewards.)
2. How much responsibility do various managerial levels assume for goal achievement? (Attempts to sabotage at some levels to high responsibility at all levels.)
3. What types of interactions occur? (Little interaction and distrust to extensive friendly interaction with confidence and trust.)
4. To what extent is there is a feeling of teamwork? (None or damaging competitiveness to substantial cooperation and cohesiveness.)

Decision process as a dimension of climate can be characterised as follows:

1. At what level are decisions formally made? (Bulk at the top and centralised to decentralised spread of decision authority and delegation.)
2. To what extent are decision-makers aware of lower-level problems? (Unaware to fully aware.)
3. To what extent is technical and professional knowledge used in making decisions? (No extent to great extent.)
4. To what extent do subordinates get involved in decisions related to their work? (No participation to high participation.)

The communication process component of climate includes these questions:

1. In what manner are orders issued or goals set? (Orders issued from above to goals established by means of group participation.)
2. How does communication primarily occur? (Formal written memos to informal verbal exchanges.)
3. How does communication flow? (Primarily downward to laterally to primarily upward.)

The control process dimension of climate is characterised as follows:

1. The extent to which review and control is concentrated. (Highly concentrated at the top to widespread responsibility for control.)
2. The extent of controls and standards. (Loose to tight.)
3. The extent to which control data are used for self-guidance. (Data used for policing to co-ordinated problem solving.)

Career Development

The top management of the organisation should plan for the career of strategic leaders and develop them in view of the significant role played by them. The following elements should be taken care of in the development of leaders:

(i) Plan for the number and kind of leaders necessary for the implementation of the future strategies.

(ii) Review of present inventory in terms of skills, talents, knowledge, aptitude and values.

(iii) Preparation of promotion, transfer and employment schedules.

(iv) Development of individual leaders in anticipation of future vacancies at higher levels.

(v) Reward system to attract and retain competent managers/leaders.

Organisation Change and Development: The next aspect of leadership implementation deals with change process. The successful implementation of new strategies requires change in the present policies, plans, people and organisational climate. Organisational development techniques help to implement the new strategies through behavioural change. The organisation development techniques include: survey feedback, confrontation meeting, team building, transactional analysis, managerial grid approach, etc.

(C) CORPORATE CULTURE

Every company has its own history, own methods of solving problems, organising activities, composition of managerial personalities and styles. An organisation's culture may be weak and fragmented, if most of the employees have no deeply felt sense of company purpose, view their jobs as a source of income and have divided loyalties. Culture of some companies may be strong and cohesive in the sense that most of the people understand the company's objectives and strategy, and know what their individual roles are. A strong culture is powerful lever for channelling behaviour and helping employees in doing their jobs in a more strategy-supportive manner. This occurs in the following ways:

(i) Employees in strong culture companies, are provided with a system of informal rules and peer pressures regarding how to behave or do the work most of the times. The absence of strong company identity and purposeful work climate in weak culture companies, results in substantial employee confusion and wasted effort.

(ii) A strong culture provides structure, standards, and a value system and provides strong company identification among employees. Thus, a strong culture turns a job into a way of life and motivates the employees to contribute effectively to the company.

Therefore, to implement a strategy, an organisation's culture must be closely fit with the strategy.

What is Corporate Culture?

Corporate culture refers to the values and patterns of beliefs and behaviour that are accepted and practised by the members of a company. Companies within the same industry and companies within the same city exhibit distinctly different ways of operating and working as each company develops its own unique culture. Impact of culture on two different types of organisations is presented in Exhibit 6.2.

Exhibit 6.2: Impact of Culture on Two Different Groups of Organisations

Dimensions of corporate culture	*Multinational subsidiaries and professionally managed companies*	*Family business and non-resident Indian companies*
1. Nature of desired managerial skills and capabilities	Emphasis on professional qualifications and rank	Emphasis on demonstrated skills, depth and quality of knowledge
2. Actual performance or results achieved	Emphasis on seniority, conformity to organisational values, loyalty, and relative fit between desired managerial behaviour and position in hierarchy	Emphasis on originality of action and thinking, innovation, and upgradation of knowledge and skills by personal efforts
3. Managerial style of planning and decision-making	Emphasis on information gathering, bureaucratic mode of functioning, risk aversion and non-entrepreneurial decision-making	Emphasis on selective information usage, intuitive and qualitative decision-making of an entrepreurial nature
4. Management systems adopted	Emphasis on use of elegant, scientific, sophisticated and rational systems which degenerate due to low usage	Emphasis on reliance on business sense and "no-frills" systems geared to quick action
5. Nature of management control	Emphasis on comprehensive, formal and written reporting and rationalisation of failures rather than resolution of problems	Emphasis on primary use of verbal reporting and remedial action

Source: M.Rokeach, *The Nature of Human values*, (NewYork: Free Press).

To manage human resources of a company effectively and efficiently, it is necessary for bringing a close culture-strategy match. Culture with a perfect match with the strategy energises employees significantly to the power and helps for effectiveness of strategy implementation. Strategy-culture mismatch results in conflict and weakens the company's performance. Therefore, the culture should be changed as quickly as possible to bring culture-strategy fitness.

1. Impact of Culture on Strategy

Culture reflects the past and environmental change. These changes bring significant modifications in corporate culture. Corporate culture in turn affects the strategy implementation either positively or negatively. Changes in strategy must be accompanied by corresponding alternations in corporate culture to implement the strategy successfully. Conservative organisations follow the controlling approach even though they have formulated new goals and plans. Exhibit 6.3 presents the impact of corporate culture on strategy formulation.

Even though, firms formulate effective strategy, the strategy may fail, if it is not accompanied by assumptions, values and ways of working that are at variance with the organisation's culture. The employees may follow the same old methods of doing the jobs, even if the strategy and organisation structures are changed, unless the culture is not modified.

Exhibit 6.3: Impact of Corporate Culture on Strategy Formulation

Organisation type	*Dominant objectives*	*Characteristics of policy-making Preferred strategies*	*Planning and control systems*
1. Defenders	Desire for a secure and stable niche in market	Specailisation; cost-efficient production; marketing emphasises price and service to, defend current business, tendency to vertical integration.	Centralised detailed control. Emphasis on cost efficiency. Extensive use of formal planing.
2. Prospectors	Location and exploitation of new product and market opportunities	Growth through product and market development (often in spurts). Constant monitoring of environmental change. Multiple technologies.	Emphasis on flexibility, decentralised control, use of *ad hoc* measurements.
3. Analysers	Desire to match new ventures to present shape of business	Steady growth through market penetration. Exploitation of applied research. Followers in the market.	Very complicated. Co-ordinating roles between functions (*e.g.* product managers). Intensive planning

Source: R.E. Miles and C.C. Snow, "*Organizational Strategy, Structure and Process,*" McGraw-Hill, 1978.

2. How Leaders Shape Culture?

Leaders can shape the corporate culture. Transactional leaders are less influential in modifying the company's culture than transformational leaders. "The transactional leader works within the organisational culture as it exists, the transformational leader changes the organisational culture."

According to Schein, leader can change the organisational culture in five ways. They are:

(i) By systematically paying attention to certain areas of business. These areas including controlling costs, improving employee productivity, improving sales, etc.

(ii) By reacting to critical incidents and organisational crises. The crises include declining sales, employee unrest, technological change, etc. The way leader deals with crisis can emphasise norms, values and working procedures etc.

(iii) By serving as a deliberate role model, teacher or coach.

(iv) By allocating rewards and status to the employees.

(v) By adopting the procedures through which a company selects, employs, and promote, retrenches and dismisses the employees. Corporate culture can be perpetuated by employing and promoting employees whose values are similar to the company's values.

Schein, also identifies primary embedding mechanisms and secondary articulation and reinforcement mechanisms. (Exhibit 6.4). The secondary reinforcement mechanisms include: organisation design and structure, organisational systems and procedures, design of physical space, stories about important events and people and formal statements of organisational philosophy etc.

Exhibit 6.4: Mechanisms for Embedding and Reinforcing Organizational Culture

Primary Embedding Mechanisms

1. What leaders pay attention to, measure, and control
2. Leader reactions to critical incidents and organizational crises
3. Deliberate role modelling, teaching, and coaching
4. Criteria for allocation of rewards and status
5. Criteria for recruitment, selection, promotion, retirement, and ex-communication

Secondary Articulation and Reinforcement Mechanisms

1. Organisation design and structure
2. Organisational systems and procedures
3. Design of physical space, facades, buildings
4. Stories about important events and people
5. Formal statements of organisational philosophy, creeds, charters

Source: E.H. Schein, *Organisational Culture and Leadership* (San Fransisco: Jossey-Bass, 1985), Chap. 10.

3. Match Between Strategy and Culture

Some parts of corporate culture may be unchangeable. The strategy-maker, in such cases should select the strategy which fits in the existing corporate culture. Once the strategy is selected, the strategy implementer should bring corporate culture into close alignment with the strategy and stabilise it there.

Aligning culture with strategy requires:

(i) Diagnosing the facets of existing culture which are strategy supportive;

(ii) Identifying the facets of present culture which are to be modified to bring match with the strategy; and

(iii) Deciding the actions to be taken by the management to modify the cultural environment and create a stronger match with the strategy.

Symbolic Actions and Substantive Actions

Managerial actions to bring the match between culture and strategy include symbolic and substantive. Symbolic actions provide the indication about the kind of behaviour and performance, strategy implementers wish to encourage. The common symbolic actions include: honouring the employees whose actions and performance serve as role models, awarding the employees for their significant contributions to the organisations and the like. Awards, rewards, ceremonies, role models are a fundamental part of a strategy implementer's culture modifying effort. Strategy implementer use symbols to build and nurture the culture. They personally conduct ceremonial events and publicly congratulate individual employees. They use every ceremonial function and every conversation to implant values, send reinforcing signals and praise good deeds.

Chief strategy implementers must be careful to lead by example. The chief executive's sincere and committed effort is necessary for reinforcing the culture through both words and deeds. Further, the task of making culture supportive of strategy is not a short term exercise. It takes time for a new culture to emerge and prevail.

Establishing Ethical Standards and Values

It is essential for a company to build a strong corporate culture on ethical principles and sound values. An ethical corporate culture has a positive impact on company's long-term strategic success. Strong values and high ethical standards nurture the corporate culture in a very positive way. Companies set forth their values and code of ethics in written documents. The kind of topics covered in these documents are presented in Exhibit 6.5. The values and code of ethics can be implemented in the following ways:

Exhibit 6.5: Topics Covered in Value Statements and Code of Ethics

Topics covered in values statements	Topics Covered in Codes of Ethics
• Importance of customers and customer service • Commitment to quality • Commitment to innovation • Respect for the individual employee and the duty the company has to employees • Importance of honesty, integrity and ethical standards • Duty to shareholders • Duty to suppliers • Corporate citizenship • Importance of protecting the environment	• Honesty and observance of the law • Conflicts of interest • Fairness of selling and marketing practices • Using inside information and securities trading • Supplier relationship and purchasing practices • Payment to obtain business • Acquiring and using information about others • Political activities • Use of company assets, resources and property • Protection of proprietary information • Pricing, contracting and billing

Source: Thompson and Strickland, *op. cit.*, p. 258.

(i) Incorporating the statement of values and the code of ethics into employee training and educational programmes.

(ii) Giving explicit attention to values and ethics in recruiting and employing to screen out applicants who do not exhibit compatible character traits.

(iii) Communicating the values and ethics to all employees and explaining compliance procedures.

(iv) Management involvement at all levels.

(v) Strong endorsement by the top management.

(vi) Word-of-mouth indoctrination.

4. Spirit of High Performance and Culture

Successful strategy implementation requires the spirit of high performance on the part of employees. Development of strong individual commitment and spirit of high performance, is therefore, essential for strategy implementation. The spirit of high performance culture results in improvement in organisational performance and organisational excellence. Organisations with a spirit of high performance are intensely human resource oriented. They treat the people with dignity and respect, encourage employees to use their potentialities, initiatives and creativity to the maximum extent in performing their work. Further, the employees are empowered in discharging their responsibilities. The companies set reasonable and clear performance expectations, use rewards and punishments, encourage the managers to develop the subordinates and grant autonomy to employees to contribute to the goals excellently. Companies must develop champions out of the people who turn in winning performances in order to create a result-oriented corporate culture.

Shared Values

The values widely shared by managers and employees are the core of the corporate culture. Fits with strategy should be created internally regarding structure, organisational skills and distinctive competence, budgets, support systems, rewards and incentives, policies and procedures and culture. The strategy can be implemented powerfully, if the fit among the administrative activities and the characteristics is strong.

McKinsey & Co., a leading consulting firm, has developed a framework for examining the fits in seven broad areas, *viz.*,

(i) strategy,

(ii) structure,

(iii) shared values, attitudes and philosophy,

(iv) approach to staffing the organisation and its overall "people-oriented",

(v) administrative systems, practices and procedures used to run the organisation, including the reward structure, formal and informal policies, budgeting and programmes, training, cost accounting and financial controls,

(vi) the organisation's skills, capabilities and core competencies, and

(vii) style of top management including how they allocate their time and attention, symbolic actions, their leadership skills, how the top management team comes across to the different levels and areas of the organisations.

McKinsey has diagrammed these seven elements which is called McKinsey 7-S framework. (Fig. 6.6). These seven elements are: strategy, structure, systems, style, staff, skills and shared values. The shared values are the core of the 7-S framework. They bond the corporate culture and give it energy.

(D) VALUES

Values influence attitudes and behaviour. 'Normally employees view that' promotions are based on either merit or seniority or merit-cum-seniority. But the employees tend to be frustrated when they know that the promotions in an organisation are based on reservations.

Thus, the values help to form attitudes, perceptions, morale and determine employee behaviour in an organisation.

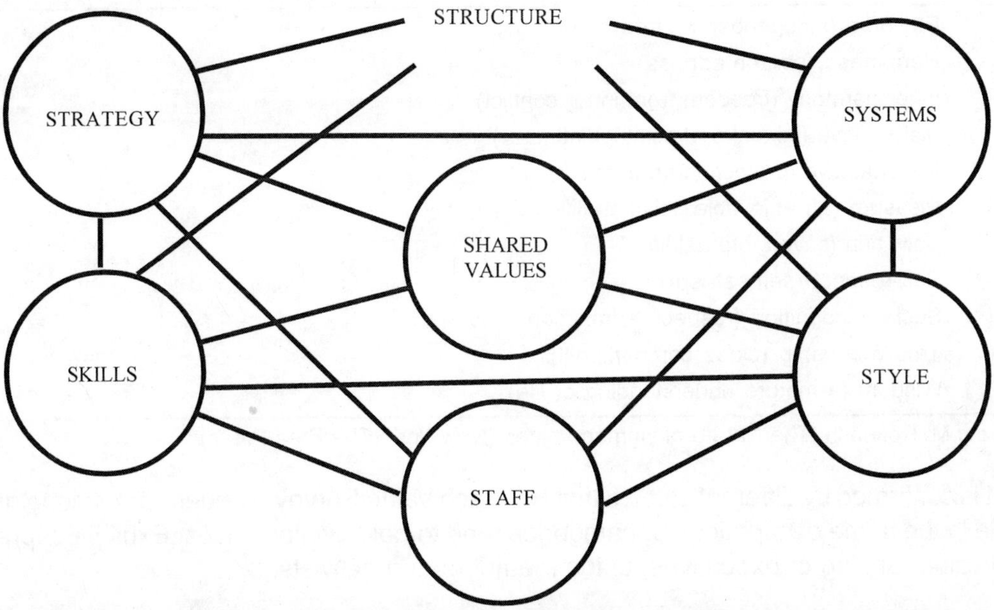

Fig. 6.6: Bonding the Administrative Fits (The McKinsey 7-S framework)

Source: Thomas J. Peters and Robert H. Waterman, Jr., *In Search of Excellence* (New York: Harper & Row, 1982), p. 10.

Types of Values

Values which influence different areas of behaviour are classified into terminal values and instrumental values by Milton Rokeach in his Rokeach Value Survey.

- Terminal values refer to desirable end-states of existence. Individuals would like to achieve these values during his/her life time.
- Instrumental values refer to preferable modes of behaviour or means of achieving the terminal values.

Exhibit 6.6 presents the terminal and instrumental values in this survey.

Exhibit 6.6: Terminal and Instrumental Values in Rokeach Value Survey

Terminal Values	Instrumental Values
A confortable life (a prosperous life)	Ambitious (hardworking, aspiring)
An exciting life (a stimulating, active life)	
A sense of accomplishment (lasting contribution)	
A world at peace (free of war and conflict)	
A world of beauty (beauty of nature and the arts)	
Equality (brotherhood, equal opportunity for all)	
Family security (taking care of loved ones)	

Freedom (independence, free choice)
Happiness (contentedness)
Inner harmony (freedom from inner conflict)
Mature love (sexual and spiritual intimacy)
National love (protection from attack)
Pleasure (an enjoyable, leisurely life)
Salvation (saved, eternal life)
Self-respect (self-esteem)
Social recognition (respect, admiration)
True friendship (close companionship)
Wisdom (a mature understanding of life)

Source: M. Rokeach, The Nature of Human Values (New York: The Free Press)

It is confirmed by different studies that Rokeach Value Survey's values vary among groups, People in the same occupations or categories tend to hold similar values. Exhibit 6.6 presents mean value ranking of executives, union members and activists.

Values in Different Cultures

Cultures vary from country to country due to variations in climatic conditions, economic conditions, physical security issues and the like. Culture, in turn, influences the formation, development and maintenance of values. Since the cultures vary across the globe, so is the case with values.

Exhibit 6.7: Mean Value Ranking of Executives, Union Members, and Activists
(Top Five Only)

Executives		Union Members		Activists	
Terminal	Instrumental	Terminal	Instrumental	Terminal	Instrumental
1. Self-respect	1. Honest	1. Family security	1. Responsible	1. Equality	1. Honest
2. Family	2. Responsible	2. Freedom	2. Honest	2. A world of peace	2. Helpful
3. Freedom	3. Capable	3. Courageous	3. Family Security	3. Courageous	3. Happiness
4. A sense of accomplishment	4. Ambitious	4. Self-respect	4. Independent	4. Self-respect	4. Responsible
5. Happiness	5. Independent	5. Mauter love	5. Capable	5. Freedom	5. Capable

Source: M. Rokeach, The Nature of Human Values (New York: The Free Press)

Geert Hofstede surveyed more than 116,000 IBM employees in 40 countries about their work related cultures. He classified the values into five categories based on his survey. They are: power distance, individualism vs. collectivism, quantity of life vs. quality of life, uncertainty avoidance and long-term vs. short-term orientation.

- ***Power Distance:*** It is a national culture attribute describing the extent to which a society accepts that power is distributed unequally in institutions and organisations.

Equal power distribution is called low power distance and extremely unequal power distribution is called high power distance.

- ***Individualism vs. Collectivism:*** Individualism is the degree to which people in a country prefer to act as individuals rather than a member of a group. Low individualism is collectivism.
- ***Quantity of life vs. Quality of life:*** Quantity of life is the degree to which values like assertiveness, the acquisition of money and material goods and competition. Quality of life is the degree to which people value relationships and show sensitivity and concern for the welfare of others.
- ***Uncertainty Avoidance:*** It is the degree to which people in a country prefer structured over unstructured situations. People with high score on uncertainty avoidance have increased level of anxiety resulting in greater nervousness, stress and aggressiveness.
- ***Long-term vs. short-term orientation:*** Long term orientation is a national culture attribute that emphasises the future, thrift and persistence. Short-term orientation is a national culture attribute that emphasises the past and present, respect for tradition and fulfilling social obligation. People with short-term orientation emphasises on tradition and fulfilling social obligations. Exhibit 6.7 presents rating of these five dimensions in different countries.

Individual values influence the organisations as well as the strategy. Organisations consist of a large number of individuals with a variety of values. The values are shaped by the organisational environment and nature of the business. Individuals will share interests and values with others within the organisations. The mode of influence of values on strategy is presented in Fig. 6.7.

Factors that Shape and Change Values: The major sources of influence of an individual's values include; external influences, the nature of business and the company culture. Fig. 6.7 shows the facts which shape and change values.

External Influences: External influences include: *(i)* values of society, and *(ii)* organised groups.

***(i)* Values of Society:** Various issues like attitudes to work, authority, and equality are constantly shaped by society at large. This process should be understood from the point of corporate strategy due to the following reasons:

(a) values of society change and adjust over time

(b) multinational and transnational companies have the added problem of coping with the different standards and expectations of different countries.

***(ii)* Organised Groups:** Individuals very often have allegiances to other groups which are very influential on their values. These allegiances are directly related to working situations like membership of trade unions or more informal like membership in clubs and social organisations.

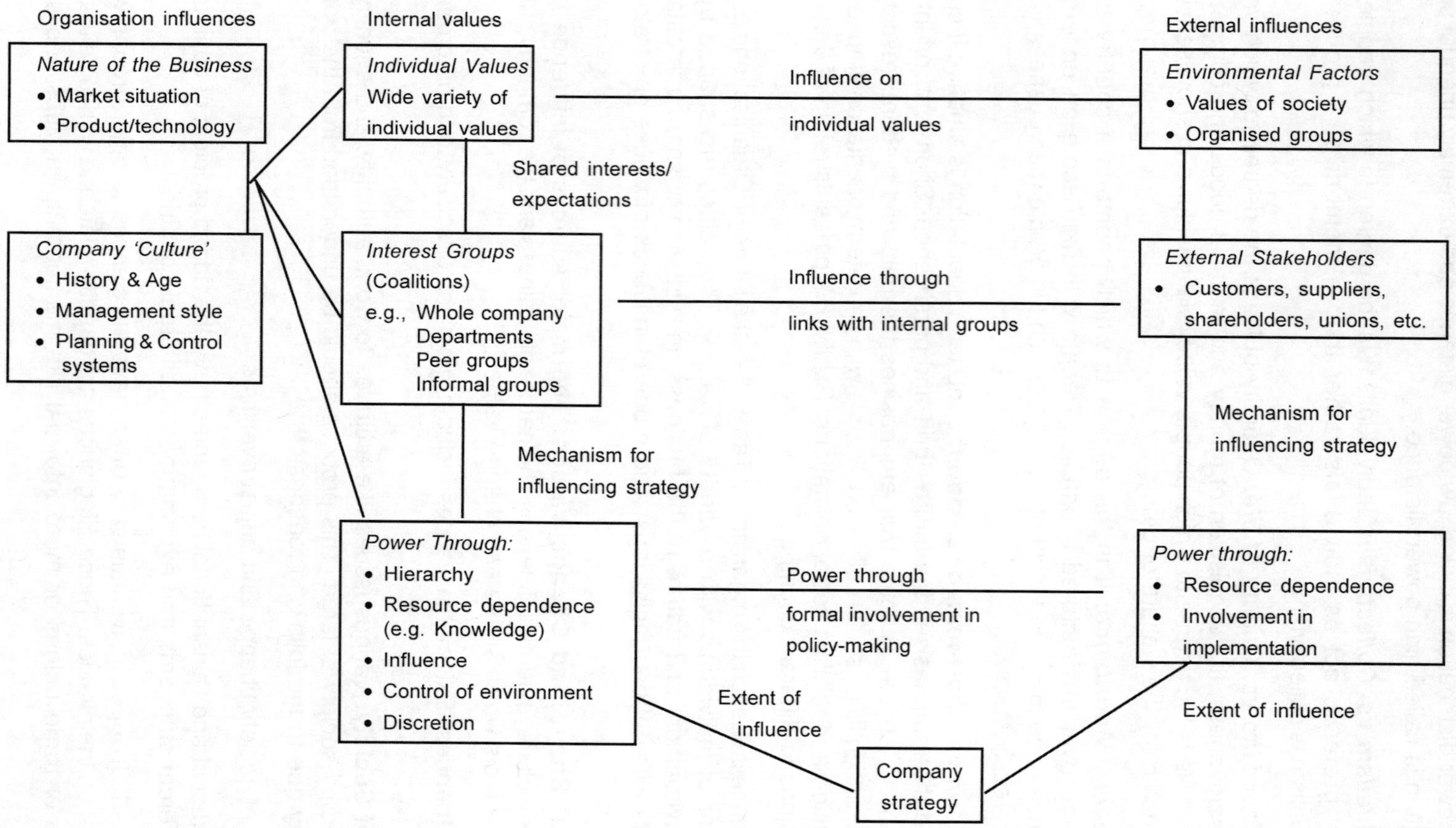

Fig. 6.7: The Mode of Influence of Values on Strategy

Source: Gerry Johnson and Kevan Scholes, *op. cit.*, p. 117.

Nature of Business

The issues concerning the nature of a business include market situation, and product/technology. These two factors are more specific to the particular circumstances of a company.

***(i)* Market Situation:** Different companies face different market situations like recession, and boom. The values of the people within the company will change depending upon the market situation. Strategic decisions, in turn, are influenced by these changed values of the people, and values of the employees.

***(ii)* Products/Technology:** Technology influences values through the product, systems of production, distribution, etc. The influence of technology on values would be in two ways *viz., (i)* The company's ability to compete in the market is determined by various factors including technology. Technology determines methods of operating and tasks to be performed by employees *(ii)* The skills required by the company are determined by the nature and level of technology. This in turn determines the kind of people required to operate the technology and their values.

(E) POWER

Power, from the view point of strategic management is extent to which individuals or groups are able to persuade, induce or coerce others into following certain courses of actions. It is helpful to know the sources of power to understand and assess the importance of power in relation to strategic management. A clear distinction should be made between the authority and power in assessing the impact of power on strategic management. It is necessary to know the sources of power to understand its impact on strategic management.

1. Sources of Power

The sources of power can be divided into two categories *viz., (i)* internal sources, and *(ii)* sources for external stakeholders as shown in Fig. 6.8.

Sources of Power

Internal Sources	*Sources for External Stakeholders*
1. Hierarchy (Formal Power) 2. Influence or Charisma (Informal power) 3. Control of strategic resources 4. Possession of knowledge/skills. 5. Control of environment (Ex: Negotiation skills) 6. Involvement in strategic implementation. (Ex: Exercising discretion)	1. Control of strategic resources (Ex: Materials, Men, Money) 2. Involvement in strategic implementation (Ex: Distribution outlets, franchise, licenses, etc.) 3. Possession of knowledge (Ex: skills) 4. Through internal links (Ex: Informal influence).

Fig. 6.8: Sources of Power

Source: Gerry Johnson and Kevan Scholes, *op. cit.*, p. 134.

Internal Sources of Power

(i) **Hierarchy:** Hierarchical positions in the organisational structure provide formal authority to the managers at higher levels. The managers with more formal authority influence the policy formulation and implementation extensively. Managers should use this power along with other types of power to make their influence efficient.

(ii) **Influence/Charisma:** Influence is an important source of power. This arises from personal qualities like charisma of the leader. Charisma is the leader's ability to influence others through his/her personal magnetism, enthusiasm and strongly held convictions. Leaders communicate these convictions and their vision for the future through a dramatic, persuasive manner of speaking. Charismatic leaders create an image of competence and success. Their personal magnetism make them role models for their employees. The more the followers admire their leaders, the more likely they are to accept their leaders' values and beliefs. This acceptance makes the leaders to exert significant influence over their follower's behaviours. The charismatic leaders are more powerful during the periods of organisational crisis and transition.

(iii) **Control of Strategic Resources:** Control of strategic resources is an important source of power. The relative importance of different resources change depending upon the strategy and situation. The leader can gain power by possessing or controlling the strategic resources.

(iv) **Expertise or Knowledge or Skill:** Expertise or knowledge is a crucial source of power for top management. Managers acquire power through achievement and performance. The better the achievement and performance, the greater will be the power of the managers. Expertise refers to a manager's ability to influence the behaviour of others. The subordinates follow the managers as they believe that their managers have command and knowledge of the problems.

(v) **Control of the Environment:** Normally, events in the company and company's internal environment affect the company's performance. Some groups or individual employees have more influence over events and company's internal environmental factors. This can be a source of power within the company. Marketing and finance managers can control the important internal environmental factors. Therefore, they play a dominant role in the strategic management whereas, the human resource manager and production manager take a back seat.

(vi) **Exercising Discretion:** Exercising discretion is a most significant source of power within an organisation. Individuals due to the nature and level of their jobs, derive power. These individual employees occupy different positions in the organisation. Strategy is to be implemented by a number of individuals across the organisation. These individuals use the power so derived in the process of strategy implementation.

Sources for External Stakeholders

So far, we have discussed the sources of power for the internal groups. Now, we discuss the sources of power for external stakeholders.

(i) **Resource Dependence:** Almost all external stakeholders like banks, financial companies, suppliers of raw materials, etc., derive power as the company depends on them for resources. The short term survival of the company is mostly dependent on any one of these stakeholders.

(ii) **Involvement in Implementation:** The importance has been shifted from manufacturing to the distribution. The distribution agencies have the power of knowledge about consumers' tastes and preferences. In fact distribution agencies determine or influence the type of product to be produced. Thus, the distribution agencies derive power by involving in the implementation process.

(iii) **Expertise:** The agencies having specialised skill or expertise that is demanded by the company derive the power for their expertise knowledge.

(iv) **Internal Links:** Internal links can provide a way for external stakeholders to influence the company's strategy. Highly authoritarian organisation normally does not provide inter links and give chance to external stakeholders to influence the strategic management process.

2. Methods of Assessing Power

It is rather very difficult to assess the power of internal individuals or groups and external stakeholders. Preffer suggests that the best way of assessing the power is to depend on indicators of power.

Indicators within Organisations: There are four indicators of power within organisations. They are:

(i) **The Status of the Individual or Group:** The position of the individual in the organisational hierarchy, and the job grade work as an indicator to assess the power. The reputation of individual or group compared to others can also be used to assess the power.

(ii) **The Claim on Resources:** The claim of the individual or group for resources in terms of share in budget, number of employees, etc., can be used to measure the power. The resources of the least powerful group normally are eroded by the more powerful group.

(iii) **Representation in Powerful Positions:** The power of the individuals and groups can be assessed by their representation in boards, committees, groups, teams, etc.

(iv) **Symbols of Power:** Power of individuals and groups can also be assessed through various physical symbols like size and location of offices, facilities like secretary, telephone, carpet, meeting tables, etc.

Indicators for External Stakeholders: The indicators to assess the power of external stakeholders are:

(i) **The Status:** The status of the external stakeholders like suppliers of raw materials, distributors can be assessed through, how quickly and to what extent their demands are met by the company.

(ii) **Resource Dependence:** Resource dependency can be measured by the proportion of the company's business with a single distributor, proportion of the raw material supplied by a supplier to the total raw materials required by the company, etc.

(iii) **Negotiating Arrangements:** The power of the external stakeholder can be assessed through whether the stakeholder invited for negotiation is allowed to interact closely or treated at arm's length.

(iv) **Symbols:** Symbols are equally valuable clues. The symbols that are used to assess the power of external stakeholders include the level of manager that deals with the stakeholder, whether, the management team wine or dine with the stakeholder, etc.

The power can be assessed relatively as high, medium and low.

(F) ORGANISATIONAL CHANGE

Change is the law of nature. It is a necessary way of life in most organisations for their survival and growth. The term organisational change implies the creation of imbalances in the present pattern or situation. Adjustment among people, technology and structural set-up is established when an organisation operates for a long time. Change could be both reactive and proactive. A proactive change has necessarily to be planned to attempt to prepare for anticipated future challenges.

Approaches to organisational change include:

- Employee participation in decision-making relating to changes
- Advanced planning and preparing all the parties for change
- Protecting employees' interests
- Encourage team work
- Cautious and phase-wise introduction of change
- Motivating the employees to welcome the change
- Sharing the benefits of change between employees and management.

1. Planning and Implementing the Change

The strategist is often called a 'change agent' as his role is to initiate the change, and help make it work successfully. Employee's support is most essential in implementing the change successfully as they are at the helm of affairs, though the strategist is an agent of change. Change is typically viewed as the required three steps, *viz.,* unfreezing, changing and refreezing. Unfreezing means that old ideas and practices need to be cast aside so that, new ones can be learnt. Change is the step in which the new ideas and practices are learnt, so that an employee can think and perform in new ways. Refreezing means that what has been learnt is integrated into actual practice.

Implementation is the institutionalisation and internalisation of a change after it has been accepted by an organisation and a decision has been taken to accept and make it part of the on-going activity. Implementation may be seen as multidimensional process. The end result of implementation is the institutionalisation and stabilisation of change. Institutionalisation is making the change permanent part of organisation and internalisation means stabilisation of the change. The implementation process should start with planning. The three important stages of implementation of change processes (See Fig. 6.9) are:

(i) Monitoring the change;

(ii) Taking action in relation to the change; and

(iii) Making necessary adjustments in the programme accepted for implementation.

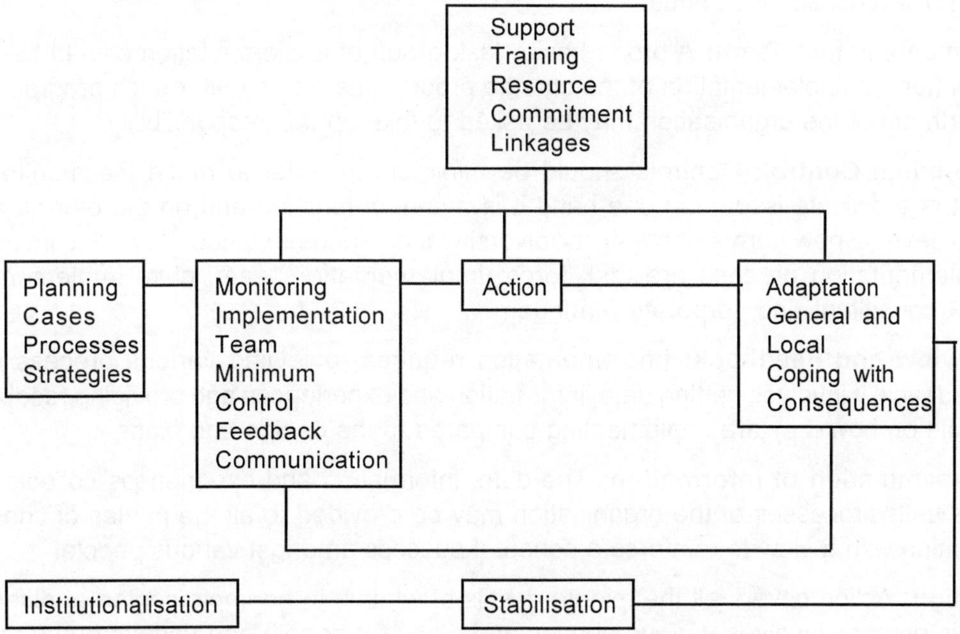

Fig. 6.9: The Model of Implementation of Change in an Organisation

1. Planning: The main objective of planning, is to have an overall understanding of the nature of implementation. Planning process refers to determining in advance the entire process of implementation of change phasing. Planning may be focussed on phasing. Phasing may be either temporal (in terms of time) or spatial (in terms of various units or the locations of the organisation).

2. Processes: Various processes involved in implementation should be decided in advance. Various stages of the process include: initiation, motivation, diagnosis, information collection, deliberation, action proposal, implementation and stabilisation (See Fig. 6.9).

Attention should be paid to the process of collaboration, increasing the capability of the organisation to face the problems of change, establishing the norms and values.

3. Strategies: Management should formulate various strategies for implementation. These strategies should focus on taking outsider's help, change agents, designing permanent organisational structures, unit/location of the organisation to be selected for initial process, openness with the environment, etc.

4. Monitoring: It is the process of "routine periodic measurement of programme inputs, activities and outputs undertaken during programme implementation. Monitoring is normally concerned with the procurement, delivery and utilisation of programme resources, adherence to work schedule or progress made in the production of outputs." Monitoring is essential to make implementation effective. Monitoring/control is to ensure that a plan proceeds according to the original design. A broader group of people should be involved in monitoring function. An independent team without having interest in change may be entrusted with the task. This team may have a continuous status.

5. Implementation Team: A broad based task group of implementation should be set-up to look after the implementation of the change programme and monitor such programme. HRD department of the organisation may be asked to take up this responsibility.

6. Minimum Control: Controls should be minimum in order to make the monitoring effective. It is a delicate issue. On one hand it is a control function and on the other it also attempts to develop new norms of creativity, diversity and experimentation. Key roles involved in the implementation process are task force, implementation team, chief implement or counterpart consultant and corporate management.

7. Review and Feedback: Implementation requires reviewing various process and provide feedback. It involves getting data, information and experiences and providing feedback to the people on how they are implementing compared to the design and plans.

8. Dissemination of Information: The data, information and experiences collected in the various units/processes of the organisation may be provided to all the parties of change implementation with a view to reinforce a sense of success amongst various people.

9. Action: Action covers all the minute details of what is to be implemented at different stages. This process involves various phases and steps for people and various group tasks in relation to change programme.

10. Adaptation: Adaptation is the combination of two main criteria of effectiveness of implementation. Adaptation may be both general in the sense that some modifications may be made in the original plan and some may be developed at later stage.

11. Support: Various types of support from all concerned will be required for the implementation of change.

12. Human Resource Development: Effective implementation of change requires new and varied technical, managerial and behavioural skills and knowledge. Human Resource development department can contribute for the enhancement of these skills through training, executive development and organisation development programmes.

13. Resources: Implementation requires support in the form of various fields like financial resources, human resources, technological support, etc.

14. Linkages: Support may also be required in terms of building linkages both with external experts, various external agencies and internal departments. Linkage among departments, implementation teams, line management and top management is essential.

15. Top Management Commitment: The most important aspect of support essential for implementing change is the support and commitment of top management. Top management should involve itself in the process of change implementation, encourage the implementation team, provide all types of resources.

Management has to get the support from employees through the following means: *(a)* Encouraging and using group force; *(b)* Development of leadership for change; *(c)* Encouraging participation and sharing views; *(d)* Maintenance of employees' security; *(e)* Effective communication; *(f)* Participation and working with the unions; *(g)* Working with the total system of the organisation which requires adopting useful and necessary changes; *(h)* Changing by evolution but not by revolution; *(i)* Adopting the change with adequate attention to human relations; *(j)* Identifying and taking care of post-change problems.

(G) ORGANISATIONAL DEVELOPMENT

Change and Development

As discussed earlier change is a must. Change occurs not only in technology, marketing but also in human values, attitudes, relationships, social system, organisational climate, culture, etc. Hence, all are aware of and are concerned with change. Changes in values, etc., have tremendous impact on organisation as changes in technology and marketing. As such the management has to meet the challenges of change. Management can effectively meet these challenges through a systematic and planned change effort. Organisation development (OD) has emerged to help the planned change for organisational effectiveness. Thus, it is said that the organisational development is the modern approach to management of change and human resource development. Organisation development (OD) concentrates on people dimensions like norms, values, attitudes, relationships, organisational climate, etc.

History of Organisation Development

Douglas McGregor served as resource person to help Union Carbide Corporation to create an OD capability where OD department was set up in 1962. French and Bell who have done most of the work on OD feel that laboratory training and survey feedback are the main stems of OD. Sensitivity training programmes were conducted to managers under the OD movement. OD is still developing and evolving as a technique.

1. What is OD?

Warren G. Bennis defines OD as, "a complex educational strategy to change the beliefs, attitudes, values and structure of organisations so that they can better adapt to new technologies, markets and challenges and the dizzying rate of change itself."

Dale S. Beach defines OD as, "a complex educational strategy designed to increase organisational effectiveness and wealth through planned inventions by a consultant using theory and techniques of applied behavioural science."

2. OD Interventions/Techniques

Organisation development interventions techniques are the methods created by OD professionals and others. Single organisation or consultant cannot use all the interventions. They use these interventions depending upon the need or requirement. The most important interventions are: Survey feedback, process consultation, sensitivity training, the managerial grid, goal setting and planning, team building and management by objectives. Other interventions are job enrichment, changes in organisational structure and participative management and quality circles.

(1) Survey Feedback: This intervention provides data and information to the managers. Attitudes of employees about wage level, and structure, hours of work, working conditions and relations are collected and the results are supplied to top executive teams. These teams analyse the data, find out the problems, evaluate the results and develop the means to correct the problems identified. The teams are formed with the employees at all levels in the organisational hierarchy, *i.e.,* from rank and file to the top level.

(2) Process Consultation: Under this method, the process consultant meets the members of department in work teams, observes their interactions, problem identification skills, problem solving procedures, etc. He feeds back the team with the information collected through observation, coaches and counsels individuals and groups in moulding their behaviour.

(3) Goal Setting and Planning: Each divisions in an organisation or branch/zonal office sets the goals or formulates the plans relating to profitability, markets share, human resources productivity, etc. These goals are sent to the top management, which in turn sends them back to the divisions/zones/branches after modifications. A set of organisation-wide goals thus, emerge thereafter.

(4) Managerial Grid: Industrial psychologist Blake and Mouton developed the managerial grid basing it on the Ohio State Study. The managerial grid identifies a range of management behaviour based on the different ways that how production/service-oriented and employee-oriented states interact with each other.

(5) Sensitivity Training: The most commonly used OD intervention is sensitivity training. It is also called laboratory training. It is called laboratory training as it is conducted by creating an experimental laboratory situation in which employees are brought together, in groups, to interact in an unstructured environment. The members are encouraged to interact with new members and new individual behaviours.

The objectives of laboratory training are:

(i) To help people understand themselves better; *(ii)* To create better understanding of others; *(iii)* To gain insight into the group process; and *(iv)* To develop specific behavioural skills.

Some people never understand why they feel and act as they do and how the others feel about them. Some people are insensitive to the effects of their behaviour upon others and their orders upon subordinates. Laboratory training helps such people to understand the impact of their behaviour on others. Most of the people concentrate on what they are going to say rather than what the others are saying. This training develops the communication skills of the employers and develops them as good listeners. It also helps the participants to form into informal groups and teams and work more effectively.

Modus Operandi of Sensitivity Training

Sensitivity training provides face to face interaction. This training is carried out by largely unstructured groups without an agenda, leader and predetermined goals. The group is given complete freedom in developing their own devices, interactions and on-going process for interaction. Sometimes, the trainer introduces certain planned activities involving one or two professional trainers set in with each "T" group. The emphasis in this training is not upon learning specific facts but upon gaining understanding of feelings, gestures, attitudes and emotions, *i.e.,* sensitivity to oneself and others.

Another type of group is encounter group. These groups involve unstructured small group interaction under stress in a situation that requires people to become sensitive to one another's feelings in order to develop group activity. These groups seek to improve understanding of self and others, group process, culture and general behaviour skills.

(6) Team Building: Most of the laboratory training takes place among the employees of the same department. These employees work together as a team. Team building is nothing but application of various techniques of sensitivity training to the actual work groups in various departments. These work groups consists of peers and a supervisor. Laboratory techniques are also applied to short-term work teams. The technique, like laboratory training, aims at improving inter-group relations. This technique is designed to improve the ability of the employees to work together as teams.

(7) Job Enrichment: Job enrichment as is currently practised all over the world, is a direct outgrowth of Herzberg's two factor theory of motivation. It is therefore based on the assumption that in order to motivate workers, the job itself must provide opportunities for achievement, recognition, responsibility, advancement and growth. The basic idea is to restore to jobs the elements of interests that were taken away under the intensive specification. However, job enrichment is significantly different from horizontal loading, referred to earlier. Horizontal loading does not enrich the task. Washing dishes, then silver ware, and then pots and pans does no more to satisfy and provide an opportunity to grow than washing only dishes. Under job enrichment there is a conscious effort to build into jobs a higher sense of challenge and achievement. In a job enrichment programme, the worker decides how the job is performed, planned, and controlled, and makes more decisions concerning the entire process. The job enrichment approach to boring jobs is to give the individual employee more autonomy in that job. Employees decide how the job will be performed and receive less direct supervision on the job. Consequently, the employee receives a greater sense of accomplishment as well as more authority and responsibility, job satisfaction. This in turn contributes for better employee performance and higher productivity.

(8) Changes in Organisational Structure: Various models of organisational structure, particularly matrix organisation, improves intergroup interaction and relations. Further, changes may be introduced in organisational structure to provide the scope for team work, group interaction and increased inter-personal relations.

(9) Participative Management and Quality Circles: Participative management and quality circles are extension to team work. They provide for voluntary formation of groups/ teams, association, interaction etc. They encourage open discussion on various problems and arriving at a commonly agreed solutions and execution of the agreements by the members themselves.

Use of a Consultant

Top managements engage a consultant or a change agent to help in establishing OD programmes when the qualified, competent and professional employees are not available within the organisation. OD professionals generally possess advanced qualifications in behavioural science and knowledge and experience in designing and conducting laboratory training programmes. The consultant examines the routine activities, provide information, help the management in designing and administering the OD programme. He also helps and trains the members to become self-sufficient in problem solving. The consultant prepares the report and submits to the top management regarding OD policy and programmes on the basis of data and information collected by him from various sources of the organisation. He also helps the organisation in executing the OD programmes. The consultant helps much in developing the members to become more effective in dealing with one another.

3. Benefits of OD

Individual employees, groups/teams and the organisations are benefited by the OD programmes. The benefits of OD include performance improvements, job specification and self-change.

OD programmes contribute to the increase in the job performance of individual employees, groups and the organisation. Impact of OD can be measured by comparing the performance of controlled group with that of non-controlled group. Group performance will be enhanced much as OD emphasises on group activity.

OD programmes encourage team work, communication skills, cooperation, interpersonal relations, openness, etc. Employees with these changing behavioural dimensions feel happy have a sense of satisfaction about the job and organisation.

OD programmes contribute to the change in behaviour, values, attitudes, perceptions, etc., by enabling the employees to understand about themselves and others in the group and organisation. This results in self-change of the employees.

Points to be Remembered

- Positive attitude is viewing and thinking realistically and positively with regard to strategy implementation.
- Leaders influence the followers through various styles all of which are oriented to strategy implementation direction.
- Corporate culture builds appropriate systems, relationships and climate necessary for efficient implementation of the strategy.
- Values influence the organisation as well as strategy.
- Power is extent to which individuals or groups are able to persuade, induce or coerce others into strategy implementation process.
- Change is the law of nature. Change before change, changes you.
- Organisation development is the behavioural changes towards the organisational and strategy implementation requirements.

Keywords

- Positive Attitude
- Leadership
- Democratic Leader
- Power
- Organisational Development
- Strategic Leadership
- Positive Mindset
- Transformational Leader
- Autocratic Leader
- Organisational change
- Values
- Organisational climate

Question for Discussion

1. What is the positive attitude? Discuss the approaches to develop positive attitudes.
2. What is leadership? Explain different kinds of leadership that are appropriate for various strategies
3. What are organisational change? How do you bring the strategic change?
4. What is organisational development? How do you use it for strategy implementation?
5. What is corporate culture? Discuss appropriate culture for strategy implementation.
6. What is power? How do you exert power in the process of strategy implementation.

References

1. W. Bennis, "*Why Leaders Can't Lead: The Unconscious Conspiracy Continues*," Jossey-Bass, San Fransisco, 1989, p. 22.
2. P. Subba Rao, "*Essentials of Human Resource Management and Industrial Relations*," Himalaya Publishing House, Mumbai, 1996, pp. 338-339.
3. Fred Luthans, "*Organizational Behaviour*," p. 398.
4. F.E. Fidler, "A *Theory of Leadership Effectiveness*," McGraw-Hill New York, 1967 and V.H. Vroom and A.G. Jago, "*The New Leadership: Managing Participation in Organisations*", Prentice-Hall, Englewood Cliffs, N.J. 1988.
5. Day and Lord, "*Executive Leadership*," p. 459.
6. J.N. Burns, "*Leadership*", Harper & Row, New York, 1978.
7. B.M. Bass, "*Leadership and Performance Beyond Expectations*," Free Press, New York, 1985.
8. *Ibid*., p. 29.
9. B.M. Bass, "Leadership: Good, Better, Best," *Organisational Dynamics*, 13, Winter 1985, pp. 26-40.
10. Thompson and Strickland, *op. cit*., p. 266.
11. *Ibid*., pp. 268-269.
12. *Ibid*., p. 270.
13. Abraham Zaleznik, "Power and Politics in Organisational Life," *Harvard Business Review*, Vol. 48, No. 3, May-June 1970, pp. 47-60.
14. Quinn, "*Strategies for Change*," p. 68.
15. Thompson and Strickland, *op. cit*., p. 271.
16. Quinn, "Strategies for Change," pp. 128-145. Quoted in *Ibid*., pp. 271-272.
17. Thompson and Strickland, *op. cit*., p. 273.
18. *Ibid*., pp. 273-274.
19. Lawrence R. Jauch and William F. Glueck, *op. cit*., p. 353.
20. *Ibid*., pp. 357-358.
21. *Ibid*., p. 360.
22. Terence F. Deal and Allen A. Kennedy, "*Corporate Cultures*," Addison-Wesley, Reading, Mass, 1982, p. 4.
23. *Ibid*., pp. 15-16.
24. *Ibid*.
25. C.D. Pringle, D.F. Jennings and J.G. Longencker, "*Managing Organisations: Functions and Behaviour*," Merrill, Colombus, Ohio, 1988, p. 594.
26. Pringle *et. al*., "*Managing Organisations*," p. 309.
27. Schein, "*Organisational Culture*," p. 30.
28. *Ibid*., p. 33.

29. Bass, "*Leadership and Performance*," p. 24.

30. Schein, "*Organisational Culture*," pp. 224-237.

31. Thompson and Strickland, *op. cit.*, p. 257.

32. *Ibid.*, p. 258.

33. *Ibid.*, pp. 259-260.

34. Peters and Waterman, "*In Search of Excellence*," pp. 240 and 269.

35. Robert H. Water, Jr., Thomas J. Peters and Julien R. Phillips, "Structure is not Organisation," *Business Horizons*, Vol. 23, No.3, June 1980, pp. 14-26. and Robert H. Waterman, Jr., "The Seven Elements of Strategic Fit," *Journal of Business Strategy*, Vol. 2, No.3, Winter 1982, pp. 68-72.

36. Gerry Johnson and Keven Scholes, *op. cit.*, pp. 121-122.

37. I.C. MacMillan, "*Strategy Formulation: Political Concepts*," West, 1978, p. 15.

38. D.E. Berlew, "*Leadership and Organisational Excitement*," in D.A. Kolb, I.M. Rubin and J.M. McIntyre (Eds.) "*Organisational Psychology*," Prentice-Hall, Englewood Cliffs, N.J., 1974.

39. Yukl, "*Leadership in Organisations*," p. 206.

40. J.R.P. French, Jr., and B. Raven, "*The Bases of Social Power*," pp. 150-167.

41. J.M. Godiwala, W.A. Meinhart and W.D. Warde, "*Corporate Strategy and Functional Management*," Praeger, 1979.

42. Samuel C. Certo and J. Paul Peter, *op. cit.*, p. 219.

43. *Ibid.*, p. 224.

44. *Ibid.*

45. T.M. Garrett, "Business Ethics," *The Times of India Press*, Mumbai, 1970.

46. Samuel C. Certo and J. Paul Peter, *op. cit.*, p. 231.

47. Gene R. Laczniak, "Framework for Analyzing Marketing Ethics," *Journal of Macromarketing*, Spring, 1983, pp. 7-18.

48. Samuel C. Certo and J. Paul Peter, *op. cit.*, p. 231.

49. D. Thakore, "How corrupt is Indian Industry," *Business World*, May 11-24, 1987, pp. 58-67, Quoted in Azhar Kazmi, *op. cit.*, p. 297.

50. Warren G. Bennis, "*Organisational Development*" Addison Wiley, Reading Mass, 1969, p. 2.

51. Dale S. Beach, "*Personnel*," MacMillan Publishing Co., New York, 1985, p. 426.

52. Stephen P. Robbins, "*Organisational Behaviours*," Prentice-Hall, New Delhi , 2007, p. 62.

***

Unit-4

Chapter - 7

Corporate Level Strategic Alternatives

Chapter Outline

(A) Strategy Formulation: Situational Analysis
(B) Stability Strategies
(C) Growth Strategies
(D) Diversification Strategy
(E) Retrenchment Strategies: Turnaround and Transformation Strategies
(F) Strategic Alliances
(G) Combination Strategy/Portfolio Restructuring
(H) Integrated Functional Strategies: Learning, Experience and Technology Curves
— Points to be Remembered
— Keywords
— Questions for Discussion
— References

Learning Objectives

After studying this chapter, you should be able to:

- Undertake strength, weakness, opportunity and threat (SWOT) analysis;
- Discuss various stability strategies;
- Analyse various growth strategies like mergers, takeovers, horizontal integration, vertical integration and joint ventures;
- Explain retrenchment strategies like turnaround strategies, captive company strategy, divestment strategy and liquidation strategy;
- Craft combination strategy and portfolio restructuring;
- Discuss various forms of strategic alliances.

(A) STRATEGY FORMULATION: SITUATIONAL ANALYSIS

Strategy formulation is often referred to as strategic planning or long range planning. This process is primarily analytical and not action oriented. The strategy formulation process is concerned with developing a corporation's mission, objectives, strategy and policy. This process involves scanning external and internal environmental factors, analysis of the strategic factors and generation and evaluation and selection of the best alternative strategy appropriate to the analysis.

Evaluation of Current Results

Henry Mintzberg, after much research found that strategy formulation is typically not a regular, continuous process. "It is small, often an irregular, discontinuous process, proceeding in fits and starts. There are periods of stability in strategy development, but also there are periods of flux, of grouping, of piecemeal change and of global change."

Performance results are generally periodic measurements of developments that occur during a given time period like return on investment, profits after taxes, earnings per share and market share. The current performance results are compared with the current objectives and with that of the previous year's performance results. If the results are equal to or greater than the current objectives and past year's results, the company will mostly continue with the current strategy otherwise, the strategy formulation process begins in earnest.

The strategic managers must evaluate the mission, objectives and policies. In fact, the strategic managers are evaluated in terms of management style, values and skills by the top management. Henry Mintzberg has pointed out that a corporation's objectives and strategies are strongly affected by the top management's view of the world. This view determines the mode to be used in strategy formulation. These modes include: entrepreneurial mode, adaptive mode and planning mode as presented in Exhibit 7.1.

Exhibit 7.1: Characteristics and Conditions of Three Modes

Characteristics	Entrepreneurial Mode	Adaptive Mode	Planning Mode
Motive for Decisions	Proactive	Reactive	Proactive & Reactive
Goals of Organisation	Growth	Indeterminate	Efficiency & Growth
Evaluation of Proposals	Judgmental	Judgmental	Analytical
Choice made by	Entrepreneur	Bargaining	Management
Decision Horizon	Long term	Short term	Long term
Preferred Environment	Uncertainty	Certainty	Risk
Decision Linkages	Loosely coupled	Disjointed	Integrated
Flexibility of Mode	Flexible	Adaptive	Constrained

Size of Moves	Bold Decisions	Incremental Steps	Global Strategies
Vision of Direction	General	None	Specific
Condition for Use			
Source of Power	Entrepreneur	Divided	Management
Objectives of Organisation	Operational	Non-operational	Operational
Organisational Environment	Yielding	Complex, dynamic	Predictable, Stable
Status of Organisation	Young, small, or strong leadership	Established	Large

Source: H. Mintzberg, "Strategy Making in Three Modes," *California Management Review*, Vol. XVI, No. 2, p.49, in Thomas I,. Wheeler and J. David Hunger, *op. cit., p. 147.*S

Entrepreneurial Mode: Strategy is formulated by one powerful individual. The focus is on opportunities rather than on problems. Strategy is guided by the founder's own vision of direction.

Adaptive Mode: This strategy formulation mode is characterised by reactive solutions to the existing problems rather than a proactive search for new opportunities.

Planning Mode: Analysts assume main responsibility for strategy formulation. Strategic planning includes both the proactive search for new opportunities and the reactive solution of existing problems.

SWOT Analysis

Underlying any successful selection of strategies is an analysis of the firm's internal strengths and weaknesses and the opportunities provided and the threats that are posed by the external environment. As explained earlier, the process of examining the firm and its environment is known as SWOT (strengths, weaknesses, opportunities and threats) analysis. The management should identify and analyse various factors (See Exhibit 7.2) to identify the strengths, weaknesses, opportunities and threats. This analysis will help the company to position itself to take the advantage of the opportunities provided by the environment and to minimise the threats posed by the environment. This analysis will also help the organisation, to emphasise on its strengths and moderate the impact of its weaknesses. Further, the organisation can uncover its strengths that have not yet been fully utilised and correct or make up for the weaknesses. Matching environmental information with the knowledge of the organisation's capabilities enables management to formulate efficient and realistic strategies for attaining organisational goals.

Exhibit 7.2: Framework for SWOT Analysis

Sources of Possible Environmental Opportunities and Threats:			
Economic Forces	Political-Legal Forces	Social Forces	Technological Forces
Industry Forces			
Possible Organisational	Strengths and Weaknesses		
Advertising	Distribution	Leadership	Product/Service Quality
Brand names	Economies of Scales	Location	Promotion
Channel Management	Environmental Scanning	Management	Public relations
Company Reputation	Financial Resources	Manufacturing and	Purchasing
Computer Information	Forecasting	operations	Quality control
System	Government Lobbying	Market Share	Research & Development
Control Systems	Human Resources	Organisational	Selling
Costs	Inventory Management	Structure	Technology.
Customer Loyalty	Labour Relations	Physical facilities/	
Decision-Making		equipment	
		Product/Service	
		Differentiation	

Source: Peter Wright, Charles D. Pringle and Mark J. Kroll, *op. cit.*, p. 70.

Corporate Profiles

SWOT analysis helps the management in determining in which business or businesses the company should be operating. The three types of corporate profiles are: *(i)* the firm can compete in one business or industry, *(ii)* the firm can compete in several related businesses or industries, *(iii)* the firm can compete in several unrelated businesses or industries. The firm benefits from the specialised knowledge, by competing in only one industry. But, operating primarily in one industry, increases a firm's vulnerability to business cycles. Firms competing in related businesses and/or markets/countries transfer the improvements in production or efficiencies in operation of one business to other businesses or markets or countries.

However, these firms also face the problems of shrinkage in consumer demand or price competition. These problems can be overcome by operating in unrelated businesses. But, the firms operating in unrelated businesses face the problems in managing diverse and unrelated businesses efficiently. SWOT analysis helps in determining which of these strategies is most appropriate for a particular firm. The strategist must analyse the firm's critical weaknesses or valuable strengths based on internal environmental analysis in the context of abundant opportunities provided or critical threats posed by the external environment. (See Fig.7.1)

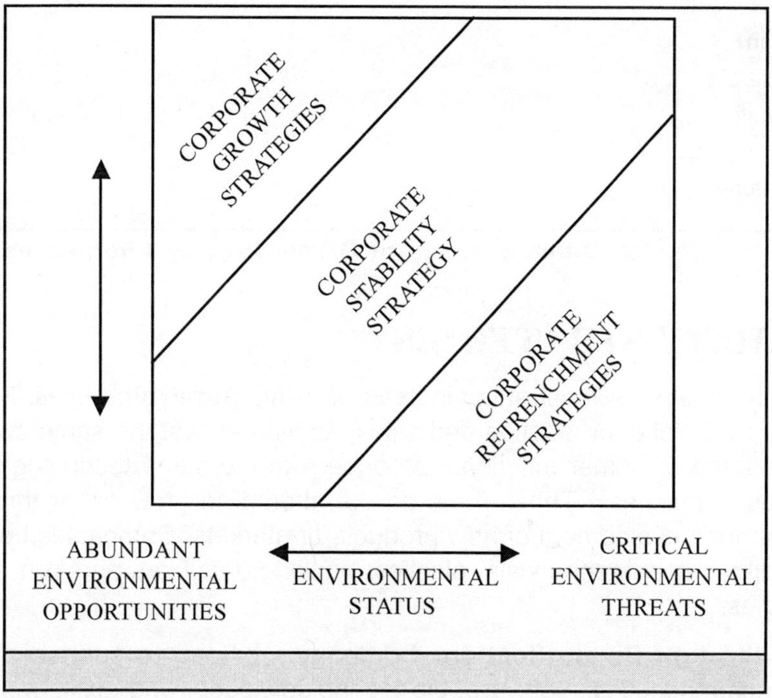

Source: Peter Wright, Charles D. Pringle and Mark J. Kroll, *op. cit.*, p. 72.

Fig. 7.1: SWOT Analysis

Strategic Alternatives

After analysing the environment and assessing the internal environment, the next step in the strategic planning process is to develop strategic alternatives to help the organisation in achieving its objectives. Different kinds of strategic alternatives are presented in Fig. 7.2. "Strategic alternatives revolve around the question of whether to continue or change the business enterprise which is currently in or improve the efficiency and effectiveness with which the firm achieves its corporate objectives in its chosen business sector." Glueck and Jauch identify four grand strategies, *viz.*, stability, expansion, retrenchment and combination of these three strategies. Now, we discuss these strategies.

KINDS OF GRAND STRATEGIES			
Stability Strategies	**Growth Strategies**	**Retrenchment Strategies**	**Combination Strategies**
• Maintenance of Status Quo • Sustainable Growth • Takeover/ Acquisition	• Internal Growth • Concentration Strategies • Mergers • Liquidation	• Turnaround • Captive Company • Transformation • Divestment	Portfolio Restructuring

- Horizontal Integration
- Conglomerate Diversification
- Vertical Integration
- Joint Ventures

Fig. 7.2: Different Kinds of Grand Strategy Alternatives

(B) STABILITY STRATEGIES

Some firms adopt stability strategy instead of using growth strategies. Firms attempt to maintain their size, level of production and sales, serving almost the same customer groups, performing the same customer functions, produce with the same technologies and operate the current lines of business. These firms do not attempt to grow either through increased sales or through the development of new products or markets. Companies belonging to mid-day industries like cement, chemicals, plastics, banking, fertilizers and iron and steel adopt stability strategies.

Stability through Diversification: Companies belong to sunrise and sun-setting industries like pharmaceutical, software, bio-technology, paper and textile mostly experience output, sales and profit swings either due to a declining demand or due to environmental uncertainties. Such companies diversify into those areas where they can experience stability in output, sales and profits. For example, DOW Chemical, Dupont, BASF and ICI diversified into plastics, fertilizers and synthetic fibers which are stable in business operations. Bayer AG purchased Roche Holding which is a consumer drug company to balance the portfolios in terms of output, sales and profits. Similarly, Bayer started the portfolios like pesticides, seeds, health care and advanced plastics. Similarly, Tata Iron and Steel Company diversified into automobiles, software, food, etc., and Reliance entered into petroleum, communication and retail business in order to enjoy the stability of earnings from different businesses.

Stability through Minor Functional Strategies: Some companies belonging to sun-setting/non-growth industries like hotel, automobile and publishing adopt minor functional strategies like service strategies, modernisation and customisation strategies in order to have stability in sales revenue and profits. For example, most of the hotels adopted the strategy of home delivery, publishing companies adopted the strategy of publishing the books based on the requirements of a specific customer group and textile companies modernised the factories in order to have stability of sales and profits.

This strategy can be of five types, *viz.*, maintenance of *status quo* and sustainable growth.

- Maintenance of *Status-Quo*
- Sustainable Growth
- Pause/Proceed with Caution Strategy

- No Change Strategy
- Profit Strategy

Maintenance of *Status Quo*

The firms adopting this strategy maintain the same level of operations. Small business firms desire satisfactory level of operations rather than growth.

Sustainable Growth: Slow growth is more desired rather than maintenance of *status quo*. In fact, it is very difficult to maintain *status quo*. Therefore, a sustainable growth strategy is more optimistic than the zero growth.

Pause/Proceed With Caution Strategy

The companies test the environment and particularly the market conditions, whenever they introduce a new product or service. At that time, they observe the reactions of the market and proceed in accordance with the positive reactions of the market. They pause the business operations including production and marketing, if the market reactions are negative. Thus, the companies follow pause and proceed strategies until the environment reaches the stability stage. Once the environment is stable, the company would follow stability strategy. Companies, thus, follow *ad hoc* strategies until the environment is under volatile conditions. Dell Computers experienced abnormal growth in demand in early 1990s and it could not manage the increased demand. Then, the company followed this strategy until it could meet the increased demand.

No Change Strategy

Companies continue the same strategy until the internal environment and external environment remain more or less constant. Even though, there would be minor changes in the environment like enhancement of opportunities or threats, there would be offset by the entry of new firms into the industry or exit of existing firms from the industry. In other words, when the opportunities increase in the form of increase in demand, new firms enter the industry. In case of increase in threats in the form of decline in demand, the existing firms exit from the industry.

Profit Strategy

Profit strategy aims at maintaining the same level of profit (earned during favourable economic conditions) even during uncertain and unfavourable economic conditions, through window dressing. Thus, the companies support themselves artificially through any one or combination of the following tactics:

- boosting up of sales revenue by presenting gross sales,
- reducing operating expenditure,
- presenting the income earned through sale of assets as operating income,

- reducing the depreciation amount by using different methods of calculation of depreciation, and
- presenting the bad debts as debtors.

Companies should use this strategy cautiously and rarely or otherwise they experience the situation experienced by Satyam Computers during late 2008.

Reasons for Adopting Stability Strategies: Firms adopt the stability strategies due to the following reasons:

(i) Managers of small businesses desire a satisfactory level of profits rather than increased profits.

(ii) Maintenance of *status quo* involves less risk than a more growth strategy.

(iii) Change of any form may disrupt the current working relationships and the consequences may be detrimental to the organisation.

(iv) Change may upset the smooth operations and result in poor performance especially, if the firm considers itself successful with the present level of operations.

(v) Changing operations to pursue a more aggressive growth strategy usually requires an increased investment and managerial support. Firms, which cannot provide resources, may continue with the stability strategy.

(vi) Some executives maintain with the stability strategy due to inertia for change.

(vii) In some cases, firms are forced to adopt stability strategy, if they operate in a low growth or no growth industry.

(viii) Sometimes, firms may find that the cost of growth is more than the benefits of the same.

(ix) Firms that dominate their industry through their superior size and competitive advantage may pursue stability to reduce their chances of being prosecuted for engaging in monopolistic practices, and

(x) Smaller firms that concentrate on specialised products or services may choose stability because of their concern that growth will result in reduced quality and customer service.

Despite these reasons for adopting stability strategy, there is a danger of pursuing the stability strategy. The danger is that the environment may change and cause the firm or its product line to become obsolete. Hence, firms plan for adopting growth strategies.

(C) GROWTH STRATEGIES

Organisations may select a growth strategy to increase their profits, sales and/or market share. They also pursue a growth strategy to reduce the cost of production per unit. Growth strategies involve a significant increase in performance objectives. These strategies are adopted when firms remarkably broaden the scope of their customer groups, customer functions and alternative technologies either singly or in combination with each other. The different types of growth strategies are discussed hereunder:

> Growth strategies include: internal growth and concentration strategies.

1. Internal Growth Strategy

Internal growth is achieved through increasing the firm's production capacity, employees and sales. Some firms prefer this strategy to the strategy of external growth as internal growth preserves their efficiency, quality and image unlike in external growth.

2. Concentration Strategies

Firms pursue concentration strategies to grow while remaining relatively simple. The total efforts of the firm are concentrated on a limited combination of customer groups, customer functions, alternate technologies and products.

Eureka Vacuum Cleaners added new functions to the vacuum cleaners like cleaning beds, cleaning domestic drainage in addition to cleaning the floor by adding a few more equipment to the original products, in order to serve the domestic customers in multiple activities. Similarly, Nokia added camera, audio and video camera, and internet facility to their mobile phones in order to meet the diversified needs of the same customer groups.

Advantages: Lauenstein and Skinner argue that most of the effective organisations focus on a narrow set of objectives. A firm can gain a competitive advantage by concentrating on a specific technology, product or market. Firms pursuing this strategy are frequently able to identify new developments and trends within the industry and respond to them. Exhibit 7.3 presents strategic alternatives available to the firms pursuing concentration strategies. However, firms change their strategies from concentration strategies despite the advantages.

Exhibit 7.3: Strategic Alternatives Available to the Firms Pursuing Concentration Strategies

Focus on Customer:

- Increase usage by present customers:
  - Increase purchase size or frequency
  - Improve product location
  - Expand product line (sizes, options, styles)
  - Expand shelf space
- Attract Competitors' Customers:
  - Increase promotional efforts
  - Initiate price cuts
- Attract Nonusers of the product:
  - Advertise new uses

Offer special prices and promotions
Increase product availability (new geographic uses)

Focus on Product:

Differentiate product from its competitors
Increase Rate of Product Obsolescence
Change styles
Change options
Change colours
Develop new uses for the product
Improve product servicing

Focus on Technology:

Develop new equipment to improve efficiency
Develop new products
Find uses for by-products
Improve quality

Source: Joe G. Thomas, *op. cit.*, p. 203.

Problems: There are certain potential problems of concentration strategies. They are:

(i) One of the greatest problems is the risk associated with putting "all the corporate eggs in one basket."

(ii) The introduction of substitute products may also be very detrimental to a firm following a concentration strategy. The substitute products can make a firm's product obsolete particularly when the firm concentrates on only one product or product line.

(iii) A company pursuing concentration strategy may also be affected by the disruption in the supply of essential and crucial raw material.

(iv) Sometimes, the market segment becomes unattractive owing to limited growth opportunities, and availability of substitute products or absence of essential resources. In such a case, a firm pursuing a concentration strategy may become locked into one area of business and become unable to move into another line of business.

Exhibit 7.4 presents the reasons for change of a firm from concentration strategies.

Exhibit 7.4: Reasons for Change of a Firm From Concentration Strategies

1. *Temptations of diversification* — Spreading risks by operating in multiple areas decreases the threat of any one area causing the firm to fail. However, diversification spreads resources over several areas, similarly decreasing the probability that the firm can be a strong force in any area.
2. *Need to meet short term goals* — When the firm is not strong in an area, managers tend to experience pressures to do what is necessary to meet the plan (budget or quota) in the short run rather than focusing on a long range success. Many times short term sales and profits can be increased by moving into new businesses.

3. *Underestimation of present opportunities* — Spreading resources too thin may cause an organization to overlook opportunities in its existing field. Similarly, resources may limit a firm's ability to capitalize on opportunities that do develop.
4. *Impatience to grow* — Small firms often feel they are too small to be important in their field. Growth becomes a primary objective. Once they have moved into other fields to increase sales and profits, however, diversified firms discover that they lack the management and financial resources needed to operate the diverse organization.
5. *Overconfidence* — A company doing well may conclude it has superior ability and can be successful in almost any business. Management often forgets the years of experience it took to earn the success being achieved. Such firms lack this experience in the new business.
6. *Misjudging success requirements* — Problems of the new business are often more complex and resistant to solution than expected. Connections between the new and old businesses are often superficial and only marginally related to the problems of the new venture.
7. *Pressure to use idle capacity* — Firms with excess resources, especially manufacturing facilities, feel compelled to put unused resources to work immediately. Rather than wait for growth to utilize the capacity, firms often rush into the first available alternative to begin using idle resources.
8. *Siren song of integration* — Forward or backward integration creates opportunities to control resources or markets and to "absorb the profits of the middleman." Many times, the acquiring firm lacks the expertise of the middleman. Furthermore, the acquiring organization rarely is able to operate the supplier/market at its most efficient capacity, thus, incurring diseconomies of scale.
9. *Dangers of pride* — Even after entering a new field that turns sour, managers are often reluctant to admit to making a mistake. Commitment to this strategy escalates. Resources are devoted to supporting the struggling venture to save the managers, pride, rather than allocating those resources to more profitable, growing projects.

Source: M. Lauenstein and W. Skinner, "Formulating a Strategy of Superior Resources," *Journal of Business Strategy*, pp. 4-10 in Joe G. Thomas, *op. cit.*, pp. 202-203.

(3) Merger Strategy

Many firms prefer to grow through mergers. Combination of two or more firms is known as a merger. When the firms of similar objectives and similar strategies combine into one firm, such combinations are called mergers. "A merger is a combination of two or more businesses in which one acquires the assets and liabilities of the other in exchange for stock or cash or both. Companies are dissolved and assets and liabilities are combined and new stock is issued." Mergers can take place within one nation or across nations.

Types of Mergers: Mergers can be classified into the following types:

(i) *Horizontal Mergers:* Horizontal mergers are combinations of firms engaged in the same business. Merger of Tata Steel with Natsteel of Singapore and Videocon with Thomson, SA, an electronics company of France are examples of horizontal merger.

(ii) *Vertical Mergers:* Vertical mergers are combination of different firms engaged in activities complementary to each other like supply of raw materials, production of goods and marketing. For example, combination of firm engaged in mining of iron ore, and iron and steel company. Merger of A. P. Lightings with Philips is an example for vertical integration.

(iii) *Concentric Mergers:* Concentric mergers are combination of firms related to each other in terms of customer groups or customer functions or alternative technologies. For example, combination of firms producing televisions, washing machines, and kitchen appliances.

(iv) *Conglomerate Mergers:* Conglomerate mergers are the combination of firms unrelated to each other in terms of customer groups, customer functions and alternative technologies. For example: combination of a publishing company and an automobile company.

Reasons/Motives for Merger

Two or more firms have to act for merger. One of them is the buyer and the other one is the seller. Both these firms have motives for combination. Availability of readymade or built-in manufacturing facilities, well known brands or brand loyalty, captive market share, loyal customers, advanced technology, efficient distribution channels, financial soundness, etc., are attractive factors resulting in the merger. Exhibit 7.5 presents the buyer's motives and seller's motives for merging.

Exhibit 7.5: The Buyer's and Seller's Motives for Merging

The buyer's motives for merging include the following:

- To increase the value of the firm's stock. Mergers often lead to increases in the stock price and/or price-earnings ratio.
- To increase the growth rate of the firm.
- To make a good investment. A firm may make a better use of funds by purchasing instead of plowing the same funds into internal expansion.
- To improve the stability of the firm's earnings and sales. This is done by acquiring firms whose earnings and sales complement the firm's peaks and valleys.
- To balance or fill out the product line.
- To diversify the product line when the current products have reached their peak in the life cycle.
- To reduce competition by purchasing a competitor (possible violation of the Sherman Act).
- To acquire a needed resource quickly – for example, high quality technology or highly innovative management.
- For tax reasons. It may be desirable to purchase a firm with prior tax losses which will offset the current or future earnings.

- To increase efficiency and profitability, especially if there is synergy between the two companies. (Synergy is discussed later in the chapter.)

The seller's motives for merging include the following:

- To increase the value of the owner's stock and investment in the firm.
- To increase the firm's growth rate by receiving more resources from the acquiring company.
- To acquire the resources to stabilise operations and make them more efficient.
- For tax reasons. If the firm is owned by a family or an individual, a merger makes it easier to deal with estate tax problems.
- To help diversify the owning family's holdings beyond the present firm.
- To deal with top management problems such as management succession for an entrepreneur or dissension among top managers.

Source: Lawrence R. Jauch and William F. Glueck, *op. cit.*, p. 229.

Critical Issues in Merger: There are four critical areas of merger. They are: strategic issues, financial issues, managerial issues and legal issues.

(i) **Strategic Issues:** These issues relate to commonality of strategic interests for mergers between the firms. Strengths of one firm may be the weaknesses of the other firm and *vice versa*. Both the firms get the advantage of the strengths of each other after the merger. Further, the impact of synergy would help both the organisations after merger to achieve the objective efficiently.

(ii) **Financial Issues:** These issues include *(a)* valuation of seller firm, *(b)* Sources of financing for merger, etc. Value of the selling firm may be assessed based on the assets, market standing, earning potential, share prices, etc. Source of financing would be based on shares through exchange of debt and equity. However, other sources of financing are used rarely.

(iii) **Managerial Issues:** Managerial issues are critical in mergers. There would be significant changes in the top management level and chief executive of the firm after merger. Further, professional management may not be given due consideration after merger. Even the staff members at middle and lower levels may also be changed after merger. To make the merger a smooth one, there should be an understanding between the buyer and seller about the top level management, staff at all levels and professional management. Further, steps should also be taken to train the employees of both the firms about the organisational culture of each other.

(iv) **Legal Issues:** Legal issues in mergers are concerned with the provisions of the various laws relating to mergers. These provisions of the laws include: Chapter V of the Companies Act, 1956, the MRTP Act and Section 72A (I) of the Income Tax Act.

Advantages and Disadvantages of Mergers

Mergers as a growth strategy are popular in many countries. There are certain advantages of mergers for both the buying and selling firms. These advantages include:

(i) The firm after the merger will enjoy the economies of large scale operations.

(ii) The firm after the merger can utilise the funds to the maximum extent and get the benefit of profit growth.

(iii) The firm will be in a position to diversify the activities, increase the level of operations and level of profits.

(iv) The more effective and efficient utilisation of resources will result in higher productivity.

(v) Revival of sick units and avoidance of mortality of loss making organisation can be possible through merger.

(vi) Entrepreneurs often find it easy to buy an existing firm with established markets rather than establishing a new company.

(vii) The merger provides the buying company an easy entry into the market along with the customers' loyalty.

(viii) The merger also helps the buying company in having easy access to the sources of raw material, finance and human resources.

(ix) The problems of procuring skilled employees and developing them can be solved through mergers.

(x) The organisational life cycle can be expanded for a longer period through mergers.

Despite these advantages, mergers and acquisitions are not always successful due to their disadvantages.

Disadvantages

(i) The psychological problems of the top management of the merging firms after merger may result in disbanding of merger.

(ii) Negative attitude of the senior partner towards the junior firm may result in the failure of the merger.

(iii) The executives of the acquired firm may get low status, low level authority and power.

(iv) Research studies find that the performance and profitability of the combined firms tend to decline compared with that of the merging firms, before merger.

(v) The mergers will lead to concentration of economic power, monopolistic conditions and thereby political power, higher prices, restricted supply, black marketing, etc.

Reasons for failure of mergers are presented in Exhibit 7.6.

Exhibit 7.6: Reasons for Failure of Mergers

Business Week reviewed a sample of firms completing mergers and identified seven reasons for the failure of mergers.

1. Paying too much for the acquired firm.
2. Assuming that a growing market or product will continue its recent outstanding performance.
3. Leaping into a merger without carefully studying its consequences.
4. Diversifying into areas in which the firm had too limited knowledge.
5. Buying too large a firm and thus, incurring an excessively large debt.
6. Trying to merge disparate corporate cultures.
7. Counting on key personnel staying after the merger.

Source: "Do Mergers Really Work," *Business Week*, June 3, 1985, pp. 88-91.

Guidelines for Effective Mergers

In view of the failure of some of the mergers due to the disadvantages discussed above, the firms should follow the guidelines for the success of the mergers. The guidelines for effective mergers are:

(i) Mergers must be carefully planned.

(ii) Human considerations should also be given sufficient care as that of financial resources.

(iii) The valuation of a merger candidate is an important process.

(iv) Legal factors must be carefully assessed.

(v) Mergers which create synergy are likely to be more successful.

(vi) The benefits of merger, the positions and the authority in the combined firm should be distributed to the people of both the firms with due considerations.

(vii) A separate plan and a detailed programme should be prepared.

(viii) Authority and responsibilities should be clearly written for executing the programme of merger.

(ix) The activities of merger should be controlled through the technique of feed-forward and management information system.

(4) Takeovers or Acquisitions Strategy

Sometimes firms want to grow through the strategy of takeover or acquisition. Takeover (or acquisition) is defined as, "the attempt (often sprung as a surprise) of one firm to acquire ownership or control over another firm against the wishes of the latter's management (and purchase some of its stakeholders)." But, in practice, takeovers can be hostile (against the wishes of the acquired firm) or friendly (through mutual consent of buyer and seller like in merger). Takeover strategy is currently the most popular strategy in India, particularly after the economic liberationisation.

Exhibit 7.7 presents the examples of acquisitions.

Exhibit 7.7

Acquirer	*Acquiree*	*Industry*
Tata Steel, India	Corus Group, UK	Steel
Hindalco, India	Novelis, Canada	Steel
Videocon, India	Daewoo Electronics, Korea	Electronics
Dr. Reddy's Lab, India	Beta Pharma, Germany	Pharmaceutical
SuzCon Energy, India	Hansen Group, Belgium	Energy
HPCL, India	Kenya Petroleum Ltd., Kenya	Oil and Gas
Ranbaxy Labs, India	Terapia SA, Romania	Pharmaceutical
VSNL, India	Teleglobe, Canada	Telecom

Advantages of Takeovers

(i) Takeovers ensure management accountability.

(ii) Takeovers provide easy growth opportunities.

(iii) They create mobility of resources from one activity to another activity.

(iv) They avoid gestation periods and problems involved in new projects.

(v) They provide the chance of survival to the sick units and provide alternatives to the disinvestment strategy.

However, the strategy of takeovers, suffers from disadvantages.

Disadvantages

The disadvantages of takeovers are:

(i) Professionalisation of the management may be replaced by money power.

(ii) Takeovers do not create any real assets to the society.

(iii) They result in monopoly and concentration of economic power.

(iv) They are detrimental to the society.

(v) Interests of the minority shareholders are not protected.

These disadvantages sometimes result in the failure of some takeovers.

Guidelines for Effective Takeovers

Prasanna Chandra recommends a six step procedure for effective takeovers. This procedure includes:

(a) Spell out the objectives.

(b) Indicate how the objectives would be achieved.

(c) Assess managerial quality.

(d) Check the compatibility of business styles.

(e) Anticipate and solve problems early.

(f) Treat people with dignity and concern.

Guidelines for effective takeover offered by an executive are presented as follows:

(i) Specify clearly the acquisition objectives, especially the earning objectives.

(ii) Workout and specify the gains of shareholders of both the firms.

(iii) Be sure that the management of the acquired company is or can be made competent.

(iv) Note the existence of important dovetailing resources but do not expect perfect compatibility.

(v) Initiate the process of merger with active involvement of the chief executive.

(vi) Clearly define the business that the company is in.

(vii) Identify and check on the strengths, weaknesses and key performance factors for both the firms.

(viii) Anticipate problems and discuss them early with the other firm so as to create a climate of trust.

(ix) Be sure that the takeover does not pose a threat to the present management team.

(x) People should be of prime consideration in planning for takeover and structuring the organisation.

(5) Horizontal Integration

Many companies expand by creating other firms in their same line of business. For example, Tata group established Tata Financial Services, Tata Capital and Tata Investment Corporation in the same line of business.

The reasons for engaging in this process of horizontal integration are:

(a) to increase the market share, *(b)* to reduce the cost of operations per unit of business through the large scale economies, *(c)* to get greater leverage to deal with the customers and suppliers, *(d)* to promote the products and services more efficiently to a larger audience, *(e)* to have greater access to the channels of distribution, *(f)* to enjoy increased operational flexibility, *(g)* finally, to take the advantage of the benefits of synergy. When the combination of two or more business units (existing and created) results in greater effectiveness and efficiency than the total yielded by those businesses, when they were operated separately, then synergy has been attained.

(6) Conglomerate Diversification

Horizontal integration strategy aims at related diversification. In other words, diversification occurs, when the existing firm creates another business unit in the same industry. But, firms may also expand through unrelated or conglomerate diversification. In other words, firms create new business units that are unrelated to its original business. For example, Gujarat Gas Ltd., created another business unit, *i.e.,* Gujarat Finance Company Ltd.

Other examples of Conglomerate diversification include establishment of unrelated businesses by Tata group like Tata Steel, Tata Consultancy Services, Tanishq Jewellery, Tata Tele Services and Tata Tea. Similarly, Aditya Birla group established unrelated businesses like Ultra Tech Cement, Indian Aluminium, Bihar Caustic and Chemicals, Idea Cellular, Birla Sun Life Insurance and PSI Data Systems.

Benefits: The benefits of conglomerate diversification are:

(a) Reduction of risks. This benefit is particularly important for businesses that operate in industries subject to rapid technological change, *(b)* economies of large scale operations, *(c)* financial stability, *(d)* increase in profits, and *(e)* attain managerial competence.

Reasons for Adopting Conglomerate Strategy

The firms adopt conglomerate strategy in order to:

(a) achieve growth rate higher than what can be realised through expansion,

(b) make effective use of financial resources with retained profits exceeding immediate investment needs,

(c) avail the potential opportunities of profitable investments,

(d) achieve distinctive competitive advantage and broader stability,

(e) improve the price-earnings ratio and bring about a higher market price of shares.

(7) Vertical Integration

Another growth strategy is vertical integration, in which new products and/or services, which are complementary to the existing product and/or service lines, are added. Vertical integration is characterised by the extension of the company's business definition in three possible directions from the existing business, *viz., (i)* backward integration, *(ii)* forward integration, and *(iii)* both backward and forward integrations. Backward vertical integration occurs when the firms acquire or create the company that supply the firm, the raw materials or components and other inputs. Forward vertical integration occurs when the firms acquire or create the company that purchases its products and/or services. Indian Railways established their own production units like Chittaranjan Locomotive Works, Diesel Locomotive Works, Integral Coach Factory, Rail Wheel Factory and Rail Coach Factory. These business units help Indian Railways to produce the coaches and engines necessary for them. Thus, these business units are the examples of backward linkage strategy. Indian Railways also established Catering and Tourism Corporation, which is an example for the forward linkage. Fig. 7.3 shows both backward and forward linkages.

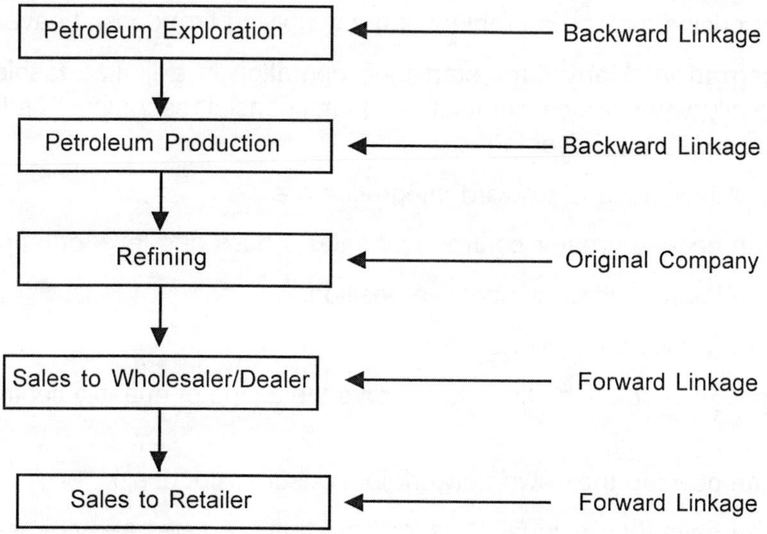

Fig. 7.3: Backward and Forward Linkages of Petroleum Refining Company

Advantages of Backward Integration Strategy

Backward integration strategy is adopted by many firms in view of its advantages. They include:

(i) Firms adopting this strategy can have a regular and uninterrupted supply of raw materials, components and other inputs.

(ii) Quality control of the raw material, components and parts can be ensured easily.

(iii) Firms can earn higher rate of return on investment in view of better use of overhead facilities and spread of overhead costs.

(iv) Firm can increase its power of negotiation with other suppliers in view of access to information on costs.

(v) Indirect taxes payable on purchase of inputs can be minimised, and

(vi) Firm can enjoy the economies of large scale operations.

Disadvantages: Though this strategy is advantageous to the companies, some companies find that this strategy is not desirable in view of the certain disadvantages associated with it. They are:

(i) Technological upgradation in one of the firms makes backward integration technically not feasible.

(ii) Technological upgradation in one of the firms, necessarily forces the management to upgrade the technology of the remaining firms. This process demands for heavy financial investment.

(iii) Adverse economic conditions in the main firm also affect the firm supplying raw materials, components, etc.

(iv) Transfer pricing may be a problem, if the supplying firm doesn't have freedom.

Forward Integration: Many firms start their operation in a limited fashion, and later expand them vertically, when they accumulate enough financial resources. The firms develop forward integration due to the advantages.

Advantages: Advantages of forward integration are:

(i) Firms can acquire greater control over sales, prices and level of output.

(ii) Firms can improve their competitive position.

(iii) Firms can reduce their overall costs.

(iv) This strategy enables the firms to improve the scope of quantity control at different stages.

(v) Firms can develop their own network for consumer feedback.

(vi) Firms can have their own facilities for providing pre-sales and post-sales service.

Disadvantages: Despite the advantages, sometimes the firms avoid this strategy in view of its disadvantages. They are:

(i) Since the firm produces the final products with its own components, and sells the final products as well as components, the firm may involve in a conflicting situation of competing with its own customers.

(ii) Sometimes it is difficult to cope up with the changes in technology,

(iii) The firm may face financial problems as this strategy demands for large scale operations.

In brief, there are many reasons for pursuing a diversification strategy and many different means to achieve that diversification. Exhibit 7.8 presents an overview of the various types of diversification alternatives available to a firm.

Exhibit 7.8: An Overview of the Various Types of Diversification Alternatives Available to a Firm

	Concentric Diversification (Related)		***Conglomerate Diversification (Unrelated)***	
	Internal	External	Internal	External
Horizontal Integration	Develop new products for current markets.	Buy a firm with products similar to existing products.	Develop totally new and unrelated products.	Merge with a firm having a distinct product line.
Vertical Integration	Move into new markets with current products.	Buy a firm with distribution channels in a new market.	Diversify into new markets with new products.	Acquire a firm that allows entry into a new market segment.
Backward:	Develop a production facility for raw materials used in current products.	Purchase facilities to produce component parts for existing products.	Develop capabilities to produce raw materials unrelated to existing products.	Acquire a producer of component parts not needed in current production processes.
Forward:	Develop retail outlets for existing products.	Acquire a retail outlet to sell existing products.	Open retail outlets that do not handle current product line.	Purchase a retail outlet that will not handle existing products.

Source: Joe G. Thomas, *op. cit.*, p. 214.

(8) Joint Ventures

Joint ventures are partnerships in which two or more firms carry out a specific project or corporate in a selected area of business. Joint ventures can be temporary, disbanding after the project is finished, or long term. The ownership of the firms remains unchanged. "Even a successful joint venture may not last forever. Nor does the collapse of a joint venture always imply failure. Actually, corporate partnerships are formed for specific and time bound objectives which, once achieved, leave little reason for the alliance to be continued. Joint ventures that last longer do so because their objectives have been redesigned."

When Do Joint Ventures Form?

Joint ventures form:

1. When an activity is uneconomical for an organisation to do alone.
2. When the risk of business has to be shared, and therefore, is reduced for the participating firms.
3. When the distinctive competence of two or more organisations can be pooled together.
4. When setting up of an organisation requires surmounting hurdles such as import quotas, tariffs, nationalistic political interest and cultural roadblocks.

Characteristics of Joint Ventures

The characteristics of joint ventures are:

(i) Every joint venture has a scheduled life-cycle, which will end sooner or later.

(ii) Every joint venture has to be dissolved when it has outlived its life-cycle.

(iii) Changes in the environment force the joint ventures to be redesigned regularly.

(iv) Joint ventures between Indian companies and transnationals also follow life-cycle.

(v) Transnationals seek to absorb their partner's competencies.

Types of Joint Ventures

1. Formation of a joint venture between two firms of the same industry of the same country.
2. Formation of a joint venture between two firms of different industries but of the same country.

3. Formation of a joint venture between two firms of two countries locating the business in the domestic country.

4. Formation of a joint venture between two firms of two countries locating the business in the foreign country.

5. Formation of a joint venture between two firms of two countries and locating the business in the third country.

Reasons for the Formation of Joint Ventures

Joint ventures are undertaken for a variety of reasons like, political, economic and technological.

1. In some countries, foreign firms are allowed to operate only if they enter into a joint venture with a local partner.

2. Size of the project may be so large and one company cannot accomplish it. Then, one firm enters into a joint venture with another firm to accomplish the project.

3. Some projects require multidimensional technology that no one firm possesses. Therefore, firms with different, but compatible technologies may join together.

4. One firm with technological competence and another firm with managerial competence join together.

5. A foreign firm with technological competence joins with a domestic firm with marketing competence.

Strategic Issues Involved in Joint Ventures

The strategic issues in the formation of joint ventures are:

1. Sharing the strengths of each other and eliminating the weaknesses of both the firms by acquiring the other's strengths. For example, the domestic firm acquires technology from a foreign company and the foreign firm acquires the knowledge of the domestic markets channels, culture, etc., after formation of a joint venture and working jointly for the objective.

2. Eliminating or reducing competition by forming a joint venture by the competing firms.

3. Increasing market share more than the sum of the market share of individual firms by forming a joint venture.

4. To acquire the strengths of the other firm in diversified industrial areas including technology, marketing, and management.

5. Unfavourable business conditions (or threats) in the existing industry may force the firm to join with the other firms of another industry.

6. Favourable business conditions (opportunities) in other industries may encourage the firm to form a joint venture with the firm of that industry.

Advantages of Joint Ventures: The advantages of joint ventures include:

(i) Firms undertake joint ventures to spread development costs.

(ii) Joint ventures allow the firms with expertise in different fields to combine their knowledge and resources.

(iii) Joint ventures are useful as a form of 'trial marriage' to see if firms can work together before undertaking a merger.

(iv) Joint ventures are more useful in entering international markets. After simple exporting activities, joint ventures are usually the next step for firms entering the foreign markets.

(v) Joint ventures provide quick access to channels of distribution, thus, reducing the marketing cost.

(vi) Partner in the domestic country (host country) assists in interpreting local customs and culture and translating the technical language.

(vii) Joint ventures reduce the investment in the host country and minimise the risk of nationalisation of business.

(viii) Joint ventures provide a means of achieving the legally required joint ownership.

(ix) Joint ventures minimise the commercial/business risk to both the partners.

(x) Joint ventures provide the facility of foreign technology to the host partner.

(xi) Joint ventures provide the chance to combine the strengths of two partners and utilise the opportunities provided by the environment. Thus, the joint ventures make the impossible things possible.

Disadvantages: Despite a number of advantages of joint ventures, some problems crop up due to joint ventures. They are:

(i) Problems of equity participation by the foreign and home partners

(ii) Foreign exchange regulations imposed by both the governments

(iii) Absence of proper coordination between/among partners

(iv) Differences of culture and customs of both the partners

(v) Division of profits with other firms

(vi) Loss of control of the other firm; and

(vii) Possible conflict and blaming each other at the time of failure

Exhibit 7.8 presents the situations when a company needs to consider diversifications

(D) DIVERSIFICATION STRATEGY

Introduction: Globalisation has given a great fillip to the diversification strategy of various corporations due to the enhanced business opportunities across the globe. Companies that adapt diversification strategy depart from the existing products/services and/or markets. In other words, companies that adapt diversification strategy, produce new products, render new services and/or enter new markets.

Diversification takes place in three forms, viz., internal, joint and external. Companies diversify internally by developing new products or services and/or markets. Companies that diversify through the form of a joint ventures, develops new products/services with the help of a partnering company. Alternatively, the firm along with other company, jointly establishes a new company in order to produce new products and/or render new services and/or enter new markets. Companies that adapt diversification strategy may acquire another company or absorb another company or merge with another company in order to diversify the business activities. Tata diversified its activities by acquiring the following companies:

- Feb 2000 Tetley Tea Company, $407 million
- March 2004 Daewoo Commercial Vehicle Company, $102 million
- Aug 2004 NatSteel's Steel Business, $292 million
- Nov 2004 Tyco Global Network, $130 million.
- July 2005 Teleglobe International Holdings, $239 million
- Dec 2005 Millennium Steel, Thailand, $167 million
- Dec 2005 Brunner Mond Group, $120 million
- June 2006 Eight O'Clock Coffee, $220 million
- Nov 2006 Ritz Carlton Boston, $170 million
- Jan 2007 Corus Group, $11.3 billion
- March 2007 Bumi Resources, $1.1 billion
- April 2007 Campton Place Hotel, San Francisco, $60 million

Source: Tata Website.

Why Diversification?

Companies diversify their activities due to various reasons. Now, we discuss these reasons:

Fast Organisational Growth

Organisations diversify their activities and operations in order to grow at a fast rate into related and unrelated areas. For example, Tata Group which was originally in the area of iron and steel diversified into automobile, telecommunications, consultancy services, and finance. Reliance diversified its activities into petroleum products, finance, telecommunications and retail business. The **Tata Group** is India's largest conglomerate company, with revenues of Rs.1,29,994 crore (US $28.8 billion) in 2006-07. The Group takes the name of its founder, Jamsedji Tata, a member of whose family has almost invariably been the chairman of the Group. The current chairman of the Tata Group is Ratan Tata, who tookover from J. R. D. Tata in 1991. The company is currently in its fifth generation of family stewardship.

The Tata Group comprises 98 companies in seven business sectors like engineering, materials, services, energy, chemicals, finance, consumer goods and information technology. 65.8% of the ownership of Tata Group is held by the charitable trust of Tata. Companies which form a major part of the group include Tata Steel, Tata Motors, Tata Consultancy Services, Tata Tea, Tata Power and the Taj Hotels.

The purpose of the diversification of these companies is to grow at a fast rate. Reliance is India's largest private sector company with a turnover of US $28 billion and a profit of US $2.033 billion for the fiscal year ending in March 2006 making it one of India's private sector *Fortune 500 company.* It was founded by the late Dhirubhai Ambani in 1966. After severe differences between the founder's two sons, Mukesh and Anil Ambani, the group was divided between them in 2006. Its diversified companies are presented in Exihibit 7.9.

Exhibit 7.9: Diversified Subsidiaries of Reliance are:

- Reliance Petroleum Limited
- Reliance Netherlands BV (including Trevira)
- Reliance Retail Limited
- Ranger Farms Limited
- Retail Concepts and Services (India) Private Limited
- Reliance Retail Insurance Broking Limited
- Reliance Dairy Foods Limited
- Reliance Retail Finance Limited
- RESQ Limited
- Reliance Jamnagar Infrastructure Limited
- Reliance Haryana SEZ Limited
- Reliance Industrial Investment & Holdings Limited
- Reliance Ventures Limited
- Reliance Strategic Investments Limited
- Reliance Exploration & Production - DMCC
- Reliance Industries (Middle East) DMCC
- Reliance Global Management Services (P) Limited

Effective Risk Management

Organisations carrying out single portfolio business face risks due fluctuations in demand for and supply for products and production factors. Diversified organizations manage risk most efficiently due to the balance between demand for and supply of its various diversified products. Therefore, organizations diversify their activities to manage and reduce risk.

Maximum Utilization of Resources

Organisations diversify the production and service activities in order to make use of manufacturing facilities and other facilities like marketing facilities and distribution facilities to the fullest extent. For example, Coca-Cola (India) Limited diversified activities by producing Kinley mineral water to make use of production as well as marketing facilities to a maximum extent.

Financial Factors

Organisations producing capital goods like machinery and equipment may face cash flow, working and liquidity problems. Such organizations diversify the activities into consumer goods and white goods industries in which cash flow and liquidity positions would be favourable. For example, Reliance which was in petroleum industry diversified into retail marketing.

To Reduce Weaknesses

Organisations possess strengths as well as weaknesses in their various internal operations as well as resources. Organisations diversify their activities or portfolios into those areas whose strengths wipe out the weaknesses of the organizations.

Technology

Organisations diversify the activities, sometimes, in order to avail the latest technology.

Formulation of Diversification Strategy

Formulation of diversification strategy resemble the practice of formulating various corporate strategies. The steps in formulation of diversification strategy include:

Conduct of Feasibility/Evaluation Studies: Organisations conduct evaluation studies in order to know the feasibility, formulate and implement the diversification strategy. The steps involved in this process include:

- Awareness and evaluation of the diversification opportunities;
- Conduct of feasibility study;
- Identifying opportunities, threats, and strengths and weaknesses;
- Selecting the diversification product;
- Procuring required resources;
- Implementing the project; and
- Evaluating the project.

Different Types of Diversification

Diversification can be of three types, viz.,

(i) Concentric Diversification,

(ii) Horizontal Diversification, and

(iii) Conglomerate Diversification.

Concentric Diversification

Companies pursue concentric diversification strategy remain relatively simple. The total efforts of the company concentrate on a limited combination of customer groups, customer functions and alternate technologies and products.

Concentric diversification strategies include producing new products that are useful to the same customer group. For example, a TV Company pursues a diversification strategy of producing DVD player. Gujarat Gas Company pursued a diversification strategy of selling gas stoves and provides finance to buy gas stoves and gas connections. Similarly, Hindustan Beverages Ltd., which produces Coca-Cola pursued concentric diversification strategy of producing 'Kinley' purified water and other beverages like 'Sprite' and 'Fanta' .

Another type of concentric diversification strategy includes producing new products or modified products by using alternative technologies or by using the same technology. For example, tomato ketchup and tomato sauce and fruit juice and fruit jam produced by the same company.

Companies that produce refrigerators also produce washing machines, air-conditioners, 'mixies' and grinders in order to make use of the same marketing channel. Thus, companies pursuing concentric diversification strategy may enter different industries, but the new products would fit the same market channel or technology.

Concept of Core Competence

The company should consolidate its production, technology, marketing, finance, human resource and research and development into competencies to enhance its competitiveness.

Core competency is something a company does have especially well in comparison to its competitors. Thus, core competency is the competency that only the company possesses, but not its competitors. It is also called distinctive competency. Thus, core competency is unique capability it gives a company in capitalizing upon a particular opportunity; the competitive edge it may give a firm in the marketplace and potential in building a distinctive competence and making it the cornerstone of strategy. Thus, core/distinctive competence are "any advantages a company has over its competitors because it can do something which they can't or it can do something better than they can".

Core Competencies

Core competence empowers a company to build competitive advantage over competitors. Core competencies include:

- Excellent quality maintenance continuously;
- Highly skilled employees;
- Perfectly committed employees;
- Lowest production cost;
- State-of-the-art technology utilization;
- Ability to provide customized service most efficiently;
- Ability to develop new products/service;
- High creditworthiness.

Benefits: Benefits of core competencies include:

- The company gets added capability in going after a particular market opportunity;
- The company gets competitive edge, it can yield in the marketplace; and
- It is potential for being cornerstone of the strategies.

Competitive Advantages of Concentric Diversification Strategy

The companies pursing concentric diversification strategy enjoy the following advantages. These companies can focus on customer:

- Increase usage by present customers
- Increase purchase size or frequency
- Improve product location
- Expand product line viz., sizes, options and styles
- Expand shelf-space
- Attract competitors' customers
- Increase promotion efforts
- Initiate price cuts
- Attract non-users of the product
- Advertise new uses of the product
- Offer special prices and promotions

Increase product availabilities by entering new markets companies pursuing concentric diversification strategy would focus on product. They differentiate product from its competitors

- increase rate of product obsolescence
- change styles

- change options
- change colours
- develop new users for the product
- improve product servicing

Companies pursuing concentric diversification strategy focus on technology

- Develop new equipment to improve efficiency
- Develop new products
- Find uses for by-products
- Improve quality

Problems of Concentric Diversification Strategy

There are certain potential problems of concentration strategies. They are:

(i) One of the greatest problems is the risk associated with putting "all the corporate eggs in one basket".

(ii) The introduction of substitute products may also be very detrimental to a firm following a concentration strategy. Substitute products can make a firm's product obsolete particularly when the firm concentrates on only one product or product-line.

(iii) Company pursuing concentration strategy may also be affected by the disruption in the supply of essential and crucial raw material.

(iv) Sometimes, the market segment becomes unattractive owing to limited growth opportunities or substitute products or absence of essential resource availability. In such a case, a firm pursuing a concentration strategy may become locked into an area of business and become unable to move into another line of business.

Change from Concentric Strategy

Firms change from concentric strategy to other strategies due to the problems associated with concentric strategy and also due to various reasons. Exhibit 7.10 presents the reasons for change of a firm from concentration strategies.

Exhibit 7.10: Reasons for Change of a Firm From Concentration Strategies

1. **Temptations of Diversification:** Spreading risk, by operating in multiple areas decreases the threat of anyone area causing the firm to fail. However, diversification spreads resources over several areas, similarly decreasing the probability that the firm can be a strong force in any area.
2. **Need to Meet Short-term Goals:** When the firm is not strong in an area, managers tend to experience pressures to do what is necessary to meet the plan (budget or quota) in the short-run rather than focusing on long-range success. Many times short-term sales and profits can be increased by moving into new business.
3. **Underestimation of Present Opportunities:** Spreading resources too thin may cause an organization to overlook opportunities in its existing fields. Similarly, resources may limit a firm's ability to capitalize on opportunities that do develop.

4. **Impatience to Grow:** Small firms often feel they are too small to be important in their field. Growth becomes a primary objective. Once they have moved into other fields to increase sales and profits, however, diversified firms discover they lack the management and financial resources needed to operate the diverse organization.
5. **Overconfidence:** A company doing well may conclude it has superior ability and can be successful in almost any business. Management often forgets the years of experience it took to earn the success being achieved. Such firms lack this experience in the new business.
6. **Misjudging Success Requirements:** Problems of the new-business are often more complex and resistant to solution than expected. Connections between the new and old businesses are often superficial and only marginally related to the problems of the new venture.
7. **Pressure to Use Idle Capacity:** Firms with excess resources, especially manufacturing facilities, feel compelled to put unused resources to work immediately. Rather than wait for growth to utilize the capacity, firms often rush into the first available alternative to begin using idle resources.
8. **Siren Song of Integration:** Forward or backward integration creates opportunities to control resources or markets and to "absorb the profits of the middleman". Many times the acquiring firm lacks the expertise of the middleman. Furthermore, the acquiring organization rarely is able to operate the supplier/market at its most efficient capacity, thus incurring diseconomies of scale.
9. **Dangers of Pride:** Even after entering a new field that turns sour, managers are often reluctant to admit to making a mistake. Commitment to this strategy escalates. Resources are devoted to supporting the struggling venture to save the managers pride, rather than allocating those resources to more profitable, growing projects.

Source: M. Lauenstein and W. Skinner, "Formulating a Strategy of Superior Resources", Journal of Business Strategy, Summer 1980, pp.4-10 in Joe G. Thomas, *op.cit.,* pp.202-203.

Horizontal Diversification Strategy

Many companies expand by creating other firms in their same line of business. The reasons for engaging in this process of horizontal integration are:

- to increase the market share,
- to reduce the cost of operations per unit of business through the large-scale economies,
- to get greater leverage to deal with the customers and suppliers.
- to promote the products and services more efficiently to a large audience,
- to have greater access to channels of distribution.
- to enjoy increase operational flexibility.
- finally to take the advantage of the benefits of synergy.

When the combination of two or more business units (existing and creased) results in greater effectiveness and efficiency than the total yielded by those businesses, when they were operated separately, then synergy has been attained.

Conglomerate Diversification Strategy

Horizontal integration strategy aims at related diversification. In other words, diversification occurs, when the existing firm creates another business unit in the same industry. But, firms may also expand through unrelated or conglomerate diversification. In other words, firms create new business units that are unrelated to its original business. For example, Gujarat Gas Ltd., created another business unit, i.e., Gujarat Finance Company Limited.

Competitive Advantages

The competitive advantages of companies that pursue conglomerate diversification are:

- Reduction of risks. This benefit is particularly important for businesses that operate in industries subject to rapid technological change.
- Economies of large-scale operations.
- Financial stability.
- Increase in profits, and
- Attain managerial competence.

Reasons for Adapting Conglomerate Strategy:

The firms adapt conglomerate strategy in order to:

- achieve growth rate higher than what can be realized through expansion,
- make effective use of financial resources with retained profits exceeding immediate investment needs,
- avail of potential opportunities of profitable investments,
- achieve distinctive competitive advantage and broader stability,
- improve the price-earnings ratio and bring about a higher market price of sharess.

(E) RETRENCHMENT STRATEGIES

The third major class of strategic alternatives available to a firm is retrenchment strategies. Growth strategies and stability strategies are generally adopted by firms that are in satisfactory competitive positions. But, when a firm's position is disappointing or, at the extreme, when its survival is at stake, then retrenchment strategies may be appropriate. Retrenchment strategies include: Turnaround strategies, captive company strategy, divestment strategy, transformation strategy and liquidation strategy.

Reasons for Adopting Retrenchment Strategies: As stated earlier, the firm's poor performance is the major reason for adopting retrenchment strategies. To be specific, the reasons include:

1. Prevalence of poor economic conditions.
2. Competitive pressures may also cause firms to curtail their operations.
3. Operating and production inefficiencies may also cause firms to pursue retrenchment strategies.

4. Inability of the firm to implement latest technology caused by technological revolution.
5. The company is not doing well or perceives itself as doing poorly.
6. The company has not met its objectives and there is pressure from shareholders, customers or others to improve performance.
7. The external environment poses threats and internal strengths are insufficient to face the threats.
8. Better opportunities in the environment are perceived in other area of business/ other markets where a firm's strengths can be utilised.

(1) Turnaround Strategy

Improving internal efficiency can be done by adopting turnaround strategy. The aim of turnaround strategy is to transform the organisation into a learner and more effective business. Turnaround means reversing the negative trend.

Indicators of Adopting Turnaround Strategy: Adoption of turnaround strategy is necessary during the adverse conditions of the firm. Specifically the indicators include:

1. Incurring losses continuously.
2. Declining demand for product and/or services.
3. Increasing cash outflows and/or declining cash inflows.
4. Declining sales and declining market share.
5. Declining production and/or productivity.
6. Increasing debt and debt service.
7. Continuous problems of working capital.
8. High rate of employee turnover and employee job dissatisfaction.
9. Significant decrease in the market price of the share. Turnaround strategy should aim at setting a reverse trend to this declining or negative situation.

Approaches of Turnaround Strategy

Approaches of turnaround strategy should concentrate on diagnosing the problem accurately and adopting a right approach. The approaches of the strategy include: *(i)* surgical, and *(ii)* Human resource development.

Surgical Approach: The surgical approach is mostly mechanic and requires a tough attitude of the top executive. The executive issues direction for change, fires employees, closes down divisions/plants, drops the product lines, replaces the machinery, issues production, controls the marketing and finance and fixes the accountability for results. This approach continues until the firm is turned around. Later the chief executive relaxes the tough environment and controls.

Human Resource Development (HRD) Approach: Human resource development approach involves:

(1) The chief executive conducts a series of meetings, encourages the managers to be open, understand each other, understand the problems and diagnose the root cause for poor performance of the firm.

(2) He encourages the employees to suggest methods of turning around, policies, gives a detailed programme through a thorough participation, and is actively involved in discussions in the form of brain-storming sessions.

(3) He encourages employees to decide the technique, acquire skills and knowledge, modify their behaviour, etc.

(4) He encourages the managers and employees to implement the solutions offered by them in a highly co-ordinated, and a committed team spirit.

(5) This team spirit is continued at least until the firm is turnaround.

This approach, though difficult, gives effective results.

Who will Manage the Process?: Basically, either the present executive and his team or a new executive will manage the process.

(i) The present chief executive along with his team will manage the turnaround process. The chief executive will be helped by the outside consultants continuously.

(ii) Since the present team is responsible for the poor performance of the business, they will withdraw on their own from the different positions. Then, the shareholders will appoint a new team to manage the turnaround process.

(iii) If the present chief executive and his team does not withdraw from the position, the shareholders will replace the existing team particularly, the chief executive. The shareholders appoint a new chief executive and the team. This new team and chief executive will manage the process.

Activities of Turnaround Process

The management should carefully undertake different activities of the turnaround process. They include:

1. Diagnosing the problem accurately.
2. Analysing the products, its quality, design, configuration, uses, suitability to the changing customer tastes, preferences and needs, etc., against the competitors' products and substitute products.
3. Analysing the production process, technology, competition, competitors' strategies, market segment positioning, etc.
4. Analysing the financial position, cost of capital, cost control, etc.

5. Feedforward of information to various decision areas and control areas.
6. Take up activities systematically, feedback and control the deviations immediately through action research.

The elements in a turnaround strategy are presented in Exhibit 7.11.

Exhibit 7.11: Matching Corporate Strategic Alternatives to Fit an Undiversified Firm's Situation Competitive Position

Market Growth Rate	WEAK	STRONG
	Strategy Options	**Strategy Options**
Rapid	*(In probable order of attractiveness)* • Reformulate single business concentration strategy. (To achieve turnaround) • Acquire another firm in the same business (to strengthen competitive position). • Vertical integration (forward or backward if it strengthens the competitive position) • Diversification • Be acquired by/sell out to a stronger rival • Abandonment (a last resort in the event all else fails).	*(In probable order of attractiveness)* • Continue single business concentration — International expansion (if market opportunities exist). • Vertical integration (if it strengthens the firm's competitive position) • Related Diversification (to transfer skills and expertise built up in the company's core business to adjacent businesses)
	Strategy Options	**Strategy Options**
Slow	*(in probable order of attractiveness)* • Reformulate single business concentration strategy (to achieve turnaround). • Merger with a rival Firm (to strengthen competitive position). • Vertical Integration (only if it strengthens the competitive position substantially) • Diversification • Harvest/Divest • Liquidation (a last resort in the event all else fails).	*(in probable order of attractiveness)* • International expansion (if market opportunities exist) • Related Diversification • Unrelated Diversification • Joint venture into new areas • Vertical integration (if it strengthens competitive position) • Continue single business • Concentration (achieve growth by taking market share from weaker rivals.)

Source: Arthur A. Thompson Jr. and A.J. Strickland III, *op. cit.*, p. 165

(2) Captive Company Strategy

A captive company strategy is another form of retrenchment strategy. This strategy is pursued when a firm sells the majority of its products to one customer (wholesaler/dealer) who in turn performs some of the functions normally done by an independent firm. Companies may undertake a captive strategy as one means of reducing labour costs and reducing the size of employees.

The customer, in this strategy, provides the product design to the captive manufacturer, who in turn, produces according to this design and supplies the products to the customer. The firm need not involve the cost of product design and marketing. The firm can also minimise the risks of marketing.

A captive strategy may also be effective for a new company. The firms with marketing problems and the small companies who cannot launch the full range of marketing activities on their own may adopt a captive strategy. However, the companies may go for their own marketing strategy after they develop their own business. The major limitation of this strategy is that the company is limited by the activities of its captor.

(3) Transformation Strategy

Another retrenchment strategy is the transformation strategy. A transformation occurs when a firm makes a major change in its outlook and operations, usually including moving from one kind of business to another. Changes in strategy are quite substantial. These strategies are difficult to implement because they require a great deal of flexibility on the part of the entire organisation.

Companies may undertake this strategy when:

1. Returns on current operations are lower than desired.
2. Opportunities in other areas are especially attractive.
3. Investments needed in the current operations exceed when the firm is willing or able to spend.
4. A strong, flexible management team exists.
5. The firm has a strong financial base to support its transformation.

(4) Divestment Strategy

Divestment is another form of retrenchment strategy. The company sells or 'spins off' one of its business units under the divestment strategy. Divestment strategy is usually adopted when the company is performing poorly or when it no longer fits the company's strategic profile.

Causes for Adopting Divestment Strategy

1. Divestment strategy is frequently used when the firm wants to increase the efficiency of a strategic business unit or a major operating division or a product line which has failed to achieve the desired results.
2. Firms may also adopt this strategy when their market share is negligible to be competitive or when the market size is too small to earn the desired profit.
3. The availability of better alternatives may also cause the firms to divest. The limited resources often force the firms to divest the resources from a less profitable business to a more profitable business.

4. The need for increased investment at later stages in providing safety facilities and infrastructure facilities causes the firms without additional funds, to divest.
5. Firms sometimes also divest parts of businesses they have acquired, as the unit may not fit in the original business of the firm.
6. A continuous increase in the cash outflows more than that of cash inflows from a particular unit forces the firm to divest that unit.
7. The firm's inability to meet the competition, causes the firm to divest.
8. The technological change and inability of the firm to invest additional financial resources forces the firm to divest.
9. Divestment of a part of the business is necessary to allow the remaining business to survive.
10. Divestment of unprofitable wings is necessary as part of the merger agreement.
11. Divestment, sometimes, is necessary to abide by the provisions of the law.

Approaches of Divestment

There are three approaches of divestment. The firm may select one approach depending upon the need for adopting this strategy.

1. Firms may pursue a divestment strategy by spinning off a part of the business as an independent entity both financially and managerially.
2. Firms may also divest by selling a business unit to another firm. Mergers are the result of one firm selling a part of its operations to another firm.
3. Another form of divestment is simply closing down a portion of the firm's operations.

Cautions in Adopting Divestment Strategy

1. Generally, the firms delay in making a decision to divest as it reflects the failure of the firms. The delay in adopting this strategy results in the financial loss of the financial sound units also. Therefore, the firms should take the decision of divesting a loss making unit at the right time.
2. The buying firm normally undervalues the assets of the divesting firm or part of the firm. Hence, the firm should find the right time, when it can get a better value of the divesting portion. Adopting divestment strategy, always is not due to business failure. It may be due to shifting from a less profit making business to a more profit making business. The delay in adopting divestment strategy may result in liquidating a portion of the business or a business unit.

(5) Liquidation Strategy

The liquidation strategy is generally considered as the most extreme retrenchment strategy. This strategy involves closing down a business organisation and selling its assets. This is the last alternative strategy as its consequences are severe. The consequences include: loss of jobs of all employees and termination of the opportunities of the firm. Adoption of this strategy implies the total failure of the firm.

Reasons for Adopting Liquidation Strategy

1. Partnership firms and small business organisations liquidate when one or more partners/shareholders want to withdraw from the business.
2. When the sole trader wants to withdraw or retire or take-up another job, he has to liquidate the business, unless one of his family members runs the firm.
3. Liquidation is necessary, when one of the partners has to withdraw and all other partners express their inability to buy the withdrawing partner's share.
4. Liquidation may also occur when a firm is worth more as closed down than surviving. In other words, the value of assets of the firm are more worthwhile than the rate of return earned by the firm.
5. Sometimes, owners may receive a "Godfather offer," for their business. The owners may receive a highly attractive offer and they feel that liquidating the business is more worthwhile. Then, the owners will adopt the liquidation strategy.

Box 7.1: It's Too Late to Save Sears

The long awaited turnaround story at Sears may never happen. Why? Because reclusive hedge fund impresario and Sears Holding Corp., Chairman Edward Lampert doesn't know how to run a retail business, says Jeff Matthews of hedge fund RAM Partners. After Sears posted a surprise quarterly loss, a Barron's report on August 24, stated the stock could fall another 50%. Lampert shot back with a letter claiming the article was "inaccurate" and "biased." Matthews says facts are facts: Shopping at Sears remains a lacklustre experience, five years after Lampert bought the company and merged it with Kmart. "They've totally lost touch with the American consumer," says Matthews, who has no position in Sears stock.

- **Lack of investment in stores.** "The stores are terrible; they don't look any better than they did five years ago. In fact, they look worse." Matthews notes Wal-Mart spends tens of billions a year on stores, while Sears is spending about $200 million. That's no way to compete.
- **No retail expert at the helm.** For more than 18 months, Sears has had an "interim" CEO, Matthews notes. Until they hire someone more permanent with retail know-how they're doomed, he says. "I kept waiting for five years: when is he going to hire the guy? Never happened."

Source: http://finance.yahoo.com/tech-ticker/article/320517/It%27s-Too-Late-to-Save-Sears-Matthews-Says?tickers=shld,azo,wmt,cost,dia,spy,XRT (Accessed on 12/09/09).

Consequences of Liquidation

Normally, large scale organisations do not adopt this strategy in view of the consequences of the liquidation strategy. The consequences include:

1. There would be a closure or elimination of an agency performing economic functions in the set-up of economic institutions of the country. Therefore, the Government does not encourage the liquidation of business, unless it is warranted.
2. All the jobs of employees will also be liquidated consequent upon the adoption of this strategy. Hence, the employees and trade unions do not welcome this strategy.
3. Different types of stakeholders of the business like creditors, dealers, financial companies, banks, customers and suppliers will have to suffer as the obligations of the firm towards them will be fully or partially unmet. Hence, these stakeholders prefer not to adopt this strategy, unless, it is a must.
4. The shareholders of the firm will forego their share capital either in full or in part. They mostly prefer running of the business than its closure.
5. Further, it would be difficult to find a buyer as it involves larger amount of finance.

In view of these consequences, the firms should adopt this strategy very carefully and in a planned way. This process would enable the company to get maximum proceeds by selling the assets and meet the obligations of the various stakeholders.

(F) STRATEGIC ALLIANCES

Strategic alliances are long term relationships between the companies designed to achieve an objective faster and more effectively than if either of the firms does so on its own. Strategic alliances are like teams that contribute to synergy. Strategic alliances are teaming and allying with other companies either of the same industry or another industry, with a view to help to perform all kinds of business/service activities necessary for a customer in the supply chain. For example, alliances among an automobile company, finance company, spare parts producing company and a service company enable them to meet a unified facility for buying and maintaining a car by a customer. Thus, alliance bridges gaps in providing a whole facility. Similarly, the alliance among road transport, Civil Aviation Authority, immigration authority and an airline company and security company enables them to provide a total facility of air travel to a foreign country.

Strategic alliances enable for entering new markets, learning new technologies, developing new products, providing product/service extensions and providing a total package of product and/or service. Strategic alliances produce both the advantages as well as risks to all partners as well as final beneficiary. Alliance relationships sometime result in turbulent environment, hence, the partners have to coordinate the activities carefully and collaborate with each other efficiently.

Characteristics of Strategic Alliances: Characteristics of strategic alliances include:

- Firms of an alliance remain independent, but join together to collaborate like a single firm, to provide the total but part by part, in the supply chain.
- Firms of an alliance coordinate with each other in addition to performing efficiently.
- Firms link with each other on a long-term basis.

- Strategies are crafted in a unified manner with a win-win attitude.
- Partners share strengths, thus eliminating the weaknesses. In other words, the strengths of one partner wipes out the weaknesses of other partner. Thus, the relationship is reciprocal.
- Alliances are for mutual benefit by pooling technology, resources, investments and bearing risks mutually and jointly.
- All firms of an alliance perform part by part, but provide all the parts of supply chain in a coordinated manner.

Objectives of Strategic Alliances

- Different partners of an alliance possess strengths as well as core competencies in various areas. In fact, the area of strength of one partner would be the area of weakness of another partner. In other words, one partner is strong in production and weak in marketing and *vice versa* would be true in case of another partner. The alliance between these two partners would ultimately bring strengths both in production and marketing. Thus, an alliance brings benefits to the alliance firms that would not be possible individually either through internal development or external acquisition.

Thus, the major objective of an alliance is to get the maximum benefit through collaboration which would be impossible either through internal growth or external growth.

- The second objective of a strategic alliance is to encourage the partners to develop new technologies, new markets, attract new group of customers and develop new products/services rather than doing by oneself all activities in the supply chain.
- The third objective of an alliance is to learn from the alliance partners how to expand and diversify into new areas in the future. Thus, alliances enable the firm to have a transnational step before actually entering into new areas.
- The fourth objective is to create and develop new resources and thereby, new core competencies. These new core competencies enable the firms to minimise or avert possible future risks. Thus, alliances reduce potential risks when a firm pursues new strategies.
- The fifth objective of alliances is to reduce the cost of establishment and operations. Firms can reduce the cost of implementing a strategy by partnering with an experienced firm in the core area of operation. For example, Air India formed an alliance with Singapore Airlines in Singapore-San Francisco route, wherein Singapore Airlines has the experience and knowledge in operations and Air India has competence in marketing in India.
- The sixth objective is to minimise or avoid risks. Firms invariably have to bear heavy risks if they develop the entire supply chain. In contrast, they share the risks by forming into alliances. The sharing of risks would reduce the burden and the risk element of the alliance firms. Sometimes, risks can also be averted, if the partner

firms have expertise in the market concerned. For example, Air Nuigini averts the risks of the Australian market through the alliance with Qantas.

Areas of Strategic Alliances

Firms form strategic alliances in the following areas:

- **New Market Entry:** Companies form strategic alliances, when they enter new markets. The firms intend to enter new markets and enter into alliance with those companies which are already in the market. For example, a new pesticides company forms alliance with the existing fertilizer company. Alliance between Coca-cola and Nestle benefitted both the companies in marketing each other's products.
- **Supply Chain Integration:** Strategic alliances are formed among the companies engaged in various operations of the supply chain. For example, the alliance among Goodman Fielder-wheat flour manufacturing company, Paradise Biscuits-biscuit manufacturing company and Food World — a retailer.
- **Design an Integrated Product-cum-Service:** Firms of different industries form alliance in order to develop an integrated product-cum-service. For example, Indian Railways along with A.P. Tourism Corporation provide an integrated service. Similarly, Apollo Hospitals and A.P. Tourism Corporation provide 'medical tourism' service.
- **Shaping Industry Evolution:** Different firms of the same industry align themselves to develop a new product. For example, Toshiba and Samsung formed an alliance to develop advanced memory chips and Intel and Hewlett-Packard joined to develop 64-bit Itanium microprocessor. Biogen and Glaxo SmithKine formed an alliance to develop tissue regeneration. Millennium Pharmaceuticals and American Home Products formed an alliance to develop genetic mapping technology. Creative BioMolecules and Biogen formed an alliance to develop kidney treatments.

Similarly, Apple iPod development, production and marketing were done by the alliance among Apple iPod, a consultant and HP. Sony teamed up with once-rival Samsung Electronics to develop the flat screen television. DaimlerChrysler joined with General Motors in USA to produce transmission and fuel cells. Ford joined with Toyota and Toshiba to produce hybrid motors.

- **Mutual Learning and Applying Technology, Methods and Systems:** Partners of strategic alliance learn technology, methods and systems from each other who has expertise and is familiar with such areas. This process helps the partners to acquire others' capabilities. For example, A.P. Lightings which was a partner and an alliance acquired the marketing methods and systems from its partner, i.e., Philips.

Forms of Strategic Alliance

Strategic alliance can take several forms. The significant among them are:

- Licensing
- Franchising
- Co-marketing

- Cross-marketing
- Co-production
- Outsourcing
- Knowledge Sharing
- Joint Ventures
- Equity Participation

Licensing: Manufacturers leases the right to use its intellectual property, i.e., technology, work methods, patents, copyrights, etc., to another partner of the alliance. For example, Coca-Cola company of USA and Coca-Cola Amatil (PNG) Limited in Papua New Guinea.

Franchising: Franchising is a form of licensing. Under franchising, the franchisee — a partner of the alliance operates the business under the name of another company called franchisor. Under franchising, the franchisee pays a fee to the franchisor and the franchisor in turn provides various facilities to the franchisee like trade marks, operating systems, product reputations and continuous support systems like advertising, employee training, and quality assurance programmes.

Co-marketing: The partners of a strategic alliance market the products jointly. For example, Air Nuigini and Qantas perform marketing on Port Moresby-Brisbane route.

Cross-marketing: Under cross-marketing arrangements, each partner helps another partner in marketing its products. For example, McDonald's helps to sell Walt Disney company's toys with happy meals. Soap manufacturers market the shampoos and toothpaste companies market tooth brushes.

Co-production: Partners of the alliance produce jointly by using the manufacturing facilities of either of them. This arrangement is mostly used when the production capacities of one of the partner are underutilized while another partner's demand is more than its capacity. Alternatively, this strategy is adopted when the size of the market is small for two or more than two produce to manufacture. For example, private electricity generating companies used to generate power for A.P. State Electricity Board. IBM used to get its production from Motorola and Toshiba.

Outsourcing: Outsourcing is the long term contracting out of non-core business processes to an outside provider to help achieve increased shareholder value. Availability of highly qualified skill pool and faster adaptation of well defined business processes leads to higher productivity gains without compromising on quality. One partner of the strategic alliance outsources the non-core business processes from another partner of the alliance in order to enable its executives to concentrate on core business processes to improve the efficiency of the process and to increase organisational capabilities. Bata outsourced its manufacturing operations to small scale industries in Kanpur and Kharagpur. Nike outsourced its production activities to small scale industries in Vietnam. Many US and European software companies, insurance companies, banks and hospitals outsourced their back-end office operations to companies in India due to the availability of high quality human resources at lowest cost.

Knowledge Sharing: Companies form alliances in order to share and then create new knowledge and thus create value to the activity. Companies from different industries are forming alliances by forming into a larger knowledge-creating web. For example, companies like Nokia, Motorola, Vodafone, Deutsche Telecom, Microsoft and other companies formed alliance in order to develop the industry's next generation of wireless telephone and data communication system.

Joint Ventures: Two or more firms form alliance to create a new business entity that is legally separate and distinct from its parents. Joint ventures are established as corporations owned by the funding partners in the predetermined proportions. The American Motor Corporation entered into a joint venture with Beijing Automotive Works called Beijing Jeep to enter the Chinese market by producing jeeps and other vehicles. Joint ventures involve shared ownership. Joint ventures provide required strengths in terms of required capital, latest technology, required human talent, etc. and enable the companies to share the risks in the markets.

Equity Participation: Strategic alliances also take through equity participation. For example, Xerox of the USA and Fuji of Japan form alliance together through equity participation, in order to explore new markets in Europe and Pacific Rim. Having studied different types of strategic alliances, now we shall study the advantages of strategic alliances.

Advantages of Strategic Alliances

- **Win-win outcomes**: Alliances and collaborative arrangements normally result in win-win outcomes to the parties.
- Alliances help in racing against rivals for **market leadership**.
- Alliances help in acquiring **new competencies**, improve supply chain efficiently and gain economies of scale.
- Alliances help in entering critical markets and building a **potent market presence**.
- Alliances help in gaining **knowledge about unfamiliar markets** and cultures through alliances with local markets.
- Alliances help in acquiring **skills and competencies** that are concentrated in certain geographical locations like software design in USA, and back-end facilities in India.
- Alliances help in acquiring **new technologies, new expertise and competencies** faster than that would be possible through internal efforts. Strategic alliances produce not only advantages, but also result in certain risks, costs and losses.

Now, we shall study the disadvantages.

Disadvantages of Strategic Alliances

Firms acquire competencies and knowledge from each other in an alliance. But, sometimes, the collaborators may turn to be a competitor after acquiring the competencies from the partner of the alliance. The alliance may turn into a most undesirable competition under such situations. The other risks and costs of alliance include:

Increase in Incompatibility of Partners: Incompatibility between partners of the alliance takes place when the partners fail to honour commitments of each other. Similarly, when the goal of the alliance is accomplished, the continuation of alliance would be at risk. Similarly, partners may not require the continuation of alliance, once they acquire the strengths from other partners. For example, Hewlett-Packard and Dell Computers formed an alliance to sell HP-branded printers. But, Dell started producing and selling printers under its own brand in 2002.

Risk of Knowledge/Skill Drain: Firms of the alliance acquire the knowledge and skill from the partners and use such skills for the development of their business. For example, Sony acquired the knowledge and skills of distinctive consumer electronics and skill from Apple, while building the laptop computers for Apple. Sony used this knowledge to enter the personal computer industry.

Risk of Dependence: Alliances sometimes can often become dependent excessively on their partner. This in turn, result in loss of skills in that area of operation in the country, in addition to extension of dependency for other lines of products. For example, the US automobile industry was extensively dependent on the Japanese automobile industry for the production of small cars. This dependency resulted in the development of skills and expertise of the Japanese while the skills of the employees of US automobile industry became redundant. The US outsourced the production of VCR and DVD to the Far Eastern Companies and development software and back-end operations to companies in India. These situations contributed to the economic downturn and consequently led to the increase in unemployment in USA.

Cost of Coordination: The success of strategic alliance mostly depends on an effective coordination of operation of the partners. In fact, the partners have to coordinate all the activities meticulously. Hence, coordination becomes a costly affair. In addition, the different cultures of the partners complicates the process of coordination. Management styles, methods, approaches and practices vary from one partner to the another partner of the alliance. Similarly, the production technologies, production systems and practices also vary from one partner to the another. These varying systems and practices result in complication of coordination and thereby, enhances the cost of coordination.

Cost of Learning: Partners should learn from each other with regard to management styles, culture, operations and production. Most of the companies feel that they know everything and as such they fail to learn. Daewoo has a similar experience with Caterpillar and Samsung with US forklift maker Clark Equipment.

Cost of Inflexibility: A strategic alliance forms after a thorough analysis of the environment and capabilities of the partners as well as competitors. But, the environmental factors as well as the capabilities of the partners may vary owing to various reasons. The partners are expected to be flexible and adaptable to the environmental shifts. Firms fail to be flexible and adaptable contributing to the failure of the alliance. IBM and Apple ¾ the partners of an alliance of development of a new operating system and multimedia technologies failed to understand the changed competitive environment of Microsoft. Consequently, the alliance failed to produce the results.

Cooperation and Competition: The firms of an alliance start with an intention of co-operation. But, when the firms acquire the competencies of the other partner, they may tend to break the alliance and compete with the partner. Thus, today's collaborator may turn into tomorrow's competitor. For example, Atlantic Coast decided to compete directly with its partner in alliance.

Shifting Loyalties of Staff: The executives and employers of the partner companies drawn for the alliance operations, may shift their loyalties from their parent companies to the alliance firm as they work closely with the alliance firm.

(G) COMBINATION STRATEGY (OR) PORTFOLIO RESTRUCTURING

This strategy is the combination of stability, growth and retrenchment strategies. Combination strategies may involve implementation of two or more strategies. In some cases, particularly during the periods of rapid environmental change, adoption of combination strategy would be necessary. Firms may liquidate one unit, develop another unit and allow the third unit to survive simultaneously to improve the efficiency of the business and maximise the profitability. Once the company's profitability is satisfactory, it may adopt a growth strategy. This strategy is common for large scale organisations with multiple units, diversified products and national or global markets. The combination of survival, growth and retrenchment strategies may be either simultaneous or sequential. This strategy is also called portfolio restructuring strategy as it is the mix and percentage make up of the different types of businesses in the portfolio. It involves both divestment and acquisition/takeover.

1. An Integrative Model of Strategic Alternatives:

We have discussed the organisational appraisal that enables us to identify the organisation's strengths and weaknesses and environmental analysis that helps to find the opportunities provided by and threats posed by the external environment. Fig. 7.4 provides an integrative model for recognising strategic alternatives that would be appropriate for a firm that evaluates itself as proposed by Joe G. Thomas.

As can be seen from this exhibit, the firms whose strengths, match with the environmental opportunities are the ideal firms. These ideal firms can adopt the strategies like concentration, vertical integration and horizontal integration.

Firms, whose strengths do not match with the opportunities provided by the environment but face with the environmental threats are the threatened firms. In other words, these firms are internally strong but externally are faced with threats from external environment. These firms may adopt the strategies like limited growth, concentric diversification, conglomerate diversification, transformation and joint venture.

FIRM'S ENVIRONMENTAL SITUATION		Opportunities are Provided	Threats are Posed
Firm's Internal Analysis	Strong	**Ideal Firm:** • Concentration • Vertical Integration • Horizontal Integration	**Threatened Firm:** • Limited Growth • Concentric Diversification • Conglomerate Diversification • Transformation • Joint Ventures
	Weak	**Opportune Firm:** • Turnaround • Concentration • Captive Company • Limited Growth • Mergers • Joint Ventures • Divestment • Liquidation	**Troubled Firm:** • Turnaround • Divestment • Liquidation

Source: Modified version from Joe G. Thompson, *op. cit.*, p. 227.

Fig. 7.4: An Integrative Model of Strategic Alternatives

The internally weak firms provided by environmental opportunities are opportune firms. These firms can adopt the strategies like turnaround, concentration, captive firm, limited growth, mergers, joint ventures, divestment and liquidation.

The internally weak firms posed which are threats by the environment are troubled firms. These firms can adopt the strategies of turnaround, divestment and liquidation. Leveraged buyouts have allowed firms to divest unprofitable segments of a business by selling them to entrepreneurs who often are able to return the segment to profitability.

Points to be Remembered

- Strategy formulation is often referred to as Strategic Planning.
- Successful Strategy Selection is an analysis of the firm's internal strengths and weaknesses and the opportunities provided and threats posed by external environment.
- SWOT analysis management determines in which businesses the company should be operating.
- Corporate level strategies include stability strategies, growth strategies, retrenchment strategies and combination strategies.

- Stability strategies include maintenance of *status quo* and sustainable growth.
- Growth strategies include internal growth, concentration strategies, mergers, takeovers/acquisitions, horizontal integration, conglomerate diversification, virtual integration and joint ventures.
- Retrenchment strategies include turnaround, captive company, transformation and liquidation.

(H) INTEGRATED FUNCTIONAL STRATEGIES: LEARNING, EXPERIENCE AND TECHNOLOGY CURVES

Efficiency means doing things right. In other words, efficiency is achieving a higher output for a given input. Prime activity of business organisations is conversion of inputs into output. Efficient business produce more for a given input compared to other businesses. In other words, the efficient businesses achieve higher productivity. Higher productivity indicates that the companies produce more for a given input compared to other firms. This in turn results in reduction in cost of production per unit. Thus, higher efficiency or higher productivity leads to reduction in cost of production per unit of output. Economies of scale are the major factor that contributes for the lower cost of production per unit.

Economies of Scale: Increase in the volume of production up to a certain stage would be possible without the increase in the investment in fixed assets. Therefore, the fixed cost per unit of production is reduced up to that stage. This reduction in the fixed cost per unit of production is a source of large scale economies. Reliance Petroleum produces larger volumes and enjoys lower cost of production per unit of output.

Division of labour and specialisation contribute for increased efficiency, higher productivity, better quality and lowest breakage and spoilage of the production process. Thus, they contribute for lowering the cost of production per unit. Thus, division of labour and specialisation contribute for the large-scale economies. Ford Motor Company by introducing greater division of labour and specialisation could produce cars on mass production. This in turn, contributed to the reduction of cost of production per car by US $ 1958.

Companies select the merger strategy in order to increase the volume of their business operations and enjoy the economics of scale. This in turn helps them to achieve the low cost leadership strategy. The merger of PNG Banking Corporation with the South Pacific Bank helped the bank to open more number of branches, reduce the costs of human resource, rent, equipment, etc., per unit and serve the customer at a less cost and at the same time increased its total profits.

Diseconomies: Companies enjoy the economies of scale up to a certain stage as increase in production beyond that stage results in disappearance of economies. This is due to the fact that production starts increasing after that stage as the company invests in additional capacities. This increase in cost of production per unit is due to the association of diseconomies.

Companies should know the stage of operation up to which they earn economies of scale and beyond which the diseconomies associate. Companies should stop their operation at this stage to maximise their large scale economies and minimise the 'diseconomies. Point QI in Fig. 7.5 is the stage where economies of scale disappear and diseconomies of scale start. Companies should stop their production/operations at this stage.

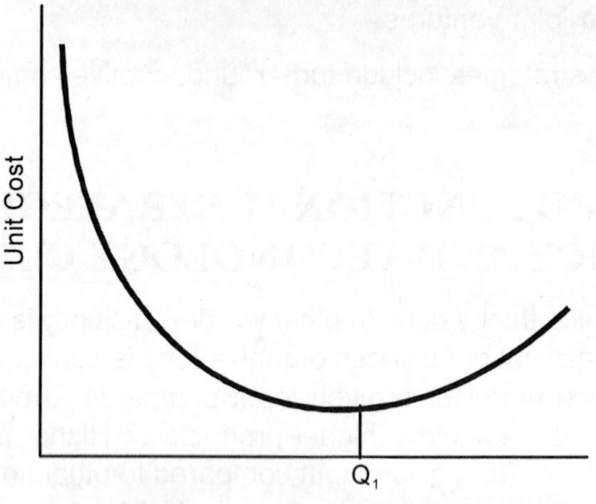

Fig. 7.5: Economies and Diseconomies of Scale

Learning Effects and Efficiency

Today, most of organisations prefer to be learning organisations. Organisations become learning organisations when their employees learn continuously. In fact, change and competition drive organisations and the individuals to be the lifelong learners. Individual employees exert superior performance when they learn higher level knowledge and acquire upper level skills, which in turn reduces the cost per unit of output. In fact, the impact of learning along with economies of scale would reduce the cost of production/operation more than that of economies of scale alone as depicted in Fig. 7.6.

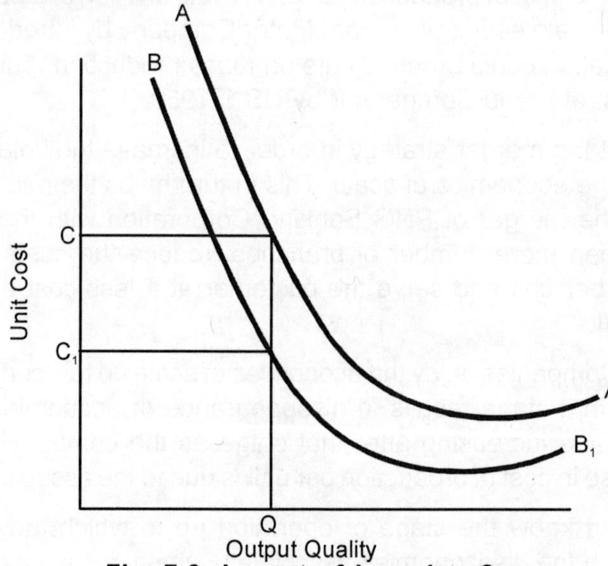

Fig. 7.6: Impact of Learning Curvee

Curve AA_1 indicates the unit cost due to economies of scale, whereas curve BB_1 indicates the unit cost due to economies of scale along with the learning effects. Unit costs is C with economies of scale and C_1 with economies of scale along with learning effects at the same level of output at 'Q'.

Experience Curve and Efficiency

When the employees do the same work continuously for quite a long period, they acquire experience, which in turn enhances the employee's efficiency. Similarly, when firms produce the same product continuously for a quite longer period, their efficiency increases along with the increase in experience. Thus, the increase in efficiency along with increase in experience result in reduction in cost per unit. The firms enjoying the benefits of experience curve along with learning curve effects and scale of economies reduce the cost much more than that of other organisations which enjoy the scale of economies along with learning curve effects and those enjoy only scale of economies. Fig 7.7 predicts the impact of the experience curve along with the learning curve effects and economies of scale.

Curve XX_1 indicates the unit cost due to economies of scale, curve YY_1 indicates the unit cost due to economies of scale and learning curve effects whereas ZZ_1 indicates unit cost due to economies of scale along with learning cure and experience curve effects. Unit cost is C_1 with economies of scale, C_2 with economies of scale and learning effects and C_3 with economies of scale, learning curve effects along with experience curve effects at the same level of output at 'Q'.

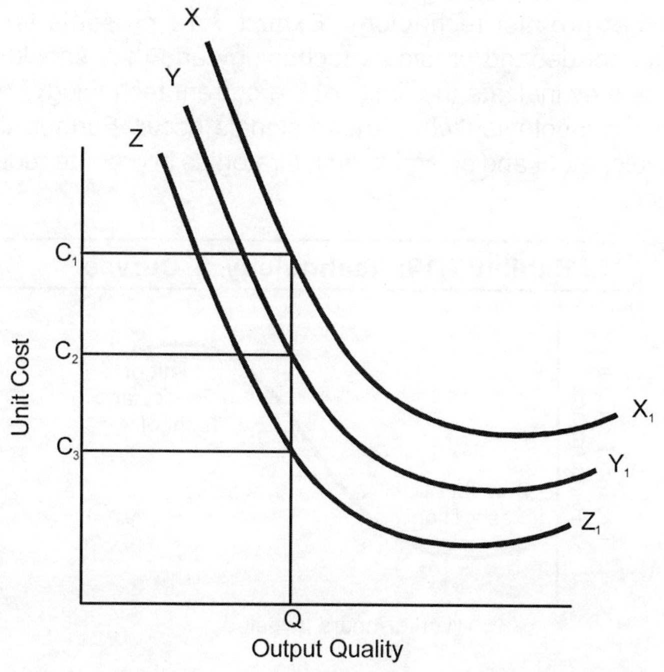

Fig. 7.7: Effects of Experience Curve along with Learning Curve and Economies of Scale

Thus, the firms enjoying the benefits of large-scale economies along with the benefits of learning curve and experience curve produce at the lowest cost per unit compared to their competitors.

Caution: However, too much experience sometimes may produce negative results of increase in unit costs. Too much experience sometimes drive the firm to produce based on the same procedure without thinking innovatively. For example, Texas Instruments which enjoyed the benefits of experience curve during 1960 and 1980 habituated to have single-minded focus on cost reduction and failed to understand customer needs and market trends after 1982. Consequently, competitors like Casio and Hewlett-Packard gained the market share for the Texas Instruments. Therefore, companies should not excessively rely on the benefits of experience curve. They should also focus on other areas of strategy like technology, customer, political, social and economics factors.

Technology Curve

Extension of learning/experience curve is technology curve. This curve plots the life cycle of technology. This curve is based on the idea that each technology has a limit or points of diminishing returns. Common danger signals appear when the limit is being approached: The relationship between the investment of man-hours and product. Performance is presented in the technology curve. Considerable R&D efforts are necessary to achieve small gains during the early days of technology development. At the later stages small efforts result in large gains. The returns begin to diminish at some point. Large efforts are necessary to get small gains in performance at this stage. These factors are vulnerable to the development of substitution of another product technology. Exhibit 7.12 presents technology S curves. Organisations should not depend on single technology and they should alert themselves to the danger signals as they indicate the limits of the current technology. The strategist should shift to the substitute technologies when these signals occur. Further, the strategist should resort to product development and diversification strategies in order to reduce the dependence on particular products.

Exhibit 7.12: Technology S Curves

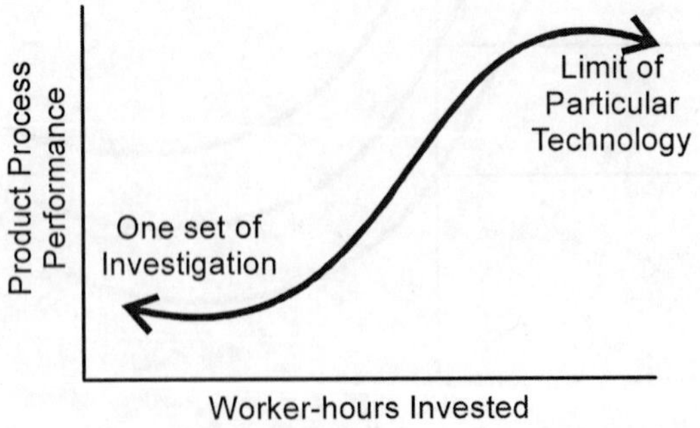

Signs of Approaching Limits
- R&D Productivity is Declining
- Most progress is in process rather than product
- R&D staff not getting along well
- Creativity seems to be lagging
- Small competitors are getting shares
- Small competitors are more innovative.

Source: R. N. Foster, *"A Call for Vision in Managing Technology"*, *Business Week*, May 24, 1982, p. 26.

Superior Efficiency vs. Customisation

Globalisation, liberalisation and privatisation led to severe competition, which in turn resulted in customisation of production and services. But, as we discussed earlier, firms can achieve efficiency and thereby low unit cost owing to large-scale economies, learning curve effect and experience curve effect.

However, the development of a flexible manufacturing technology or lean production could meet the challenges of customisations and the probability of increase in unit cost. Flexible manufacturing technologies designed, "to reduce set up times for complex equipment, increase the use of individual machines through better scheduling and improve quality control at all stages of the manufacturing process". Research also suggests that low unit cost of production like that of standardised and mass production could be achieved with customisation. As such, the term mass customisation has been coined. The once upon a time's conflicting objectives, viz., low cost and differentiation, became harmonious and compatible objectives with the help of flexible manufacturing technology.

Customisation also contributes to the low unit cost as the firms can reduce inventory handling and maintenance cost, breakage and spoilage of material and cost of maintenance of market intermediaries and logistics as customisation eliminates market intermediaries. In addition, flexible manufacturing, adopt efficient systems of inventory management just-in-time to reduce the unit cost.

Superior Efficiency and Marketing

Companies adopt different kinds of marketing strategies in order to retain customers as the cost of attracting a new customer is four times more than that of retaining an existing customer. In addition, companies prefer to eliminate the market intermediaries to the greatest extent possible in order to reduce the cost of marketing.

In addition to cost reduction, companies prefer to introduce innovations in product design, pricing, place of market and promotion in order to achieve efficiency in customer convenience and acceptance.

Human Resource and Superior Efficiency

Different human resource strategies contribute to enhance employee contribution to organisational efficiency and also for the reduction in cost of human resource per unit. Balanced job design incorporating the achievement and recognition needs of employers reduce supervision and motivation cost and enhance employee's self-motivation and commitment.

- Employee referrals and online recruitment enhance recruitment effectiveness and reduce the cost.
- Self-managed teams would result in synergy which contributes to the higher productivity, lowering unit cost, quality improvement and reduction in the need for supervision and control.
- Employer branding inspires the best of the prospective employees to seek employment in the company, which in turn results in the employment of more qualified and competent human resources.
- Employee empowerment enables the employers to make use of the best potentialities, reduce the organisational hierarchies, and speed up the decision-making and implementation process.
- Employee competency mapping allows the managers at various levels, in various departments and locations to spot out and utilise the competencies of employees.
- Employee training strategies enable the employees to develop their skills and knowledge in tune with organisational strategies. This in turn makes the skills readily available for implementation of strategies.
- Discriminative remuneration enables the high performers to contribute significantly for the enhancement of productivity as well as quality. This in turn motivates other employees to, enhance commitment and organizational loyalty. To sum up, it contributes to employee job satisfaction.
- Online training strategies as well as collaborative efforts for training reduces cost, increases benefits and conveniences and augment the fit between organisational training needs and performance.
- Variety of benefits improves employee's sense of belongingness, enhances employee's commitment to the jobs and organisation, which in turn contributes for the cost reduction and quality improvement.
- The strategies of flexi-time, flexi-workplace and flexible work provide convenience to employee, enhance innovation and reduce cost.

Information System and Efficiency

Information technology including Internet brought paradigm shift in all functional areas of businesses like manufacturing, marketing, finance and human resources. Information technology enables the companies to locate the manufacturing facilities in a number of locations across the world. These enabled the companies to increase productivity and reduce the cost. Cisco, Dell and IDBI Bank use web-based information for efficient and low cost coordination. Web-based program provide easy interaction with the suppliers of raw material, marketing intermediaries and customers.

Web-based programmes provide absolute coordination among various machines, production processes, and warehouses, reducing the processing time, deviations from standards and breakage/wastage. Thus, information technology and internet enhance efficiency.

Now, we shall study the contribution of functional strategies for achieving a superior quality.

Superior Quality

Various functional strategies contribute to the product reliability and product attributes. Product reliability as promised contributes to product quality. Total Quality Management (TQM) is a continuous process of improvement for individual, groups and the total organisation. TQM works horizontally across functions and departments, involving all employees from top to bottom and extends backwards and towards to include the supply chain and customer-chain.

The quality emphasis, initially, was on quality control as a defensive mechanism. However, today, the emphasis is shifted to strategic quality management. The dimensions of quality of products include:

- Performance of the products in terms of operating characteristics.
- Product features, though they are not as vital as product primary operating characteristics, are important.
- Reliability: Reliability is the successful functioning of the product uninterruptedly for a particular span of time.
- Durability: Durability is the expected operational life of the product.
- Conformance is meeting of the established standards by the process and individual components of the product.
- Serviceability: Serviceability is related to the ability to be repaired at a fast rate, availability of spare parts, competence to undertake repair and courtesy to carry-out the repair.

The dimensions of quality in services include: reliability, tangibles, responsiveness, assurance and empathy.

Why Superior Quality? Achieving efficiency in superior quality is essential due to the cost of poor quality. Costs of poor quality include cost of prevention, cost of detection/appraisal and cost of failure. Cost of failure can be internal failure costs and external failure costs. Internal failure costs are those associated with producing defective products that are identified prior to shipment. External failure costs are those associated with producing defective products that are identified after deliverey to the customer.

Organisations initiate total quality management (TQM) in order to avoid the costs of quality failure.

Total Quality Management

As mentioned earlier, total quality management is a continuous process and an organization, wide approach that focuses on producing superior quality products and services. TQM is an integral part of an organisation and encompasses all the functional areas and levels in an organisation including input suppliers.

The primary element of TQM are leadership, employee involvement, products/ process excellence and customer focus. TQM in its turn enable for achieving all-round superior quality.

Leadership: TQM process involves vision, mission, and strategy communication which are the functions of an efficient leadership. A leader can formulate and implement quality strategy with full commitment by involving and inspiring the employees and suppliers.

Employee Involvement: Employee involvement is the entire TQM process. The employees should be involved in data and information gathering, decision-making, problem identification, idea generation, development of viable solutions and the like.

Product/Process Excellence: Product or process excellence includes quality in product design, analysis of field failures, statistical process quality and other analytical tools.

Customer Focus: Customer focus is in quality, which means conformance to the customer needs. Therefore, customers' demand and views should be taken into account in quality design and maintenance.

Six Sigma: Motorola introduced quality improvement programme in order to produce very high quality programmes. This quality improvement programme is known as "Six Sigma", whose goal is to reduce process variation to the point where the defects rate is only 3.4 per million products.

Deming suggests TQM philosophy on the following five-step reaction:

- TQM reduces/avoids the costs of poor quality and thus, reduces/costs of production,
- Improvement in productivity;
- Improved quality enables market share and enjoys a high margin or higher price and high profit,
- Improvement in market share and stability in business,
- Company can create more employment opportunities.

Advantages of Superior Quality: Achieving superior quality and total quality brings the following advantages:

- Producing a qualitative product reduces the quantity of defects, which causes the yield to increase,
- Producing the right product the first time reduces the number of rejects and time and money spent on network,

- Making the production employees responsible for quality, eliminates the need for inspection
- Improvement of quality converts the wastage of employee hours and machine time into the manufacturing of good products and better service. Improvement in quality naturally and inevitably begets improvement of product.

Superior Customer Service

Pre-sales and post-sales customer service assume greater significance in an integrated approach of all functions and in formulating overall functional strategies. Customer service differentiates the product from that of the competitor. Customer service also includes product serviceability. Therefore, product features, durability, conformance, and technical compatibility in terms of availability of spare parts and technical skills, competence of service employees and courtesy of the service employees to carry-out the maintenance activities of the product functioning.

Company should focus on customer's current and prospective needs, design and develop products based on such needs. Customers, themselves may not know their needs in most cases.

Therefore, company based on its innovations, research and development efforts should identify such needs. Company leadership should also focus on customer needs. In addition, leader should inspire employees to develop positive attitude and mindset of employees towards customer focus.

As we discussed in production strategies, and low cost strategy, customisation of products also brings low cost owing to flexible manufacturing technology or lean production and flexible machine cells. Customisation of products/services enhances the quality of customer service.

Recession and Customer Service: Superior customer service helps the company particularly during recession by enhancing customer retention. In addition, superior customer service and customisation diverts the customer's mind from low price requirement, infrequent purchases, postponement of purchase, shift to low priced products to the product of the company that renders superior customer service during the boom and recessionary periods.

Superior Guarantee

Problems of functioning, quality, etc., occasionally arise and result in less than acceptable product/services. Companies, in order to avoid the consequences of these problems to customers, guarantee the customer against acceptable quality and functioning gains, which provides a competitive advantage over the competitors. A service guarantee is more challenging to provide than a product guarantee. There are five desirable characteristics that are to be included in a service guarantee. They are:

(i) The guarantees should be unconditional, with no exceptions.

(ii) It should be easily understood and written in simple language.

(iii) The guarantee should be meaningful by guaranteeing what is important to the customer and making it worth the customer's time and effort to invoke the guarantee, should he or she be dissatisfied.

(iv) The guarantee should be convenient to invoke and not require the customer to appeal to several layers of bureaucracy.

(v) The customer should be satisfied promptly, without a lengthy waiting period.

Conclusion: Strategies at functional level, viz., production/operations, marketing, finance, human resource and information bring integrated strategies. These strategies include achieving superior efficiency that results in producing at the lowest cost, superior quality, superior customer service and superior guarantee. These strategies enable the company to achieve its business unit level and corporate level strategies efficiently.

Keywords

- Stability strategies
- Internal growth
- Mergers
- Acquisition
- Conglomerate diversification
- Joint ventures
- Captive company
- Liquidation
- Sustainable growth
- Concentration strategies
- Takeover
- Horizontal integration
- Vertical integration
- Turnaround
- Divestment
- Portfolio restructuring

Questions for Discussion

(1) What is SWOT analysis? How do you use SWOT analysis in crafting strategies?

(2) What are the Stability Strategies? Discuss their advantages and disadvantages.

(3) What are Growth Strategies? Discuss their pros and cons.

(4) What are Joint Ventures? Explain the circumstances under which the joint ventures are appropriate.

(5) What is a Merger? Explain the circumstances under which the mergers are appropriate.

(6) What is Acquisition? Explain the circumstances under which the acquisitions are appropriate.

(7) What are Retrenchment Strategies? Discuss each of them.

(8) What is Turnaround? Explain the circumstances under which the turnaround is appropriate.

(9) Discuss Combination Strategies in detail.

References

1. Henry Mintzberg, "Planning on the Left side and Managing on the Right," *Harvard Business Review,* July-August, 1976, p. 56.
2. Thomas L. Wheelen and J. David Hunger, "*Strategic Management and Business Policy,*" Addison-Wesley Publishing Company, Reading, 1986, p. 146.
3. Henry Mintzberg, "Strategy Making in Three Modes," *California Management Review,* Winter 1973, pp. 44-53.
4. Thomas L. Wheelen and J. David Hunger, *op. cit.*, pp. 146-147.
5. Peter Wright, Charles D. Pringle and Mark J. Kroll, "*Strategic Management*", Allyn and Bacon, Boston, 1992, p. 70.
6. W.F. Glueck and L.R. Jauch, "*Business Policy and Strategic Management*", McGraw-Hill, 1984, New York, p. 209.
7. *Ibid*., p. 241.
8. Joe G. Thomas, *op. cit.*, pp. 197-198.
9. Peter Wright, Charles D. Pringle and Mark J. Kroll, *op. cit.*, p. 76.
10. Joe G. Thomas, *op. cit.*, pp. 203-204.
11. Lawrence R. Jauch and William F. Glueck, *op. cit.*, p. 229.
12. Harry Levinson, "A Psychologist Diagnoses Merger Failure", *Harvard Business Review*, March-April, 1970.
13. Thomas Hogarty, "The Profitability of Corporate Mergers", *Journal of Business,* Vol. 4, No. 3, 1970, pp. 317-327.
14. Lawrence R. Jauch and William F. Glueck, *op. cit.* p. 231.
15. Arthur A. Thompson Jr., and A.J. Strickland III, *op. cit.*, p. 90.
16. Prasanna Chandra, "*Financial Management: Theory and Practice*", Tata McGraw-Hill, New Delhi, 1987, pp. 660-661.
17. Willard Rockwell Jr., "How to Acquire a Company", *Harvard Business Review,* Vol. 46, No. 5, October 1968, in P.K. Ghosh, *op. cit.*, p. 218.
18. Peter Wright, Charles D. Pringle and Mark J. Kroll, *op. cit.*, p. 73.
19. H. Igor Ansoff, "*Corporate Strategy*", McGraw-Hill, New York, 1965, p. 127.
20. P.K. Ghosh, *op. cit.*, p. 185.
21. Peter Wright, Charles D. Pringle and Mark J. Kroll, *op. cit.*, p. 76.
22. Sundeep Khanna, "Paradigm Shifts in Partnership", *Business Today* 7-21, October 1996, p. 81.
23. Thompson and Strickland, *op. cit.*, pp. 92-93.
24. Sundeep Khanna, *op. cit.*, p. 80.
25. S. Jain, "*International Marketing and Management*", Mass: Kent; Boston, 1984.

26. Peter Wright, Charles D. Pringle and Mark J. Kroll, op. cit., p. 77.

27. Glueck and Jauch, *op. cit.*, p. 219.

28. P.N. Khandwalla, "Two Routes to Turnaround", *Business World,* 12-25, April, 1989, pp. 17-19.

29. G.A. Mirchandani, "Turning a Business Around", *Business India,* March 7-20, 1988, p. 110-11 in Azhar Kazmi, *op. cit.*, p. 168.

30. "Despite Ford Venture, Mexico Faces Struggle to be Competitive", *Wall Street Journal,* January 11, 1984, p. 1. In Joe G. Thomas, *op. cit.*, p. 218.

31. Joe G. Thomas, *op. cit.*, pp. 220-221.

32. Peter Wright, Charles D. Pringle and Mark J. Kroll, *op. cit.*, p. 78.

33. Joe G. Thomas, *op. cit.*, pp. 219-220.

34. *Ibid.*, pp. 221.

35. *Ibid.*, pp. 226.

36. Arthur A. Thompson and A.J. Strickland, *op. cit.*, p. 180.

37. "Steel Entrepreneurs Seek Profits in Plant that Big Firms Discarded as Uneconomical", *Wall Street Journal,* May 15, 1984, p. 33. in Joe G. Thomas, *op. cit.*, p. 228.

***

Unit-5

Chapter - 8

Strategic Evaluation and Control

Chapter Outline

(A) Introduction

(B) Process of Strategic Control: Strategic Audit

(C) Reluctance to Use Strategic Control

(D) Strategic Control and Environmental Factors

(E) Strategic Information Systems

(F) Implementing Strategic Control

(G) Guidelines for Successful Maintenance of Strategic Control

— Points to be Remembered

— Keywords

— Questions for Discussion

— References

Learning Objectives

After studying this chapter, you should be able to:

- Understand the concepts of control, strategic control and the purpose of strategic control;
- Explain the process of strategic control;
- Understand why some managers are reluctant to use strategic control;
- Discuss various factors that affect the strategic control environment;
- Know the kinds of information necessary for strategic control;
- Understand how to implement strategic control;
- Know how to maintain strategic control successfully.

(A) INTRODUCTION

Once the strategy is formulated and implemented, there is no guarantee that the strategy is implemented as it is designed and the strategy generates the results as aimed at. Therefore, the strategist has to evaluate the strategy and its programme to assess whether the implementation of the strategy is as per the strategic plan. Further, a number of deviations either in the external environment or in organisational environment may take place. These deviations, may necessitate a change in the strategy. These changes also require a strategic evaluation and control.

1. Definition of Control

Control consists of making something happen the way it was planned to happen. According to Henri Fayol, control consists in verifying whether everything occurs in conformity with the plan adopted, the instructions issued and principles established. It's objective is to point out weaknesses and errors in order to rectify them and prevent recurrence. It operates on everything, things, people, actions. The control function includes three procedures, *viz., (i)* measuring actual performance, *(ii)* comparing actual performance to standards, and *(iii)* taking corrective action to ensure that planned events actually occur. Fig.8.1 shows the model of control process.

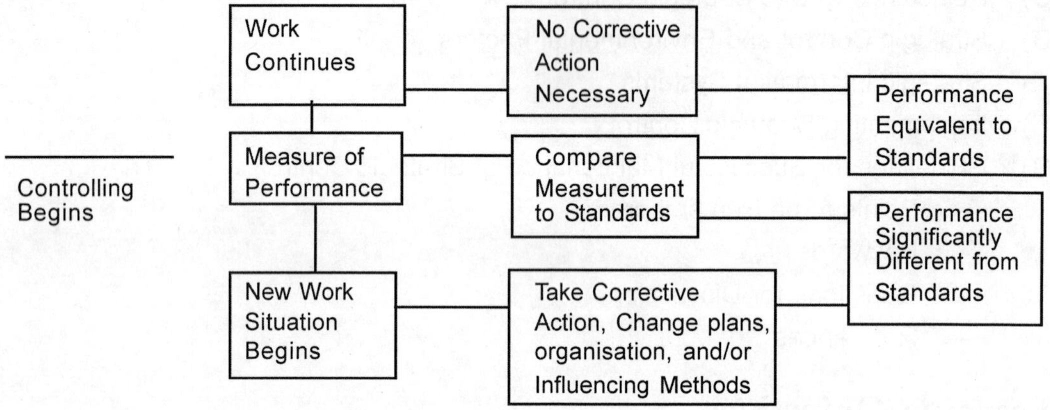

Source: Samuel C. Certo, "*Modern Management*," 1994, p. 436.

Fig. 8.1: General Model of Control Process

Three Types of Control: There are three types of managerial control, *viz.,* preliminary control, concurrent control and feedback control. These three types of managerial control are presented in Fig. 8.2.

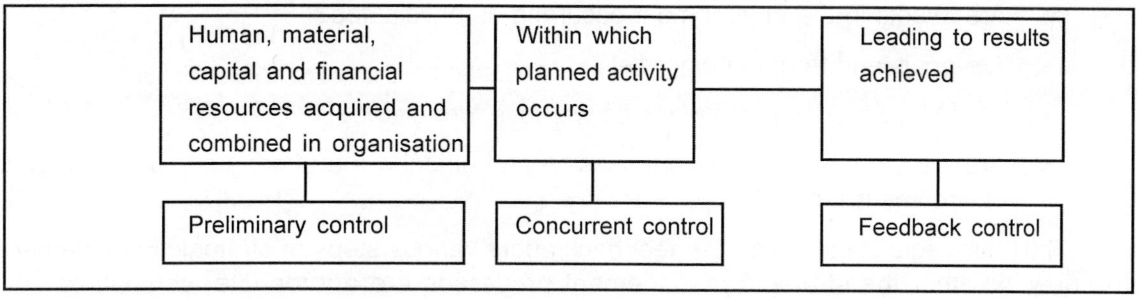

Fig. 8.2: Three Types of Managerial Control

Preliminary control focuses on preventing the possible deviations in the quality and quantity of resources. Human resources must meet the job requirements. The materials must meet acceptable levels of quality and other specifications. Financial resources must be available at reasonable cost in the right time. Concurrent control monitors ongoing operations to ensure that objectives are pursued.

Feedback control methods focus on end results. Corrective action is directed at improving either the resource acquisition process or the actual operations.

2. Strategic Control

Strategic control focuses on monitoring and evaluating the strategic management process to ensure that it functions in the right direction. The strategic control aims at achieving the results planned at the time of strategy formulation. Strategic control is a special type of organisational control.

3. Purposes of Strategic Control

The basic purpose of strategic control is to help top management to achieve strategic goals as planned. To be specific, the purposes of strategic control are to answer the questions such as:

- Are our internal strengths still holding good?
- Have we added other internal strengths?
- Are our internal weaknesses still holding good?
- Do we have other weaknesses?
- Are our opportunities still opportunities?
- Are there new opportunities?
- Are our threats still existing?
- Are there new threats?
- Are the decisions being made consistent with policy?
- Are there sufficient resources to achieve the objectives?

- Are events in the environment occurring as anticipated?
- Are goals and targets being met?
- Should we proceed with plans as we have formulated?
- Are the organisational vision, mission and objectives appropriate to the changing environment factors?

Thus, strategic control provides feedback about various steps of strategic management to know, whether the strategic management processes are appropriate, compatible and functioning in the desirable direction.

We have discussed managerial control and strategic control. Exhibit 8.1 presents the differences between strategic control and budgetary control and Exhibit 8.2 depicts the differences between strategic control and operational control.

Exhibit 8.1: Differences Between Strategic Control and Budgetary Control

Strategic Control	*Budgetary Control*
Time period is lengthy — ranging from a few years to over ten years.	Time period is usually one year or less.
Measurements are quantitative and qualitative.	Measurements are quantitative.
Concentration is internal and external.	Concentration is internal.
Corrective action is on-going.	Corrective action any be taken after budget period has elapsed.

Source: Wright, Pringle and Kroll, *op. cit.*, p. 202.

Exhibit 8.2: Differences Between Strategic Control and Operational Control

Attribute	*Strategic Control*	*Operational Control*
1. Basic question	"Are we moving in the right direction?"	"How are we performing?"
2. Aim	Pro-active, continuous questioning of the basic direction of strategy	Allocation and use of organisational resources
3. Main concern	"Steering" the organisation's future direction	Action control
4. Focus	External environment	Internal organisation
5. Time horizon	Long-term	Short-term
6. Exercise of control	Exclusively by top management, may be through lower-level support	Mainly by executive or middle-level management on the direction of top management
7. Main techniques	Environmental scanning, information gathering, questioning and review	Budgets, schedules and MBO

Source: Adapted from J.A. Pearce III and R.B. Robinson, *Jr. Strategic Management: Strategy Formulation and Implementation* (3rd edn.), (Homewood, Ill. Richard D. Irwin,), pp. 404-419. Quoted in Azhar Kazmi, *op. cit.*, p. 319.

(B) PROCESS OF STRATEGIC CONTROL

The strategic control process consists of six steps (Fig. 8.3). Top management, initially must decide what elements of the environment and the organisation need to be monitored, evaluated and controlled. The three key areas to be monitored and controlled are: the macro-environment, the industry environment and internal operations.

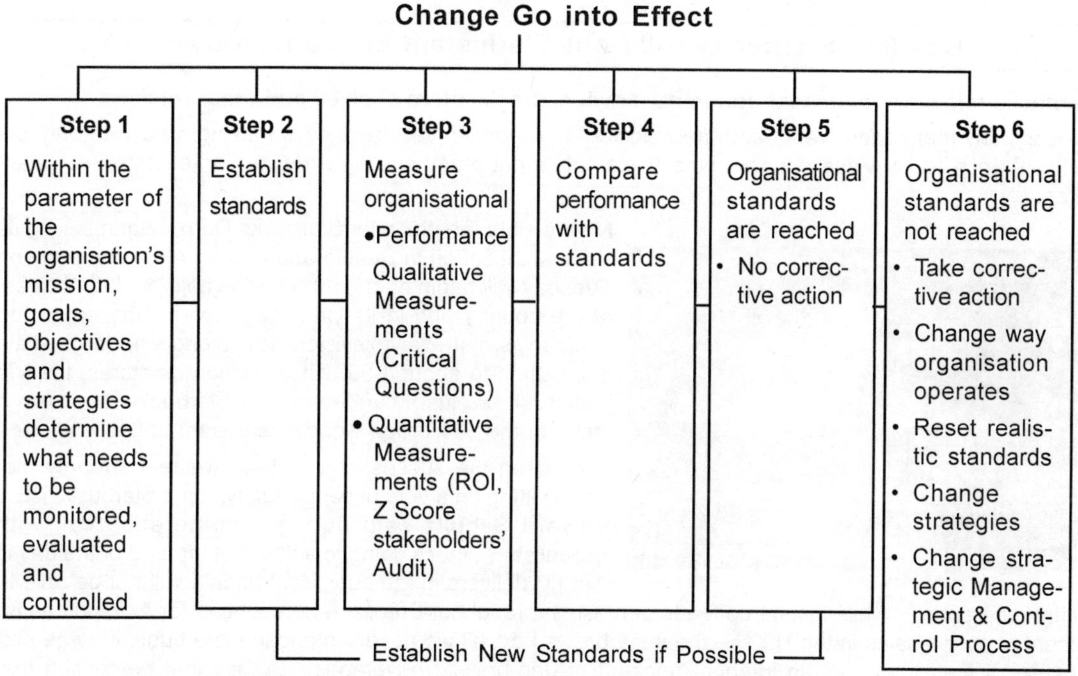

Source: Modified Version From: Wright, Pringle and Kroll, *op. cit.*, p. 202 and Samuel C. Certo and J. Paul Peter, *op. cit.*, p. 150.

Fig. 8.3: Strategic Control Process

Step 1: Key Areas to be Monitored

Macro-environment: As stated earlier, one of the key areas to be monitored is the macro- environment of the company. This area should be focussed first. Normally, individual companies cannot influence the environment significantly. But, the external environmental forces must be continuously monitored as the changes in the environment influence the strategic implementation process of the company. As discussed in the earlier chapters, continuous strategic fit between the company and its external environment is necessary. Therefore, strategic control is essential.

Strategic Monitoring and Control Includes: Modifying any one or more of the areas like company's mission, objectives, goals, strategy formulation and strategy implementation. The modification depends upon the nature and degree of changes and shifts in the environment.

Industry Environment: The strategist also monitors and control the industry related environment. The environmental forces may not be as they were planned. The changes in the environment may provide new opportunities or pose new threats. The strategy, therefore, should be modified accordingly. Thus, the purpose is to modify the company's strategy, goals and operations in order to capitalise the new opportunities and defend against the new threats effectively. The industry environment of the future should be considered by the top management for the purpose of strategic evaluation and control (See Box 8.1).

Box 8.1: Starbucks rolls out Via instant coffee nationwide

Starbucks releases Via instant coffee nationwide, stocks store shelves and other retailers

The company that added "venti" and "frappuccino" to American vocabularies is making a push throughout North America to convince connoisseurs to sample what many see as a down-market drink — instant coffee.

Nearly eight months after Starbucks Corp. began selling its Via instant coffee in Seattle and Chicago, the company on Tuesday will begin offering the dissolvable drink to the rest of the country and in its Canadian stores. Backed by the company's first-ever television ads, along with large-scale distribution to about 1,500 sites outside its stores, the Via launch shows just how determined Starbucks is to own a stake in the $21 billion worldwide instant coffee market.

"Based on the success we've had, we feel strongly that we're sitting on a very big opportunity," said Starbucks CEO Howard Schultz said during a conference call with journalists. "What's going to sell Via at the end of the day is that (it) delivers in the cup. Most people will not be able to tell the difference." While instant coffee is pervasive throughout Europe — accounting for as much as 80 percent of coffee sales in the U.K. — the insta-brews haven't won over American taste buds, in large part because of their image as an inferior knock-off of drip-brewed beverages. But it's that perception that Starbucks executives are trying to change. They hope the skinny cylindrical 3-packs ($2.95) and 12-packs ($9.95) of coffee that dissolve in water will eventually be as prevalent on store shelves as its packaged coffee is now. The coffee is available in Colombia and Italian Roast flavors, and more varieties are expected to be introduced in the future. While experts see opportunity for Starbucks, they also see challenges.

Bob Goldin, an analyst at the Chicago-based food consultant Technomic Inc., said Starbucks faces twin hurdles of perception and price. The Starbucks instant comes in just shy of a dollar a cup, compared with the pennies it costs for a cup of home-brewed joe. Marshaling vendors like camping store chain REI and office supply chain Office Depot Inc., will help the company get the product in the hands of new customers. Via also will be sold inside Costco Wholesale Corp. and Target Corp., stores and to big food vendors like Compass and Aramark. The offensive is also taking to the air, where passengers onboard certain United flights on Tuesday will be able to sample the drinks. In late October, United travelers will be able to buy 3-packs of the coffee from flight attendants while cruising at 30,000 feet. Vendors will be able to set their own prices for Via, but the company recommends similar prices to what the product will be sold for in Starbucks stores. Next year, Via will appear on grocery store shelves, which along with bulk stores account for roughly two-thirds of Starbucks' packaged coffee sales. Executives wouldn't release data on how Via's performed during its eight months on the market, but said early sales in the two U.S. cities — as well as in London — have exceeded expectations.

Among the surprises so far are the various uses of the drink discovered by consumers, executives said. Some people are buying the ground coffee to cook and bake with, while others are mixing it with cold water or milk. Schultz said it's also being bought by teachers to keep in lunchrooms and desks and by physicians who want a quick cup of coffee in a hospital. The introduction of Via comes at a particularly trying time for Starbucks, which has seen its revenue slide for the last three consecutive quarters. Meanwhile, profits have fallen in five out of the past six quarters.

Hit by increasing competition and a recession that's caused caffeine addicts to switch to cheaper drinks, the gourmet chain's also had to close hundreds of stores and lay off workers as it tries to regain its financial swagger. Whether or not Via will be a home run remains to be seen, particularly as competitor Nestle SA ramps up marketing of its own single-serve instant Nescafe coffee. Goldin said the product will need more widespread sales than vendors such as Office Depot, REI and United can offer. If Starbucks can get Via in front of enough consumers, then it could have a chance for the beverage to succeed. "They're trying to find a breakthrough and I give them credit for that," he said. "But it's easier said than done. I think they're going to have some challenges."

Source: http://finance.yahoo.com/news/Starbucks-rolls-out-Via-apf-273848205.html?x=0

Internal Operations: The strategist has to evaluate the internal operations continuously in view of the changes in the macro-environment and industry environment. The strategist has to introduce changes in internal operations when the changes in the environment affect the strategy.

Step 2: Establishing Standards

Evaluating an organisational performance is normally based on certain standards. These standards may be the previous year's achievements or the competitor's records or the fresh standards established by the management. Qualitative judgements like the qualitative features of the product or service in the last year may be used. Quantitative measures like return or investment, return on sales may also be used for judging the performance. Companies should establish the standards for evaluating the performance of the strategies taking several factors into consideration (See 8.2).

Box 8.2: Volkswagen L1 Concept: 240 miles per Gallon

A one-liter car? This moniker describes a car that uses one liter of fuel—about a quarter of a gallon—to propel a car for 100 kilometers, or 62 miles. The one-liter car's fuel economy translates to almost 240 mpg, and VW has had such a car in its sights for some time now. In 2002, outgoing VW CEO Ferdinand Piëch, now head of the company's supervisory board, drove a cigar-shaped prototype from VW headquarters in Wolfsburg to a shareholders' meeting in Hamburg.

Now the idea of the one-liter car has been resurrected. VW's biggest news at the Frankfurt auto show was the L1 concept, a prototype that "is close to production" and "will be developed," the company says. Three ingredients were needed to make it happen: a supremely efficient powertrain, great aerodynamics, and lightweight engineering.

As to the powertrain, VW has opted for a two-cylinder, 39-hp turbo-diesel engine combined with a 8-hp electric motor. There is a stop/start system and a seven-speed dual-clutch transmission. The L1 can reach 100 mph, but fuel economy at that speed drops to a shameful 1.38 liters per 100 kilometers, or 170 mpg.

The front-wheel-drive L1's aerodynamics are optimized by the two-seat layout with the occupants sitting in a row. The result is a car that is relatively long, quite low, and extremely slim. The monocoque and body is made of carbon fiber, and total weight of the L1 is a mere 838 pounds. We think that the seating configuration will likely be changed as development progresses; two people sitting behind each other is too unusual for prospective buyers.

Even so, the L1 looks refined and close to series production, which couldn't be said of the 2002 concept. It could be on the market as soon as 2013, Volkswagen sources tell us. The L1 may seem ironic to those who remember that VW is also responsible for Bugatti, which makes the fastest production car in the world, the Bugatti Veyron, and which just unveiled the W-16 Galibier sedan concept. But if you think about the styles of both Piëch and current VW chairman Martin Winterkorn, this contradiction seems logical: These guys both tend to go to extremes. And we submit that the Volkswagen L1 is a more significant step in saving resources than are heavy gasoline-electric hybrids.

Source: http://autos.yahoo.com/auto-shows/frankfurt_auto_show_2009/1106/Volkswagen-L1-Concept

The standards may include:

- Quality of Products/Services.
- Quantity of Products to be Produced.
- Quality of Management.
- Innovativeness/Creativity.
- Long term investment value.
- Volume of sales and/or market share.
- Financial soundness in terms of return on investment, return on equity capital, market price of the share, earnings per share, etc.
- Community and environmental responsibility in terms of amount spent on community development, variety of facilities provided to the community, programmes undertaken for the environmental protection and ecological balance, etc.
- Soundness of human resource management in terms of number of employee grievances, employee satisfaction rate, employee turnover rate, industrial relations situation, etc.
- Ability to attract, develop and retain competent and skilled people.
- Use of company's assets.
- Production targets, rate of capacity utilisation, design of new products, new uses of existing products, rate of customer complaints about the product quality, suitability of ingredients, etc.
- Corporate image among the customers and general public.
- Market place performance.
- Standards relating the organisational variables include freedom and autonomy, level of control, responsibility, formal organisation and degree of formality, informal organisation.

Step 3: Measuring Performance

The strategist has to measure the performance of various areas of the organisation before taking an action. Strategic audits and strategic audit measurement methods are useful to measure the organisational performance.

Strategic Audit

A strategic audit is an execution and evaluation of organisation's operations affected by the strategy implementation. Strategic audit may be very comprehensive, emphasising all facets of a strategic management process. It may also be narrowly focused, emphasising only on a single part of the process such as environmental process. Strategic audit may be quite formal adhering to organisational rules and procedures. It may be quite informal providing freedom and autonomy to the managers to take decisions. The strategic audit must work to integrate related functions. Hence, the strategic audits are carried out by cross-functional teams of managers.

There are no universally accepted single method of strategic audit. Each organisation can formulate its own method depending upon its need. Exhibit 8.3 presents a worth while set of general guidelines on how to conduct a strategic audit.

Exhibit 8.3: How to Conduct a Strategic Audit

A strategic audit is conducted in three phases: diagnosis to identify how, where, and in what priority in-depth analyses need to be made; focussed analysis; and generation and testing of recommendations. Objectivity and the ability to ask critical, probing questions are key requirements for conducting a strategic audit.

Phase One: Diagnosis

1. Review key documents such as:
   (a) Strategic plan
   (b) Business or operational plans
   (c) Organisational arrangements
   (d) Major policies governing matters such as resource allocation and performance measurement
2. Review financial, market, and operational performance against benchmarks and industry norms to identify key variances and emerging trends.
3. Gain an understanding of:
   (a) Principal roles, responsibilities and reporting relationships
   (b) Decision-making process and major decisions made
   (c) Resources, including physical facilities, capital, management and technology
   (d) Interrelationships between functional staff member and businesses or operating units
4. Identify strategic implications of strategy for organisation structure, behaviour patterns, systems, and processes — define interrelationships and linkage to strategy.
5. Determine internal and external perspectives.
   (a) Survey the attitudes and perceptions of senior and middle managers and other key employees to assess the extent to which they are consistent with the strategic direction of the firm. One way to accomplish this task is through carefully focused

interviews and/or questionnaires to ask employees to identify and make trade-offs among the objectives and variables they consider most important.

(*b*) Interview a carefully selected sample of customers and prospective customers and other key external sources to understand their view of the company.

6. Identify aspects of the strategy that are working well. Formulate hypotheses regarding problems and opportunities for improvement based on the findings above. Define how and in what order to pursue each.

Phase Two: Focussed Analysis

1. Test the hypotheses concerning problems and opportunitists for improvement through analysis of specific issues. Identify interrelationships and dependencies among components of the strategic system.
2. Formulate conclusions as to weaknesses in strategy formulation, implementation deficiencies, or interactions between the two.

Phase Three: Recommendations

1. Develop alternative solutions to problems and ways of capitalising on opportunities. Test these alternatives in light of their resource requirements, risks, rewards, priorities, and other applicable measures.
2. Develop specific recommendations to produce an integrated, measurable, and time-phased action plan to improve strategic results.

Source: Adapted from A.J. Prager and M.B. Shea, "*The Strategic Audit*," in The Strategic Management Handbook, ed. K.J. Albert (New York: McGraw-Hill,), pp. 8-14.

Strategic Audit Measurement Methods

Generally accepted methods may be used to measure organisational performance. These methods can be broadly divided into two categories, *viz.*, *(i)* Qualitative Methods and *(ii)* Quantitative Methods. Exhibit 8.4 presents Key Strategy Evaluation Questions.

Exhibit 8.4: Key Strategy-Evaluation Questions

1. Do you feel that the strategic-management system exists to provide service to you in your day-to-day work? How has it helped you in this respect?
2. Has the strategic-management system provided the service that you feel was promised at the start of its design and implementation? In which areas has it failed and excelled, in your opinion?
3. Do you consider that the strategic-management system has been implemented with due regard to costs and benefits? Are there any areas in which you consider the costs to be excessive?
4. Do you feel comfortable using the system? Could more attention have been paid to matching the output of the system to your needs and if so, of, in what areas?
5. Is the system flexible enough in your opinion? If not, where should changes be made?

6. Do you still keep a personal store of information in a notebook or elsewhere? If so, will you share that information with the system? Do you see any benefits in so doing?
7. Do you think that the strategic-management system is still evolving? Can you influence this evolution and, if not, why not?
8. Does the system provide you with timely, relevant, and accurate information? Are there any areas of deficiency in this respect?
9. Do you think that the strategic-management system makes too much use of complex procedures and models? Can you suggest areas in which less complicated techniques might be used to advantage?
10. Do you consider that there has been sufficient attention paid to the confidentiality and security of the information in the system? Can you suggest areas for improvement of these aspects of its operation?

Source: K.J. Radford, *Information Systems for Strategic Decisions*, 1978, pp. 220-21.

Qualitative Organisational Measurements

Qualitative measurements are in the form of non-numerical data that are subjectively summarised. These measurements are organised and provided to the strategists for decision-making and strategy control action. Critical questions are designed to reflect important facets of organisational operations. Answers to these questions form as the basis for measurements. There are no universally acceptable list of questions by all companies. However, Exhibit 8.5 presents a list of useful questions of quantitative organisational measurements.

Seymour Tilles in his paper on, "How to Evaluate Corporate Strategy," mentioned several important questions to measure organisational performance qualitatively. These questions include:

1. *Is organisational strategy internally consistent?* Internal consistency is concerned to the cumulative impact of various strategies on organisation. Are strategies conflicting with each other. Strategies should also be judged by their relationship with other organisational initiatives.
2. *Is the organisation's strategy consistent with its environment?* Normally, organisational strategies are formulated based on the industry's environment and general environment.

Similarly, the strategies are modified based on the environmental changes. The strategist should see, whether the strategies are consistent with the present and future environmental factors or not? These environmental factors include: Present and future regulations of the Government, Customers taste and preferences, trends of labour supply, technology changes, competitors products and demand. Many organisational problems can be solved easily, if the management brings the balance between the strategy and the environment.

Exhibit 8.5: Sample Questions for Qualitative Organisational Measurement

- Are financial policies with respect to investment, dividends, and financing consistent with the opportunities likely to be available?
- Has the company defined the market segments in which it intends to operate specifically with respect to both product lines and market segments? Has it clearly defined the key capabilities it needs to succeed?
- Does the company have a viable plan for developing a significant and defensible superiority over competitors based on these capabilities?
- Will the business segments in which the company operates provide adequate opportunities for achieving corporate objectives? Do they appear attractive enough to draw an excessive amount of investment to the market from potential competitors? Is the company providing adequately for developing attractive new investment opportunities?
- Are the management, financial, technical, and other resources of the company really adequate to justify an expectation of maintaining superiority over competitors in key capabilities?
- Does the company have operations in which it cannot reasonably expect to outperform competitors? If so, can managers expect these operations to generate adequate returns on invested capital? Is there any justification for investing further in such operations, even just to maintain them?
- Has the company selected business segments that can reinforce each other by contributing jointly to the development of key capabilities? Do competitors combine operations in ways that give them superiority in the key resource areas? Can the company's scope of operations be revised to improve its chances against competitors?
- To the extent that operations are diversified, has the company recognized and provided for the special management and control system this requires?

Source: Milton Lauenstein, "Keeping Your Corporate Strategy on Track," *Journal of Business Strategy 2*,

3. Is organisational strategy appropriate, given organisational resources? Strategy implementation invariably requires the allocation of sufficient resources. Therefore, the strategist should enquire, whether the existing organisational resources are sufficient to carry out a proposed strategy? The strategist should not implement the strategy, without the allocation of sufficient money, material, machines/technology and human resources.

4. Is the time horizon of the strategy appropriate? Organisational strategies are formulated to achieve specific goals within a time framework. The strategist should require whether the time framework, under the existing circumstances is realistic and acceptable? Organisational goals cannot be achieved satisfactorily, if there is inconsistency between these two variables:

Qualitative measurement methods are efficient and are useful. But applying them relies mostly on human judgement. Conclusion based on such methods should be drawn carefully due to the subjectivity of the judgement.

Quantitative Organisational Measurements: Under quantitative organisational measurements of the performance of strategy implementation is taken place in the form of numerical data. The numerical data can be summarised and organised to draw conclusions and to recommend strategic action. Quantitative measurements can be used to evaluate:

(i) number of units produced per time period,

(ii) cost of production, cost of marketing,

(iii) productivity and production efficiency levels,

(iv) Employee turnover, absenteeism levels,

(v) sales and sales growth market shares,

(vi) Profit-gross, net, earning per share, dividend rate, return on equity, market price of the share,

(vii) Cost of production,

(viii) cost of marketing, etc.

Organisations design and use their own methods to evaluate the performance quantitatively. The commonly used methods include:

1. Return on Investment: Return on Investment is widely used as a measure of organisational performance

$$\text{Raturn of Investment (ROI)} = \frac{\text{Amount of Incomper year}}{\text{Total Investment during that year}}$$

Management calculates the return on investment for consecutive years or consecutive quarters and compares the values over the period to measure the performance. ROI as a measure of organisational performance. It has its advantages and limitations (Exhibit 8.6). Managers can use the ROI alongwith other measures of organisational performance in view of its limitations.

Exhibit 8.6: Advantages and Limitations of ROI Performance Measures

Advantages

1. ROI is a single comprehensive figure influenced by everything that happens in a firm.
2. It measures how well the division manager uses the assets of the company to generate profits. It is also a good way to check on the accuracy of capital investment proposals.
3. It is a common denominator that can be compared among many entities.
4. It provides an incentive to use existing assets efficiently.
5. It provides an incentive to acquire new assets only when doing so would increase the firm's return.

Limitations

1. ROI is very sensitive to depreciation policy. Variances in depreciation write-offs between divisions affect their ROI performance. Accelerated depreciation techniques reduce ROI, conflicting with capital budgeting discounted cash flow analysis.
2. ROI is sensitive to book value. Older plants with more fully depreciated assets have relatively lower investment bases than newer plants, increasing ROI. (Note also that inflation can skew asset values and ROI.) Managers might be tempted to hold down asset investment or dispose of assets in order to increase ROI performance.
3. In many firms that use ROI, one division sells to another, so transfer pricing affects the measure. Expenses incurred affect profit. Since, in theory, the transfer price should be based on the total impact on firm profit, some investment center managers are bound to suffer. Equitable transfer prices are difficult to determine.
4. If one division operates in favourable industry conditions and another division operates in an industry with unfavourable conditions, the former division will automatically look better than the other.
5. ROI reflects a short time span. The performance of division managers should be measured in the long run. This is top management's time-span capacity.
6. The business cycle strongly affects ROI performance, often despite managerial performance.

Source: Excerpt from James M. Higgins, *Organisational Policy and Strategic Management: Text And Cases.*

2. Weighted Performance: This quantitative measure numerically weights and sums five performance measures to arrive at an overall score.[10] The score becomes a basis for classifying companies as healthy and unlikely to go bankrupt or as sick and likely to go bankrupt.

The formula is $Z = 1.2 \times 1 + 1.4 \times 2 + 3.3 \times 3 + 0.6 \times 4 + 1.0 \times 5$.

Z = Index of overall financial health. The five variables are explained in the Exhibit 8.7.

Exhibit 8.7: Variables for Z Score

X_1 = Working capital/Total assets	Frequently found in studies of corporate problems, this is a measure of the net liquid assets of the firm relative to its total capital. Working capital is the difference between current assets and current liabilities. This variable explicitly allows for liquidity and size characteristics. Ordinarily, a firm experiencing consistent operating losses will have shrinking current assets in relation to total assets.
X_2 = Retained earnings/Total assets	This measure of cumulative profitability over time relies on balance sheet figures. It implicitly considers the age of a firm. For example, a relatively young firm will probably show a low RE/TA ratio because it has not had time to build up its cumulative profits. Therefore, this analysis

may seem to discriminate against the young firm, since its chance of being classified as likely to go bankrupt is relatively higher than another, older firm. This is precisely the situation in the real world, though. Failure is much more likely in a firm's earlier years; over 50 per cent of firms that fail do so in the first five years of existence. Note, however, that the retained earnings account is subject to manipulation via corporate quasi reorganisations and stock dividend declarations. A basis could be created by a substantial reorganization or stock dividend.

X_3 = Earnings before interest taxes/total assets

In essence, this ratio measures the true product-and ivity of the firm's assets, abstracting from any tax or leverage factors. Since firm's ultimate existence is based on the earning power of its assets, this ratio appears to be particularly appropriate for studies dealing with corporate failure. Furthermore, insolvency occurs when total liabilities exceed a fair valuation of the firm's assets, with value determined by the earning power of the assets.

X_4 = Market value of equity/

Equity is measured by the combined market value of all shares of stock, preferred and common, while liabilities include both current and long-term debt. Book values of preferred and common stockholders' equity may be substituted for market values. The substitution of book values, especially for the common stock component, should be recognized as a proxy without statistical verification, however, since the model was built using market values (Price × Shares outstanding). The measure shows how much the firm's assets can decline in value (measured by market value of equity plus debt) before the liabilities exceed the assets and the firm becomes insolvent. For example, a company with equity worth $1,000 and debt worth $500 could experience a two-thirds drop in asset value before insolvency. However, the same firm with $250 in equity would be insolvent after a drop of only one-third in value.

X_5 = Sales/Total assets

This capital-turnover ratio is a standard financial ratio that illustrates the sales-generating ability of the firm's assets. It is one measure of management's capability in dealing with competitive conditions.

Note that variables X_1, X_2, X_3, and X_4 should be inserted into the model as decimal fractions; for example, a Working capital/Total assets ratio of 20 percent should be written as 0.20. The variable X_5, however, is usually a ratio greater than unity; for example, where sales are twice as large as assets, the ratio is 2.0.

Source: Adapted from Edward I. Altman and James K. LaFleur, "Managing a Return to Financial Health," *Journal of Business Strategy*, 2, No. 1 (Summer 1981), pp. 31-38.

3. Stakeholders' Audit: Stakeholders are the people who have a stake in the company. They are interested in the company's activities as they are significantly affected by the company's objectives. The organisational stakeholders include:

(i) shareholders or owners of the company who are interested in dividend, market price, the share,

(ii) Trade unions and employees interested in favourable wages, benefits, conditions of employment and better quality of work life,

(iii) creditors interested in company's liquidity position and ability to repay the debts with interest in right time,

(iv) suppliers interested in retaining the organisation as a good customer,

(v) government interested in keeping the organisation as a good tax payer, maintaining the congenial industrial relations, maintaining the ecological balance, and contributing to solve the social and economic problems of the country,

(vi) social interest groups such as consumer protection associations and environmental protection associations

(vii) customers who expect a qualitative product/service at a reasonable price, prompt service and favourable conditions of sales.

Stakeholders audit is one of the measures of organisational performance. Exhibit 8.8 provides stakeholder groups and measures to assess both the short run and long run impact they may have on organisational performance.

Step 4: Compare Performance with Standards

Once the performance of the different aspects of the organisation is measured, it should be compared with the predetermined standards. Standards are set to achieve the already formulated organisational goals and strategies. Organisational standards are yardsticks and benchmarks that place organisational performance in perspective. The strategists should set standards for all performance areas of the organisation based on the organisational goals and strategies. Normally, the standards vary from one company to the other company. Further, they also vary from time to time in the same company. The standards developed by General Electric can be used as model standards. These standards include.

1. Profitability Standards: These standards include how much gross profit, net profit, return on investment, earning per share, percentage of profit to sales the company should earn in a given time period.

2. Market Position Standards: These standards include total sales, sales-region-wise and product-wise, market share, marketing costs, customer service, customer satisfaction, price, customer loyalty shifts from other organisations' products etc.

3. Productivity Standards: These standards indicate the performance of the organisation in terms of conversion of inputs into outputs. These standards include capital productivity, labour productivity, material productivity, etc.

4. Product Leadership Standards: These standards include the innovations and modifications in products to increase the new uses of the existing product, developing new products with new uses, etc.(See Box 8.2).

Box 8.2 World's Largest Passenger Jet Makes U.S. Debut

Some of my earliest childhood memories involve my tiny face pressed up against the inside of an airplane, looking down at the passing land below. While flying these days is often a hassle with long lines, frustrating security and a complete lack of service, there is still that little kid in me pressed up against the window. Today that little kid got a big treat: A close look at the first U.S. landing of the A380, the world's largest commercial airplane.

The double-decker plane flown by Emirates Airlines touched down at New York's JFK airport at 4:29 p.m.. Crowd of reporters and VIPs cheered and then eagerly waited as the mammoth plane taxied to the terminal. More than 70 ground crew were on hand to quickly unload and then reload the plane for its return to Dubai. Many had cell phone cameras out to capture the moment. The plane was escorted in by police cars and dwarfed everything along its way. The A380 was also greeted by two airport firetrucks with water cannons that gave it a ceremonial wash. The A380 is unlike any other plane before.

The average first class ticket on the route goes for $14,635, business for $9,571 and coach for $1,477. While that is the same as the service on the airline's Boeing 777 routes, there are substantially more of these high-end seats to sell. The four-engine jumbo jet can carry up to 850 passengers, although most airlines plan to fly closer to 500. This plane put an end to the Boeing 747's astonishing 40-year reign as the world's largest passenger jetliner.

Emirates configured its A380 for 489 passengers. Most are in coach but there are 76 business-class seats and 14 private suites in first-class with electronic doors for privacy. They also get showers, their own mini-bar, a 23-inch high-definition TV screen, your own wardrobe and meals on demand. Singapore Airlines was the first to fly the A380, launching service in October. It now flies the planes between Singapore and London and Sydney and Tokyo. Dubai-based Emirates is the second to fly the jet, but the largest of Airbus' 17 customers. By the way, not one of them is an American airline.

Source: http://news.bbc.co.uk/2/hi/uk_news/england/west_midlands/7536527.stm (02/08/08)

5. Human Resource Standards: Human resource standards include providing competitive salaries, benefits and different aspects of quality of work-life. These standards also include human resource performance, productivity, turnover rates, absenteeism rates, etc.

Exhibit 8.8: Stakeholder Groups and their Impact on Organizational Performance

Stakeholder Category	Near-Term Performance Measures	Long-Term Performance Measures
Customers	Sales (value and volume) New customers Number of new customer needs met	Growth in sales Turnover in customer base Ability to control price
Suppliers	Cost of raw material Delivery time Inventory	Growth rates of Raw materials costs Delivery time
Availability of raw materials	Inventory	

		New ideas from suppliers
Financial Community	EPS[a]	Ability to sell strategy to Wall Street
	Stock price Number of "buy" lists[b] ROE[c]	Growth in ROE
Employees	Number of suggestions Productivity Number of grievances	Number of internal promotions Turnover
Congress	Number of new pieces of legislation that affect the firm Access to key members and staff	Number of new regulations that affect the industry Ratio of cooperative to competitive encounters
Consumer advocates	Number of meetings Number of hostile encounters Number of coalitions formed Number of legal actions	Number of changes in policy due to consumer advocates Number of calls for help initiated by consumer advocates[d]
Environmentalists	Number of meetings Number of hostile encounters Number of coalitions formed Number of Environmental Protection Agency complaints Number of legal actions	Number of changes in policy due to environmentalists Number of calls for help initiated by environmentalists

a Earnings per share.

b Lists from which financial brokers recommend stock purchases for their clients.

c Return on equity.

d Calls in which consumer advocates attempt to enlist others in action against a company.

Source: Adapted from Edward Freeman *Strategic Management: A Stakeholder Approach*, Boston: Pitman Publishing,

6. Employee Attitude Standards: Employee attitude standards include employees' favourable attitude towards the nature of work, organisation, salaries, benefits, working environment, quantity of work-life, treatment by superiors, etc.

7. Social Responsibility Standards: All organisations discharge their responsibilities towards different sections of the society. These standards are related to the services of the organisations towards community, government, employees, suppliers, creditors, etc.

8. Standards Reflecting Balance between Short-range and Long-range Goals: Short-range and long-range strategies should be balanced successfully. Standards in these areas should bring balance between short-range and long-range goals.

Step 5: Take No Action if Performance is in Harmony with Standards

If the performance of various organisational areas match with the standards, the strategist need not take any action. He should just allow the process to continue. However, he can try to improve the performance above the standards, if it would be possible, without having any negative impact on the existing process.

Step 6: Take Corrective Action, if Necessary

Strategist should take necessary corrective action, if performance is not in harmony with standards.

The strategists compare the performance with standards. If they find any deviation between the standards and performance, they should take corrective action to bridge the gap between the standards and performance.

Causes of Deviations: It is very easy to conclude that someone made a mistake, when deviations are identified. But, the deviation may be the result of an unexpected move by a competitor, a typical whether patterns or changes in external environment. Therefore, the strategist should consider the following before making a decision, in this regard:

- Was the cause of deviation internal or external?
- Was the cause random, or should it have been anticipated?
- Is the change temporary or permanent?
- Are the present strategies still appropriate?
- Does the organisation have the capacity to respond to the change needed?

Corrective Action: Corrective action may be defined as change in a company's operations to ensure that it can more effectively and efficiently reach its goals and perform up to its established standards.

Strategies that do not achieve standards produce three possible responses, *viz., (i)* to revise strategies, *(ii)* to change standards, and *(iii)* to take corrective action in the existing process without changing standards and strategies. Strategy change may require a 'fine tuning' of the existing strategy or complete changes in strategies. If it is realised that the existing standards are unrealistic under the present conditions, the strategist should reset the standards taking the existing conditions into consideration.

Corrective action may be as simple as increase in the price or may be as complex as change the chief executive officer. Deviations require re-examination of the company's mission, objectives, relationship to its environment, internal strengths, weaknesses and strategies (See Box 8.3).

Box 8.3: Where Wal-Mart went wrong

Late 2006, Mukesh Ambani-promoted Reliance Retail opened its first store in Hyderabad. Around the same time, Wal-Mart Stores Inc., the world's largest retailer in terms of sales, announced its partnership with Bharti Enterprises to begin operations in India. Eighteen months hence, Reliance Retail is a 600-store chain, while Wal-Mart, which had planned to start operations by the year-end, has deferred the launch to 2009. Our August announcement (to start by 2008-end) was a statement of intent," said a Bharti Wal-Mart spokesperson. "As we get closer to execution, we are investing significant resources to better understand the nuances of the market and closely studying the existing supply chain infrastructure." In fact, Wal-Mart showed extreme alacrity when it overtook British supermarket chain Tesco Plc., which was earlier in talks with Bharti. In November 2006, the US retailer was able to clinch the deal with the Indian business house in a record three months, rendering Tesco's over a year-long talks futile. Nonetheless, it took the two companies 10 months just to decide the formats in which the joint venture would roll out the operations. Ambani opened its first retail store five months after the initial announcement. Ending the speculation of Bharti being the franchisee for Wal-Mart's front end operations, the companies signed an agreement to establish Bharti Wal-Mart Private Ltd, an equal joint venture for wholesale cash-and-carry and back end supply chain management operations in India in August 2007. "In the case of one or two clients, we saw that it takes a long time in such joint ventures to even synchronise the calendar for every one for discussions," said Arvind K Singhal, chairman of Technopak, a business consulting firm. "These international retailers are also facing some degree of crisis in some of their markets, which would take away their attention," he added. Wal-Mart argues that the delay is because India is the first market that it is entering organically in the last 10 years. "It took us time to understand the nuances of the market through customer research and get our agreements in place," said the Bharti Wal-Mart spokesperson. However, analysts have a different opinion about the slow pace of Bharti Wal-Mart's rollout plan. "It took time because Wal-Mart was evaluating if it could be brought to the front end," said an analyst with a leading domestic brokerage. Wal-Mart inked the pact with Bharti when the industry was expecting some amount of foreign direct investment (FDI) in multi-brand retailing and Tesco was seen taking the lead from Wal-Mart. The government allowed 51 per cent FDI in single brand retail stores in 2006 and some amount of FDI was also expected in multi-brand retail. However, FDI in multi-brand retailing was not allowed amidst opposition from political parties expressing concern of negative impact on small kirana shops. However, 100 per cent FDI in the wholesale cash-and-carry model remained intact. This left only one route for multi-brand international retailers, such as Wal-Mart, Tesco, and Carrefour, to open its stores under own brand name: to find a franchise. The franchise route has been open for the foreign retailers. However, it did not attract Wal-Mart and it chose to partner Bharti for the cash-and-carry operation, which it could have gone alone under government guidelines. However, Wal-Mart insists that its India joint venture is out of choice and not compulsion. Bharti Enterprises, through a separate subsidiary, also moved into front end retailing under the brand name Easy Day, which opened its first store only last month in Ludhiana. It has got three stores now and more will follow.

Source: http://www.rediff.com/money/2008/jun/02walmart.htm(Accessed on 02/06/2008)

Further questions useful in establishing reasons for deviations and in identifying possible actions are depicted in Fig. 8.4.

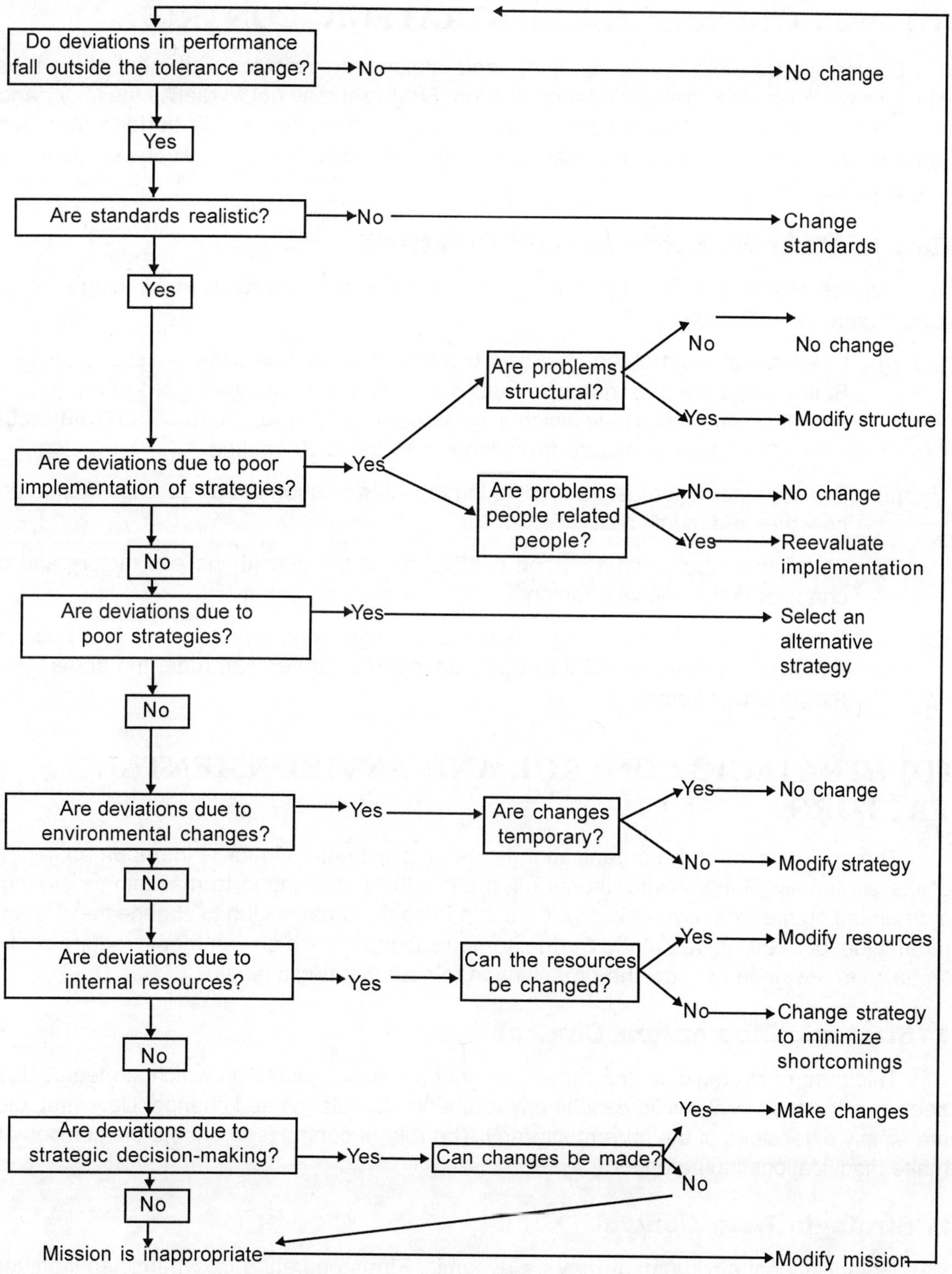

Source: Joe G. Thomas, *op. cit.*, p. 340.

Fig. 8.4: Determining Reasons for Deviations

(C) RELUCTANCE TO USE STRATEGIC CONTROL

Strategists are motivated to formulate and implement strategies. But most of them are reluctant to perform the strategic control function. Strategist may not *(i)* realise the importance of strategic control, *(ii)* have time to conduct long term analyses, *(iii)* perform long-term performance as being of equal importance to short-term performance, or *(iv)* be evaluated on long-term basis.

How to Make Strategic Control Creative?

Lorange, Morton and Ghoshal make the following recommendations for keeping strategic control creative and viable.

(i) Use strategic control teams drawn together from various parts of the organisation. Better follow the informal organisation structure and the cross lines of authority to draw individuals with new insights. Composition of the strategic control team should change regularly to assure fresh ideas and avoid stagnation.

(ii) Top management must be involved in the interpretation of key success factors and how they are monitored.

(iii) Strategic control must focus on bottlenecks in the critical success factors and on changes in the success factors.

(iv) Flexibility must be obtained within the strategic control process so that budgets, formats, agendas, and other organisational procedures can meet the demands of the particular control context.

(D) STRATEGIC CONTROL AND ENVIRONMENTAL FACTORS

The environment of the organisation is the greatest determinant of the appropriateness of the strategies. Stable environments often allow the organisation to maintain its strategic momentum or direction. Dynamic environments force the organisation to change the strategic momentum or direction frequently. Further, organisations in such environments require control techniques designed to allow the organisation to make strategic leaps.

1. Strategic Momentum Control

This form of strategic control reconfirms that the assumptions on which strategies have been constructed are still valid despite environmental turbulence and change. New strategies are simply extensions of the current strategy. The role of control is to enable the company to make modifications in strategies.

2. Strategic Leap Control

Organisational environment may be dynamic. Firms operating in dynamic environment probably have major shifts in strategies and their assumptions may require more drastic changes. Lorange *et. al.*, label this form of strategic control needed as the 'strategic leap'. Developing and maintaining control in such an environment need new strategic rules and to cope with emerging environmental realities. Therefore, the strategies, under dynamic environments should redefine the rules for developing and operationalising strategies. There are four forms of strategic leap control, *viz.*, *(i)* strategic issue management, *(ii)* strategic field analysis, and *(iii)* systems modelling, and *(iv)* scenarios.

***(i)* Strategic Issue Management:** Strategic issue management involves the identification of one or a few key issues that are perceived as crucial to an organisation to achieve its performance objectives. Strategic issue management is designed to reduce the chances of an organisation being caught unaware by a major environmental change. These control techniques encourage the company to remain sensitive to potential environmental changes, plan appropriate actions for changes and avoid becoming locked into a particular course of action.

***(ii)* Strategic Field Analysis:** It is a way of examining the nature and extent of synergies that exist or are lacking between/among components of an organisation. This examination allows the managers to exploit the opportunities provided by the environment.

***(iii)* Systems Modelling:** Systems models are typically computer-based models trying to capture the administrative realities of an organisation and how it interfaces with its environment.

***(iv)* Scenarios:** Scenario planning focuses on qualitative aspects of the organisation broad trends, describing alternative major scenarios and developing an assessment of which scenario is most likely.

Moving from Momentum to Leap and *Vice Versa*

The environmental factors may change from stable to dynamic and *vice versa*. The strategist should also change from momentum to leap control and *vice versa* depending upon the nature of the environment.

(E) STRATEGIC INFORMATION SYSTEMS

Accurate and reliable information about various measures of organisational performance is highly essential for successful strategic control. Organisations should develop and implement formal system to collect valid, reliable and timely information. There are two information systems, *viz.*, Management Information Systems (MIS) and Management Decision Support Systems (MDSS).

1. Management Information System (MIS)

A management information system is a formal computer-assisted organisational function designed to provide managers with information to help their decision-making. The important use of such information is to support strategic control. There are six steps in the operation of MIS (Fig. 8.5).

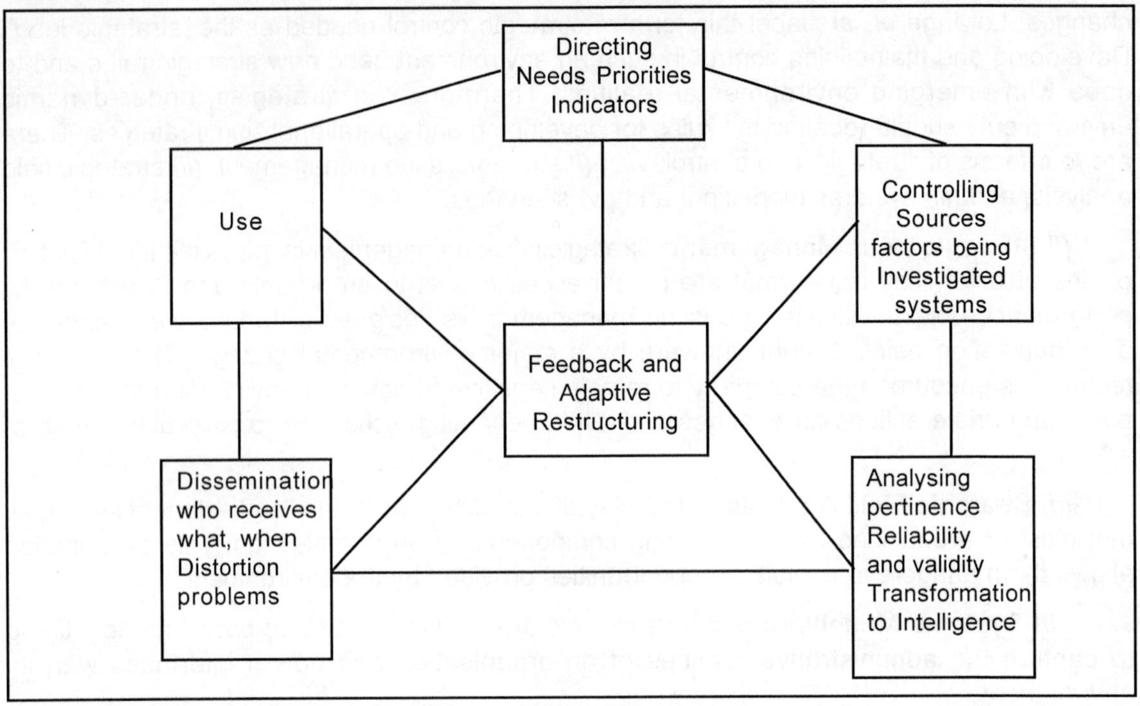

Source: Samuel C. Certo and J. Paul Peter, *op. cit.*, p. 152.

Fig. 8.5: Major Steps in Operating an MIS

Managers at different levels of the organisation perform different functions and therefore, they need different kinds of information. MIS should be flexible to provide different kinds of information to the managers at various levels. Exhibit 8.9 presents typical activities performed by top management, middle management and junior management.

Exhibit 8.9: Typical Activities of Managers at Various Organizational Levels

Organisational Level	*Characteristics of Activities*	*Sample Activities*
Top management	Future oriented Significant uncertainty Significant subjective assessment Strategic management emphasis	Establishing organizational direction Performing environmental analysis Developing organisational strategies Marking short-term forecasts Budgeting Human resource planning
Middle management	Somewhat future oriented (less than top-management activities) Emphasis on implementation of strategies	Assigning jobs to specific workers Managing inventory

	Emphasis on daily production Emphasis on daily performance that reflects organizational strategy and contributes to attaining long-term goals	Supervising workers Handling worker complaints Maintaining organisational procedures and rules

Source: Samuel C. Certo and Paul Peter, *op. cit.*, p. 153.

Since the success of the strategic control depends on the efficient functioning of MIS, the strategists should monitor the functioning of MIS continuously. The strategists should be aware of the symptoms of a malfunctioning MIS (Exhibit 8.10) and set the MIS in the right direction and in right time.

Exhibit 8.10: Symptoms of a Malfunctioning MIS

Operational Symptoms	*Psychological Symptoms*	*Report Content Symptoms*
Large physical inventory adjustments	Surprise at financial results	Excessive use of large tables of numbers
Capital expenditure overruns	Poor attitude of executives about usefulness of information	Multiple preparation and distribution of identical data
Unexplained changes from year to year in operating results	Lack of understanding of financial information by nonfinancial executives	Disagreements among information from different sources
Uncertain direction of company growth	Lack of concern for environmental changes	Lack of periodic comparative and trend information
Unexplained cost variances	Excessive homework	Late information
No order backlog awareness		Too little or excess detail
No internal discussion of reported data		Inaccurate information
Insufficient knowledge about competition		Lack of standards for comparison
Purchasing parts from outside vendors that the firm could make itself		Failure to identify variances by cause and responsibility.
Failure of investments in facilities, or in programs such as R&D and advertising		Inadequate externally generated information

Source: Institute for Practitioners in Work-Study, Organization, and Methods, Middlesex, England, Management Sciences 4, No. 5 pp. 15-24.

2. Management Decision Support System

A management decision support system is an independent set of decision aids that helps managers make relatively unstructured, perhaps non-recurring decisions. Fig. 8.6 presents information needs of executives responsible for strategic control in their firms and the internal functions responsible for finding, interpreting and passing on critical information to top managers.

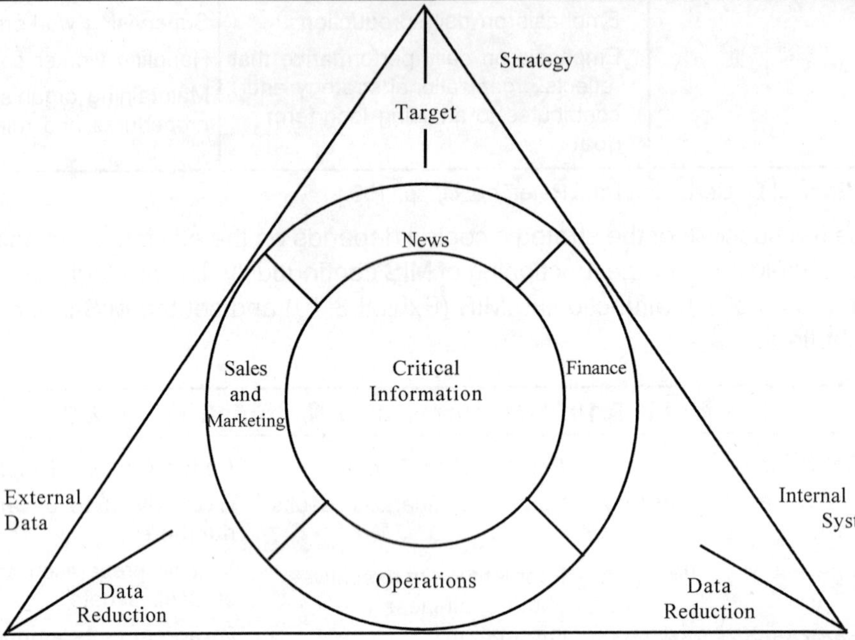

Source: Robin Matthews and Anthony Shoebridge, "*EIS - A Guide for Executives*," Long Range Planning, Vol. 25, No. 6, p. 98.

Fig. 8.6: Information, Executives and Strategic Decision Making

(F) IMPLEMENTING STRATEGIC CONTROL

Strategic control is the primary responsibility of the strategist who formulated the strategy. However, it is the responsibility of all members of the organisation. All employees participate in the strategy implementation. Therefore, all employees can contribute to the control of strategic implementation process.

1. Role of the Strategy Planning Staff

Normally, the role of strategy planning, formulation, implementation and control go hand-in-hand. But, in some companies the roles of planning and control of strategy are separated. This practice is unfortunate as performing these two functions separately by two managers is too often inflexible and bureaucratic. Planning without control eliminates feed forward and control without planning eliminates feedback.

The best results of strategic control are achieved when the planning and control staff work as a team. When a strategic control team members represents a cross-section of the organisation, a number of advantages are likely to occur. Better judgements and insights should result from a diverse group. The team serves as a sounding board for the ideas of individual managers. Involvement in implementation and control gives other members a better comprehension of the problems associated with the new strategy.

2. Role of Top Management

Top level managers are primarily responsible for strategy formulation, analysis and implementation. Therefore, they should understand strategic control and take actions implies in the control process. Top managers should have a vision about the possible changes in the environment and their possible affect on the current strategy and feed this information forward to the staff at the ground. They must be committed to the strategic control process. Top managers are in leadership position and as such they should influence the organisational members in strategic control process.

(G) GUIDELINES FOR SUCCESSFUL MAINTENANCE OF STRATEGIC CONTROL

Successful maintenance of strategic control is important from the long-run point of view. Fig. 8.7 presents the variables that are important to maintain successful strategic control. According to this model, top managers must ensure that four interrelated organisational variables are consistent and complementary. They are: *(i)* organisational structure, *(ii)* reward system, *(iii)* information systems, and *(iv)* organisational value systems or cultures.

Quinn argues that implementing strategy and controlling its progress are actually a series of incremental steps. Quinn suggests that the managers should do the following to implement strategic and control the strategy successfully.

1. Create Pockets of Commitment: Executives provide broad goals, a proper climate, and flexible resource support. By allowing various groups to develop and present proposals for strategies, managers are able to build commitment among the groups to support the strategy finally selected.

2. Maintain Objectivity: Managers should avoid taking a stand on issues too early in the generation and evaluation process. When managers take a position, the generation of new alternatives often ceases and the evaluation of existing alternatives is often biased by the position of the top manager.

3. Eliminate Options Two Levels Down: Managers can maintain their position of neutrality and avoid rejecting proposals by encouraging, discouraging, or killing options through subordinates.

4. Crystallize Focus and Consensus: By controlling membership on committees, managers are able to influence, and if desired, receive the proposals wanted. Properly selected committees can broaden support for and increase commitment to new strategies.

5. Empower Champions: Managers are given responsibility for developing new ideas and programmes early. As the programme is evaluated and gains support, these individuals tend to become committed to the programme or strategy. Once it is given final approval, these managers are then willing to champion the strategy and to guide it through whatever hurdles are necessary to get it operating effectively.

6. Develop Strategies Incrementally, but Not Piecemeal: Part of management's responsibility is to make certain that strategies are integrated and appropriate for the environment in which the firm is operating. Strategies may be developed in incremental steps, but they must be made to fit together in a unified, integrated, and cohesive whole.

7. Recognise Continuing Dynamics: Strategies do not remain constant and fixed for long periods. Part of the executive's responsibility is to gain consensus and support for the new strategy, but at the same time room must be maintained to modify or terminate the strategy. Managers should use discretion in making certain that the organisation does not become overcommitted to the new strategy and unwilling to change at some future point.

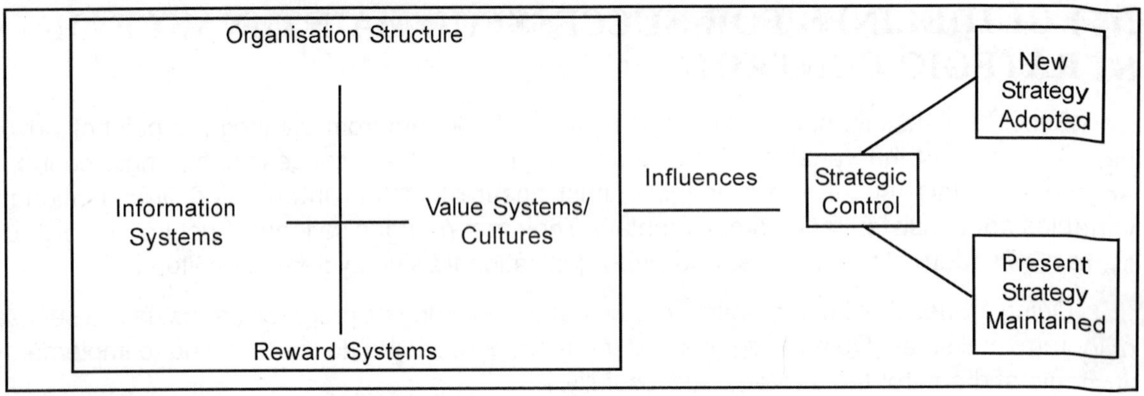

Source: Samuel C. Certo and Paul Peter, *op. cit.*, p. 156.

Fig. 8.7: Variables Important to Maintaining Strategic Control

Points to be Remembered

- Control consists of making something happen the way it was planned to happen.
- Strategic control focusses on monitoring and evaluating the strategic management process to ensure that it functions in the right direction.
- The three key areas to be monitored and controlled are the microenvironment, the industry environment and internal operations.
- Strategic audit is an execution and evaluation of organisation's operations affected by the strategy implementation.
- Performance should be compared with predetermined standards.
- Take no action, performance is in harmony with standards
- Take appropriate correction action, when the performance is inferior to the standards.
- Strategies are motivated to formulate and implement strategies.
- The environment of the organisation is the greatest determinant of the appropriateness of the strategies.

Keywords

- Control
- Standards
- Corrective Action
- Microenvironment
- Strategic Audit
- Stakeholder's Audit
- Strategic Momentum Control
- Strategic Control
- Quantitative Measures
- Microenvironment
- Qualitative Standards
- Weighted Performance
- Strategic Leap Control
- Management Information System

Questions for Discussion

(1) What is strategic control? Discuss the purpose of strategic control.

(2) Discuss the process of strategic control in detail.

(3) Why are some managers reluctant to use strategic control?

(4) What are the factors that affect strategic control?

(5) Discuss the information requirements of strategic control.

(6) How do you implement strategic control?

(7) How do you maintain the strategic control successfully?

(8) Discuss the actions you take to implement strategic control successfully.

References

1. Robert N. Anthony, "*The Management Control Function,*" Harvard Business School Press, Boston, 1988.
2. Henry Fayol, "*General and Industrial Management*," Pitman Publishing, London, 1949, p. 107.
3. Peter Lorange, M.F.S. Morton and S. Ghoshal, "*Strategic Control*," West Publishing, St. Paul, Minn, 1985.
4. Lawrence L. Steinmetz and H. Ralph Todd Jr., "*First Line Management*," Richard D. Irwin, Homewood, 1986.
5. Fred R. David, *op. cit.*, p. 325.
6. Lawrence R. Jauch and William F. Gleuck, *op. cit.*, p. 377.
7. Samuel C. Certo and J. Paul Peter, *op. cit.*, p. 139.
8. Peter Wright, Charles D. Pringle and Mark J. Kroll, *op. cit.*, p. 203.
9. Samuel C. Certo and J. Paul Peter, *op. cit.*, pp. 139-140.
10. Seymour Tilles, "*How to Evaluate Corporate Strategy*," Harvard Business Review, July-August 1963, pp. 111-121.

11. R.E. Freeman, "*Strategic Management: A Stakeholder Approach*," Pitman, Boston, 1984, p. 25.

12. R. Kaufman, "*Preparing Useful Performance Indicators*," Training and Development Journal, September 1989, pp. 80-83.

13. Robert W. Lewis, "*Measuring Reporting, and Appraising Results of Operations with Reference to Goals, Plans and Budgets,*" in Planning, Managing and Measuring the Business: A Case Study of Management Planning and Control at General Electric Company, Controllership Foundation, New York, 1955.

14. Joe G. Thomas, *op. cit.*, pp. 338-339.

15. Samuel C. Certo and J. Paul Peter, *op. cit.*, p. 149.

16. R. Hodgetts and M. Wortman, "*Administrative Policy,*" Wiley, New York, 1980, p. 128.

17. Lorange, Morton and Ghoshal, "*Strategic Control,*" p. 138.

18. *Ibid.*, pp. 10-11.

19. *Ibid.*, p. 11.

20. Joe G. Thomas, *op. cit.*, p. 346.

21. Lorange, Morton and Ghoshal, *op. cit.*, pp. 104-106.

22. *Ibid.*, p. 112.

23. Samuel C. Certo and J. Paul Peter, *op. cit.*, p. 153.

24. Lorange, Morton and Ghoshal, *op. cit.*, p. 139.

25. Samuel C. Certo and J. Paul Peter, *op. cit.*, p. 156.

26. J.B. Quinn, "*Strategies for Change*," Irwin, Homewood, 1980, pp. 126-138.

***